D1345736

LAST OF THE GIANTS

Also by Mick Wall:

Prince: Purple Reign
Lemmy: The Definitive Biography
Foo Fighters: Learning to Fly
Getcha Rocks Off
Love Becomes a Funeral Pyre: A Biography of The Doors
Lou Reed: The Life
Black Sabbath: Symptom of the Universe
AC/DC: Hell Ain't a Bad Place to Be
Enter Night: Metallica – The Biography
Appetite for Destruction
When Giants Walked the Earth: A Biography of Led Zeppelin
W.A.R.: The Unauthorised Biography of W.Axl Rose
Bono: In The Name of Love
John Peel: A Tribute to the Much-Loved DJ and Broadcaster
XS All Areas: The Autobiography of Status Quo
*Mr Big: Ozzy, Sharon and My Life as the Godfather of Rock, by
Don Arden*
Paranoid: Black Days with Sabbath & Other Horror Stories
Run to the Hills: The Authorised Biography of Iron Maiden
Pearl Jam
Guns N' Roses: The Most Dangerous Band in the World
Diary of a Madman: The Official Biography of Ozzy Osbourne

LAST OF THE GIANTS

The True Story of
Guns N' Roses

MICK WALL

Copyright © Wallwrite 2016

The right of Mick Wall to be identified as the author
of this work has been asserted in accordance with
the Copyright, Designs and Patents Act 1988.

This edition first published in Great Britain in 2016
by Trapeze
an imprint of the Orion Publishing Group Ltd
Carmelite House 50 Victoria Embankment
London EC4Y 0DZ
An Hachette UK Company

1 3 5 7 9 10 8 6 4 2

A CIP catalogue record for this book
is available from the British Library.

Hardback ISBN: 978 1 4091 6721 1
Trade Paperback ISBN: 978 1 4091 6722 8

Typeset by Input Data Services Ltd, Bridgwater, Somerset

Printed and bound by CPI Group (UK) Ltd, Croydon, CR0 4YY

Every effort has been made to fulfil requirements with regard to
reproducing copyright material. The author and publisher will be
glad to rectify any omissions at the earliest opportunity.

www.orionbooks.co.uk

For Axl, you won

WHAT THE CRITICS SAY
ABOUT MICK WALL

LEMMY: THE DEFINITIVE BIOGRAPHY

'Wall's vision of Lemmy as a rock'n'roll stalwart who made no concessions is vivid to the last.' *THE GUARDIAN*

FOO FIGHTERS: LEARNING TO FLY

'Wall turns his attention to the Foo Fighters, charting the band's rise – or, more accurately, Dave Grohl's journey from punk rock everyman to stadium rock hero. Classic.' *ROLLING STONE*

GETCHA ROCKS OFF

'Wall understood like no one how to really get close to the stars . . . In the end he even wrote down the truth about Axl Rose only to be called a "motherfucker" in the Guns N' Roses song 'Get In The Ring'. This was actually an accolade, as it proved how well he had hit the nail on the head.' *ROLLING STONE*

THE DOORS: LOVE BECOMES A FUNERAL PYRE

'Jim Morrison was the Terrible Angel of the American Sixties, and his latest biographer Mick Wall tells his story with a passionate, wide open drive, like Jim's famous Shelby GT Ford Mustang with a nitrous oxide hookup. Here James Douglas Morrison emerges more and more as a stand-up, reciting American poet, and an artist whom this author makes you really feel for.'

STEPHEN DAVIS, *AUTHOR OF HAMMER OF GODS*

LOU REED: THE LIFE

'Mick Wall has written in a rough and unsentimental style that suits his subject, and he doesn't gild Reed's more unpleasant aspects.'

THE TIMES

AC/DC: HELL AIN'T A BAD PLACE TO BE

'Mick Wall has a habit of delivering gold-standard biographies that pull no punches, and in the wake of his Zeppelin and Metallica books he has pulled off a splendid hat-trick in *Hell Ain't A Bad Place To Be.*'

RECORD COLLECTOR

ENTER NIGHT: A BIOGRAPHY OF METALLICA

'It takes a writer of Mick Wall's pedigree and calibre . . . to present the whole wild, wonderful and emotionally draining tale all over again and make it as consistently fascinating and momentous as *ENTER NIGHT* . . . the definitive account of heavy metal's biggest band of all.'

CLASSIC ROCK

WHEN GIANTS WALKED THE EARTH

'So this is the big one: a fat, juicy biography of the biggest band ever . . . Mick Wall, the veteran rock journalist, lays it all bare in a book that can only be described as definitive.' *DAILY TELEGRAPH*

CONTENTS

ACKNOWLEDGEMENTS

Heartfelt thanks to all those that helped make this book a reality, either directly or indirectly, over time and space: Linda Wall, Anna Valentine, Robert Kirby, Malcolm Edwards, Alan Niven, Doug Goldstein, Vicky Hamilton, Emma Smith, Kate Walsh, Marleigh Price, Jessica Purdue, Krystyna Kujawinska, Mark Handsley, Craig Fraser, Mark Thomas, Jon Hotten, Dave Everley, Joe Daly, Vanessa Lampert, Steve Morant, Ian Clark, and John Hawkins. Last but hardly least, the five original members of GN'R.

PART ONE

Down on the Street

'Give up all hope, all illusion, all desire . . . I've tried and still I desire, I still desire not to desire and hope to be without hope and have the illusion I can be without illusions. Give up, I say. Give up everything, including the desire to be saved.'

Luke Rhinehart, *The Dice Man*

1

DO YOU KNOW WHERE THE FUCK YOU ARE?

Los Angeles is full of ghosts. Take a drive through West Hollywood, along Sunset Boulevard and its many tributaries, and names and places from the past return, some urgent, some distant, all able to conjure those ghosts by their mere mention. Tower Records, bankrupt since 2006; the Hyatt on Sunset, once known and feared as the 'Riot House', now a sanitised boutique hotel called the Andaz West Hollywood; the Roxy, the Rainbow Bar and Grill, the Whisky a Go-Go, the Troubadour . . . all still standing, but existing on the fumes of their shared, impossible to replicate pasts; nasty joints like the Coconut Teaszer and Gazzarri's, now long gone; Sunset Strip Tattoo, relocated from its ramshackle shop opposite the Hyatt some way further down Sunset; the buildings that once housed the Starwood and the Tropicana and the Cathouse and the Seventh Veil now rebranded and reused; the 24-hour Ralphs supermarket that had so many aspiring musos walking its aisles it was known as 'Rock'n'roll Ralphs'; the Capitol Records building, the Geffen Records building, each monuments to a vanished industry. And the side streets with their stories: North Clark, where once both Mötley Crüe and Guns N' Roses lived in the cheap apartments that lined it; Alto Loma, where the 'hidden oasis' of the Sunset Marquis hotel lay – Hunter S. Thompson used to call that place 'the Loser's Hilton', so many and varied were the touring bands and LA rich that partied in the cabanas by the rippling pool . . .

West Hollywood is a different place now, and ironically, given the turbo-charged, try-hard heterosexuality of the late 1980s, one of the city's best-known LGBT districts. But for anyone who remembers its ghosts and who saw the place in its 1980s heyday, this is the town where anything that could happen did happen. Where everything was coooool, baby, one minute, then out of control the next.

Imagine arriving here, as W. Axl Rose and many thousands of others did, from the Greyhound Bus terminal in North Hollywood and seeing the Strip for the first time at night. The atmosphere of the place came at you like a bullet in the back, a supercharged mix of ambition and abandon, hedonism and desperation: it was like a permanent first night away from home, no responsibility, no tomorrow, no fucker telling you what to do or what to wear or where to go, a heady blast of freedom, intoxicating and scary. The levels of bullshit and testosterone were off the charts. Everyone was in a band, or starting a band or thinking about it, or else they were a budding promoter or a DJ or a VJ or a manager. In a pre-internet age, cheap photocopied flyers were the best form of communicating who you were and when you were playing – by the end of the night, discarded A5s would be blowing down Sunset like tumbleweed. Bands formed and broke up and reformed again with this guy replacing that guy, this name instead of that one, one crazy dude after another. Loose collectives looking for the magic formula, the glory moment at which the touchpaper would ignite and they could begin their climb from a paid-for slot on the bottom of the bill.

It could happen, and it did: look around and you could even see the people that it had happened to – David Lee Roth, singer with LA's biggest home-grown band, Van Halen, ligging with his manager, Pete Angelus, in the Rainbow; Vince Neil, a Mexican kid from the wrong side of town now somehow singing his way to

4

platinum heaven with Mötley Crüe, dragging the mud-wrestling girls from the Tropicana back to his house to party; Robbin Crosby, Ratt's blond bombshell of a guitarist, propping up the bar at the Troubadour, surrounded by chicks and chicks-with-dicks . . . and until the gods pointed their fingers and decided that this was your fate, there was an itinerant life of cheap places to crash, sofas to surf, rehearsal space to find. There was some movie doing the rounds saying 'lunch is for wimps' . . . well, so were breakfast and dinner out in Hollyweird, California. Any spare dollars – and who had those? – were allocated to booze, partying and flyers long before loose change was scraped up for fast food or whatever cheap shit was left on the shelves after midnight at Ralphs. The true Hollywood vampires knew girls who would buy their groceries and offer up their beds while they were busy trying to climb the greasy KY pole . . .

This was a very particular life in a very particular time and place and it was being projected outwards from these few neon streets to the rest of the world. Rock rags like *Hit Parader, Circus, RIP, Spin* and *Kerrang!* helped build the myth. Video clips that began on *Headbangers Ball* then crept onto mainstream, daytime MTV. Radio stations like KNAC – blasting out Poison, W.A.S.P., Ozzy Osbourne – saw their playlists picked up across America. People saw and people heard and they came in their thousands to be part of it. Axl stayed only a few weeks, freaked out by the place and its people, walking around with 'a can of mace in one hand, a piece of steel in the other' like the hayseed Indiana boy he was, but somehow he knew that he had to come back . . .

Young Bill Bailey, just turned 18 years old and not yet W. Axl Rose, was a smalltown cop's nightmare. In Lafayette, Indiana, in the late 1970s, most of the teenage troublemakers were of the usual sort: bored, drunk, pumped full of hormones and not particularly bright. It didn't take the FBI to catch them. Bill Bailey was different. He was bright – very, in fact – and his rebellion had both a root and a reason. It wasn't that they couldn't arrest him. It was that they couldn't stop him, couldn't make him respect their authority, or anyone else's. He ran up 20 arrests by his estimate ('I was guilty on five'), although Tippecanoe County Court records state that he spent a total of ten days in the county jail as an adult over a period from July 1980 through September 1982, on charges of battery, contributing to the delinquency of a minor, public intoxication, criminal trespass and mischief. When he finally hitchhiked out of town, back to LA and away from the torture of his early years, he was technically skipping judge's bail. He would not return for a very long time.

If Axl Rose is the last great rock star, then Bill Bailey is the sad, sweet, clever, abused and angry child that Axl left behind in Lafayette. Yet he lives on in every onstage meltdown and backstage bust-up, in every act of intransigence and temper. And he surfaces in the untold moments of kindness and vulnerability, in the love songs with which he lays himself open and protects so fiercely. He's there in the lyric to 'One in a Million' – '*Police and niggers that's right / Get out of my way*' – and to 'Sweet Child o' Mine' – '*She's got a smile that it seems to me / Reminds me of childhood memories . . .*'. He's there in his choice to cover a Charles Manson song on the *Spaghetti Incident?* album, and he's there again in his need to emulate the songwriting of Elton John and Freddie Mercury. He's there in the desire to control every element of Guns N' Roses, from the ownership of the name to the safeguarding of the musical legacy. It's easy enough to make the link between a young Bill Bailey dreaming of one day having the freedom to sing somewhere other than the bathroom of his family home out of earshot of his religious zealot father, and the glistening edifice of *Chinese Democracy*, a record so singular and out of time that it could only have been the work of a reclusive rock star taking the

6

chance to offer his version of a perfectly realised artwork to the world, uninterrupted by anyone.

It began on 6 February 1962, when he was born William Bruce Rose to a pretty 17-year-old single mother named Sharon Lintner, who was still in high school, and a Lafayette bad boy, also called William Rose, who definitely wasn't. Before Bill was two years old and with any certain memory of what happened, William and Sharon may or may not have legally married, and, when they split in 1964, he may or may not have been abducted, briefly, by his natural father, and sexually abused by him, too. When, many years later, he bought into 'regression therapy', Axl would claim that 'I didn't like the way he treated me before I was born, so when I came out I was just wishing that the mother-fucker was dead . . .' And also that William Rose had 'fucked me up the ass . . . I remember a needle. I remember getting a shot. And I remember being sexually abused by this man and watch-ing something horrible happen to my mother when she came to get me.'

The reality of this is for Axl to know. If it happened, little Bill did not recall it. Sharon met and married Stephen Bailey a year later, and Bill would grow up believing that Stephen was his nat-ural father.

And Stephen Bailey was another doozy in the dad stakes, a case of out of the frying pan and into the fires . . . Known to some of his friends at church as 'Beetle', he was, to give him his full title, the Reverend L. Stephen Bailey and his faith was of the fire-and-brimstone kind. He preached at the Pentecostal church that stood on a gravel road in the farming country outside of town, where heaven and hell were tangible destinations, transcendence and sin both real and alive, where people writhed on the floor and spoke in tongues and the word of God was there to be spread, where Puritanism was desirable and rock'n'roll music, alcohol, premarital sex and most other kinds of pleasure most certainly weren't. Young William and his half-siblings, Stuart and Amy, who came along early in the Bailey marriage, made the eight-mile trip to church every Sunday morning, Sunday evening and Wednesday night as a minimum, and usually more often.

When, during the elementary school years, William began having vivid nightmares about living in a house with his mother and a strange man who did bad things, he was told that the dreams were sent by the devil. Of the endless trips to church he remembered: 'We had tent meetings, we had healings. We saw blind people read. People would talk in tongues. There were foot-washings, the whole bit.' At home, Stephen Bailey ruled his family with God-fearing rhetoric and an iron hand. William was struck in the face for watching a woman in a bikini in a TV adver-tisement. The television itself was thrown out soon afterwards. The Bailey kids got to listen to the radio once a week on a Sunday afternoon when Stephen and Sharon had some 'special time' in the bedroom. When he was asked, many years later, if he could recall any happy memories of his childhood, Axl replied, 'As in a good time? Wow! I guess it would be when the three of us kids were playing and getting along with my stepfather, wrestling around, kind of getting away from whatever was going on and all relating and having fun as little kids.'

That was all, and beyond it nothing. The family environment exerted its own socialising force. The kids began to police one another if they saw or said anything sexual. They were disciplined and conditioned by Stephen, and Sharon always seemed to take his side. He played them Jimmy Swaggart tapes on his reel-to-reel tape machine, making them listen to the jaded old fraud over and over. By the time William was ten years old, he knew the Bible well enough to win the church contest for youngsters, and he was invited to sermonise. Learning to speak in front of a crowd, and later to play piano and sing, Bill somehow found an identity. He knew it had to do with the music he practised time and again for church recitals. One time, in the car, Barry Manilow came on the radio singing 'Mandy' and the chorus was so catchy he joined in. His reward was a fat lip from Stephen, because the song was 'evil'. Hey, if you got a smack to the jaw for singing 'Mandy' then what power did this music have? He got hold of a small radio from Sharon – probably one of the times she was feeling guilty about Stephen – and began listening to it under his bedcovers at night, and the tiny world of Lafayette and school and church opened up: he heard Elton John, Queen, Led Zeppelin, Billy Joel . . . He heard the words and sensed how the melodies made him feel. He understood these things had power, whether he was singing in church to get the congregation to raise the old wooden roof so that Stephen could have them at fever pitch for his sermons, or whether some guy like Freddie Mercury or Robert Plant was standing in front of many thousands and having them stand up and cheer and faint and scream out in tongues . . .

Once the connection was made, his life began to change. The shy, nerdy kid that walked everywhere in Sunnyside Middle School with his back stooped and his eyes cast down, white shirt starched and black trousers pressed, transitioned into a rebellious, semi-delinquent kid at Jefferson High, fast with his temper and his fists, noted for that 'psycho' look in his eye that warned off even the toughest boys. He learned more about the power of music then. Stephen knocked him from the piano stool when he played Zeppelin's 'D'Yer Maker'. He got hold of an Elton John songbook and marvelled at the way the tunes were constructed ('ten fingers of the weirdest chords in the world'). He looked at rock magazines like *Creem* in the drugstore on his way to his piano lesson and there he discovered other magazines, too, like *Oui*, which had arty pictures of beautiful women, right at the time he began to feel his dick tingle at the thought of the girls at school. And then he met Jeff Isbell.

If Bill was learning what cool was and how you might figure out a way to become it yourself some day, Jeff seemed to have been born that way. Three months younger than Bill, he had the same beaky nose and sharp-planed face as Ronnie Wood or Johnnie Thunders, and he was rock star skinny, just like his all-time hero, Joe Perry, the guitarist in Aerosmith. He loved the loose-hipped vibe that the Stones and Aerosmith had, a sort of effortless, gun-for-hire cool that came from hanging just behind the beat. It was a style he'd find was his own, too, once he started out on guitar, but when he and Bill first met, they found a shared love of other stuff as well, music like ELO and David Bowie, and cool British bands who didn't get on the US radio so much – Nazareth and Thin Lizzy. And AC/DC. Wait, they were Australian? Cool . . .

Jeff was a drummer back then, and from musical roots. He'd been born in Florida, but his father, who had Native American blood somewhere on his side of the family, moved them to the countryside outside of Lafayette before Jeff started school, which meant, back in the early Seventies, no neighbours for ten miles in all directions down the unmade gravel roads – 'far out in Bumfuck', as Izzy would recall many years later. When his mother and father split the sheets soon afterwards, Jeff, his mom and his brother, Joe, moved into town, which at least offered him the chance of some sort of social life. His grandma encouraged his musical ambition, and on his thirteenth birthday, the longed-for drum kit arrived. Jeff's best pal had an older brother who ran with the hooligan crowd. They liked to take over an old farmhouse to party, and when they were all good and drunk, they'd ask the skinny, beaky little kid to come up and jam on the drums with them. 'That was my first adrenalin rush,' Izzy recalled. 'Other than that, my life was completely boring.'

He fought that boredom by retreating into music and learning tricks on his skateboard. He started to grow his hair. He felt somehow that he was destined for life in a band, far away from

Lafayette. He was hanging around a school corridor one day in ninth grade when 'I heard all these books hit the ground, yelling, and then he went running past. A bunch of fucking teachers chasing him down the hallway . . .'

The next time he saw Bill Bailey they were sitting next to one another in Driver Education class, and their friendship began. Jeff was in some school band or other, just a bunch of guys who didn't really have a name, and he thought that his crazy new friend might make a frontman. 'I thought, well, here's a guy who's completely crazy, he'd be a fucking great singer,' he told me many years later. 'We had to coax him a bit [and] it didn't go so well in the early days. Sometimes he would just come over and stand around, like he was embarrassed. Or he'd start to sing and then he'd just leave. Walk out and I wouldn't see him again for, like, three days! Some things don't change, huh?'

Jeff understood. He may not have been as academically gifted as Bill, but he was an astute reader of people and from an early age was settled in his own skin. When he and I spoke a decade after he'd quit Guns N' Roses, his recollection of this high-school friendship gave an insight into Axl's adult character: 'He had long, red hair, he was a little guy and he got a lot of shit. I think he never got laid, too, in school. I hate to bring this up cos this is getting nasty. But he never got no pussy at school, Axl. So now the guy's a big fucking rock star, he's got the chicks lined up, he's got money and he's got people . . . and the power went to this guy's head. I mean, he was a fucking monster! Nuts! Crazy!'

All that came later, though. It wasn't rock fans but the Lafayette police Bill first started getting noticed by, in the mid-Seventies. He was 15 and 'because I was one of the smartest, the cops thought I was the ringleader'. His juvenile records remain sealed but he was arrested at least four times before he was 18, once in his own backyard. He started drinking and popping pills at 16, smoking joints when he could get them. By the time he discovered the truth about his parentage, Bill Bailey wasn't just living on the wrong side of the tracks – he was ready to jump the rails completely. He'd been shuffling through some old papers in a drawer at home when he discovered that Sharon's High School Diploma listed her surname as 'Rose' and not her maiden name of Lintner. He kept searching and found insurance documents that gave 'Rose' as his surname too. When he confronted his parents that evening, he got a part of the truth: he was told that his real father had hurt his mother and then disappeared, to where, no one knew or cared. 'Your real father does not get brought up,' Stephen warned him when he continued to press for information.

He was at a vulnerable age, and the discovery struck at the heart of his identity and demolished his sense of self. Suddenly, the strange dreams he'd had as a child of living somewhere else with his mother and another man made sense. Relieved, too, perhaps, that the tyrannical Stephen Bailey was not his real father, Bill changed his name immediately, albeit unofficially, to 'W. Rose' – heartbreakingly, the 'W.' was because he didn't want to share a full first name with a natural father who had abandoned and maybe abused him. His behaviour, though, worsened. His mood swings became so extreme that a psychologist diagnosed an intermittent psychosis. His grades dropped off a cliff-edge and then he quit school altogether. He couldn't get a job, because all of the stores in the mall knew him as a shoplifter. The police 'beat the crap' out of him, he said, and tried to run him out of town. Stephen Bailey finally kicked him out of the family home under the ridiculous pretence of him having 'too-long hair' and so he went to stay with his grandmother. He started hanging around in Columbian Park, just behind his grandma's house, with Izzy and his pals: David Lank, who would take one of the early trips to LA with him, Mike Staggs, another local musician who would also take the trip west, Monica and Dana Gregory, Anna Hoon, whose younger brother Shannon would later find fame in Blind Melon, and Gina Siler, who met Axl on her seventeenth birthday, when he was 20, and became his first serious girlfriend.

To all of his friends, the twin sides of his personality were apparent. Monica recalled his beautiful piano playing. Dana remembered 'the vibe he gave off' – bad enough to earn the warnings from the local cops. Jeff saw both sides: 'He was just really fuckin' bent on fighting and destroying things. Somebody would look at him wrong and he'd just start a fight. If it wasn't for the band, I just hate to think what he'd have done.'

Something had to give. Jeff moved to LA in 1981 and found his own new name – Izzy. And Bill followed a year later, the first few trips terrifying and aborted, the city just too vast and imposing and hostile, but with the threat of some proper jail time hanging over him and nothing much to keep him in Lafayette, he made the move permanently in December 1982, with Gina Siler in tow. A new life needed a new name, and W. Axl Rose was born. As he later explained, 'I am "W." Rose because "William" was an asshole.'

Much has been made of 'Axl Rose' as an anagram of oral sex, but the truth was, A.X.L. was the name of one of Dana's bands – a band Bill had been desperate to join – and he simply took the letters for himself. 'I had a small apartment in Huntington Beach,' Izzy recalled, 'and Bill used to come down and crash on the floor. He was always coming out to visit [and] getting lost. Then, at the end of '82, he came back out with this girl and rented an apartment. That's when he finally stayed . . .'

Unbeknown to Axl and Izzy, unbeknown to the world, Saul Hudson and Steven Adler were there waiting for them. After relocating from the drear environs of his father Tony's native Stoke-on-Trent when he was four years old, Saul had grown up in the boho enclave of Laurel Canyon, in a house on Lookout Mountain Road. Leaving behind the scarred landscapes of the Potteries, where the coal-mining industry made its presence most obviously felt in the slag heaps which littered the horizon, young Saul now found himself in the same hippy paradise then occupied by rock denizens of the day like Jim Morrison, Frank Zappa, Joni Mitchell and Crosby, Stills and Nash (and Young). Indeed, a wooden shack in the Canyon was then every turned-on couple's desire in those dreamy, incense-lit days. By the time Slash arrived in 1970, what had been a rundown, overgrown semi-wilderness had been transformed by musicians looking for cheap places to hang out and get high, to play their music beneath the bird-of-paradise plants, thickets of pepper trees and pines, and reinvent themselves as the love generation. It was the place where Elektra Records' exec Barry Friedman would famously phone all his neighbours and get them to drop the needle on the new Stones album, all at the same time, until the Canyon rang out with their groovacious sounds.

It was a childhood and a life that Axl might have craved, one of barefoot freedom and unfettered creativity, a house always full of music, dope and colourful characters. Tony Hudson, an ambitious young artist, had met Ola Oliver, an African-American clothing designer, in Paris. Ola left the little family in Stoke soon after Saul was born to return to LA and lay the foundations for their life there. When she was joined by her husband and son – and soon by a new addition in Saul's younger brother, Ash – Saul seized on to this new existence. 'My first memory of LA is the Doors' "Light My Fire" blasting from my parents' turntable all day long,' he later recalled. One of his early babysitters was David Geffen, whose hugely influential record label Guns N' Roses would one day sign to. Tony designed the *Court and Spark* album cover for Joni Mitchell, who lived just up the road, and who used some of Saul's animal drawings to make a book of her poems. Ola's clothing design really took off, and she worked with Joni, and David Bowie during his Thin White Duke phase, and then Ringo Starr and Carly Simon. Things were going so well, the family moved down the hillside to a swish apartment on Doheny Drive, just off Sunset, where Saul was introduced to everyone from Diana Ross and Stevie Wonder to John Lennon and Bill Cosby. Ola would take Saul to shows at the Troubadour and onto various TV and film sets where she was working and he felt the magic, especially when he saw a stage full of gleaming musical instruments laid out and ready to go.

Now calling himself Slash, adopting a nickname given to him by the actor Seymour Cassel, a family friend – 'Because I was always running around the place, at lightning speed' – when Tony and Ola's relationship began to hit the rocks, Saul would take long walks with his father. He learned of their split over a meal in Fatburger. Although his parents remained on amicable terms, and lived close to one another, 'the only stability I knew was gone', and he began staying for extended periods with his grandma, Ola's mother, who was also called Ola. 'I had to redefine myself on my own terms,' he later remembered in his memoir, especially when it became clear to him that his mother was engaged in a brief but intense affair with Bowie that began shortly after he'd signed to appear in the film *The Man Who Fell to Earth* and Ola was hired to design the costumes. 'Inside I was still a good kid,' he said, 'but on the outside I became a problem child.'

By the time he was 12, Saul was drinking, smoking, even having sex. He began to seek the stability of a new family and found it in the suddenly hip sport of BMX biking with some older kids he'd met at a shop called Spokes and Stuff. 'All of us but two – they were brothers – came from disturbed or broken domestic situations,' he'd recollect. They'd ride all over – Laurel Canyon, Culver City, the La Brea Tar Pits – and especially Laurel Elementary School, where they'd spend their evenings hanging in the playground and smoking weed. Within a year he'd picked up another bad habit: kleptomania, lifting books, comics, tapes, art supplies . . . until it came to an embarrassing end at Tower on Sunset, when he was caught with pockets full of tapes which were laid out for his mother to see when she was summoned to collect him. 'She didn't say much and she didn't have to,' he reflected. 'She was over thinking I could do no wrong . . .'

Saul also struck up two key friendships during this restless period, the first an enduring one with Marc Canter, whose family owned the famous Canter's Deli in West Hollywood. Canter would be on hand in the early days of Guns N' Roses, often paying for flyers or buying guitar strings when money was short. The second was with a rough-and-tumble blonde kid named Steven Adler, who rocked up one evening in the Laurel Elementary playground, and who soon found himself as a classmate of Saul's at Bancroft Junior High. The pair were, according to Saul, 'instantly insepa-rable'. Soon they were snorting 'locker room' – a cheap form of amyl nitrate – before class, and then bunking off to smoke dope and wander the streets of Hollywood bullshitting one another about music, forming bands and hustling money.

Steven was a Valley Boy who'd arrived in California at the age of seven from Cleveland with his mom, Deanna, and his older brother, Kenny. His natural father was an Italian 'gangster wan-nabe' called Mike Coletti, who had, in the Catholic tradition, ori-ginally named Kenny 'Joseph' after his own father and Steven 'Michael' after himself. When Deanna left Mike, the family moved in with her mother, Lilly, who insisted that, in the Jewish tradition, the children were not named after living family – thus Michael became Steven, and Joseph became Kenny. No matter how quickly the famously easy-going young Steven shrugged it off, this was a deeply unsettling period of his life which would leave its emotional scars.

Soon he was, in his own words, 'a crazy, wild, fucked-up kid' who was essentially uncontrollable. When the claustrophobic apartments and biting winter winds of Cleveland got too much,

Deanna headed west to join an older sister in SoCal. Steven's course was set at the age of 12, on a day trip to Disneyland's Magic Mountain: Kiss made a special appearance and hit him like a tidal wave. Deanna remembered Steven in the car on the ride home. '"Mom," he said, "When I grow up, I want to be a rock star." I just said, "That's nice, Stevie . . ." And I thought that would be that . . .'

But Steven knew deep in his bones that it wasn't anything to do with being 'nice', and soon he was convincing his new friend Saul of it, too. 'We'd dip school nearly every day,' he recalled. 'Me and Slash would walk up and down Sunset and Hollywood Boulevards and each day we had this thing where we'd take a different type of alcohol and we'd walk up and down, up and down, and what we'd be talking about was how we'd be living when we were rock stars. It was like this dream that I always knew would come true. We'd go out and meet chicks – older women – who would take us back to their Beverly Hills homes. They'd give us booze, coke, they'd feed us, really. All we'd have to do was fuck them. Occasionally a guy would pick me up. In return for a blow job, I'd get a little dope and thirty or forty bucks.'

Adler would also have darker experiences with some predatory paedophiles who hunted for young flesh in Hollywood, admitting in his autobiography that he'd been picked up on Santa Monica Boulevard by two men who took him to an apartment where he was 'hurt quite badly . . . They didn't beat me up but they did everything else and it was quite devastating.'

The one thing he really had going for him was the music. It was Steven who finally got a guitar into Saul Hudson's hands. 'I lived about five or six blocks from Santa Monica Boulevard, so if I was with Slash, we'd always get back to my house first,' he said. 'I had two rooms – a living room and a bedroom – and I'd always sleep in the living room. In the bedroom, I had this guitar and a little amplifier that I was learning to play, and one day I just showed it to Slash. I knew two chords and two scales and I tried to play along to *Kiss Alive* – strike all of the Ace Frehley positions, man! Well, Slash just fell in love with that guitar. I gave it to him, and within a week he was writing songs. He was just made for the guitar. *Made* for it. I just wanted to be a rock'n'roll star. The guitar was too complicated for me . . .'

Everything was too complicated for Steven. And it didn't get any simpler when he and Slash met a couple of strange cats from out of town with the even stranger names of Izzy and Axl.

Gina rented an apartment in West Hollywood and Axl used it to store his stuff and as a crash pad when he wasn't hanging out-side the Troubadour or the Starwood, watching enviously as local celebs like Mötley Crüe or Ratt or even David Lee Roth caused little ripples to run through the crowds of kids that gathered around. Axl would later claim that no one spoke to him 'for two years', but Gina understood what he was doing, even as they drifted apart and she grew increasingly alarmed at his anger. 'He was born to be a musician, nothing else,' she said. The chaos of his life soon proved too much for her. Gina moved out and Izzy moved in. While Axl was still the cowboy-booted hick with the crazy eyes, Izzy already had the LA thing down. He looked like a star an age before he was one: jet-black hair, beanpole legs and, when he played, guitar slung low around his knees like Keef or Joe Perry.

Axl finally got a gig on the strip when a short-lived spell with the going-nowhere-fast Rapidfire resulted in a set at Gazzarri's. It would set in motion a slow-moving chain of events that brought the members of Guns N' Roses together. When Rapidfire lost traction, Axl resolved to develop his partnership with Izzy, who was in turn keen to start a band with a young guitarist calling himself Tracii Guns. Tracii was one of the best on the Strip, fluent in Randy Rhodes-style shredding as well as dirty rock'n'roll, and already had something on the go, so he recommended Izzy to one of his high-school friends, Chris Weber. Chris and Tracii had attended Fairfax High together, where Tracii had a band called Pyrrhus and two other pupils, Saul Hudson and Steven Adler, had a pick-up outfit called Road Crew.

Izzy and Chris met one night in the parking lot at the Rainbow, and spent a few hours talking. The next day, they began to jam. Four of the five future members of Guns were now, in the last months of 1983, in one another's orbit for the first time. It would take another two years for the band to coalesce as they splintered and then re-formed in the casual, try-to-make-it-happen atmosphere of the Strip.

Slash and Steven had created Road Crew almost in name only. Steven only had a set of pots and pans to hit at first, but once he had a kit and a beaten-up old car provided by his grandma, they were on the same footing as most of the other kids. In fact Slash, with his curls cascading around his face and his guitar slung down by his crotch, was already drawing admiring – and jealous – glances for his natural ability. He seemed to be able to play right from the first minute he picked up a guitar. His sphere of reference, musically, stretched from Rufus to the Rolling Stones, from Stevie Wonder to Led Zeppelin, but as a guitarist he felt as ardently about Aerosmith as Izzy did, and that root of influence would prove important.

As far as Izzy and Chris were concerned, Axl Rose became a serious proposition after he laid his low baritone and shattering scream over some songs that they'd written inspired by *Rock in a Hard Place*, Aerosmith's 1982 album. Axl's wild unpredictability was, however, already evident. Chris and Izzy had even called their band A.X.L. and had the name spray-painted on a wall along the Strip in big letters, yet he still walked out without warning. 'Axl was so full of energy that he would shake, literally tremble, when he got up there to sing,' Chris remembered.

He was soon back, changing the name to Rose and then the more atmospheric Hollywood Rose, and by mid-1984 they had a demo that contained the first seeds of at least one major song, the future *Appetite for Destruction* track 'Anything Goes', in 'My Way, Your Way'. They played a few riotous shows and then Izzy quit to join London, a legendary Strip band with one apparently permanent member in the giant singer Nadir D'Priest and a revolving-door policy for the rest, who had included the soon-to-be-famous Nikki Sixx of Mötley Crüe, Blackie Lawless of W.A.S.P., Fred Coury of Cinderella, and many more. Membership of London, however brief, was almost a rite-of-passage moment, and when Izzy realised his mistake and left, he discovered that Axl had been poached – or was about to be – by Tracii Guns for *his* new band, which he called LA Guns, only for Axl to fold soon afterwards and reform Rose with Izzy. It was permanent midnight out there for these nascent Strip bands. No one stayed anywhere for long, everything was real until it wasn't.

When Slash and Steven got to hear about Tracii's desire to work with 'the best singer in Hollywood at the time', according to Slash, and when Steven picked up a flyer for a show at the Troubadour with Rose towards the bottom of a 12-band bill, he and Slash went along. A few days later Steven was introduced to Izzy through a mutual friend, Lizzie Grey, who was playing guitar in London at the time, and when Axl fired Chris Weber soon after *that*, Steven talked his way into bringing Slash down to a Rose rehearsal at a notorious punk space called Fortress. They began to jam but then Izzy took off halfway through, and Slash and Axl struck up a short but intense friendship that ended with Axl crashing at Ola's house – at least until he'd outstayed yet another welcome.

Hollywood Rose managed a few shows until Slash quit after a disastrous gig at the Troubadour where Axl went for a guy in the crowd, and Tracii Guns really did get his man when Axl then joined LA Guns and further severed his connections with Slash by sleeping with Slash's on-off girlfriend Yvonne – although Slash's call to confront Axl came when Axl was at work during a spell at Tower Video and ended with Axl getting Slash a job as a conciliatory gesture . . .

Slash, in the meantime, had auditioned for a preening bunch of new arrivals, a band from Pennsylvania calling themselves Poison. They were pushing the glam look to the edge, with towering bleached blonde hair and full eyesore make-up and, as Slash recalled, the first question they asked him was, 'You don't wear those shoes onstage do you?'

But then Axl pulled Izzy into LA Guns . . . Slash and Steven returned to Road Crew . . . Slash left Road Crew to join Black Sheep . . .

This was how it went on the Strip in 1985, bands started, bands ended, you left one and formed another and, somewhere along the way, something would happen that would make the whole world open up for you like a key in a lock . . . That's what you told other dudes anyway, as you lolled around pretending to know what the fuck you were doing. By the spring, Axl was again working with Tracii Guns and drummer Rob Gardner. They hooked up with Izzy once more and a flyer appeared which read: 'It's only rock'n'roll – LA Guns and Hollywood Rose present the band Guns N' Roses. March 26. Doug Weston's Troubadour'.

Twelve people saw the show, of whom four had paid the $2 admission.

And then the key to the lock did show up. His name was Michael McKagan, although since childhood he was known to his family – of which he was the last child of eight – as 'Duff'. By the time he arrived in Los Angeles in September 1984, driving in his ancient Ford Maverick from his native Seattle via a few days at a squalid punk squat in San Francisco, Duff was 20 years old and had been, by his estimation, in 31 different bands. He was leaving behind a chaotic start in life, first the happy racket of a big, working-class family in which his father – much older than the fathers of his contemporaries – was a Second World War vet, a fireman and something of a local hero, and then, once he'd come back from school soon after his mother had begun a course at a local college and found his old man in bed with the woman next door, all of the pain of a family break-up.

He started getting panic attacks that he medicated with alcohol and then drugs. He found solace in Seattle's DIY punk scene. Duff could play anything – drums, guitar, bass – and if he couldn't do that he was happy to roadie, or load gear or whatever else got him out of the house. He could also smile like his hero Sid Vicious – that corrupted Elvis curled lip – and had taken to wearing a padlock chain around his neck. He was 15 when he formed his first band, The Vains, playing bass, releasing one single a year later, 'School Jerks'. At the same time he played guitar in another punk outfit, The Living, who once opened for Hüsker Dü. The same year he also began drumming with The Fastbacks, playing on their 1981 single, 'It's Your Birthday'. Then he was in the charmingly named The Fartz, who only got as far as making demos – until Duff got famous and someone had the great idea of releasing them as an album.

It was only when The Fartz became 10 Minute Warning that they achieved any real measure of punk immortality, though. By now Duff was back being the guitar player. 10 Minute Warning were at least different, still punk, but slower, heavier, more oppressive, paving the way for proto-grunge acts like Green River and Soundgarden to follow. Duff later claimed that if he'd known Seattle was going to explode the way it did in the early Nineties, that he would never have left town. But that wasn't true. Duff was tall, good-looking, blonde, and looking for a good time all the time. He also liked to dress up. He had about as much in common with Kurt Cobain and his ilk as diamonds with rust.

In LA he stayed with his brother, found a job as an apprentice server in a Black Angus steakhouse and began to get a handle on the scene. It was bigger than Seattle, because LA was vast and sprawling, but it worked the same way. Almost everyone he met seemed to be a guitarist so he figured bass gave him a better chance of gaining a foothold, and with the feeling in his bones that punk, for the moment at least, was dead, and this new rock'n'roll vibe on the Strip was his to grab hold of and shake, he picked up a local music newssheet, *The Recycler*, and answered an ad.

'The name to call was Slash, so I assumed he must be a punk rock guy like me,' Duff later recalled. They met at Canter's Deli, Duff in a floor-length leather coat with an anarchy symbol on the back that he'd blacked out with a Sharpie, Slash and Steven with long hair and girls in tow. They ended up at Slash's mom's place, Duff immediately appealing to Ola's mothering instincts, and they had a warm week or so of building a friendship if not a band, taking in a night at the Troubadour watching LA Guns. But Duff had his worries about Steven's playing and the direction of Road Crew – the only one of the bunch who'd actually recorded and could play both guitar and drums – and so they agreed to shake hands and go their separate ways, Slash's number on a piece of paper in Duff's pocket.

After he got laid off by the Black Angus, Duff found work as a delivery driver, and while he was doing his rounds one day he ran into Izzy, who told him about this new band he had that was kind of an amalgam of LA Guns and this other thing with a very good, if kinda crazy, singer. As it turned out, they'd just lost a bass player and hey . . . don't you play bass? And in the way that things happen, Duff found himself at a rehearsal of Guns N' Roses. He liked Axl right away, tuned straight into his restless energy, and as soon as he heard him let rip into the mike, 'I knew in an instant that this dude was different and powerful and fucking serious . . .'

They played some shows, and although they were good, Duff got the sense that Tracii and Rob were happy being big fish in a small pond, playing the same gigs around West Hollywood over and over until something happened. That wasn't the punk way. In Seattle, where there weren't any major-label guys always hovering at gigs, you didn't wait for things to happen because they never did, and so Duff pulled Axl and Izzy aside and suggested a road trip, a string of gigs up the West coast, finishing off in Seattle. It would be an adventure, he told them, and a way to find out if things were going to fly away from the heady hothouse of LA.

'I could tell immediately that Izzy knew what I was up to,' Duff said, looking back. 'He knew this was a way to test the links in a band and find the weak ones.' They found them. Tracii and Rob bailed ten days before the tour, freaked, Duff felt, by the plan to get in a car, drive to the show and let the rest – food, a place to sleep, gas money, etc. – take care of itself. He felt around in his pocket for a phone number and called that guy Slash. 'Don't worry,' he told Axl and Izzy, 'I know who we can bring in.'

The key slid into the lock and turned. Slash and Steven had three rehearsals with Axl, Izzy and Duff, played a raucous one-off on 6 June at the bottom of the bill in the Troubadour to get loose, and Guns N' Roses were ready to go on tour. They had a couple of friends, Danny and Jo-Jo, whom they'd enlisted as roadies, and Danny's car, a snarling Buick Le Sabre with a trailer on the back.

It broke down 100 miles later. Danny and Jo-Jo were delegated to stay behind with it, as the band that would soon become the biggest in the world hit the road with their thumbs out. It was chaos. They missed all three gigs booked between LA and Seattle, but somehow strung together enough rides to arrive, triumphant, hungry and reeking to high heaven, at the Gorilla Gardens, for their first ever show outside LA. Barely ten people saw them, but this time it didn't matter. There was booze, dope and Duff's punk friends to party with, and more importantly they had made it, and made it together, through a 1000-mile odyssey of rides in trucks, sleeping at roadsides; starving, cold, tired, wired and looking, in Duff's excellent phrase, 'like hungry wolves'. They were a band.

When the promoter at the Gorilla Gardens tried to welsh on their $200 guarantee – 'You haven't sold any tickets' – Axl set light to some paper towels and tried to burn the place down. The bouncers chased them into the streets and they ran, screaming from the joy and adrenalin, into another club, where they attempted unsuccessfully to commandeer the equipment of the band playing there – a local outfit Duff knew called Soundgarden. That failed too, but when Duff's friend Donner organised a ride back to LA, they returned happy, and, as Duff said, 'A genuine band. A gang with the shared experience of a road trip gone wrong, an out-of-town gig and the knowledge that we were fully committed to Guns N' Roses.'

2

WHERE THE GIRLS ARE PRETTY

Although it was Duff McKagan who had booked what Guns N' Roses were already calling 'the Hell tour' to Seattle, once they returned to LA, one thing was clear: with Tracii Guns out of the picture, the band had a leader, and that leader was W. Axl Rose. 'Axl always had this kind of *vision* of where he wanted to be,' Slash would tell me. 'What he wanted the band to be. He didn't like people he thought were trying to hold him back.'

With Tracii now out of the way, and the other band members unready to challenge a guy so seemingly set in his own mind, Axl was ready to assume leadership. Sure, Duff was determined to keep pushing forward; like Axl, he wanted to rehearse regularly and get the show on the road as soon as possible, but he would yield to the singer in terms of writing. Slash and Izzy, who were more involved in the writing process, were so laidback (and increasingly strung-out) that they would often just leave him to it once things were up and running. And they both owed him: Axl had sold himself and Izzy as a pair, even when Slash had visions of a one-guitarist band, and in turn Slash had already blown it with Axl once and couldn't afford to lose a singer that good again. Only Steven seemed able to talk back to Axl, but then Steven really didn't give a fuck – about anything.

Anyhow, it often helped if bands had a dominant personality: the Stones had Jagger, the Beatles had John Lennon, and so on through the history of rock. Sometimes, as with Metallica, the dominant business force (drummer Lars Ulrich) and the dominant musical force (singer-guitarist James Hetfield) were different but complementary. As Guns N' Roses evolved, W. Axl Rose would become both. His desperate need for control, though, seemed to be of an entirely different order to that of most maniacal bandleaders. In the years to come, Axl would talk of the profound damage his dreadful childhood had done to him. And of his attempts, through various forms of therapy, to try to repair at least some of that damage. Right now, though, the other members of Guns N' Roses only knew the bad-ass guy that didn't take shit from nobody. Not even them. But the band would learn that his sudden and uncontrollable mood swings were there to be indulged – at least if they wanted a tolerable working atmosphere and the easy rock star life they'd always dreamed of. 'We call him the Ayatollah,' Slash would tell me when we first met, every part of his face smiling except the eyes. 'With Axl, it's always been *his* way or the highway.'

After the Hell Tour came the Hell House. And like the creation of a star, the Hell House was to suck in a lot of dark matter before it emitted the white heat and light of the Guns N' Roses who were ready to make their first records. There are always torrid tales that surround the creation of a rock'n'roll legend, but in the Hell House bad things happened, things that do not reflect well on anyone involved – however famous and lauded they were to become. The building was located in West Hollywood, behind 7508 Sunset Boulevard near the junction of North Gardner Street, a one-room space of around 12 feet by 12 feet that was officially designated a 'storage area' (it's now behind a shop called the Russian Bookstore). Just over the road was the Guitar Center, and nearby the Mesa/Boogie amp showroom. It wasn't a dwelling space at all: it had a roll-up aluminium door, no bathroom, kitchen or air conditioning, and until Izzy and a couple of friends found some lumber abandoned behind the unit and used it to build a rudimentary gallery that just about slept three if you lay very still, was entirely unrecognisable as one.

Anyone needing the toilet had to use the communal facility 50 yards up the street. It was a terrible place, one you'd only consider if you were young, broke and living day to day with some fucked-up dream in your head. Izzy described it as 'a fucking living hell . . .' Slash, having lost a job working on a newsstand and its attendant chance to crash at the apartment of the stand's manager, was forced to choose between the Hell House or homelessness and even then sometimes took the latter option, sleeping in the Tower Records parking lot rather than the squalid, overcrowded nightmare that the House became.

It started out as a rehearsal space. They had been getting by using a room in Silver Lake owned by Nicky Beat, a Strip-scene drummer who'd spent about ten minutes in LA Guns. 'Nicky wasn't necessarily seedy,' Slash recalled. 'But he had a lot of seedy friends . . .' Guns N' Roses connected with various of those – the 'underbelly' as Slash called it – and some would follow them back to the Hell House. Their lives were chaotic and becoming more so, and yet the chaos fired them. In the Hell House they wrote and worked up most of the songs that would appear on *Appetite for Destruction*, plus a few that would hold over for *Use Your Illusion*, too. Izzy had the riffs for 'Think About You' and 'Out ta Get Me'; Slash had the opening chords and riff to 'Welcome to the Jungle'. 'That song, if anything,' Slash explained, 'was the first real tune that the band wrote together . . .'

Duff and Steven spent many hours jamming along to rock and funk, forging their groove, and the rhythm of 'Rocket Queen' came from one of those extended jams. And they wrote quickly. 'Out ta Get Me' and 'Welcome to the Jungle' took little more than an afternoon to assemble. When they got to the Hell House, the fierce work ethic continued. 'We rehearsed a *lot* of hours,' Duff recalled. In the small concrete space with their amps turned up, 'our shitty gear sounded magical, clear and *huge*'.

They had no PA and played so loud Axl would have to scream lyrics and vocal melodies into his bandmates' ears in order to get his ideas across. Axl and Slash were the first to become permanent residents in the garage. Izzy, Duff and Steven had girlfriends that they were living with, but they still spent most of their waking hours there. As the band began to establish itself as one of the best new acts on the Strip, they dragged others towards the Hell House too. There was West Arkeen, a musician neighbour of Duff's, cut from the same cloth as the band and ultimately close enough to Axl to co-write 'Yesterdays', 'The Garden' and 'Bad Obsession', as well as 'It's So Easy'; Del James, a biker turned writer and a pal of West's, who began to hang with Axl and wrote short stories that were adapted for various lyrics and ideas, most notably the video for 'November Rain'; Todd Crew, who played bass in another Strip band called Jetboy; Robert John, a photographer and friend of Axl's whose work would become synonymous with the band's early years; Jack Lue, another photographer, closer to Slash; Slash's friends Mark Manfield and Ron Schneider; Duff's Seattle pal Eddy, who quickly tapped into Izzy's heroin supply and was exiled back to Washington State; Marc Canter, still a true Guns believer who was to have a key, if unsung, role in Guns' development during the Hell House era; Vicky Hamilton, a promoter and would-be manager with an eye for talent – she had booked early shows for Mötley Crüe and Poison – and the key to those precious slots at the Troubadour that Guns had begun to covet while they schlepped their wares at Madam Wongs (a Chinese restaurant) and the Stardust Ballroom (miles from West Hollywood); plus a revolving cast of bands that got to know of Guns N' Roses as the new noise on Sunset (literally – the rehearsals were audible from ten blocks away): musical misfits like Faster Pussycat, Redd Kross, London, the rest of Jetboy and a stack of others, followed of course by girls who liked guys in bands, and then guys who liked girls that liked guys in bands, an ever-growing scene that centred around the Hell House and a cheap, dark Mexican restaurant across Sunset called El Compadre, and the Seventh Veil strip club, where the band became friendly enough with the girls to start having them come and dance on stage with them.

The scene itself fuelled creativity, sparked songs: when the entire band went to visit Lizzie Grey, who lived on Palm Avenue, an infamous street that ran between Sunset and Santa Monica (Slash: 'more than a few sleazy chicks lived there, a few junkie girls we knew lived there . . .'), Lizzie passed around a bottle of cheap fortified wine called Night Train, a formidably alcoholic brew known for its ability to get the very broke very blasted very quickly. They began screaming the words 'I'm on the night train' as they walked up Palm Avenue, with Axl extemporising along. The next morning back at the Hell House, they nailed the entire thing, words and music.

One of the regular visitors to the Hell House, Slash's childhood buddy Marc Canter, recalled seeing the band work on that early material. 'A lot of the songs would start with some idea from Izzy like "My Michelle" – the spooky intro part of "Michelle" was total Izzy but without Slash we wouldn't have gotten the harder riff that followed it. Axl would hear these unfinished songs and just know exactly how to work within them. Duff and Steven would then make the songs truly swing and really flesh them out with their ideas. You could say as some have that Axl was the most important, [but] if you took any one of those guys out of the equation it would have drastically changed all of those songs. It was truly a democracy in the beginning, at that time in 1985 or 1986 they were all on the exact same page.'

All of the lyrics came from real-life situations or people. 'My Michelle' was named after Michelle Young, who went to school with Slash and Steven and was a friend of Slash's first serious girlfriend, Melissa. Michelle had a brief fling with Axl, who then immortalised her early life in the brutal opening couplets: '*Your daddy works in porno / Now your mummy's not around / She used to love her heroin / But now she's underground*'.

The idea, ironically, had come from Michelle herself, who'd once remarked to Axl how wonderful it would be to have someone write a song about her, after listening to 'Your Song' by Elton John with him. 'We were driving to a show I think it was,' she described in 2014, 'and that song came on and I was like, "Oh, that's such a beautiful song! I wish someone would write a song like that about me." And then, lo and behold, came "My Song",' she laughed.

It wasn't so funny, though, she admitted, the first time she heard the lyrics. 'I heard it when I was at my dad's house. I was in my bedroom [when] Axl called. He would always call me and sing me new songs. He would play this drumbeat on his knee and sing and snap to me on the phone whenever he had a new song, he would call me and sing a little and ask my opinion of it.' This time, though, she didn't know what to say. 'I was so out of it at the time, I was always high back then so when I heard it and heard the lyrics I was like, "Oh, it's fine, it's cool . . . do whatever you want."' She laughed again then added, 'I didn't really honestly think that the album was going to be *that* huge or even that that song was gonna be on their album for that matter.'

According to Slash, writing in his memoir, 'Michelle loved the attention it brought her. Back then it was the best thing that had happened to her. But like so many of our friends that were drawn into the dark circle of Guns N' Roses, she came in one way and went out another. Most of them ended up going to jail or rehab or both (or worse).' According to Michelle, though, 'when the song came out I can say it was never a blessing, it was always a curse, let's just say'.

The reasons for some of the Hell House's depravity were economic. The rent was 400 dollars a month. With only Duff working anything other than spasmodically, they learned to survive on
next to nothing. 'We could usually dig up a buck for a bottle of
Night Train,' said Duff. 'Which would fuck you up. For $5, we'd all
be gone.' Slash had procured a hibachi grill on which they'd cook
up hamburger meat. On Saturdays they'd line up with all of the
other Hollywood waifs and strays for the Salvation Army Mission's
free food handout. They discovered the all-you-can-eat-for-a-dollar
buffet at Rage, a well-known West Hollywood gay club. 'We tried to
live off $3.75 a day,' Axl told me in one of the first interviews we did.
'Which was enough to buy gravy and biscuits at Denny's diner for
a buck and a quarter, and a bottle of Night Train for a buck and a
quarter, or some Thunderbird. That was it. You survived.'

Or at least, you did at first . . . Once word got out that the alley
behind the Hell House was deserted at night, a tiny urban black
hole in the midst of West Hollywood, it became the place to go
once the clubs closed for the evening. 'Between us and the other
bands, the alley began to attract a lot of drugs, booze, girls and
other musicians. Strippers from the neighbourhood constantly
came by, often bringing Quaaludes, Valium, coke or booze to
share,' recounted Duff. Soon, from the early hours until day-
break, hundreds of people were gathered there to party. The band,
seizing their chance as proprietors, began buying cheap beer and
selling it at marked-up prices. Soon they were making enough to
pay the rent for the month.

Some of the women were ruthlessly exploited. If one of the
band was having sex with her, another would be stealing her
money. 'There was a lot of indoor and outdoor sex,' said Axl. 'I
used to fuck girls just so I could go stay at their place,' admitted
Slash. 'We sold girls,' said Izzy. 'If one of the guys was fucking a
girl in our sleeping loft, we'd ransack the girl's purse while he was
doing her. We *managed*.'

'We'd talk girls into climbing into the loft,' said Axl, 'and someone would hit the lights and go, "All right! Everyone in the loft either get naked or leave . . ."'

Heroin, the subject of another of Axl's salutary lessons in how not to live, 'Mr Brownstone', had now arrived and was about to cut a swathe through the band. Izzy was not only using but openly dealing, another source of income. He claimed that Joe Perry had once come by to score, just before he cleaned up and Aerosmith began their commercial resurrection. Slash noticed that Steven 'seemed like he was drunk', when he showed up at rehearsals, despite not having been drinking. It transpired that a girl he was sleeping with, in an apartment further up on Gardner Street, and her roommate had got Steven into smack, and once Slash started dating the roommate, he was soon doing it as well. In addition to heroin and all of the pills and booze, a creepy crack dealer named Philippe also became a fixture.

The squalor was overwhelming. 'At one point we had the band and four other women living in this one room,' said Axl. 'The nearest bathroom [the communal facility in the alley] had been destroyed by people throwing up. I used to shit in a box and throw it in the trash, because the bathroom was so disgusting.' The depravity spilled over. They would get horribly fucked up at shows. Slash threw up behind his amplifier at a gig at Raji's. Axl started a fight with someone in the crowd. He also got barred briefly from the Rainbow – some achievement – and the band earned a reputation for drunken obnoxiousness, bumming drinks, starting fights, aggressively panhandling at their own gigs. The West Hollywood Sherriff's Department became aware of the parties in the Gardner Street alley, and heard the tales of drug dealing and other anti-social behaviour.

Then, in December 1985, came a dark and serious incident that signalled the end of the Hell House era. A 15-year-old girl named Michelle entered the rehearsal space one day, and, according to an interview Axl later gave to the *LA Weekly*, 'started fucking with our equipment'. There was some kind of scuffle and the girl ended up running naked along Sunset Boulevard. Michelle was known to the band. She'd hung around the Hell House periodically, along with lots of others, and had found herself in the wrong place at the wrong time. Axl's version of events was that 'this hippy chick wandered in and started fucking with our equipment trying to break stuff . . . So eventually she wound up running down Sunset naked, all dingy, and didn't even know her own name.'

Slash, in his autobiography, published, of course, many years later, offers: 'My memory of the events is hazy but from what I remember she had sex with Axl up in the loft. Towards the end of the night, maybe as the drugs and booze wore off, she lost her mind and freaked out intensely. Axl told her to leave and tried throwing her out. I attempted to help mediate the situation to get her out quietly, but that wasn't happening.'

A naked, underage girl running away from adult men along one of the busiest streets in Los Angeles was not going to go unnoticed, and within hours the LAPD were back at the Hell House with the girl, looking to ID her assailants. Everyone in the house was brought outside except for Axl, who hid behind some equipment along with another girl. 'While the cops are out there harassing everybody, asking their stupid questions, I'm with this girl behind the amp and we start going at it,' he later boasted. 'That was the rush! I got away with it! It was really exciting.'

The police left, warning the band that Axl needed to turn himself in. Within a few days the garage had been raided and searched. The band was told that the girl and her parents were pressing charges of statutory rape (a minor is considered by law as incapable of giving consent to sexual intercourse) against Axl and Slash. There were rumours that the garage was under surveillance from undercover officers, and also the LAPD vice squad. Despite Axl's bravado, he and Slash quickly skipped the scene when reality – and the possibility of a mandatory five-year jail sentence – hit home. Slash retreated to an apartment Steven was sharing with a new girlfriend, Monica, who was a stripper at the Seventh Veil – and who Slash later claimed he and Steven had '*awesome* threesomes' with – while Axl slept rough in West Hollywood, making use of the Tower Records parking lot and bathrooms in gas stations and cheap restaurants.

They were now afraid to play live in case Axl or Slash or both were arrested at the gig. They cancelled a show at the Music Machine, and did not take any further bookings. Growing desperate, Slash rang Vicky Hamilton, their sometime promoter/manager, and begged her to take Axl in for a few days. Hamilton had a one-bed apartment at 1114 North Clark Street that she'd secured with settlement money she'd received for relinquishing an interest in the management of Poison, who were now in the process of breaking big. She was sharing with a friend in need, Jennifer Perry, and working as an agent for Silver Lining Entertainment as well as helping Guns N' Roses out on an ad hoc basis. (Even before Guns headed out on the Hell Tour, Hamilton had 'made myself available for the band 24/7. They would often come by my apartment to check in'.) That arrangement became more solid as soon as Axl showed up as a fugitive from the LAPD.

'I got a call from Slash,' she elaborated, 'asking if Axl could stay and I asked why. Slash had replied: "Well, it's kind of important . . . the cops are looking for him." "Why are the cops looking for him?" "He had a girl up in the loft, and I guess they had sex, but then he got mad at her and locked her outside without her clothes and she went to the cops and said that he raped her." I was stunned and didn't know what to say. Slash sort of begged so I said, "Okay, for a few days." Minutes later Axl walks through the door carrying a plastic garbage bag and a little suitcase full of all his worldly possessions.

'"Oh, my God . . . Thank you so much, Vicky, you have saved my life," he said. I asked him what happened and he said very little, other than "It was stupid, involving a girl . . . It won't happen again," Axl promised. He didn't give me any more information. Everything I heard about the incident from that point on was hearsay.'

The Hell House era was done. Over the next few months, Hamilton's tiny one-bedroom apartment became the de facto crashpad/centre of operations for Guns N' Roses, with the fugitive Axl and Slash in semi-permanent residence in the tiny lounge (at least when Axl wasn't ghosting around the darkened booths at the Rainbow, where his ban had been rescinded) and the rest of the band dropping by constantly for councils of war. Hamilton even found Axl a lawyer to represent him on the rape charge.

After a few months of this, she wrote in her illuminating memoir, *Appetite for Dysfunction*, 'my apartment looked like a cyclone had hit it. There were McDonald's cartons, cigarette butts, cigarette burns, and empty alcohol bottles everywhere. There was a jar of mayonnaise on the windowsill in the kitchen, as I still hadn't got around to buying a refrigerator. One of my neighbors had posted a note on the window saying, "Kids, don't use that mayonnaise. It will make you sick. It needs to be refrigerated." I would wake up in the morning and step over bodies in sleeping bags to get a drink of water. Most of the time, I could tell that they had company in their sleeping bags as I could hear them having sex. The bathroom was the worst of it. The walls had caught all the blue/black hair dye from Slash and Izzy's dye jobs. The bathtub had an indefinable scum on the inside surface. You couldn't sandblast that stuff off. I got in the habit of taking a trash bag to the shower with me to stand on while showering.'

Although Hamilton recalls several visits from the police and many, many lawyers' phone calls, the rape charges were withdrawn at some point during this period. The case against Slash was given a court date but later dropped. Axl did have to find a suit and appear at a court hearing, but his case was also dropped through a lack of hard evidence. Instead, when word of the incident swept along the Strip, instead of damaging them, it seemed to fuel Guns N' Roses' reputation as rock'n'roll outlaws, the real, no-fucks-given kind of deal that so many other bands were just throwing shapes pretending to be. A wild rumour circulated that the charges had been dropped after Axl slept with the mother of the girl concerned. No one seemed bothered that a 15-year-old had been through a harrowing experience, whatever the detail. Instead, the toxic edge of the Hell House simply generated more heat. Once the threat of prison time began to recede, they even played on it, producing a flyer with the words, 'Send donations to Guns N' Roses – Keep us out of jail fund' along the bottom.

The flyer, painstakingly produced by Slash in Vicky Hamilton's living room, was headed 'Move to the City' and advertised the band's return to the Strip at the Troubadour on 4 January 1986. That show, and a follow-up at the Roxy two weeks later, took Guns N' Roses to a tipping point. They were now pulling hundreds of people to their gigs, with hundreds more locked out, mooching around in the street just to say that they were there. Guns looked like street urchins given a last-minute makeover in the ladies' bathroom, Axl in biker chaps, wiggling his ass in a snaky move he'd cribbed from Richard Black, the singer in Shark Island, Izzy like Johnny Thunders' long-lost twin, Duff in his heavy leather punk gear, Slash wearing last week's jeans, hiding behind his curls, Steven at the back, the blonde himbo with the goofy grin . . . and they sounded like nothing else out there. They had a depth and purpose that set them apart from Poison or Ratt or Faster Pussycat or any of the other bands about to do the same old glam metal thing. Instead they were the successors to Aerosmith or the Stones, a classic one-off rock'n'roll band with unique heart and tone. The set was diamond-hard and built around the material they'd worked up in the Hell House.

Walking on to an ear-splitting intro tape, 'What's That Noise' by the Stormtroopers of Death, they would start with 'Reckless Life', reworked from the Hollywood Rose-era 'Wreckless', and then 'It's So Easy', 'Move to the City', 'Out ta Get Me', 'Rocket Queen' (now complete with lyrics inspired by Barbi Von Grief, a girlfriend of Axl's who also influenced much of their look and who would often dance onstage with the band), 'My Michelle', a slow and sinister new number called 'You're Crazy', Axl's overwrought ballad 'Don't Cry', climaxing with 'Welcome to the Jungle' and 'Paradise City'. They would throw in Aerosmith's 'Mama Kin' or Rose Tattoo's 'Nice Boys' for flavour, and as a hat-tip to their influences. As a club band Guns N' Roses were now at their peak.

'The phone was ringing constantly for the guys,' recalled Vicky Hamilton of the growing intensity that would ultimately lead to the band being signed. 'Aside from all the girlfriends, club bookers were calling, industry insiders were calling, writers, A&R reps, publishers and agents were calling. Keep in mind that the cellphone did not exist. Everyone had a landline, and if someone was on the phone, you received a busy signal . . .'

The band's business arrangements were as casual and tangled as everything else they did. Before moving into Vicky Hamilton's cramped apartment, they'd had another sort-of manager called Brigitte Wright, who also represented Jetboy, but after Vicky had hidden them from the cops, put them up, booked them gigs, helped Slash make flyers and small ads for *BAM* magazine, promoted shows, and taken a week-long job in the booking office at the Roxy 'because Guns were bleeding me dry', it seemed only fair that she should officially have the role of Guns N' Roses' manager. At least, to everyone in the band except Axl, who always somehow managed to avoid the conversation. Yet Vicky had a verbal agreement from Slash, and all of the band's 10x8s and flyers carried her name and number, but she'd been bruised in the past by her experiences with Mötley Crüe and Poison, and when her friend John Harrington, one of the promoters at the Roxy, urged her to get something in writing, she knew that he was right.

Hamilton called a well-known music biz attorney named Peter Paterno, who looked after a lot of first-time deals for bands on the Strip. He gave her a draft contract for herself and the band to sign, but 'The band stalled in working out the agreement with me, so I started getting pissed. I felt thoroughly taken advantage of. They were living at my house for free . . . I was booking their shows, feeding them, clothing them . . . with *my* clothes. Getting them legal representation, getting Axl's charges dropped, buying them cigarettes, helping them create their flyers and advertisements . . . I must be crazy. I told them that they had to negotiate and sign an agreement with me right then, or they had to move out . . . immediately. They agreed to negotiate.'

But the wolves were circling . . . Kim Fowley, the legendary Hollywood sleaze-ball who'd made his name producing novelty hits in the Sixties for one-night-stand acts like Bee Bumble and the Stingers, then in the Seventies creating and producing The Runaways, arrived at Hamilton's apartment and offered Axl a traveller's cheque for $7500 and a contract to sign over the publishing rights to three songs. According to Hamilton, Axl actually thought this might be a good idea, as he wrote 'hundreds' of songs. She quickly dissuaded him. 'The buzz got out,' said Slash. 'And we kept getting invited out to meet these idiots from record companies. One label we were talking to, I was saying, "It sounds kinda like Steven Tyler", and the chick goes, "Steven who?" All of us just looked at each other and went, "Uh, can we have another one of those drinks?"'

Hamilton took the band to meet with Paterno. Slash was so hungover that he vomited from the rail of the tenth-floor patio down the side of the building. A few days after the meeting, Paterno told Hamilton that he should handle the band's legal negotiations and that she should find another lawyer to represent her in establishing a management agreement. 'I was furious, but too naive to realize that I was being played,' remembered Hamilton in her memoir. 'Things were moving so fast and every day we were being wined and dined by different record companies. Yet I did not have a negotiated contract with the band, and apparently I did not have a lawyer any more either. The band told me not to worry, that they were going to take care of me. I believed them to a fault.'

From living in a garage and fucking girls for food and rent, Guns N' Roses were now taking meetings with record company representatives who were talking giddying sums of money. 'The Chrysalis fucking brains came along and said we'll give you guys $750,000, and we just said, yeah, but have you ever heard us play?' Duff related. 'And they were like, "No, but . . ." So we were like, "See ya!" Suddenly there was this little label war, everybody trying to get us to sign – we had a lot of great lunches.'

After the Roxy show, Hamilton took a meeting with Peter Philbin at Elektra, where Axl warned him 'not to take too long' in offering a deal. Although Chrysalis had not struck a chord with Duff, they began to edge further along the road with an executive there named Susan Collins. After an extravagant lunch at the Ivy, Collins took the band to meet her boss, Ron Fair. It was a meeting that became one of the most infamous in the history of the era, and one which illustrated both the ambition and the attitude of W. Axl Rose.

Vicky Hamilton's eyewitness account is vivid: 'Axl sat and propped his legs up on Ron's desk, sporting his snakeskin cowboy boots . . . with fresh duct tape so the sole would stay together. Ron smiled at Axl and then introduced himself to the whole band. His hard sell began with why the band should sign with Chrysalis. He then took out a pad of paper and drew a big dollar sign on five sheets of paper and handed each band member a sheet. "This is what you will get when you sign with Chrysalis." Axl looked at me and whispered in my ear, "Is he fucking kidding us?"'

Vicky asked exactly how much money Ron was talking about. But Ron didn't have a number, just sputtered, 'A lot!' Then told them he'd get back to them after he'd spoken to the label's legal-affairs department. Unimpressed, Axl blew out his cheeks, turned to Collins and told her with a straight face: 'If you'll run down Sunset Boulevard naked, we will consider signing with you.'

Susan Collins said nothing as she showed the band the door. But when they played the Troubadour again on 28 February, Hamilton counted 16 A&R representatives in the audience. The day had begun inauspiciously, when Axl and Steven had got into a fight in Hamilton's apartment over who should clean up, but the show was as taut and frenzied as usual. Outside the venue, Paterno introduced Hamilton to a young A&R man from Geffen named Tom Zutaut. He looked anomalous amongst all the rockers, short-haired and cherub-faced, still young. Geffen had taken him on after he'd persuaded Elektra to sign Mötley Crüe, and he'd come up with their first significant hit, a cover of Brownsville Station's 'Smokin' in the Boys Room'. Now the Crüe were poised to go multi-platinum, and Zutaut's ear for a hit was zinging again. He later claimed that he knew Guns N' Roses were going to be the biggest band in the world after just two numbers: 'Welcome to the Jungle' and 'Nightrain'.

In fact, Zoots, as he was known, had already been tipped off about the band by his pal Joseph Brooks, the influential KROQ radio DJ and former owner of the hip Hollywood record store Vinyl Fetish. 'I dragged A&R people to their gigs and played the 'Welcome to the Jungle' demo on my [KROQ] show,' he said. A memory Zutaut shares. 'Joe at Vinyl Fetish was like, "There's this new band called Guns N' Roses – you should check them out." I went to see them at the Troubadour and there were a lot of A&R people. So I left after two songs . . . On my way out I said [to one of the other A&R people], "They suck – I'm going home", knowing full well I was going to sign them to Geffen come hell or high water.'

The day after the Troubadour show, Zoots called Axl and invited the band to his house, where he cut straight to the chase and offered them a deal. At first Axl did his best to play it cool. The more they talked, however, the more Axl warmed to the kid-faced Geffen exec. Zutaut made two smart moves. The first was to let them know how much he loved Aerosmith, and how Geffen were about to resurrect their career (which they went on to do, in spectacular style). If Guns N' Roses signed to Geffen, they would be label mates with their heroes. The second was to throw the name of Bill Price into the mix as a possible producer. Price had worked with the Sex Pistols, which both excited Axl and proved to him that Zutaut saw the band in the same way that they saw themselves.

Impressed by Zutaut's knowledge of music and his obvious passion, Axl made him a bravura counter-offer: 'If you can get us a check for $75,000 by Friday night at six p.m. we'll sign with you. Otherwise, we're going to meet with some other people.'

When Zutaut returned to his office and spoke to his boss, the label's president, Eddie Rosenblatt, he once again played his hunch and tried to convince Rosenblatt that, although the request was highly unconventional, W. Axl Rose had the kind of potential that you tore up rule books for. Rosenblatt, who had been around the block enough times to own the building, resisted. So Zutaut asked for a meeting with David Geffen himself, and, amused and impressed by his desire, Rosenblatt agreed. Putting his case all over again, Zutaut watched helplessly as Geffen laughed out loud at his urging that Guns were going to be the biggest rock'n'roll band in the world. 'David, I swear to God,' Zutaut insisted. 'I have no doubt about it, and you have to make this happen. I have to have this cheque for $75,000 by Friday at six.'

Geffen, who had created a corporation out of playing his own immaculate hunches, nodded his head. He was entirely unaware that he'd just agreed to cut a cheque for the same little kid, Saul Hudson, he'd once babysat up in Laurel Canyon.

Zutaut called Axl, only to be told that should Susan Collins walk naked down Sunset Boulevard before 6 p.m., Guns N' Roses would be signing with Chrysalis. Tom Zutaut sweated until 6.01 p.m., constantly peeping through his office blinds and half expecting to see some kind of traffic pile-up on the Boulevard below.

Later that night, Axl, Slash, Izzy, Duff and Steven dutifully showed up at his office and signed the deal memorandum that Zutaut shoved their way across his desk. By midnight it was done: Guns N' Roses had signed a major, long-term recording contract with Geffen Records. Kim Fowley recalled Axl swanning into the Rainbow that Friday night brandishing a photocopy of the Geffen cheque. 'He said, "Look, we got our deal." I said, "Congratulations", and he said, "Buy me a drink – I don't have any money."'

Vicky Hamilton would be left behind in the wreckage. The months before the band signed with Geffen had been a whirlwind, and came at some cost to her. She had borrowed $25,000 from Howie Hubberman, who owned a store called Guitars R Us, and used it to buy equipment and clothes and to help finance a couple of cheap demos that had been handed around to A&R scouts just before the feeding frenzy began in earnest. She worked every contact she had to do so. She got a tape to John Kalodner, Geffen's chief scout, long before Zutaut had fallen for the band. She'd helped to get Kiss mainman Paul Stanley in front of Axl to talk about producing them – a meeting that went south almost immediately when Stanley had suggested rewriting a couple of songs. She'd given them everything she had to give and more. And they took it and never even said goodbye.

Except for Axl. At the end of March 1986, Guns had played a show in support of another of their long-time heroes, Johnny Thunders, out at Fender's Ballroom in Long Beach – a druggy, unpleasant experience. It just after that when Axl invited Vicky out for dinner – just the two of them – at the Rainbow. She told me how Axl had explained that he planned for Guns N' Roses to be bigger than Queen, bigger than Elton. And that for that they needed 'a real heavy hitter as a manager, and that wasn't me. I was okay with that if that's the way they wanted to go. But what about all the time and effort I'd put into them? Didn't that count for something? What about all the money I owed?'

Axl told her: 'I really intend to pay you back, and give you a bonus on top of that, but I am not sure that you will be our manager once we sign a deal. You are really great on a local level, but I don't know if you have what it takes to take us to the top, to worldwide success.'

Hamilton countered by offering to go into partnership with a more experienced manager, and set up a meeting with Doc McGhee and Doug Thaler, who were managing Bon Jovi, the Scorpions and now Mötley Crüe. It was a disastrous morning, with a couple of the band, red-eyed and hungover, nodding out on the McGhee Entertainment office sofas while Doc and Doug asked them about their plans. McGhee had enough of that on his hands with Mötley Crüe, and passed.

As Tom Zutaut upped his efforts to sign the band, he offered Hamilton a job as an A&R scout at Geffen. 'He said to me, "If you come to work at Geffen, you will be too busy scouting talent to manage Guns N' Roses, so we will have to find them a new manager. I will get you an office, somewhere off campus, not on the Geffen lot. You can still manage and scout, but you will have to give up Guns N' Roses and let me find them a big-time manager,"' she recounts in *Appetite for Dysfunction*. 'I told him that I would think about it. Meanwhile, he was courting the band and inviting them to his house to party. Sometimes I would come home in the middle of the afternoon and find Tom in my living room with the band. I was sad and depressed at the thought of letting GN'R go, but continued to mull over my options. I came to the decision that I should take the deal that Tom Zutaut was offering.'

Guns N' Roses played two sets at the Roxy on 28 March, shows that Hamilton had originally designed as showcases but that now became celebrations of the Geffen deal. She helped the band cash their advance cheque – the band ended up with about $7500 each. Vicky got nothing. 'The guys were running around town buying clothes, getting tattoos, buying musical equipment, all the while partying to the extreme. I was broke, sitting in my destroyed apartment, not sure how I was going to pay that month's rent, or buy groceries. Howie Hubberman handed me $500 and told me to go check into a hotel somewhere . . . I really needed a couple of days away from the band to get my head together.'

As Hamilton was eased out of the band's future, Guns N' Roses met the press for the first time, and – perhaps as an augury – things went catastrophically wrong. Hamilton had organised a cover story with *Music Connection* magazine, a story written by Karen Burch, who met the band at Vicky's apartment in North Clark Street and conducted an entertainingly spiky interview that began badly when she asked the band their ages. When the piece came out –'Days of Guns N' Roses: Face to Face with LA's Friskiest Bad-Boy Band' – it emerged with the warning: 'This issue's cover is running against the wishes of Guns N' Roses, according to Axl Rose', which was true. Having taken a dislike to the idea of the story, he'd waged a week-long campaign of harassing phone calls to Burch in an attempt to spike it, and once the magazine was published on 14 April 1986 composed a rambling letter of complaint about everything from the 'insincerity' of the photographer to the 'unrecorded sexual prodding' of Burch.

It was an absurdly self-regarding missive, written floridly – 'where the pen acts, and so often is in actuality, as the knife' – and filled with concocted reasons why Burch had left a 'foul stench' with her work. It began a pattern that would persist through his dealings with the press, and was another sign of the mercurial behaviour that was about to assert its grip on the band and its running. It was strange, as the piece, read today, looks as fine a prompt as any for a band receiving its first cover story from a major American music magazine.

Soon afterwards Hamilton received an eviction notice, and would move out of North Clark Street and down into a bungalow in West Hollywood, a blessed relief, even though she was still struggling to make the rent. It was now clear that she would not be managing Guns N' Roses, although she still booked their shows while Zutaut used Geffen's A&R resources to handle the band's day-to-day needs. His first attempt at finding a new manager for them was Arnold Stiefel, Rod Stewart's representative, which ended rapidly when the band trashed a house Stiefel rented for them. Back to square one, and with their reputation already damaged with a couple of leading management companies (Doc McGhee having also passed), Zutaut organised another house on Fountain Avenue, a famous Hollywood thoroughfare that runs parallel with Sunset Boulevard. Axl didn't like it and for a while kept breaking into Vicky Hamilton's to crash on the couch, but once her eviction notice was enforced, the pair stopped speaking. She got her gig working for Geffen, and also a heartening phone call from Ola Hudson, Slash's mother, thanking her for looking after the band, but although Slash, Steven and Duff publicly expressed their gratitude, she was never repaid the money she'd spent on Guns N' Roses, and three years later would launch a suit against the band.

Guns N' Roses played the first show at the refurbished Whisky a Go Go in April 1986, a night that carried all sorts of significance. They were supported by Faster Pussycat, a band Hamilton was soon shopping, and who Axl had insisted go on the bill. He was also in the first throes of a serious, adult relationship – with Erin Everly, the 20-year-old model daughter of singer Don Everly – and was feeling the tension of it all. He and Steven Adler got into another fight on the afternoon of the gig. Nobody could remember exactly why.

Tom Zutaut had invited Aerosmith's co-manager, Tim Collins, out from New York to see the band with a view to handling their affairs. 'I didn't really want to,' Collins admitted, but he was in a position where Aerosmith's own relationship with Geffen was just developing and he felt that he should at least take a look out of courtesy. Along with Aerosmith's 'Toxic Twins', Steven Tyler and Joe Perry, Collins had recently got clean, and after one look at Guns N' Roses backstage, surrounded by dubious characters and barely dressed young girls, 'I immediately felt the narcotic vibe of this band and knew that I was at serious risk of relapse if I wasn't careful.'

Collins brought the band to his suite at the La Dufy hotel, where they stayed up all night. He was impressed with Axl, but when he finally got into the bathroom after the numerous visits paid by Izzy and Slash, he found blood on the ceiling and realised that at least one of the band was mainlining heroin. 'Frankly, I was scared of them,' Collins told the American writer Stephen Davis, and despite pressure from David Geffen himself, he passed. Zutaut also tried Rod Smallwood, the straight-talking, Yorkshire-born, Cambridge-educated manager of Iron Maiden, but Smallwood had a stake in Poison, who were now label mates with Maiden at EMI, and he passed too. 'There was just something about them

I wasn't quite sure of,' he told me. 'The singer did most of the talking but it wasn't anything he said, so much, that put me off. Just something about them that wasn't quite right, some vibe that was just . . . wrong.'

Guns N' Roses' reputation for being 'unmanageable' grew.

The chaos continued through the summer of 1986. Plans to record in London with Bill Price were scrapped, in part for budgetary reasons but also because Zutaut recognised the lunacy of letting Guns N' Roses loose in a foreign land. David Geffen asked Price to come to LA, but Bill, who'd just got off producing Pete Townshend's latest album and was already involved making demos with The Jesus and Mary Chain, decided against it. Mötley Crüe's producer, Tom Werman, also passed, as did Bob Ezrin, who'd worked with Lou Reed and Roger Waters yet found the prospect of working with this band of Hollywood weird-kidz too much. A meeting with Cheap Trick's guitarist, Rick Nielsen, ended with Izzy kicking Nielsen in the balls after a tequila binge. Zutaut even approached Mötley Crüe's bassist, Nikki Sixx, as Nikki explained: '[To] see if I could give the punk-metal they were playing at the time a more commercial, melodic edge without sacrificing credibility. They were just a punk band, he told me, but they were capable of being the greatest rock'n'roll band in the world if someone could help them find the melodies to take them there. I was too much in agony trying to slow my down my drug intake to consider the idea . . .'

Finally they found someone at least willing to enter the studio with them when Nazareth's guitarist, Manny Charlton, engineered a long session at Sound City in Hollywood. The band's fierce work ethic was stimulated by the presence of one of Izzy and Axl's high-school favourites, and the session produced 27 songs, including most of *Appetite for Destruction*, plus a batch that would be held over for *Use Your Illusion*, most notably Axl's cherished ballad 'November Rain'.

It was the breakthrough Zoots needed, and he was heartened by their work rate. When they headlined the Troubadour on 11 July, Axl was able to tell the crowd that not only would Guns N' Roses be making a record for Geffen, but they would be releasing some of the Sound City sessions on an indie label to let their fans on the Strip get a taste of how LA's hottest live band would sound on vinyl.

Before it happened, Zutaut rode his newly arrived good luck and forged two relationships that would catapult the band way beyond the few miles of Hollywood streets that had become their world. The first of those was with Alan Niven, a New Zealand-born, English public school-educated free spirit who had escaped from the future in the military that his father had laid out for him by learning to play guitar and write songs. While he waited for fame to strike, he parlayed his growing musical connection into a job for Caroline, the distribution wing of Richard Branson's fledgling Virgin Records empire, a job that took him from London to Miami to Gothenburg then later LA, then later still . . . anywhere he damn well pleased.

'By the time I was done with school and they were done with me, I was head of house,' Niven says now. 'School prefect, all that bullshit. At the end of that period I became completely and utterly disgusted with pleasing adults who I felt were hypocritical and letting me down. So that was where my sense of anti-authoritarianism blossomed and bloomed. Am I going to go to Sandhurst, with the family tradition? Fuck, no! I'm going to go and get high and see if somebody's going to be actually kind enough to get me laid.

'In those days we talked of consciousness expansion and the idea was not to get fucked up but to learn faster and comprehend more deeply and more quickly. We were marching through the doors of fucking perception. We were going to be the better generation. Then in the Seventies along came cocaine and all that shit went out the window.'

Though they didn't know it yet, Axl Rose was about to meet his match. The one that helped light the fire that would consume them all, and the one he would later blow out – and, with it, everything else.

3

CHICKEN À LA LSD

Talking years later, after the war was over but the casualties were still being counted, Izzy Stradlin put it like this: 'Alan Niven came along. Thank God he came along because he took us on. He probably looked at us and said, well, they're a mess. But I think he'd been there maybe himself and saw potential. He worked with us and whether anybody says it or not he became like the sixth, silent, member.' In fact, the 33-year-old Alan Niven was already the sixth, not-so-silent member of a soon-to-be-platinum LA band named Great White, a band he'd rescued from the dumper of a failed career as a wannabe heavy metal band and singlehandedly resurrected them into what they were by 1986: a more groovy, blues-influenced rock outfit with a back pocket full of potential hits. Having had the audacity to re-sign the band to the parent group (Capitol Records) of the label that had just dropped them (EMI America), Niven had completely made the band over, co-producing their comeback album, *Shot in the Dark*, co-writing four of the six original numbers on there and hand-picking the two covers, including their scorching version of the track 'Face the Day', originally by Australian rockers The Angels, whom Niven had also worked with.

More, Niven had taken it upon himself to personally promote the track to the two most influential rock radio stations in

California at the time: KMET and KLOS. '"Face the Day" was *the* song of the year in LA in 1986,' he recalls now. 'Twenty or so labels in town and they all had huge budgets and slush funds and piles of coke and they're going, "How the fuck is this guy getting all this airplay?" So in the perception of the huge industry giants along Sunset Boulevard, they're kind of looking at me like, "Has this guy got a little bit of magic and mojo in his blood?" And that kind of helped with getting done what I needed done with GN'R. That and the English accent!' He laughs. 'Walk into a room and remember that you once lived in Oxfordshire. They daren't say boo to you because you sound like you've stepped out of PBS.' When Tom Zutaut, whom Niven had first met when they were both instrumental in getting Mötley Crüe a deal with Elektra, four years before, added him to the 'cattle call' in his search for new management for Guns N' Roses, Niven admits he was reluctant to get involved, only agreeing to take the meeting 'because Zoots was a friend'.

Like most of the people who make it in LA, Alan Niven was a guy from elsewhere. He'd been living in Sweden for two years, working for Virgin/Caroline, when an independent LA-based distribution company called Greenworld recruited him. 'It was one of those moments where you knew you were fucked,' he recalls. 'Because I knew if I didn't go I'd spend the rest of my life wondering what would have happened if I'd gone to LA.' What happened was he struck oil almost immediately, doing the deal which allowed a raw, out-of-control West Hollywood band called Mötley Crüe to release their first album, on their own Leathür Records label, *Too Fast for Love*, in November 1981, as part of a 'pressing and distribution' deal with Greenworld Niven brokered with the band's manager, Allan Coffman. 'I arrived in LA and Mark Wesley, one of the Greenworld partners, gave me the Mötley cassette. "Piece of Your Action" came on and I went, okay . . .' Niven didn't even use lawyers for the contract, drawing it up himself.

'Allan Coffman was only interested in getting the $15,000 cash advance we scraped together.'

Alan Niven first met Tom Zutaut, then working as a junior talent scout for Elektra Records, at the 1982 National Association of Music Merchants (NAMM) convention at the Century Plaza hotel. 'I had these Mötley Crüe posters in my booth,' Niven relates, 'and [Tom] said that he wanted to talk to me about the band. And I said, "Well, come and have dinner."' Niven was living with his then wife in a little cottage in Palos Verdes, overlooking the ocean, out towards Catalina Island. Zutaut arrived for dinner one Friday evening – and didn't leave until the following Monday. Niven laughs as he recalls the special meal he had prepared for them: 'I cooked him my roast chicken à la LSD. My thinking at the time was, well, we'll find out who this guy is pretty quickly . . .'

They both ate the chicken. Wild peacocks roamed the area near the cottage and Tom was convinced they were wearing diamond earrings. 'He had this *incredible* crush on Belinda Carlisle and he lay in front of the little fireplace in the cottage watching the flames telling me just how much he adored her. He wanted to be a success so as he could marry her. That was Tommy and I slipping off from the dock and going out into the ocean together . . .' After that, Tom would go down to the cottage most weekends. 'We spent a lot of time together. My then wife then went and worked as an assistant to him for a while. You know, we were pals, we were friends. We had plans. One day we wanted to run a record label ourselves, together.' When Niven helped Zutaut sign Mötley Crüe to Elektra, 'That opened the door to the A&R department for him.' Niven, meanwhile, had been a key player in the emergence of the Enigma label, which grew out of Greenworld, in 1982, signing Berlin, who would go on to major international success with 'Take My Breath Away', and had been instrumental again in helping Zutaut sign Dokken to Elektra, a band who would also go on to platinum success in the US in the mid-Eighties.

At the time Zoots began twisting his arm about managing Guns N' Roses, though, via Niven's Stravinski Brothers company, Alan was fully committed to Great White. 'I was looking at it and going, this means I've got to fragment my time and energy. And I'm really, really scared to do that, because it took an awful lot to get Great White another record contract. It went against all conventional wisdom. You fuck up on your debut record, you're done. And I'd got a sense of what needed to be done and how to do it.' With Great White there was now a workable plan in place. With this raw new outfit from the streets, the only plan that suggested itself was to hope for the best. 'I'm looking at GN'R and going, I don't expect this band to be anything more than a really great underground band. It wasn't going to be a radio-friendly band and it had so much attitude and was so raw, I knew it was going to be a lot of hard work. [But] I was the last desperate management throw by Zoots as Rosenblatt was threatening to drop Guns without even recording an album.' Tom told Alan later that when he signed on to be manager, Geffen's president, Eddie Rosenblatt, had warned him: 'This guy gets this thing looking like it could be productive within three months or they're gone.'

Niven went to meet the band for the first time, at their new home, a house in Laughlin Park, in the plush Los Feliz area of LA, which Rod Stewart's manager, Arnold Stiefel, had rented for them before getting cold feet. 'A well-known Sunset stripper was leaving as I arrived,' Niven recalls. 'Iz was there and Slash. But no one else. Iz nodded off. Slash showed me his fucking snake. I hate fucking snakes. As I expected, it was a somewhat haphazard circumstance.'

When Niven arranged to go and see the band play, Axl didn't show up for the first gig – or the second gig. As he explains: 'Having signed a contract to work with the band in September of 1986, the very next show that the band were to perform was to open for Alice Cooper at the Arlington Theatre in Santa Barbara.

Alice was to perform a minor market one-off show as a conclusion to his pre-production for a tour. He needed someone to open and it was a good opportunity to get Guns on a decent-size stage; they had only played the LA clubs to this point.

'I rented a big old Lincoln car to drive everyone the hundred miles out to Santa Barbara. When I went to pick up Axl he said he'd rather travel with the photographer, Robert John, and follow the band caravan out to the show. "No worries," I thought. "Now the car will have a little more space." How foolish of me. Set time drew near and there was no Axl. The band were anxious. I thought he was merely running late. Ten minutes before show time there was still no singer. At that point I left my "waiting for Axl" watch in the parking lot behind the theatre and went to the band dressing room. Everyone was miserable.

'"We can't play," said Slash. Izzy just stared at his feet. "I don't give a damn," Niven told them. "We're booked to play and play we will. You sort out who is going to sing what, but you fuckers are going on." The band dejectedly traipsed onto the stage and Duff and Izzy did their best to carry the vocal load. 'I may be wrong but I think even Slash took a go at one of the microphones. All in all it was probably the very worst gig the band ever did. As I stood in the audience I could hear the muttering of punters making negative comments – "I heard there was a buzz on this band. Man, they *suck*." Maybe so, but at that moment Slash, Izzy, Duff and Steven won my heart for their effort in a ridiculous situation.

'Axl later claimed he turned up just as the band went on. We never saw him, though, either before or after the set and we'd left passes at the door and his name on the backstage entrance. But there you have it. Ax has always had a difficulty in getting to the show on time, if at all. From that moment, however, my commitment was even more clearly to the band, to the whole, rather than the one prima donna fronting it.'

The development of that commitment was sorely tested on the very next gig. Booked to open for the Red Hot Chili Peppers on the UCLA campus, only 12 people turned up. 'Twelve! I counted them. So I'm thinking, this is great. What the fuck have I got myself into with Tom Zutaut and his fucking band? Either the singer doesn't turn up or the fucking audience doesn't turn up. This is going to be great . . . Izzy stuck to me like glue. He was like, "We've got one manager from the bottom of the barrel. The last guy possible has agreed to do this. If we lose him we're done." And they would have been.'

Over time, says Niven, Izzy became 'the one I could always count on for timely and pertinent input. When I wanted to know what somebody from the band felt about a particular situation, he was the one I talked to more than anybody else. It was him and Duff that caught my eye over both Slash and Axl, when I first went to see them. Because they had an amazing . . . they just exuded this *incredible* sense of cool when they were onstage. They weren't working it. I was riveted with that confidence and insouciance.'

There was never any doubt, however, over who the leader of the band was, its main focus and truth-giver. Axl, he says, 'really did have his moment of incredible androgynous beauty. Most people look at me like I'm barmy. But most people when we're having a conversation about Guns, where appropriate I'll go, "Well, you fucking tell me. What did Guns N' Roses stand for?" And they look at me like, "They *stood* for something, you know, apart from appetites and indulgences?" And I go, "Fucking right they did! That's why I connected to it, and if you don't understand that then you've missed the point."'

He describes the night Tom Zutaut came to him at his beach-side cottage and virtually begged him to take the band on. 'I'll never forget it . . . He sat by the window and he looked at me and said, "Niv, this is gonna be the end of my career. I'm gonna end up with egg on my face." And he's talking about throwing them off the label and saying, "I desperately need help." Well, what did that tell me? Obviously, in huge fucking neon letters that these people are legitimately, authentically anti-authoritarian. If you know a little bit about me, that's just like, okay, I'm in. There were aspects to Axl's behaviour that I found excessively abusive of others, even considering the difficulties of whatever might have occurred in his childhood.' In the end, though, Niven simply 'believed that if I could keep some kind of discipline in place, we could sell half a million records'.

The first key move Alan Niven made as the new manager of Guns N' Roses was finding them a producer who would get the best out of them in the studio: an engineer-turned-producer from Baltimore named Mike Clink, who'd apprenticed at one of LA's most famous studios, the Record Plant, where he'd worked under Ron Nevison, a solid-gold, commercial hit-maker who had produced multi-million-selling records by Heart, Survivor, Europe, Ozzy Osbourne, Eddie Money and Jefferson Starship. Clink understood what sounded good on the radio, 'But I knew what to do with Guns,' he said. 'They played me records they liked. Slash had Aerosmith; Axl had Metallica's *Ride the Lightning*.'

Clink took the band to Rumbo Recorders, an environment in which Zutaut hoped and prayed they could only do limited damage. It was located in Canoga Park, north-west of Hollywood in the Valley, and shared a parking lot with the Winnetka Animal Clinic. 'I put them in an apartment when we were making the record,' Clink recalled, 'and they destroyed it. One night they locked themselves out, so they put a boulder through a window. They thought it would look like somebody had robbed the place. When they finally got kicked out, there wasn't one thing left intact. It looked like somebody was remodelling and had knocked down the walls.' Or as Slash later told me: 'We partied really hard, but when we were in the studio, we were pretty much together. There was no doping and all that stuff.'

Axl had known Erin Everly for a matter of weeks before the band entered the studio with Mike Clink, but it quickly became apparent that the relationship would be a significant one for them both. Erin, of course, was no friend from back home like Gina Siler, or one of the many lost girls on the Strip who found their way to the Hell House. She was part of Los Angeles' elite, and lived in a different, more rarefied society, the daughter of a music legend, Don Everly, and the actor Venetia Stevenson, and the granddaughter of the director Robert Stevenson and the actor Anna Lee. In Axl, Erin had found the ultimate good girl's bad boy, the singer of the most dangerous and dirty band in Hollywood. In Erin, Axl found an escape from all that. As Duff noted: 'Axl continued to drop out of sight for days on end, a result of his erratic moods. Sometimes it was as if he was on speed, bouncing off the walls; then he would sleep for three days . . . I was always aware of what a fundamentally different type of person he was from me.' But then Duff was now 'an alcoholic'. Slash was strung out on heroin, along with his partner in grime, Izzy. Steven was a more general kind of fuck-up. He'd been living off his wits, sleeping on roofs, bundled in the corner on floors, for so long, wasted or sober it was all the same to him.

During their short-lived tenancy in Arnold Stiefel's rental house the divisions in their lives became obvious – at least they would have been had Slash and Izzy been *compos mentis* enough to notice. While their rooms quickly became little more than drug dens, lit first by naked bulbs and then finally by nothing at all, Axl retreated to the top of the house, where he furnished his bedroom properly and padlocked the door. Now that he had Erin, there was further reason to withdraw from the chaotic, druggy, hedonistic lifestyle that the band were falling deeper into. Yet the relationship would ultimately become volatile and destructive for both Erin and Axl. Many years after they separated, Everly auctioned some of the letters and notes that Rose had written to her, and they are an enlightening little snapshot into their world: 'FROM AN ASSHOLE' was the tag with one florist's delivery; 'Sorry for being hard on you, you didn't do anything wrong . . .' begins another, 'I just became frustrated with my predicament and didn't know how to verbalise my feelings'; 'Ya didn't need to play it so tough – I should have known better – I never realised how much you cared and wanted me . . .' and so on.

While the last months of their marriage would be marred by rage and accusations of violence, the notes show in Axl a gentleness and a willingness to both compromise and apologise that his bandmates and those in other areas of his life may have found surprising.

It was precisely these feelings, imbued in this new and adult relationship, that he was to reflect in a new song, one of the last written for *Appetite*. It's a measure of the gap that was developing between singer and band that their initial reaction to his 'Sweet Child o' Mine' was less than enthusiastic. 'Joke' was the word that cropped up most often. Slash had begun playing the carnival intro guitar figure as 'a joke', and described the process of writing and rehearsing the song as 'like pulling teeth. For me, at the time, it was a very sappy ballad.' Duff agreed, also calling the new song 'a joke. We thought, "What is this song? It's gonna be nothing."'

'It *was* a joke,' Slash went on. 'We were living in this house that had electricity, a couch and nothing else. The record company had just signed us and we were on our backs. There was a lot of shit going on. We were hanging out one night and I started playing that riff. And the next thing you know, Izzy made up some chords behind it, and Axl went off on it. I used to hate playing that sucker.' But Axl heard something in the music that fitted his lyrical idea. Like much of his early writing, it was directly autobiographical, but tenderly so. He was prepared to be reveal-ing and romantic – *'Her hair reminds me of a warm, safe place / Where as a child I'd hide'* – in a song that played against type. And he knew exactly how it should sound, too: 'I'm from Indiana, where Lynyrd Skynyrd are considered God to the point that you ended up saying, I hate this fucking band,' he told me. 'And yet for "Sweet Child" I went out and got some old Skynyrd tapes to make sure that we'd got that heartfelt feeling.'

Axl's refusal to take no for an answer paid off, becoming a significant turning point for both singer and band. When the song later became the engine that drove *Appetite for Destruction* forward, played endlessly on radio and looped on MTV, it was enough to convince Axl he should never again listen to what anyone else had to say about one of his songs – including Slash. Maybe especially Slash. It was also noticeable that Axl was closer artistically and in terms of friendship to West Arkeen. Arkeen was one of the great characters on the LA scene, the kind of guy who seemed to flourish in the pre-grunge, pre-austerity excesses of the late Eighties and early Nineties (sadly he wouldn't make it out of 1990s, dying of an opiate overdose at just 36 in 1997). He'd first met the band when he lived next door to Duff, and grew es-pecially close to Axl and Slash, who would say of him: 'for a long time, he literally was the only one we could trust'. But while they were close, Slash never wrote with Arkeen. 'We hung out and jammed a couple of times but there was only a couple of songs I was ever around where I was there with Axl and we were all play-ing together,' he said. While an unnamed 'friend' would later tell the veteran American rock biographer Stephen Davis that Arkeen was 'a strange, shadowy figure, very private and withdrawn. A weirdo. But Axl rated him – highly. You'd see Axl playing stuff for West, getting his opinion on what they were doing.'

Axl, already separated from his band by their enthusiastic chemical excess and becoming surer of his artistic judgement, began to hear of Tom Zutaut's growing concerns over the state of Guns N' Roses, and had other things on his mind than the so-called strangeness of his friends. Mike Clink had been to see Zutaut in August 1986 to tell him that the early pre-production sessions were going nowhere because Slash wasn't showing up. The summer had become one long fall into the depths of addiction. Slash had been so out of it at a Geffen photo shoot that he had to be physically held upright for the session. He nodded out one night at the band house and had to be revived. There were stories of nightclub fights, and of Axl threatening to leave the group. 'There was a point where I fucking stopped playing guitar,' Slash admitted. 'I didn't even talk to my band except for Izzy, because we were both doing it.'

Zutaut began to worry that his bosses would start to think that investing in the most dangerous band in the world was just too, well, *dangerous*. Making and promoting a record would cost them north of $500,000 when production and marketing were thrown on top of a recording budget of more than $300,000. It was a lot of money to risk on hopeless junkies – and Tom was the man risking it. He read the band the riot act, recalling that 'as much as you can threaten junkies' he did, telling them that he was on the verge of dropping them before they'd even released anything. If the ship was going down, Zutaut wasn't going down with it. Slash and Izzy had brief spells in rehab as a result, which kept their worst excesses at bay for a few weeks at least. And after they'd wrecked the apartment at Rumbo Recorders by putting a boulder through the window, Mike Clink drew the line. 'I'd never come into contact with guys like that,' he admitted. 'During our first meeting, they were spitting over each other's heads. They really were living on the street, that reckless life. But I pushed them hard and had a rule: no drugs in the studio.'

Clink made a sort of Devil's bargain: deliver the goods, and he would ignore their destructive behaviour away from Rumbo. He was happy for them to work all night – their usual pattern – just as long as they were working. 'He kept us at arm's length,' said Slash. Ultimately it would prove a wise call – once Clink was able to tell Zutaut that songs were going down on tape, the record company's nerves began to settle.

The final legalities of the Geffen deal were completed when the band inked their full 62-page contract, binding them to the company. Alan Niven signed his deal, too, and took Guns for a boozy evening at Barney's Beanery to mark the occasion, impressing them with both his capacity to hold his drink and his tales of encounters with the Sex Pistols when he'd worked for Virgin. 'I had a little silver single plaque in my office for "Something Else" [from *The Great Rock'n'Roll Swindle*]. Duff noticed that so I was all right. Later he came to find out that the very first time the Pistols got airplay in America was when I placed a copy of "Pretty Vacant" on the turntable of WMMS [in Cleveland].'

These were important moments for Guns N' Roses. They received the rest of their advance money from Geffen, and their hand-to-mouth hustling existence – although not yet dead – was eased as they became corporate assets. And it was a symbolic moment for Axl, who signed the contracts with his new name, changed by deed poll from the loathed William Bruce Bailey to W. Axl Rose. It was his break with the past, a new start and a statement of his determination to forge a new life on his own terms.

The album sessions would not begin in earnest for another few weeks. The band continued to gig around LA, their headline shows at the Troubadour, the Roxy and the Whisky sold out and packed to the rafters with fans wanting to see if the rumours that buzzed on the streets were true – Slash was *dead*; Izzy was *in rehab*; Axl had *quit*. The answers appeared right there in front of them, the shows were that weird mix of intensity and sloppiness that Guns N' Roses were making their own. When Guns headlined the Street Scene festival in a park downtown, the atmosphere reached such a peak, stoked by Axl's exhortations, that the show was stopped after a few songs by the fire marshals, and all of them, including Mike Clink, began to wonder how they might get that same feeling down on tape.

While they wrestled with that, Alan Niven turned his attention to the first recordings that Guns N' Roses would issue to the waiting world – the 'indie' release that Axl had promised from the stage of the Troubadour back in July. The notion of an 'indie' record was hollow, a dress-up designed to ape the genuine article like Mötley Crüe's *Too Fast for Love* or Poison's *Look What the Cat Dragged In*, two dirt-cheap, dirty-sounding records that had earned their creators major record deals. Guns already had a major record deal. And surprisingly for a band so sold on authenticity, there was an element of artificiality to the 12-inch EP *Live?!*@ *Like a Suicide*, released in December, that Axl in particular would quickly see through and denounce. It wasn't a live record at all; instead its four tracks were pulled from some early sessions at Pasha studios in Hollywood, when the band had briefly tried out Spencer Proffer as a producer, and Take One in Burbank with Hans-Peter Heuber and Alan Niven engineering and mixing. Informed by Geffen that they wouldn't pay to record a GN'R show, crowd noise was simply added to these studio recordings, taken, Duff admitted, from the Texxas Jam festival held annually over the 4 July weekend in Houston. Niven chose the label name – the confrontational UZI Suicide – safe in the knowledge they wouldn't have to use it again. Geffen pressed 10,000 copies and released it (they claimed) on 24 December – in fact it had come out nine days earlier in order to allow fans to get it before Christmas.

'I wasn't sure I would get away with it but no one called us out,' says Alan Niven now. 'Plus, my success with indie releases was one of the reasons Geffen came to me.' There was also the knowledge that it was one thing to be signed to a major label, quite another to get them on the case building momentum. Alan knew it didn't just come to new artists. They almost had to force the label's hand, no matter how good the contract they'd just signed appeared to be. It wasn't an end in itself, merely a toehold. 'So that when *Appetite* came out there was already some awareness of who they were. Some expectation. I said, "Here's the kicker, they cannot have the word 'Geffen' on them. The boxes cannot have [Geffen distributers] 'WEA' on them. They've got to be as if I'd had them pressed [independently]. There can't be anything linking this to WEA or Geffen."'

The one thing that all of this artifice couldn't disguise was the music. *Live?!*@ Like a Suicide* lasts for less than 14 minutes and features just four songs, but the street-level appeal that had packed Hollywood's clubs over the summer of 1986 was obvious. It opened with a faked stage intro – '*Hey fuckers, suck on Guns N' fuckin' Roses!*' – but the faking ended there. Reluctant to waste their best material on an EP, the two original songs, the opening 'Reckless Life' and 'Move to the City', came from the Hollywood Rose era, and featured a co-writing credit for Chris Weber. They were teamed with a couple of covers, a vicious take on Rose Tattoo's 'Nice Boys' ('*Nice boys – don't play rock'n'roll*' runs the chorus, while the verses are pertinent takes on girls brought low by hanging out with said boys) and a nod to their main inspiration with Aerosmith's 'Mama Kin', an act of homage that quickly aligned them with a deeper history than the here-today-gone-later-today hair metal scene. All that really tied Guns to the Strip were the cover images, on the front Axl, face almost entirely obscured by his towering, primped hair, leaning on Duff's shoulder, and on the rear a deliberately sleazy line-up shot styled by 'rocket queen' Barbi Von Greif, which was all *de rigueur* leather and cowboy boots.

Live?!@ Like a Suicide* sold out immediately, mostly in Hollywood. But, crucially, it found its way to the critics, too, with the band's first national and international reviews appearing in *RIP*, *Circus* and, in the UK, *Kerrang!* – all of which recognised Guns N' Roses as the real deal, in its rawest form. Strikingly, the one dissenting voices' was Axl's, who had hit out at the idea almost from the start: 'It's the most contrived piece of shit we've done . . .' he said. 'It ain't no live record. If you think it is, you're crazy or stupid.'

When he uttered those words in December 1986, Axl was in a position that artists sometimes find themselves in – aware that the work just being heard by the public has already been left well behind by their newer endeavours. Everything about the *Appetite for Destruction* sessions, from the very first demoing of the songs, was a giant step forward from the punkish, lo-fi racket of *Live?!**@ *Like a Suicide*. Yet the die was cast, especially at Geffen: these guys were a feral pack, trailing destruction down the Strip and even to the doors of the Geffen offices – staff were aghast at one appearance which saw them accompanied by a naked girl, still wet, wrapped in a shower curtain. Then there was the day-to-day prosaic detail of their existence: casual sex in an era of AIDS, hard drugs, constant in-fighting, outrage in clubs and bars . . . there was at least one serious discussion between Axl and Slash over drug use affecting performance. Doubts were expressed over Steven Adler's ability even when sober. One executive urged Zutaut to get the record done quickly before the band's inevitable self-immolation.

Navigating this path was Mike Clink, who not only had a terrific pair of ears but a hard-earned degree in rock star psychology. Having read the band the riot act over drugs in the studio, he set about getting the real Guns N' Roses down on tape. Clink was intent on 'capturing the band's essence, not beating it into the ground', and so all the tracks were initially recorded as-live, with the aim of nailing the song while the band were still feeling it, with overdubs kept to a minimum. Slash, already a fan of the way that Clink had engineered Michael Schenker's guitar sound on one of his favourite records, UFO's *Lights Out*, was quickly taken with the producer's way of working: 'He knew how to direct our energy into something productive,' he recalled. 'His secret was simple: he didn't fuck with our sound. He worked hard to capture it perfectly, just as it was.' Duff was equally happy: 'With my favourite punk bands the bass was the loudest thing and led the way,' he said. 'And [on] the songs that would make up *Appetite*, the bass was the loudest, roundest thing on the recordings. It had a lot of space.'

Yet Mike Clink's skills weren't just technical. Recognising Axl's attention to detail and latent perfectionism, he handled the singer's contribution entirely differently. As Axl later told me, what people didn't hear immediately 'is that there was a perfectionist attitude' to the recordings. 'I mean, there was a definite plan to that. We could have made it all smooth and polished. We went and did test tracks with other producers and it came out smooth and polished – with Spencer Proffer. And Geffen Records said it was too fucking radio. That's why we went with Mike Clink. We went for a raw sound, because it just didn't gel having it too tight and concise.

'Cos Guns N' Roses onstage, man, can be, like, out to lunch. Visually, we're all over the place and stuff and you don't know what to expect. But how do you get that on a record? But somehow you have to do that. So there's a lot more that's needed on a record. That's why recording is my favourite thing, because it's like painting a picture. You start out with a shadow, or an idea, and you come up with something that's a shadow of that . . . And then you add all these things and you come up with something you didn't even expect. Slash will do, like, one slow little guitar fill that adds a whole different mood that you didn't expect. That's what I love . . . You use the brush this way and allow a little shading to come in and you go, "Wow, I got a whole different effect on this that's even heavier than what I pictured. I don't know quite what I'm on to but I'm on it", you know?

'"Paradise City", man,' he continued, 'That's like, I came up with two of those first vocals – there's five parts there – I came up with two and they sounded really weird. Then I said, look, I got an idea. I put two of these vocal things together, and it was the two weirdest ones, the two most obtuse ones. And Clink's like, "I don't know about that, man . . ." I'm like, "I don't know either, why don't we just sleep on it?" So we go home and the next day I call him up and now I'm like, "I don't know about this." But he goes, "No, I think it's cool!" So now he was the other way. So then we put three more vocal parts on it and then it fit. But the point is, that wasn't how we had it planned. We don't really know how it happened.'

Clink was realistic about the band's habits too. He, Alan Niven and Axl had homes to go to at the end of each day, but stranded in the 'tedious' Valley, Slash, Izzy and Steven, plus studio techs Porky and Jame-O and a giant minder/driver named Lewis, hired by Alan Niven to limit any damage, would go out and disrupt whichever local bar they could find that they hadn't disrupted already. Through the fug of their hangovers, Clink would quietly have a word when he felt an individual wasn't playing at his best and shepherd him in later to redo their part. Slash had a slightly bigger problem when it came to laying down his lead-guitar lines. During his chaotic, druggy, sofa-surfing summer of '86, he'd sold or otherwise lost most of his instruments. Now, although he felt Izzy, Duff and Slash had essentially finished their parts during the initial Rumbo 'as-live' sessions, he was struggling for the sound he wanted. On the final day at Rumbo, Alan Niven provided the answer, turning up with a beautiful flame-top Les Paul replica that he'd got from Jim Foot, a guitar maker in Redondo Beach. Slash loved it and after a search of rental shops with Clink found the right Marshall amp and the pair spent some happy time in Take 1 studio rerecording and overdubbing together. The guitar has remained Slash's main studio instrument ever since, although as he admitted in his autobiography, even he has been unable to replicate the exact sound he and Clink got for *Appetite* . . . never mind all of the wannabes who've attempted to kick-start their careers by aping it: 'The size and shape of the room, the soundboard used in recording, as well as the molecular quality of the air all play a part – humidity and temperature affect a recording tremendously . . . It is more than just setting up the same equipment in the same booth because, believe me, many have tried.' Happy at last with his sound, Slash worked at some pace, nailing, he reckoned, a song a day. And happy to be back on the right side of the Hollywood Hills, Duff would hang at the studio while Slash worked before the pair disappeared into the night together. From the first song Slash overdubbed, 'Think About You', to the last, 'Paradise City', this was the pattern they repeated.

Alan Niven made another smart intervention when he suggested tightening up, in 'Welcome to the Jungle', the original two repetitions of the *'when you're high . . . and you . . . never wanna come down . . .'* section to just one. At the time the band knew nothing of his creative involvement with Great White. 'It's a very good thing that none of us were aware of that,' Slash said, 'because that session might not have gone so well and "Welcome to the Jungle" would be a very different song . . . It never bothered me once we found out about Alan's connection to Great White, but it had quite a negative, snowball effect among other members of our band.' Meaning Axl.

That lay ahead, a problem for another day. Along with 'Sweet Child' the *Appetite* sessions would produce one more late-breaking, self-lacerating Guns N' Roses tune, a song that Slash and Izzy began to – well – cook up, after the Geffen deal was signed and then finished in the studio. The lyrics, which they presented to Axl scrawled on a brown paper bag, were essentially a description of their days on dope, a repetitious existence of escalating usage – 'I used to do a little but a little didn't do it, so a little got more and more . . .' – and helplessness – 'He's been knocking . . . He won't leave me alone . . .'. They called it 'Mr Brownstone', a sledgehammer reference to what was going on, and set it to a shuffling, Bo Diddley verse section alongside an urgently rising chorus, and when sung by Axl it seemed to turn from a confession into a warning. It was ruthlessly autobiographical, a full stop, along with 'Sweet Child', on the band's lives to date: '[The record] is a storybook of what this band went through in Hollywood; trying to survive, to when it was finished,' Slash said. The 30-odd songs stretched from 'November Rain', which Axl had begun writing back in Indiana, and 'Anything Goes', which he and Izzy had started in the very early days of Hollywood Rose, right up to 'Mr Brownstone' and 'Sweet Child'.

The job now was to parse those 30 songs down to a single album, to dig through to the essence of the band. Tom Zutaut was firmly of the view that it needed to be a hard rock album, with a maximum of one ballad. Alan Niven was in agreement – his plan was to build a core fan base for what he still regarded as an 'underground' band. Axl was of the opinion that they wanted a classic, 'live'-sounding record that captured a moment in time. He understood that big, romantic songs as close to his heart as 'November Rain' and 'Don't Cry' would have to wait for their time – which wasn't now.

The Clink sessions had been an outstanding success. Even in their raw, unmixed state, it was obvious that the producer had fulfilled every brief, and, what's more, he had put himself on the line to do it, catching the easy-going, do-it-right-now immediacy of Steven, Duff and Izzy, working one-on-one with Slash on his solos and then going straight to 18-hour days recording Axl's vocals, which were the most complex parts on the recordings.

Speaking soon after the record was released, Axl explained: 'I sing in about five or six different voices that are all part of me, it's not contrived. I'm like a second baritone or something. I used to take choir classes and stuff and I'd always sit there and, since I could read music, I'd try to sing other people's parts and see if I could get away with it. We had this teacher who was pitch-perfect, or whatever you call it. He had ears like a bat, man, like radar. So in order to get away with singing someone else's part, you'd really have to get it down. Or else he'd know . . .' It was true, too: from 'It's So Easy' to 'Sweet Child' to 'Welcome to the Jungle', Axl's vocal range and natural ability to inhabit a lyric and sell the song, owning the narrative, would become a huge part of the record's appeal.

Soon after New Year, Alan Niven took Slash to New York to meet with candidates to mix the songs. They had dinner with Rick Rubin, who had just put Aerosmith in front of a new generation with the groundbreaking Run DMC cover/collaboration of their decade-old song 'Walk This Way'. 'We just shot the shit,' Slash remembered, 'because he'd already passed on mixing us. A lot of people passed on mixing us – and, once again, all of them regretted it later.'

Alan Niven briefly considered doing the job himself and mixed a trial version of 'Mr Brownstone' that Izzy in particular liked a lot, but ultimately band and manager elected to go with the team of Steve Thompson and Michael Barbiero, experienced engineers who had worked mostly on dance and pop club remixes but who produced a thunderous take on 'Mr Brownstone' as an audition piece. They found themselves in Media Sound studios in Manhattan's midtown, playing host to the band *sans* Steven but plus Niven and Zutaut and assorted crew and girls, most of whom were put up at the Parker Meridian hotel, where they shared rooms. The material was pared down to that which would make the album, with Niven keen to stockpile the leftovers. One by one, the early versions of 'November Rain', 'Pretty Tied Up', 'Civil War', 'The Garden', 'Dust and Bones', 'Yesterdays' and 'Don't Cry' fell away. Among the last to go were 'Back Off Bitch' and 'You Could be Mine', which until quite late was thought to have good potential as a first Guns N' Roses single.

Thompson and Barbiero had developed a unique way of working: Barbiero set up a basic mix before Thomson joined him at the desk and they began playing the song through, Thomson working on the guitar and vocal dynamics while Barbiero controlled the foundations. With four hands on the faders, they'd take pass after pass at the songs until everyone was happy. '[They were] amazing,' enthused Slash in his autobiography. 'They had a system, pretty much an unspoken language, between them. Steve was the energetic, in-your-face guy, and Michael was the reserved, analytical, calculated guy. And they got on one another's nerves constantly, which somehow fuelled their creativity.'

Slash had arrived in New York with an arm in plaster having fractured his wrist – as only he could have done – thumping the floor to try and get a record to stop skipping while he was having sex with a girl at one of Duff's friend's houses in Seattle. He had one night out with Steve Thompson, where he'd felt supremely out of place in a New York disco called China Club clad in his top hat and leathers, but the differences between the band and Thompson and Barbiero were evident and best illustrated by a notorious incident in the mixing of 'Rocket Queen'. Adriana Smith, a friend of Slash's from LA, found herself in New York and hooked up with the little crew at the Parker Meridian, spending her nights in the room shared by Slash and Axl and her days drinking in the studio. When Axl decided that the 'Rocket Queen' mix was lacking something, he turned to Smith, as she reminisced many years later: 'Basically, Axl propositioned me in the studio. I was really drunk and although we were both seeing other people at the time, he had a really creative interest for this song and wanted to give it an edge and I was the girl to do it. I did it for the band.'

'We lit some candles for atmosphere,' Slash said, 'and she and Axl went out into the live room, got down on the floor by the drum riser, and we recorded the performance . . .' Michael Barbiero was less impressed: 'I didn't want to be around for recording a girl getting fucked,' he said. 'That wasn't the high point of my career. So I set up the mikes and had my assistant record it. If you look at the record, it says, "Victor 'the fuckin' engineer" Deyglio. So it's literal.' Axl and the band simply thought it was funny. Or as Duff later put it: 'She was a goer. She knew how to work a microphone.'

Work done, they retreated to LA for a couple of homecoming shows, the first at the Whisky and the second at the Roxy, shows that would essentially mark the end of Guns N' Roses as an LA club band. They didn't quite know it yet, but they had outgrown those few miles of tiny clubs, however resonant their history. In the necessary lull between completed mixes and the final track-listing and sequencing of the record, which would take place in May 1987, Alan Niven instituted a plan, one which had been working in the music business ever since Chas Chandler brought Jimi Hendrix to London in the last months of 1966. British audiences, if they could be persuaded to get behind the latest US sensation, imbued them with a cachet that could travel back over the Atlantic and offer some glamour to otherwise familiar local boys. 'In terms of the development of the band, it was key to my strategy that we connected well in the United Kingdom,' says Niven. 'It was about creating a perception that it was not just a bunch of Hollywood fuck-ups, it was a band that had international appeal.'

It was time for another Alan Niven masterstroke. He struck a deal with Geffen's president, Eddie Rosenblatt, to personally distribute all 10,000 copies – records and cassettes – of the *Live ?!*@ Like a Suicide* EP. Then turned up in a van to pick them all up. 'Eddie told me later, when I loaded that van up and disappeared down the road, he rather wondered if he'd ever see me again.' Niven sold the lot to an independent distribution company called Important and picked up a cheque for $42,000. Then he went back to Eddie with the cheque. 'I pulled it out and waved it at him behind his desk. He went to hold it and I pulled it away from him. I said, "This takes us to England." And he sat there and looked at me for a moment. I said, "This pays for our first trip to England, *okay*?" And he goes, "Okay." And I gave him the cheque. And that's how we paid for the three Marquee shows.'

The Marquee was the emblematic rock dive in London's Wardour Street. Since the dawn of the Sixties, every major rock artist from the Rolling Stones and Jimi Hendrix to David Bowie and the Sex Pistols had played there. Getting Guns N' Roses to play their first shows outside America there was a major coup, the kind of outside-the-box thinking that would earmark GN'R as somehow different – smarter, cooler – than their LA contemporaries. 'It was essential to me to bring them to England,' says Niven. 'It was essential to me to get ahead of the pack.' Faster Pussycat were also recording their major label debut; LA Guns were not far behind. Other West Hollywood charmers like Jetboy were snapping at their heels. 'It gave me a clear message: get ahead of the pack.'

To help set the scene for their London debut, Geffen brought some of the British rock press to LA. *Sounds*, the inkie weekly known – unlike its more illustrious rivals *NME* and *Melody Maker* – for its uninhibited love of hard rock and heavy metal, carried the first UK interview with Guns N' Roses, the band bemoaning what they saw as a fake LA scene (Axl taking the chance to stick the knife into Poison; Slash claiming Van Halen as the only real rock band to emerge from the city) before the writer, Paul Elliott, concluded accurately that 'raising hell has regained some of its glamour'. *Time Out* were next, London's leading arts, culture and listings magazine left somewhat open-mouthed after a trip to West Arkeen's latest residence, a biker crashpad on Poinsettia Street that several members of Guns used as a place to hang out and sleep in. It was, if anything, even worse than the Hell House, and quickly got the same moniker, Slash describing it as, 'more gruesome than anything else I've seen in a first-world country'. It didn't stop him frequenting the place, and telling the *Time Out* reporter that he was there because he'd just ditched his girlfriend, as her 'boobs were too big'.

Niven made sure he was on hand for both encounters, ensuring that to the outside world, newly exposed to this phenomenon, Guns N' Roses came across exactly as they were: cocky, rowdy, wild and so far unstopped.

4

FIVE SKULLS AND A DEATH'S HEAD

The effect of the first wave of serious British press coverage of Guns N' Roses would be magnified just as soon as Europe got up close and personal with them, but before it happened the final choices that would turn Mike Clink's sessions into *Appetite for Destruction* were made. The record was sequenced, a job that in the last days of vinyl and albums having a very clearly delineated side one and side two (on the finished artwork, the band would label these 'G' and 'R') required a great deal of thought and an artist's touch. The best records, the kind of great and deathless albums Guns were trying to follow, had not just dynamics but a sense of narrative.

'Welcome to the Jungle', with the furious intensity of its knife-slashing opening riff (itself almost cathartic after the tease of Slash's guitar intro) and its story of a wide-eyed country boy stepping off the bus and into the alien city, was an obvious opener. 'Paradise City', the upside of the dream, was its perfect counterpoint to close side one. Then 'My Michelle' to open side two, its story about Michelle Young blisteringly frank and unblinking, was bookended by the record's final track, 'Rocket Queen', inspired by another of the band's noir-ish Hollywood circle, Barbi Von Greif ('I wrote this song for a girl who was gonna have a band and she was gonna call it Rocket Queen. She kinda kept me alive for a while', as Axl told *Hit Parader* in 1988). In between, it was all killer no filler, don't-bore-us-get-to-the-chorus solid gold: side one's triple hook to the liver of 'It's So Easy' (bad girls, worse drugs), 'Nightrain' (bad booze, worse girls) and 'Out ta Get Me' (slithering urban paranoia with undertones of Axl's real-life troubles with the law) before the withering self-critique of 'Mr Brownstone'. And then side two's flipside to the hedonistic excess: after 'My Michelle', the sweetness of Izzy's 'Think About You' (*'Somethin' changed in this heart of mine / And I'm so glad that you showed me'*); and then Axl's 'Sweet Child o' Mine' (*'She's got eyes of the bluest skies . . .'*); 'You're Crazy' (*'Looking for a lover in a world that's much too dark . . .'*); and then 'Anything Goes' to puncture the balloon, a descent back into the Hell House days (*'Panties round your knees / With your ass in debris'*).

The overall effect was of a mad ride through the life of the band, mostly tough and defiant but occasionally touching and vulnerable, a record that achieved a truthfulness in its voice that eluded all of the other preening hair bands on the Strip. All of the qualities that would make it so successful and so loved came built in: the wild lifestyle that gave the songs their street-level honesty; the volatile combination of personalities that could stretch the band to breaking point in terms of its personal relationships also provided a controlled fury in the music that couldn't possibly be faked. Izzy and Steven's loose, half-a-beat-behind, rhythmic groove, Duff's punkish attack, Axl with his five voices for any occasion and Slash's pyrotechnic lead playing, all caught at a very particular time and in a very particular place, worked in a way that this sort of art should work: on the central nervous system, triggering instant releases of adrenalin. It wasn't there to be intellectualised or critiqued; LA and the scene on the Strip weren't about that. Axl in particular may have had artistic pretentions that he would go on to try to fulfil, but the band's first record was a straight-up body punch, fraught and dazzling, made in a moment and for the moment, not for any kind of posterity.

It was almost impossible to see it as a major commercial hit. It lacked the fluffiness beloved of mainstream radio. Alan Niven wasn't even sure if they'd get budget for a video clip, even if they could find a song that could be cleaned up enough for public consumption – the record had at least 12 audible 'fuck's including, in 'It's So Easy', Axl's unequivocal *'why don't you just . . . FUCK OFF . . .'*

Mike Clink, though, was certain both he and the band had excelled themselves and that the album would be a success despite its obvious commercial challenges. 'I said to Tom Zutaut at Geffen, "This is going to sell two million copies." He said, "No, it's gonna sell five million!"' According to Barbiero, 'Sweet Child o' Mine' had 'sounded like a hit to all of us. So much so that I remember Axl asking me when we were finished if I thought the album would actually sell. I told him that, despite the fact that it was nothing like what was on the radio, I thought it would go gold. I was only off by 20 million records.'

The album title that so effortlessly summed up Guns N' Roses in the late 1980s was one of the only things on the record that wasn't theirs. Axl had a postcard depicting a painting by the LA artist Robert Williams, a graphic, cartoonish image of a robot standing over an apparently sexually assaulted woman, her shirt torn, scratch marks on her exposed breasts, her panties around her calves, while above them hovered an avenging vision of hell with red claws and dagger teeth. Williams had called it *Appetite for Destruction*. Axl wanted not just Williams's title, but the rights to use the painting as the album cover, too, and Zutaut duly negotiated a deal with the artist. Within the Geffen rank and file, however, there was an immediate disquiet about the idea. The climate around censorship in America in 1987 was heated. Tipper Gore, wife of the US senator and future Vice President Al Gore, had used her public profile to launch the Parents Music Resource Center (PMRC) after finding her 11-year-old daughter listening to a notorious Prince track, 'Darling Nikki' ('*I met her in a hotel lobby / Masturbating with a magazine*'). Gore had parlayed her outrage into some Congressional hearings and the stickering of albums with a 'Parental Advisory' warning. It was effectively a badge of honour for most artists, especially those in rap and the more outré rock bands, but however dismissive the artists may have been, Geffen were acutely aware of both Guns' reputation in the industry and of the uncompromising content of the record. They feared that if it had a cover like the Williams painting it wouldn't be stocked by major retailers such as WalMart and Sears, and that others – Tower Records, for example – might be reluctant to display it prominently. Then there was the whole of the South of the country, deep in the Bible Belt, where Geffen's salesmen knew that it would be impossible to get the album into racks without protest. The issue would float on, unresolved, as the planned spring release slipped back to summer.

Then Guns N' Roses arrived in London for three shows at the Marquee, the first on 19 June, and then the 22nd and 28th. They were jetlagged, hungover, testy, some of them not long out of rehab. For Slash it was a return to a country he barely remembered (when he was in a state to remember anything). The others had never left America. Alan Niven and Tom Zutaut, both far more worldly, at least in terms of culture and travel, were soon dealing with the same kind of shit they got in LA: Duff threw Steven up against a wall for making stupid remarks about Robert John, who'd paid his own way on the trip; Slash arrived in the midst of a five-day bender and needed two days' sleep. He got drunk again at a party to celebrate the release of Bob Dylan's film *Hearts of Fire*, and caused a ruckus; Axl had a brief scuffle with the security staff at Tower Records after he felt faint from the effects of anti-histamine tablets and lack of sleep and sat on some steps, unwilling or unable to move when requested.

The growing fractiousness was in part due to the desire Guns had to prove themselves. They were in the city of the Rolling Stones and the Sex Pistols. The infamous UK music press was primed and ready to take down this latest bunch of LA wannabes. But the London branch of Geffen was behind them in a way that the US branch could not be. They had issued a limited-edition double A-side of 'It's So Easy' and 'Mr Brownstone', knowing that it had no chance of any radio play, but, as their label manager Jo Bolsom told me: 'We knew the music press would pick up on it, which they did, and that it would reinforce the band's reputation as being wild and out there, so it did its job. It also sold quite well. We only pressed up about 10,000 copies initially anyway.'

Before the first show at the Marquee, before a packed Friday night crowd, Alan Niven gave the band a pep talk. 'I sat those little fuckers down and I said, "Listen, they're gonna look at you as a bunch of poser LA wankers. They're gonna test you. They'll spit at you. They'll yell at you. And if you blink, you're fucking dead. You give it as good as you get.' And god bless the Marquee audience, that's exactly what happened. Until Axl and Duff threatened to come offstage and fuck with a couple of people. From that moment on it was a love affair.'

It was their London agent, John Jackson, who came up with the idea of doing the first Marquee then leaving it for a few days until the weekly music press came out with their reviews, then follow that with two more shows, the following week. It was a clever plan, but it nearly backfired when the first show fell distinctly short of the kind of wild-eyed impact everyone had been predicting. Whether it was the pressure or the jetlag or the history or the disorienting effect of being thousands of miles from home, the first Marquee show was a flop, a real stinker.

'It's great to be in fucking England, finally!' Axl told the audience from the stage, as Slash wrung the last of the life out of set-opener, 'Reckless Life'. The crowd response was perhaps down to excitement, perhaps due to the edgy atmosphere, perhaps even a flashback to the punk years: a hail of spit and plastic beer glasses were hurled stagewards, causing Axl to stop the next number, fittingly 'Out ta Get Me'. 'Hey, if you wanna keep throwing things we're gonna fucking leave,' he screeched. 'So whaddaya think?' he challenged them. Another glass clattered noisily into Steven's drum-kit. 'Hey, fuck you, pussy!' Axl cried, pointing his finger angrily at the drunken culprit and yelling more obscenities out of range of the microphone. It was an inauspicious beginning. The set restarted with 'Anything Goes', but the fragile connection between band and audience had been lost. The singer took it badly, calling the evening 'a total nightmare', upset that he'd 'failed' in the hometown of bands he revered.

Poor reviews duly appeared in both *Kerrang!* and the *NME* just a few days later.

The *NME* review was written by Steve Sutherland, a distinguished journalist who would go on to edit the paper, but who nonetheless was no particular fan of LA rock in general or of Guns N' Roses in particular, and who was withering about them. Axl took the review personally, rang the office and threatened to visit Sutherland (who later wrote that he took 'an early lunch' as a precaution). More hurtful to Axl – because he knew in his heart it was true – was Xavier Russell's review for *Kerrang!*, which said plainly that 'Guns N' Roses blew it, pure and simple.' Although Russell, who had heard an early tape of *Appetite* . . . mitigated his critique by calling the record 'truly wonderful' and speculating that the performance may have been different had the crowd not thrown beer cans at the band from the off. As Axl himself would tell me when they returned to tour the UK a few months later, 'It was the first magazine that really came out and supported us big time. When you said we were good, I believed you guys. So if you say a gig sucks, I believe that too . . .'

At least they had two more shows to rescue themselves. The band moved from a hotel to a rented flat in Kensington, which settled them down a little. Axl's friend Del James, and Todd Crew, the now former Jetboy bassist and Slash's drug buddy, arrived in town and the Guns gang mentality kicked in. The final show in particular was a triumph, the band adding epic new versions of AC/DC's 'Whole Lotta Love' and Bob Dylan's 'Knockin' on Heaven's Door' to the set, and *Kerrang!* showing its faith in the band by commissioning another review: '[They were] raw, savage, furious, emotional, dangerous, rebellious, vibrant, hungry, intoxicating . . . firmly in the tradition of the Stones, Aerosmith, Rose Tattoo, Sex Pistols, Motörhead [and] AC/DC,' it almost yelled. The band returned to LA better, wiser and a little more aware of how wide the world was. Peter Makowski, a veteran music writer who had been around almost every big rock band of the 1970s and '80s, spent time with them in London, and offered a good insight into what the band were like on their first trip outside the US: 'The excitement came more from their image and the way they connected with an audience,' he told me. 'Rock was going through a very safe phase, Bon Jovi were the big sensation, Iron Maiden still ruled. Guns N' Roses appealed to the fans left cold by that stuff. The disaffected punk and metal fans that were hungry for something a bit more real, and suddenly here it was at last.'

Offstage, he said, the band, 'seemed like a fairly normal bunch of people. I took Izzy to Ladbroke Grove to buy some reggae albums, and got to know Axl a little bit. He was the quietest of the bunch, almost shy, I thought, if you can imagine that now. In terms of drugs, there was a fair bit of drinking but I never saw them use anything heavy. Then, a few days after the first show, Slash phoned one night to ask if I could get him "anything". I thought he meant hash and I said I'd see what I could do. Then Izzy rang and said, "Whatever you do, don't get Slash any gear"

– meaning heroin. "He's only just stopped and it's too risky." That was the first time I realised they might have a problem.'

Just as Alan Niven and Tom Zutaut had planned, the fine detail of the UK visit and the odd dodgy review in the *NME* meant nothing in America. What carried weight was the fact they'd been there and done it. As Izzy said soon afterwards: 'Everything just took off. Word spread and we had a platform at last.' Soon after returning to America they flew to New York to be seen at the New Music Seminar, and to have some merchandise meetings and talk with their new booking agents, ICM. It was there that their lifestyle would again cast a dark shadow over the romantic 'most dangerous band' image, and where the death of Todd Crew would illustrate, starkly, the sordid realities of the junkie existence.

Slash had travelled to New York with a porn actress called Lois Ayres, who he'd been seeing in LA and who had flown east with him to perform at a couple of strip clubs. Ayres was booked into the Milford Plaza on Eighth Avenue, and Slash decided to stay with her. They were awoken at seven in the morning by a phone call telling them that Crew was in reception and asking for Slash. He was in a bad way. He'd been fired by Jetboy and had just broken up with his long-term girlfriend. 'He arrived at my door already fucking drunk,' Slash recalled in his autobiography, 'with a full litre of what we liked to call Toad Venom in one hand: vodka and orange juice disguised in a 7 Up bottle.'

By Slash's account, he was unwilling to leave Crew alone and took him to all of his meetings around Manhattan, stopping off also at a Western Union so that Crew could pick up some money. Crew was drunk to the point where Slash had to prop him up and help him walk. Nonetheless by early afternoon they were done, and wandered into Central Park, where they ran into three musician friends. From there they went drinking and the idea to score some heroin was raised. The three musician friends disappeared to buy heroin in the East Village and, Slash said, all five then went to the apartment of the Plasmatics' bassist, Chosei Funahara, where Slash cooked up some smack for himself and Crew. From there the pair bought a case of beer and entered a cinema in Times Square to watch *Jaws 3D*. Crew left halfway through to phone his former girlfriend, and Slash found him passed out by the payphones. He took Crew back to the Milford Plaza, where later, Slash claimed, they were visited again by the three musicians they'd met in the park.

As he recounts in his autobiography: 'They were all set to shoot dope and hang out and Todd suddenly perked up and was eager to join in. It was another losing battle, so I got onboard. I shot almost all of my dope because this stuff still had yet to kick in. At the same time I was monitoring Todd to be sure he didn't have too much, because he'd been drinking heavily for about eighteen hours. I can't say what happened for sure, but I'm almost positive he got a shot from someone else who was there that night when I wasn't looking. What I gave him wasn't strong enough to cause what happened.'

What is known to have happened next is that Crew OD'd and slipped into unconsciousness, and the other three musicians fled, leaving Slash alone to try to revive him. He threw him in the bath, doused him in cold water and slapped him until he came round, whereupon he put him to bed. He called Robert John in LA, and then 'a girl named Shelley who worked at ICM'. By Slash's account he was still talking to Shelley when Crew once again stopped breathing and this time could not be revived. 'Todd, all of twenty-one years old, died in my arms . . .'

Paramedics arrived about 40 minutes later and removed the body. Slash was questioned by police at the hotel for some hours, and afterwards Alan Niven collected him and flew with him back to LA. News of Crew's death spread quickly through the Hollywood rock crowd, and, as Slash admitted, many blamed him for what had happened. He attended Crew's funeral in Oakland, where 'I had to deal with finger-pointing from Todd's obviously distraught family – everybody thought the death was my fault.' Crew's family would hire a private investigator to try to find out what had happened in New York, and after Slash had published his account of the death in his autobiography in 2007, it was questioned again by another member of Jetboy, the guitarist, Billy Rowe, who told the Blabbermouth website: 'There's definitely some loopholes in the story.'

Whatever the truth, regret was all that was left. Axl confessed to his, in that he hadn't spoken to Crew about his habit while they were in London, as he'd intended to do. Slash said that 'it really fucking scared me'. And yet it would not be enough to stop him using. A bunch of junkies shooting up and one turns blue. Happens every day in New York, LA, London . . .

Nevertheless, Todd Crew's death hung over the US release of *Appetite for Destruction* three days later. Initially, as many had foreseen, nothing much happened. It was a record at odds with what was playing on rock radio – big hits from Aerosmith, in their new, AOR-friendly incarnation, Heart, Def Leppard, Whitesnake . . . There was as yet, though, no single or video in America to help boost the album's profile, and when the first pressing of the record, 30,000 copies, went out in the Robert Williams sleeve they were almost immediately rejected by major retailers. 'All that people saw was a girl with her knickers pulled down – not the karmic retribution in it,' claimed Niven. Williams himself had foreseen the problems the band would have. 'I told Axl he was going to get into trouble,' he asserted. Intriguingly, he said that his main concern was that 'None of the guys in this band were too articulate, so [I knew] they would direct the media to me to defend the cover.'

In the event, Geffen circumnavigated the problem by simply moving the image on new pressings of the album from the front cover to somewhere inside; while the front was freshly adorned by another cartoon-like image – on a plain black sleeve was featured Axl's newly minted tattoo of a death's-head cross studded with five skulls, each of which represented a different member of the band. The alternative 'black sleeve' was also made available to record retailers in Britain after WH Smith banned the original sleeve from its shelves and Virgin Megastore in London refused an in-store display.

It was another indication of what kind of world *Appetite for Destruction* was released into: post-AIDS, post-Reagan, third-term Thatcher, a world in which rock had become a shiny, happy, big-haired thing in which stars got married, worked out and lived more like Tom Cruise than Keef Richards. A world where marketing was more important than A&R; videos more 'market penetrative' than tours. Neither *Rolling Stone* nor the rest of the mainstream media saw fit to acknowledge the release. Until *Appetite* really began to move months and months later and it suddenly became achingly hip to possess a copy, it was ignored. Yet it was the first truly potent chronicle of urban street life that had existed outside of the realm of hip hop and rap since the decade began; and a genuine return to the raw, untamed, visceral values of rock in its pre-MTV heyday. It would shatter the post-Live Aid image of do-gooder rock stars like Sting and Bono and Peter Gabriel, preaching to the converted. It was unreasonable, anarchic, a response to a world of music that in Axl's phrase has 'sucked fucking dick since the Sex Pistols'.

It was liberating to hear, to play loud with the summer windows wide open, and, for a music writer, the band were liberating to write about and be around, a throwback to why we'd all got into this industry in the first place. Although the corporate machine was soon to close around them – no one would sell any records without it – in a way it would happen on Guns N' Roses' own terms, with them presented as pretty much what they were. All that would be concealed was the real darkness behind the image: the excesses of the Hell House, the reality of junkie life, the death of Todd Crew . . .

At first, though, there was just the low hum of the rock press and its universally excellent reviews, and some early adopters. Most notable among them were another British band cleaning up on the US circuit, the Goth poseurs turned unreconstructed, Rick Rubin-produced rock monsters, The Cult, who were filling arenas all over the US with thumping, derivative yet bullshit-free songs like 'Love Removal Machine' and 'Wild Flower'. Guns N' Roses were offered, and accepted, the opening slot on the next leg of one of their apparently endless tours, beginning in August 1987 in the rock'n'roll outpost that was Halifax, Nova Scotia. The whole thing nearly came to nothing, though, when Axl thought he could take a Sten gun across the Canadian border, and forced the band into cancelling a show when he was refused entry.

Maybe he was still under the influence of the nerve-shredding video the band had just made for 'Welcome to the Jungle', which would, like the album, go nowhere – at least, not at first – before becoming recognised as probably the best, certainly the most shocking, rock video of 1987. An Englishman, Nigel Dick, directed, and ended up with a suggestively violent film that would ultimately be heavily censored before it ever made it to any kind of rotation on MTV. It was quite an achievement, on all sorts of levels.

Geffen had grudgingly put up $75,000 for Guns N' Roses to shoot a video for what would be their first single in America. And only then because Tom Zutaut was pestering them so much Eddie Rosenblatt ended up telling Alan Niven to call off his attack dog. Nevertheless, $75,000 was about half what most new artists might expect to get to shoot their all-important debut video. It meant they certainly wouldn't be able to shoot the storyboard Alan wanted for that price. 'So what I did was I butted "Jungle" against a Great White video shoot for their next single, "Lady Red Light", and used the same director, the same equipment, the same crew.'

Great White were on a roll. Their recent single, 'Rock Me', had become a staple of rock radio in America that summer. 'It meant we got to a second Great White video fast.' In the video and film world you did four-day rental deals. If you took it for even one day more they would charge you for another four. So Niven booked a four-day rental on 'Lady Red Light', 'then immediately went into "Jungle", so I could [offset] my shortfall on "Jungle" and kind of sweeten it across the whole board. By running four days in a row [two with each band] with the same production company I was able to amortise costs. Without that there would have been no "Jungle" video. And its form, with its socio-political content, was crucial to a perception of authenticity.'

With the financials sorted, Alan and Tom sat together at Geffen working on ideas for the video. 'Tom says, "What are we gonna do?"' Niven begins. 'And in that moment, I came up with the three steals – *Midnight Cowboy*, *The Man Who Fell to Earth* and *Clockwork Orange*.' The *Midnight Cowboy* steal was there in the opening scene of Axl getting off the bus with a straw hanging out of his mouth, the country boy arriving footloose in the big, bad city. The *Man Who Fell to Earth* steal was evidenced in the scene where Axl is seen viewing multiple TV scenes (using free news footage). And the *Clockwork Orange* steal, the climactic scene of a straitjacketed Axl forced to sit in front of TV images of sex and violence. Until he is 'cured'.

Alan Niven says he 'bullied' Nigel Dick into doing the 'Jungle' video. 'He didn't want to do it.' But 'Rock Me' by Great White had got significant airplay and by the autumn of 1987 their *Once Bitten* album had gone gold, heading for platinum, 'and Nigel wanted to keep his relationship with me'. As it turned out, MTV paid scant attention, only playing the video during the graveyard hours between midnight and 6 a.m., and then only grudgingly.

If the band was to make any headway outside LA, it was going to be the hard way – on the road. The bill with The Cult was a good one, though. They had been invited onto the tour personally by Cult frontman, Ian Astbury, after he had witnessed one of their Marquee shows in London. 'He spent more time in our dressing room than his own,' said Axl. Between The Cult's sudden metamorphosis from Goth-punk British invaders to arena-pleasing American rock goliaths and Guns N' Roses' everything's-cool, post-punk trip, for those in the know this was the must-see show of the summer holidays.

Behind the scenes, though, Axl was so intent on making the band's first major tour a success he was driving everyone else crazy. Alan Niven sighs heavily. 'Third date on the Cult tour, up in Canada, I flew up to see how it was going and spend a week on the tour. I'd just dropped my bags on the bed in the hotel room and there's this bang on the door. I go to open the door and there's Izzy, he looks a bit disconsolate. He brushes past me, walks into my room, and he flops into the sofa. I go, "What's up, Iz?" He looks up at me and he goes, "He makes us fucking miserable every fucking day." Three days into their first national tour. My response was, "Come on Iz, it's Ax. You know how he is. At least he's here. Let's go."'

A year into his own involvement with the band, Niven was painfully aware how uncomfortable Axl could make the others feel, when his mood wasn't right or his anxiety was high: insecurities he hid behind a barrage of angry tirades or days spent sulking in the shadows. Niven says the only time he and the singer ever came close to bonding was later on the Cult tour, when they arrived back in LA for a show at Long Beach Arena. 'It was an almost unique moment. We were sitting in the bus after the gig and I had to zip from Long Beach to somewhere else, where Great White were playing. And Axl looked at me and he said, "I miss you" – because I'd been running around doing other things. And he looked at me and he said, "I miss you." It was the only time that I ever got a statement like that from him.'

Even with a new cover on *Appetite*, Niven and Geffen were fighting to get it any attention. Tom Zutaut began to despair of the album selling enough copies to justify his faith in signing them, and his mood darkened further when David Geffen expressed his doubts, having finally listened to the record and found it 'unpleasant'. Zutaut did everything he could to put on a brave face to the Geffen promotions department, as though a complete lack of TV and radio exposure was all part of the plan, never wasting an opportunity to inform the head of promotions, Al Coury, that *Appetite* was merely a 'slow-burner'. Coury remained unconvinced. Zutaut told Niven to keep the band out on the road, keep them working, and so when they had the chance to jump on the next Aerosmith tour to Europe, it seemed like the perfect marriage of bands, and a chance to repeat the trick of building a buzz overseas that they could use when Guns returned home.

Except Aerosmith cancelled at the last minute. According to their co-manager, Tim Collins, the last straw was when Joe Perry told him he'd once bought heroin from Izzy Stradlin. With Aerosmith's newfound sobriety only ever one drink away from cracking and the band finally achieving all of the commercial success that their habits had denied them for a decade, he wasn't taking any chances. Meanwhile, their new album, *Permanent Vacation*, which had come out at the end of August, looked set to be their first major hit since their Seventies heyday, and the European dates were scrapped in favour of a gargantuan American tour now slated to begin in New York on 16 October.

Cue panic. It would take weeks for Niven to find another major tour for GN'R to piggyback on to, and with no video action and radio interest to help fill the void he feared the album would be dead in the water by the time the band got busy again. He discussed it over the phone with John Jackson, in London: 'John, out of a combination of humour, genius and sarcasm said, "Why don't you come and headline yourself?" I went, "If we can, let's do it."' John called Alan back the following night and said he thought they could pull it off. Five theatre shows in the UK splashed with posters. Plus some high-profile club shows around mainland Europe, with each town on the tour swamped in posters. 'That was that awesome fucking poster of the skulls and cross. And we blanketed the cities we were playing with those posters. They looked fucking amazing. And we pulled it off.'

They just needed one more thing: another band with similar appeal to help fill out the venues. Once again, John Jackson came to the rescue when he suggested Faster Pussycat, a shrewd choice given that they were being talked of with almost the same excitement as Guns in the UK rock press. Says Niven: 'It worked pretty good because it was just Faster Pussycat, what threat are they? Except that when we got to Germany it became very apparent to me that the record company thought [Faster Pussycat's manager] Warren Etna was the shit. And it took the Germans ages for them to come off of their high fucking horse and do something with *Appetite*.' That was the only serious glitch, though, to what was a bold new plan. 'How many people do that now? Go and headline the UK when you've sold 7000 records?'

After the indifference of Canadian ice hockey arenas, the opening shows at Hamburg's Markthalle and Amsterdam's gorgeous wooden former church the Paradiso were bustling, vibe-rich sellouts. Steven Adler would tell me later that Amsterdam was the first time he'd used heroin (a claim he'd later contradict in his autobiography, recalling he'd first shot up years before at the former Fleetwood Mac guitarist Bob Welsh's house in Laurel Canyon). Nonetheless, the story he told proved that Todd Crew's death had done nothing to still the band's use: 'We were bumming around the red light district, amazed that hookers actually advertised it in store windows. We stopped by a hash bar, ordered off a menu and got high. On the way out, this Dutch dude recognises us and invites us to a party. We follow the stranger to his townhouse on one of the canals. Everything's cool until Slash and Izzy disappear into another room. I know what they're doing – and I'm tired of being left out. I walk in and Izzy and Slash are already flying. I turned to Slash and said, 'Do me." He ties up my arm and stabs me. Halfway through the syringe, I was already freefalling and told him to take it out. This would be the night I most regret in my life. But at that moment it felt so damn good.'

They flew to England, where ticket sales in Nottingham and Manchester were slower. The Manchester Apollo show, where they had closed off the balcony for lack of ticket sales, was where I met them for the first time, immediately after they'd stepped off the stage. Standing in the dressing room, it seemed like the clock had been turned back 15 years; they were dressed like old-school rock stars, all hats and scarves and skull rings – and they were acting like them too.

'Hey, man,' said Steven. 'Where can I score some loods?'

Here was a guy barely into his twenties asking for Quaaludes – the drugs *du jour* for early-Seventies American concert-goers; heavy-duty tranquillisers that made falling down stairs seem fun.

'You can't get loods in England,' I told him.

'What!' he cried. 'You're fucking kidding me! What *can* you get then?'

'Mandrax,' I said. 'Mandies. Or reds – Seconal. That's probably the nearest equivalent.'

'Cool,' he said, 'so how can I get me some red Mandies, dude?'

Then Izzy ambled over. 'Hey, man,' he drawled, 'I smell pot. Who has pot?'

Someone passed him the joint and he clung to it like a drowning man. Slash shambled up, his face almost entirely obscured by the top hat and the cascade of curls that showered from underneath it. In his hand was clamped a half-full bottle of Jack Daniel's.

'I bet you go to bed with that thing . . .'

'Sure,' he said, 'I like to wake up to it, too. It's the only way . . .' He paused and glanced around. ' . . . I can handle *this*.'

I was introduced to Axl as we passed on the stairs. I'd only seen the pictures and the reality was surprisingly small, his pinched, freckled face and upturned nose giving him a vulnerable quality the stage lights had kept hidden. Of all the band he seemed to be the most self-contained and grown up; the one most certain of who he was and what he was trying to achieve. 'I wanna thank you and the magazine you're from for everything you've done for this band,' he told me, gripping my hand firmly. 'And I wanna tell you how much it means to me, cos I read your shit, man. I know who you are.' He delivered the lines sincerely, in a low voice. I believed what he said. 'You coming to see us in London, too?'

'London' was perhaps the most significant moment in the band's career as a live act, up to that point, a show that would go down as one of those 'I was there' gigs. The Hammersmith Odeon (as was: it's now known as the Apollo) was the capital's landmark gig, a transition point between clubs and arena as well as a gig almost every significant rock band had on their CV, most of them numerous times. Its capacity was 3500, and Guns were ultimately maybe 200 tickets short of a sell-out, a sign of how far they'd come in a few months. Axl dedicated 'Knockin' on Heaven's Door' to Todd Crew. The reviews of a ferocious show that climaxed with Axl playing Duff's bass while Slash soloed were overwhelming. Guns went back to America with some momentum at last.

There was also a new and increasingly significant figure on the scene: their tour manager, Doug Goldstein, whom I also met for the first time on those UK dates. Doug would 'put a lot of good energy in', according to Alan Niven. 'Dougie was really reliable to me initially. He was someone I trusted. He had patience and he wasn't a fucking nine-to-fiver. I didn't run an LA management company. I was involved in a way of life, as far as I was concerned. And he fit with that.'

Goldstein was the 26-year-old son of a retired policeman who had studied international marketing at North Arizona University. After college, Doug had worked in events security, and in 1984 he was appointed chief security recruiter for the Olympic Games. Since then he'd made his way into the music biz handling security for Air Supply, Van Halen, David Lee Roth, Black Sabbath and Heart. At first glance he may have seemed like an odd appointment: short-haired, clean-shaven, with a moustache . . . 'Izzy was convinced that Niven had hired a cop,' he says now with a chuckle. Perhaps because of this, Izzy was the only member of the band that Doug readily admits he never really established a bond with. Interesting, too, as Izzy was the one member Alan Niven felt he most related to.

Goldstein soon got a handle on the rest of them, though – beginning with Steven. The drummer's nasty habits were already becoming hardcore, but Doug just liked him. They had met at a specially arranged band dinner at El Compadre. 'That was Slash's spot. That and Hamburger Hamlet, Slash's other spot.' After the meal, Doug and Steven went to jump in a car, 'a big truck with a camper shell'. They both dived into the back of the truck. 'Steven goes, "No wait. There's room upfront." I go, "No, I'm getting in with you." He goes, "Dude, I'm just the drummer." And I go, "Yeah? I'm just the fucking tour manager, which means you're my boss." And that was all it took. He was like, "Oh my god. Somebody's treating me like I'm their equal and/or they're below that."'

Duff was cut from the same cloth as Steven, thought Doug: a wannabe rock star living life as he'd read about it in rock magazines. When the band came to Doug complaining that Duff had been wearing the same leather pants on- and offstage for three months, he handled it the best way he knew how. 'We're travelling in a bus. It stinks. The band is coming to me saying, we don't give a fuck what you have to do, lose the fucking pants!' So, at the next gig, 'I sent the runner out for a pair of gym shorts. Duff comes offstage and I'm in hiding. I wait until he goes to take a shower and I grab the leather pants and take them out to a dumpster at the back of the venue. He gets out and he's like, "What the fuck's going on?" I came in and said, "I'm sorry. We all voted. You have to lose the leather pants!" He was so upset because he had promised his then wife Mandy that he was going to wear the same pants on and off stage for the whole tour.'

The relationship Doug Goldstein would have with Slash was more complicated. Today, Slash likes to blame Doug for the break-up of the original GN'R line-up. Back in the late-Eighties and early Nineties, however, it is no exaggeration that the guitarist owed his life to his intrepid tour manager. They also became close in other ways, working side by side often, during those times, which were many, when Axl either couldn't be found or simply didn't want to know. 'He doesn't get the credit for it but Slash really was the guy that helped me run that band. No question. He'd pass out in a chandelier at four a.m. and he'd be at my door knocking at ten a.m. saying, "What do we have to do today?" We'd sit down and do all the radio interviews. I'd pick out him and Duff and we'd go and do in-store [appearances], Steven when he was in the band still. People think that Axl was the overall visionary, and Axl's an artist but he's not . . . he knew where he wanted to go but Slash was the guy that really put the plan into place.'

Goldstein also credits Slash for much of the band's early, iconic artwork. 'Nobody knows this and I don't know why but Slash has done probably ninety-five per cent of the band's artwork. Merchandising, I mean, everything. He's a brilliant artist.

He's a *brilliant* artist. He was the merchandise company's dream because they didn't have to pay people to do artwork. He came up with it all.'

Goldstein had his own opinions about Slash. 'The derivation of the top hat has a lot of different stories behind it but I have my own theory. When we went to Hawaii he wouldn't go outside; it was like he was avoiding getting tanned. Back then you didn't see many African-Americans in the rock'n'roll scene.' So are you saying you think Slash was self-conscious about being half black? 'Yep.' Hence 'the hair in the eyes, the top hat and all of it'.

The most significant relationship Doug Goldstein would forge with Guns N' Roses, though, was with W. Axl Rose. Where Alan Niven would appear increasingly at loggerheads with the flame-haired singer, Goldstein, with his more emollient approach, would quickly become Axl's go-to guy in all matters relating to both the business of the band – and, increasingly, his own, almost ritualistically tangled personal affairs. Put simply, Axl, who never trusted anybody, trusted Doug. 'Implicitly. No question. I'm the guy he'd call at three o'clock in the morning and say, "Dougie, can you talk?" I'd say, "Sure." "Come to my room." So I'd go down to his room and we'd just sit around till, like, five, six in the morning, discussing different ideas.'

Initially, this good-cop/bad-cop routine would work in everybody's favour. Stephanie Fanning, then working as assistant to Alan and Doug at the Stravinski offices in LA, recalls how, 'In the very beginning with Alan and Doug they could not have been [more] perfectly matched for each other. As far as Alan being on the business side, he's meeting with the record company, he's meeting with the attorneys. He's meeting with all of the business side of things and he is doing an amazing job. Then there's Doug, being the social guy. "Hey, how are you? I'm Doug Goldstein, GN'R's tour manager." Knew everybody's name, shook everybody's hand. There was nothing that you felt like he couldn't take care of for you, make you happy, everything just felt in control and taken care of.'

Goldstein elaborates: 'When I first was hired on, Niven was like, "I'm having the typical rock'n'roll issues." "Like?" "Well, like they're busting up hotels." I said, "Give me two months and I can fix that." He said, "Okay, yeah, you got it." So Stevie breaks a lamp in his room. I tell him, "Steven, this is the way I handle things. We've got to pay for it. We don't break shit and leave."' He took Steven downstairs to the hotel reception, where Doug explained to the guy behind the desk that they had broken a lamp and would like to pay for it. 'The guy asks for $150. I go, "No way. That's a seventy-dollar lamp." The guy says, "No, it cost us $150." I go, "I don't give a fuck. I've been travelling most of my life, I know what this lamp is worth so I'm gonna give you seventy-five bucks and we'll call it a day." The guy's like, whatever, fine. So Stevie goes back and tells everybody, "Doug saved me seventy-five bucks today."

'So I do that. You know, a television here, a lamp there. I do that for, like, six weeks. Finally Slash breaks a TV. So he calls me.' Doug took him down to reception, told the manager on duty that they'd accidentally broken a TV and that they'd like to pay for it. 'The guys says okay, and that the set cost $350. I go, "No way." And Slash is waiting for me to bring it down, right? I go, "Not a chance. That is *not* a $350 TV. That's a $700 TV." Slash is like, "*What?*" I go, "Slash, shut up. I do this for a living and I *know* a $700 TV when I see one." The guy is like, "No, really. Just give me $350." I go, "Shut up! I do this for a living." I go, "Slash, I'm gonna have to take $700 of your money." So now it's not even a band deal, I'm taking it out of his personal income. He was fucking livid! But I tell you what. Nobody broke *shit* after that.'

After another month of club shows, the cards started to fall their way once more. Mötley Crüe were about to go out in support of a Number 2 hit album, the multi-platinum *Girls, Girl, Girls*, and Whitesnake had been booked as the support act. But Whitesnake's *1987* album was breaking out too, also reaching Number 2 on the *Billboard* chart and about to be catapulted to greater sales with a hit single 'Is This Love'. When Whitesnake pulled out of the Crüe tour to play headline shows of their own, Niven and Zutaut used their Crüe connections to have Guns N' Roses step in as last-minute replacements. Although the Crüe and Guns would soon be at the centre of one of rock'n'roll's most infamous feuds (which would in turn have its knock-on effects for me), they were for a couple of brief months the perfect match, Crüe at the peak of their trashy appeal, Guns hungry to knock them off their coke-encrusted perch.

As Guns wound around America, *Appetite* at last began to ascend the Billboard Hot 100, first in the high 60s, then creeping, by December 1987, up to Number 59, with sales approaching 200,000 albums. Not at all bad for the debut album by an underground band with zero radio support. This jump came on the back of yet more drama. In Lakeland, Florida, the band filmed a slot for MTV, for the *Headbangers Ball* segment. Alan Niven and Doug Goldstein realised that the band were in no fit state to be taped. Slash and Izzy were on some distant smack planet – where they'd been joined by Mötley Crüe's bassist, Nikki Sixx – Duff was drinking himself into oblivion most days and Axl was unpredictably contrary whenever confronted by the press, and so damage limitation was entered into. The band were filmed playing 'It's So Easy', Goldstein did an interview in an attempt to put a bright shiny face on a bunch of obvious fuck-ups, before MTV finally got to confront the band face to face in the dressing room as Mötley Crüe took the stage, a piece that rapidly degenerated into an unairable few minutes of drunken swearing and laughter. It finally made the air, heavily cut, years later when *Appetite* was the biggest-selling rock record on the planet.

Back on the road with the Crüe, Axl found himself in trouble again. This time in Atlanta, where police actually walked on stage and arrested him during the second song for attacking one of the arena security guards, who, Axl claimed, had been beating up the band's friends in the audience. He was held for questioning backstage while the rest of the band were left to get on with their 45-minute set as best they could. A roadie hurriedly hauled on-stage helped out with some of the vocals, while Slash contributed a 15-minute guitar solo and Steven managed a longer-than-usual drum solo to fill in the gaps. After the show, Axl was incandescent with rage, claiming he had been the victim of trumped-up charges. 'In Atlanta I dived in and I had police saying I hit them,' he fumed. 'I never did, but I had to plead guilty because we didn't have any money at the time. Lie? Yes, I guess I did lie once. I lied and said that I hit four cops. I guess we should reopen the case and take me to trial for perjury. But I didn't have $56,000 to pay them off under the table.'

The Crüe tour ended in predictable disaster back in LA. Both bands returned home together. Guns were due back out with Alice Cooper a few days later, and Slash holed up in the Franklin Plaza hotel. Nikki Sixx joined him, where they were both shot up by a local smack dealer introduced to them by Robbin Crosby of Ratt. Sixx immediately overdosed and Slash found himself once again dragging a corpse into the shower in an attempt to bring it back to life. Sixx was luckier than Todd Crew – the paramedics arrived in time to restart his heart with needles full of adrenalin, and he took off into the night, calling Slash on the phone the following day to thank him for saving his life. Sixx would immortalise the night on Mötley Crüe's next album in a song called 'Kickstart My Heart'. Slash would do everything to try to forget about it. Until next time . . .

5

MUCH TOO HIGH

1988 would be the year that the lives of everyone connected to Guns N' Roses would be changed for ever. For the five band members it was the moment when their dreams of rock stardom became an inescapable reality. By 6 August, *Appetite for Destruction*, led by the single 'Sweet Child o' Mine', would have topped the *Billboard* chart for the first time (it would return on a further three occasions) and was in its first of three solid years – 147 weeks – within the Top 200. The band was on tour with Aerosmith (Tim Collins having negotiated entirely separate travel and accommodation for both acts) and about to fly to the UK to appear at the Donington Monsters of Rock festival, where they would encounter another terrible low. Newly immortal, until that moment, they thought the worst was behind them. They were wrong.

The year had begun in the studio. Eddie Rosenblatt had urged Niven to make another record, something the manager had forcefully resisted, taking the view that they'd sold almost 250,000 albums without a proper single, video or marketing campaign, and – not unreasonably – asked Rosenblatt what he thought they might sell should they get one? Instead, with Mike Clink, the band cut some acoustic songs for a prospective stop-gap EP or a bunch of B-sides: a sweet ballad of Axl's called 'Patience'; a blackly comic tune they'd debuted at the UK shows, 'Used to Love Her'

('... *but I had to kill her!*', a lyric inspired by Axl's fondness for 'shock comic' Sam Kinison); and 'One in a Million', an obnoxious Rose rant that also began in Kinison-esque humour but quickly descended into something far less funny, storing up trouble for the band later on). They also recorded a rangy acoustic, much longer and doubly vitriolic version of 'You're Crazy' that Clink liked as much as the electric version on *Appetite*.

Between times there were one-off shows. They opened for Great White at KNAC's second anniversary show, where Cinderella's drummer, Fred Coury, sat in for Steven Adler, who'd broken his hand in a barroom brawl following a show opening for Alice Cooper in Minneapolis a week before Christmas. Then there was an unannounced 'secret' show billed as the Drunk Fux, which featured the five-man band plus Axl acolytes Del James and West Arkeen, performing an impromptu set of covers – including a first public performance of a new song, 'Yesterdays', a ragtag blues shuffle Axl had recently banged together with Del and West and another street kid, named Billy McCloud, and which Axl announced he and the band would be recording the following week. (They didn't.) There was also a hurriedly arranged Thursday night gig at the Cathouse on 21 January – Steven's first full gig back behind the drums, essentially a glorified rehearsal for three shows in Scandinavia supporting Mötley Crüe.

Essentially, though, the band was treading water. Again Eddie Rosenblatt urged Niven and Zutaut to consider getting another album ready to go, based on the latest session with Clink. 'No way, this record's just beginning,' Zoots told Eddie. 'We haven't even scratched the surface yet. There's a Number One single that is buried on the second side of the album. The promotion people have not even listened to it!' Zutaut was referring to 'Sweet Child o' Mine', but by then neither Rosenblatt nor anyone else at the company was prepared to listen.

Exasperated, Zutaut appealed directly to David Geffen, who asked simply: 'What is the one thing that I could do to help you?' Zutaut replied, 'It would help if you could get the "Welcome to the Jungle" video played on MTV.' Geffen said he would do what he could and put a call through to MTV's chief executive, Tom Freston, an old friend who owed him a favour. Freston accordingly agreed to air 'Welcome to the Jungle'. Just one proviso: MTV would play it only once, at 3 a.m. on the East Coast, midnight on the West Coast. After that, all bets were off. However, within minutes of the video airing for the first time a week later, the phones began to light up at the network as their switchboard became overloaded with calls for repeat plays from overexcited fans. Within a month, 'Welcome to the Jungle' had officially become one of the most-requested videos on MTV that year.

At the same time, in another weird example of the kind of synchronicity that seemed to bless their professional relationship, Alan Niven had managed to wangle Guns N' Roses into a live appearance on MTV. Originally the station had approached Niven about filming Great White live at The Ritz in New York for an MTV Special that would also be broadcast live across several radio stations. It seemed like a no-brainer. Great White's *Once Bitten* album had just gone gold in America and MTV wanted to get in on the ride. Alan said yes on one condition. 'My other band opens, okay?' The MTV producers agreed.

In the weeks leading up to the show in February, however, 'Welcome to the Jungle' had begun its own heavy rotation, moving the needle on the dial of the *Appetite* album, too, which was also now approaching gold status for over 500,000 sales. Suddenly Alan Niven was presented with the unique situation of having two hot'n'heavy acts steaming up the US charts. On the eve of the show, he decided the 'smart call' was 'to flip the bill order'. He goes on: 'Guns had just gone white hot. I went to Great White and said, "What's the fucking rule? Be a hard act to follow before you follow a hard act."' So they switched places and Great White opened the MTV Special instead. Both bands played the same length of time but there was no doubting afterwards who the stars of The Ritz were that night.

'There's a couple of moments in [the Great White] set that still give me goosebumps when I play back the tapes,' insists Niven. 'To the point where Slash ran into the dressing room after they played and said, "You fuckers! How do we follow that?"' But not only did GN'R follow that, 'To a lot of people that is the apex of watching Guns N' Roses. Imagine all the fucking faces, cognoscenti and industry fuckers that were there at the show. I'm not the greatest at the social bit but I'm having to work the room and be nice to everybody and try to remember who fucking everybody is.' Next thing, he got a tap on the shoulder. 'Goldstein panicking saying Axl can't find his bandana. "He wants you to go into the crowd and find him one." So I did. I went into the crowd and found one. He didn't like that one so I went and found another one. Second one was okay. Slash is aware of all this. So what would your state of mind be when you went out on stage? Good god, half the fucking time each was seething at the other. And The Ritz was the classic example. Yet most people think that's the apex of GN'R live on film. Yet not everybody was happy with Axl at that moment. But what's his muse? His muse is confrontation. His muse is conflict. He's a power tripper.'

Whatever the background, the results were dynamite, and can still be seen on YouTube today. Niven is right. This was Guns N' Roses, at their earliest, now classic best. When Slash dived into the audience at the climax of 'Rocket Queen', you could almost touch the heat from the crowd, escaping, hissing like bad gas from the manholes of New York City.

With his star rising fast, instead of making him feel more at ease, Axl Rose's on- and offstage behaviour was becoming increasingly erratic. He became more difficult and demanding, attempting to control every situation, even those involving large crowds, by losing his temper: he would walk offstage if something offended him and have to be coaxed back. A fortnight before the end of the tour, he didn't take the stage at all. It happened at the second of two shows they were to headline, 12 and 13 February, at the Celebrity Theatre in Phoenix. The first show had ended prematurely when Axl walked off at the end of 'Nightrain' and refused to come back out for an encore. No one knew quite why, putting it down to another of Axl's weird head-trips.

The following afternoon, however, he barricaded himself in his hotel room with his then-girlfriend, Erin Everly, and refused to come out. 'We tried everything to get him out,' says Niven. 'We banged on the door and shouted, "Come on, dude, we got a gig. Come out!" and he'd shout back, "Fuck off!" I don't know if Axl and Erin were fighting. That was probably something that happened more often than not, but he refused to come out no matter what we said.'

As opening band, T.S.O.L. – a Californian punk-metal band signed to Niven's former label, Enigma – completed their 40-minute set, Niven pushed them back onstage to try to buy some time. 'Finally, these poor guys in T.S.O.L. came offstage after playing Beatles covers. They looked at me mournfully and said, "We've played absolutely everything we know. We're beat. Can we quit now?" That was the moment I had to walk onstage and say, "Tonight's performance by Guns N' Roses, unfortunately, will not occur due to a medical emergency." Immediately, people started throwing shit at me and it got ugly fast. The crowd rioted and it spilled out into the parking lot, and at least one car was turned over and set on fire.'

When they got back to the hotel, led by a seething Steven Adler, they told Axl he was fired, to which he responded with the classic 'You can't fire me, I was leaving anyway . . .' Then he called the band's bluff, took a car to the airport and left them to stew. 'For about three days, it really did look like the band was over,' says Alan Niven. But the tactic worked. He and Slash talked on the phone a few days later and Axl was back, but the pattern was set. Axl had asserted his authority, established his indispensability, and clearly demonstrated his willingness to exercise his power over and emotional control of the band. Steven Adler would later reflect, 'It was the greatest time of my life, but one of the guys – I don't need to name him – made it so difficult for us all. Quite often he made the best and most exciting times I'll ever experience feel like a complete pain in the ass. Besides the loneliness and sadness I felt when I was excluded, the worst thing was to play in front of [thousands of] people and have the guy storm offstage in the middle of the first song. With no warning, he'd throw the microphone to the floor, then leave. And not come back. Quite rightly, the audience would boo, and it was an awful feeling to know there was nothing the rest of the band could do about the situation. You'd go backstage and get in a fight with the guy. He'd say, "Fuck you" and get on a plane and you'd have to cancel a lot of other shows. It's all coming back to him now because he's the one who looks bad. But at the time it reflected badly on all of us.'

So much so it almost holed the GN'R bandwagon beneath the waterline. Says Niven: 'I lost what I had just had to compete with our own fucking agent for, which was the opening slot for AC/DC. I'd got AC/DC to agree to do that. [But] that invitation was rescinded when they heard about the Phoenix riot.'

As ever, Axl felt his actions were entirely justifiable. 'I guess I get mad because of some form of fear about my own weaknesses,' he once said in a moment of deep clarity. 'Everybody has theirs, and mine happen to be in what I do. And what I do is sing and run and get my picture taken. I've always needed high maintenance to keep my act together. Nothing really comes naturally to me except the desire to sing. I used to jump ship every three days. And I wasn't crying wolf. It would usually come down to, I was leaving but there was no place to go. What am I gonna do, go to Paris, do poetry? Look at art museums and hope that not going after what I set out to do didn't eat me alive? Go pump gas? I was leaving to pump gas a few times, and ready for it. Then, I don't know, something in me would go, "You can deal with this now." It just took time to be able to deal with it. A lot of my anger came from people not understanding that I needed that time.'

As Tom Zutaut had been telling anyone who'd listen, 'Sweet Child o' Mine' was the single that would properly break *Appetite*. Now they were listening. At the start of April, a couple of weeks before the album broke the US Top 10 for the first time, Guns N' Roses shot a video for 'Sweet Child' at the Ballroom in Huntington Park, taking their girlfriends along, including Erin Everly, who'd inspired the lyrics, and Duff's girlfriend, Mandy, whom he'd marry the following month. Albeit mimed, 'Sweet Child' is a near-perfect rendition of everything that made the band so captivating, from Axl's cobra-swaying dance to the cigarette dangling from Izzy's thin lips, to Slash coaxing then bullying his trusty Les Paul copy through the guitar solo: this was Guns N' Roses at their dizzy, seductive peak. Even now, decades later, its power remains undiminished. Alan Niven realised that this was their moment: 'They got to a point where they got a momentum that you knew was going to be unstoppable, and for me that was in the spring of '88 . . .'

And yet, as with almost every other crucial milestone in their harum-scarum story, the 'Sweet Child' video so nearly didn't happen. In fact, as far as Axl was concerned, it didn't happen at all the way he originally envisaged it. Alan Niven takes up the story.

'Eddie Rosenblatt had begrudgingly put up $35,000 to do a second video. Thirty-five grand for a video in those days was zero. Great White's first video had a budget of over 100k.' Axl, though, having done one video, 'was now Martin Scorsese' and had his own idea for the kind of video he wanted for 'Sweet Child.' Nigel Dick was again the director. Alan told him straight: they were going for a no-frills, straight, as-live performance video. No storyboards. No nothing but the band and the song. 'Nigel found a room in central LA, three inches deep in pigeon shit and had it cleaned up.' The only snag was that Axl, who'd had no ideas for 'Jungle', had several for 'Sweet Child'.

In an effort to manage expectations, Niven set up a dinner for him, Nigel and Axl. Then sat listening patiently as Axl outlined his ideas for the video in excruciating detail. 'I told Nigel just to say yes to whatever Axl suggested,' Niven smilingly recalls. 'We start with the detail of a printed newspaper that had something to do with him and Erin lying in the gutter. Then the car tyre goes over leaving perfect tracks . . .' He pauses and sighs. 'By the time we were in the cornfields of Kansas, fucking Nigel is sitting at the table with eyes bigger than goose eggs. "Yeah, we can do that. Yeah, we can do that . . ." We come to the end of the meal and Axl is really happy because *War and Peace* is going to be remade starring him and Erin.'

As Niven reached for the bill he told Nigel, in front of Axl, to thumbnail it and give him an estimate for how much he thought Axl's ideas for the video would cost, and fax it to Alan's office in the morning. 'Nigel faxes this thing through the next day and it's something like $285,000.' Alan called Axl with the news. When he told him how much it would cost, 'I could just hear the suck of oxygen out of Axl's lungs. He said, "What are we gonna do?" I said, "Don't worry, we'll get it done. We can't do this at the moment but we obviously will get a video done."'

To his credit, Axl then came up with the idea of including all the girlfriends in the video, knowing that if he were to include Erin in the shoot there'd be hell to pay if the other band members couldn't bring their girls along for the ride too. Niven and Dick, meanwhile, made plans to shoot the as-live video they'd already discussed. At 5 a.m. after filming for several hours, 'Axl realised that none of his desires were being fulfilled in this shoot, and that basically it was a bad shoot, and he stormed off. I looked at Nigel and he said, "Don't worry, I think I've got enough."' He explains: 'Nigel had been concerned because we only had a budget for a single camera. So he had an idea. "What if I bring in a couple of Bolexes" – 16mm handheld film cameras – "and anybody can pick up a Bolex and shoot footage?" I said, "You're a fucking genius!"'

There were three Bolexes, loaded all the time, left lying around so anyone from the band's entourage could pick up one of the cameras and run around and shoot things. Nigel Dick also shot in both colour and black-and-white. Over the next couple of days, Alan and Nigel sat through hours of the footage. Niven instructed Dick to make two videos, one 'best-shot' predominantly in colour with flashes of black-and-white, and a second completely in black-and-white, except for the very last image, in which Axl turned into colour. It was an inspired move. When MTV called Niven a few weeks into its heavy rotation of the first 'Sweet Child' video, saying it had reached the end of its shelf life and would now be downgraded to a much lower level of rotation, Niven told them: '"Fine, you're gonna have another edit on your desk by the end of the day." And they did and we got another six weeks of airplay on the subsequent video. Two for thirty-five grand!'

The result was 12 weeks of heavy rotation for what would become the most iconic video of the late-Eighties rock era – a feat that would eventually send 'Sweet Child' to Number 1 on the *Billboard* chart, the band's first and only singles chart topper. Joy, however, was not unconfined, at least not for Axl and Slash, who bristled at seeing the near six-minute album version of the song edited down to a more 'radio-friendly' four-minute version, something they achieved by effectively neutering Slash's elongated guitar solo. 'I hate the edit of "Sweet Child o' Mine",' Axl would later complain in *Rolling Stone*. 'Radio stations said, "Well, your vocals aren't cut." [But] my favourite part of the song is Slash's slow solo; it's the heaviest part for me. There's no reason for it to be missing except to create more space for commercials, so the radio-station owners can get more advertising dollars. When you get the chopped version . . . you're getting screwed.'

Back on the road, the band got bumped from the opening spot on the next David Lee Roth arena tour – and for exactly the same reasons AC/DC had bumped them: 'Too much hassle, man', as he told me, though behind the scenes many suspected it was more to do with the fact that the increasingly insecure Roth, who's post-Van Halen solo career had hit a serious bump in the road, simply feared the competition – Alan Niven again found himself having to scrabble to come up with Plans B, C and D. He'd managed to bridge the gap in their touring schedule by getting them their first national TV slot on Fox's *The Late Show*, where they stole the show with the new, snake-hipped 'You're Crazy', *sans* swear words, and a hopped-up version of 'Used to Love Her' that even left Axl smiling. For the next few weeks, though, they would be on their own, headlining small theatres and auditoriums, with the backing of German sheet-metallists UDO, and Zodiac Mindwarp, then big briefly in the UK, and whose neo-biker image provided a neat bridge between UDO's generic heavy metal garb and GN'R's soulful living-on-the-Strip mien. The crowds loved the shows, but it was like the English tour all over again, the band punching above their weight, using the tour as a lifeline until something better came along. Niven, meanwhile, was trying to square the circle by also keeping tabs on Great White – still the more prominent of his two acts – who were then touring sold-out American arenas in support of Whitesnake. He was so busy, 'I swear to God there were a couple of times I passed myself at LAX.'

Then, out of the blue, a little taste of tomorrow – and another odd blast of synchronicity. Great White's *Once Bitten* and Guns N' Roses' *Appetite for Destruction* had both originally been scheduled for release on the same day in July 1987. Sensibly, Eddie Rosenblatt had delayed the release of *Appetite* by four weeks, to give Alan Niven time to 'gasp for oxygen'. Since then the latter had been lagging behind the former, in terms of sales, if not prestige: *Once Bitten* had gone gold in the US in November; *Appetite* had gone gold the following March. Now, suddenly, in April 1988, they had caught up with each other.

'They both went platinum on the same day,' says Niven. It was Thursday, 7 April 1988 – exactly a week after GN'R's eye-catching appearance on *The Late Show* and just a few days before they shot the 'Sweet Child' video. That night Great White opened for Whitesnake at the LA Forum in Inglewood. The final night of the tour, there was a party afterwards. That morning, Alan Niven had got a phone call from Capitol saying they had just shipped their millionth copy of *Once Bitten*. Niven was ecstatic: vindication at last for his faith in a bunch of no-hopers he'd almost single-handedly now turned into million-selling rock stars. Then that evening, as he was walking into the LA Forum to see Great White, Eddie Rosenblatt showed up (like GN'R, Whitesnake were signed to Geffen) and made straight for Niven. 'Congratulations,' said Eddie, 'we just moved the millionth copy of Guns N' Roses.'

Now Niven was truly knocked out. He had to stop walking and check what condition his condition was in. On top of everything, 7 April also happened to be his thirty-fifth birthday. He blurted out the good news to Eddie, who just stood there and gave him the gimlet eye. 'Well, somebody's living life right,' said Eddie.

The next day, though, it was back to business. Most pressing: finding another big tour to get Guns N' Roses latched on to. When Iron Maiden's manager, Rod Smallwood – a pal of Niven's but another manager who'd turned down the opportunity to manage GN'R early on, claiming there was 'just something not right about them' – offered the band ten shows opening for Maiden in

Canada in May, plus another 22 across America throughout June, Niven grabbed it with both hands. Yet things started to go wrong almost immediately.

The first inkling he had that things were about to turn bad, says Niven, was when he got a phone call from Izzy going, 'Niv, there's some fucker with fucking horns on his head and they've got cardboard icebergs on stage. What the fuck are we doing here?' Doug Goldstein laughs as he recalls: 'So we get on the [Maiden] tour and first day, swear to god, the scrims [backdrop props] behind the band were robotic ducks. It's kind of early in the day and Axl's never usually there but for some reason he's there earlier in the day. And he comes up to me and he goes, "No photographs the entire tour. There's not a fucking chance, man. No way. *Zero*, Doug. And if I see one camera I'm fucking bailing." I said, "Why?" He said, "Dude, I don't even need to tell you why. If you can't figure it out then you're a fucking idiot."'

He goes on: 'I hadn't been up to see it yet so I asked Slash, why is Axl is upset? He goes, "Doug, all I can tell you is I'm with him on this one." I go, "Come on! Why in the fuck are we on this tour? It's all about promotion. It's all about getting out there and bashing the headliner." That's what you do as an opener. He goes, "Look, Doug, I'm just telling you, I agree with him." So I go to my last resort – Duff. I'm like, "Come on, Duff, buddy, I need to rally the troops." He goes, "Yeah, yeah. Let's walk out here and see what the issue is."' But when, on their way to the stage, Iron Maiden's singer, Bruce Dickinson, came out of his dressing room 'wearing these knee-high frilly boots, Duff looks at me and goes, "I don't even need to see it, Doug. I'm in with the two of 'em. No photographs."'

But, as Alan Niven points out, 'Sweet Child' hadn't hit big yet and although the band had the buzz, it was important to build and keep them on the road. 'Also,' he says, 'if you've got a bunch of fucking addicts, it's easier to wrangle with their asses if you've got them on a mobile facility like a bus. If they're in LA they're scattered everywhere. The one time I went through cold turkey with Slash, we had him in our guest room, counting out his Valiums, cleaning the puke out of his mouth, getting him through the week. What does the fucker do the minute he's through the week? He calls up COF for a fucking car and he goes to find his dealer. If I can keep them on the bus and keep them moving I've got a better chance of keeping them alive.'

Guns N' Roses simply met Iron Maiden at the wrong moment for both bands. Huge throughout the rest of the world and noted for their relentless work ethic, the veteran British metal act had never quite cracked America in the same way as they had everywhere else. Their current album, *Seventh Son of a Seventh Son*, had only just made gold status and ticket sales for the early part of the tour had been slow. Guns N' Roses not only had a bigger album, but as soon as they joined the tour, ticket sales picked up. Soon the feeling within the GN'R camp was that they were the real headline act here. Duff even took a week off to get married to his girlfriend, Mandy Brixx, at the end of May, leaving the Cult's bassist, Kid Chaos, to fill in. It was impossible to imagine them treating – for example – Aerosmith in the same way, a band they actually related to and respected.

Axl, in particular, loathed every moment he was on the road with Maiden. As if affirming every doubt and second thought he had about the validity of doing the tour, the first night at the Moncton Coliseum, on 13 May, he cut the set short after the Maiden fans kept booing and throwing things at them. When a beer can bounced off his arm during 'Knockin' on Heaven's Door', he told the crowd that he didn't like 'warm beer, especially not Alpine'. Then he stormed off, yelling, 'Fuck you, Moncton!' The following night at the Metro Centre, in Halifax, before 'Knockin' on Heaven's Door', an enraged Axl told an audience member he could suck his dick then challenged him to come up onstage for a fight. In Ottawa, Axl was in such a foul mood he began ranting into the mike about trying to kill someone before 'My Michelle'.

By the time the Maiden tour had reached Seattle at the start of June, it looked like Axl and the band had finally settled into their new temporary home. They were including 'Sweet Child' in their short, punchy set, and the band was starting to play a little freer, without the anxiety and tension that had marred the Canadian shows. The closer the tour got to LA, though – to home – the worse Axl's moods were becoming again. I was there at the two nights at Irvine Meadows, a 17,000-capacity outdoor amphitheatre in Long Beach, California, where GN'R were supposed to open for Maiden, and when I arrived the disquiet was obvious. Things had degenerated to the point where the two bands were hardly speaking. The brace of Irvine shows should have been a glorious homecoming for Guns N' Roses. Instead, both their appearances were cancelled when Axl succumbed to 'voice problems'. The rumourmongers whispered that there was nothing wrong with his voice. Axl simply resented opening for a band he now considered smaller than Guns N' Roses, something which Doug Goldstein now strenuously denies.

'He used to blow out his pipes all the time. When you go through seven different cycles of your vocal cords, from stretching and compressing, that guy's just built to fail.' Axl found himself sitting in the surgery of an otolaryngologist, Dr Joseph H. Sugarman – coincidentally, the brother of the former Doors biographer Danny Sugarman. 'He wanted to operate on Axl and Axl's like, "Fuck you."' Instead, Axl put himself in the hands of Dr Hans von Leden, an ear, nose and throat specialist who taught at UCLA and USC and treated voice disorders in singers, attorneys, teachers, politicians, pastors and other professionals. 'Hans von Leden was this old German guy working out of UCLA, the president of the Otolaryngology Association. And the guy was like [German accent], "No! Don't ever let anybody operate on your vocal cords.

We can heal them!" So that was it. He was Axl's guy. He had zero fucking clue who Axl was. Axl brought him a platinum record. He was like, "What is zis?" He had no idea. Cute little guy, probably weighed 100 pounds dripping wet.'

In the event, all 15 of the remaining shows GN'R were to have done with Iron Maiden were cancelled, along with a handful of shows that were to have followed in Japan. While Axl took care of his voice, the rest of the band did what they always had done, away from the road. Got high. Git low. Gone round and round wherever you go . . . Slash was staying at the Hyatt on Sunset under the name Mr Disorderly. Steven was staying there, but under his own name. I was in a hotel across the street: the plusher Mondrian. I arranged to meet Slash for an interview one morning at 11 a.m. and we walked across Sunset Boulevard back to my hotel (where there was an expense account waiting – they might have been famous but the money hadn't started rolling in yet). He told me he'd just been 'smoking a foil' before meeting his dad for breakfast. That is, smoking heroin. We bumped into Steven hanging around outside. Asked what he was doing, he just smiled, shook his blond head. 'Ah, you know, man. People to see, places to go.' Though not Axl, who was home with Erin. Or Duff, who was home with his new wife, Mandy. Or Izzy, who . . . actually, nobody knew where Izzy was at. Like Slash and Steven, Izzy had *nothing* to do, except get wasted.

By then everybody in LA seemed to know their names, or at least their faces. The 'Sweet Child' video was gathering momentum on MTV and all the rock magazines were now splashing their out-of-it faces across their into-it front covers. As Slash and I took a table inside the bar at the Mondrian, next to the pool, a bunch of bikini-clad young girls surrounded us. 'Hey, Slash, can I get your autograph?' 'Sure, baby.' 'Hey Slash, my girlfriend Melissa says she went out with you?' 'Uh . . . sure, baby . . . maybe . . .'

'Hey, Slash . . .' He stood there patiently signing his name on various areas of their bodies, sometimes adding a little drawing of a bad man smoking a cigarette. Or maybe a skull playing guitar . . . Or something that looked something like that anyway . . . It was pretty clear he didn't really know what he was doing any more.

He told me he'd just been saying goodbye to his father, Tony, when I'd arrived to meet him. 'He was telling me to keep my feet on the ground and stuff. I told him, I'm cool. I know what it's all about. I mean, look at me. T-shirt, jeans, boots, that's me, man. That's all there is. Besides, we haven't had any money yet. We just get these phone calls – yesterday it was 35,000 sales, today it's 91,000 sales. It freaks my ass out.' Acknowledging that part of the band's appeal lay in the notion that it might end tomorrow, Slash concluded, somewhat prophetically, 'Actually, I'd *rather* it collapsed. I'd rather be as good as possible in the amount of time that you can do it, and do it to the hilt. Then fall apart, die, whatever . . .'

Slash smiled as he said this. Hidden behind all that hair I couldn't tell if his eyes were smiling too, or just his mouth. Like all the best jokes we both knew it contained more than its fair share of truth, the seeds of future past. But for now, off the road, with the album fast on its way to its second, maybe even third million, everybody's good mood had returned. Even Axl's. 'The funny thing about Axl,' says Doug Goldstein, 'he has a *fantastic* sense of humour. Nobody knows that about him. He is *hilarious*. Because he has that high intellect, I always say you can tell when someone is intelligent by their sense of humour. Because if you're daft that synapse doesn't take place in the brain. Or if it does, it's very delayed, and he is so bright that he just, bang, fires them off one after another.'

He recalls Axl phoning him around this time with an important question. 'I'd always told him, don't read the press. So he calls me and says, "Dougie, I know you told me to never read the press but I couldn't help it. Everybody says that success has turned me into an asshole." I started laughing. He says, "Why are you laughing?' I go, "What do you want me to say?" He goes, "I want you to tell me the truth. Do you think the success has turned me into a prick?" I go, "All right, you want the truth? Axl, when I first started working for you, you were the biggest asshole I've ever met in my life. But you weren't publicised and nobody knew it. Now you're just a highly publicised asshole but you're not nearly as difficult to work with as you were back then." He just laughed at me.'

More and more, Doug Goldstein was the man to keep everybody's spirits up on the road. It was also while the band was off the road that summer, waiting for Axl's voice to heal, that Goldstein found himself spending more time with Slash, while they were both holed up at the Hyatt. 'Not only do we have not enough money for a Sunset-facing view, our rooms are so small you had to go out into the hallway to change your mind. So I'm in my room and all of a sudden I hear all of these sirens, so I look out the backdoor and some guy had taken a dive off the roof. Slash calls me and he's crying, saying, "Did you look out the window?" I said, "Yeah." He says, "Fuck, man. I'm so bummed." I go, "No, man. I hear you. What a horrible way to go. I tell you what, why don't you come to my room and we'll talk about it." He says, "Yeah, okay, give me, like, five minutes." So he walks in and then standing on the heater, which is, like, by the window, I have two signs in my hand: 9.0 and 9.5. He was like, "You're fucking sick, man!" I said, "Well, it wasn't a bad dive."'

The serious stuff was left to Alan Niven. Having seen GN'R bumped from both the AC/DC and David Lee Roth arena tours, and having been forced to withdraw from the Iron Maiden jaunt, but with an album, *Appetite*, and single, 'Sweet Child o' Mine', now looking like the biggest hits of the summer, he saw only one possible option left for the band to capitalise on their possibly once-in-a-lifetime position. 'I went to Eddie Rosenblatt at Geffen and said, "Look, there's only one other tour left. We *have* to have it. I need it. *You* need it!" And that was the Aerosmith tour.'

With three hit singles in the US that year and their first million-selling album since the Seventies, Aerosmith were now approaching the apex of the same steady climb they had begun a year earlier when they cancelled their European tour, effectively dumping GN'R in the process. The difference in their respective fortunes between then and now, though, just 12 months later, was enormous. With sales of *Appetite* now overtaking those of *Permanent Vacation*, having both bands on the same bill guaranteed a sell-out wherever it alighted in America that year. The fact they were both on the same label made it, on paper at least, a no-brainer.

The only snag was that the five members of Aerosmith had now all been on the wagon for two years. While the five members of Guns N' Roses didn't actually appear to know what a wagon was. What Alan Niven was relying on was that, as he says, 'Most people live in abject fear of David Geffen.' And that Tim Collins 'was very compliant with the suggestions and wishes of David Geffen and Eddie Rosenblatt. He was *extremely* compliant. I think I might be one of the few that couldn't be bothered. But, anyway, I went to Eddie and said we *have* to have it.'

Niven's request was granted. 'Eddie's looking at me going, "Okay, kiddo. I hear you."' On one condition: that nobody from the GN'R camp, including most of all the band themselves, would be allowed to be seen drinking or – God forbid – doing drugs anywhere on tour where the Aerosmith entourage might be within sight. Or, as Niven puts it now, chuckling darkly, 'They had turned Aerosmith into candy-asses . . . there's restrictions about who can come backstage. What they can drink . . . And they took out Guns N' Roses as support?' He almost chokes with laughter. 'Fucking un-fucking-believable. Are you kidding me? Poor Tim is sitting there going, "I've got to run a clean machine and take *that* fucking crew?" But he does it.'

Then Niven hit on an idea that made him wheeze even more with laughter. To bond with Tim and try to reassure him that all will be well on tour and that his boys won't corrupt Tim's newly clean boys, Alan takes him to . . . his gun club! 'I pull out my .44 Magnum and I say, "Try this. You'll find it empowering." He took one shot with my .44, dropped it and stumbled back about four paces. Eventually he got a little more comfortable, enough to shoot my .25 Beretta that I used to keep in my pocket. So he's shooting my little bip-bip-bip-bip-bip gun and he's comfortable with that.' Alan had deliberately decided not to give Tim the little gun and allow him to work his way up. 'I put the .44 Magnum in his hand. You want a little bit of symbolism? You gonna fuck with us? We're Guns N' Fucking Roses.' He laughs. 'It's no wonder people have negative things to say about me. I must have been a total shit.'

But if Niven thought his problems were over, he was sorely mistaken. 'So we got the Aerosmith tour,' he goes on. 'Everybody's happy – except Axl.' As the first date in Chicago, in July, came closer, 'Axl locked himself in his apartment and wouldn't communicate with anybody.' In desperation Niven told Izzy to go there and talk Axl down. 'Get him to come. It's gonna be good. It's gonna be cool.' Izzy did as his manager asked, but when he got there Axl wouldn't even let him in. 'They tried talking through the door and that wouldn't work and Izzy came back and reported that to me.' Izzy told Alan: 'He's locked up in his bedroom and he won't come to the door.' Alan asked if there was any way Izzy could talk to him in his bedroom and Izzy said, 'Well, there's a tree outside his fucking bedroom window.' Niven looked at him and said, '"Go climb the fucking tree and talk to him!" So Izzy goes off. He climbs the fucking tree and there's Izzy hanging in the fucking tree, going, "Come on, dude, it's Aerosmith, it's gonna be cool. Let's go. We all wanna go." And Axl's like, "FUCK OFF! I DON'T WANNA DO IT!" True story.'

What now? Sitting in his office, surrounded by his staff and other band members, waiting for his decision, he was faced with a stark choice. Doug was there, Izzy was there, as was Stephanie Fanning. Chitchatting, 'trying to figure out what the fuck was going on'. Niven sighs deeply. 'I had this general rule of thumb. That if Axl was yelling at me it was like, whatever. But when he spoke softly, quietly, my ears really opened and I became incredibly attentive to what he was saying. Because I knew I was hearing from the centre of his consciousness.

'This was probably Wednesday. The first Aerosmith show was the Sunday evening. I had to push the button for the trucks to leave with the equipment the next morning if we're gonna be there, and we were trying to evaluate what to do. Steph stuck her head into my office and she was pale. Very drawn. She looked at me and she said, "Axl's on the line." I looked at her face and I went, "Oh fuck . . ." I picked up the phone and this very soft voice said, "Niv, I – just – can't – do – it. Cancel the tour." I said, "Okay, Ax", and I put the phone down.'

He told the others what Axl had just said. They all looked at him. 'I sat there for a moment. Then I went, "You know what, I signed a contract for five fucking individuals. Five people applied their signature to my contract. Not one. The other four want to do this. The one we can't go onstage without tells me he can't do it." I felt in a complete and utter bind. And then, where these things come from, God alone knows. But I'm staring at the table and there are these two red dice staring back at me . . .'

Niven had just returned from a Great White show in Las Vegas. He had some dice on his desk, from the Aladdin, where they'd stayed. As he sat there wondering what the hell to do about the Aerosmith tour, he recalled reading Luke Rhinehart's classic novel, *The Dice Man*, as a young man in the Seventies. 'He thought all our neurosis came from the conflict of choice. Am I gonna be a gentleman or am I gonna stick it up her ass? If I let the dice decide I will not feel guilty or neurotic about what I do.'

Alan Niven rolled the dice. 'I sat in front of everybody and said, "Here goes . . ."' He said he would give Axl 'the weight of the odds. If I throw a ten or less we're done. And I think it might be over. If I throw an eleven or a twelve, we're all going. And we'll be there. And if he's not there then it's entirely on him.'

He threw an 11. 'I said, "That's it. Send the trucks. Send the crew. We fly out. We're going." And we all went.'

They didn't even send Axl plane tickets for the trip to Chicago. 'We just left a message saying we were going. That we would be there and he could join us if he wanted to. It was up to him to sort it.'

Alan Niven admits he 'had no fucking idea' if Axl would call his bluff. The stress, he says, 'was mountainous'. But Axl did arrive, on the morning of the show. Alan Niven was sitting eating breakfast at the hotel when he heard 'the clank, clank, clank' of Axl's jewellery. 'He comes marching in, in his shorts and his forty-eight pounds of jewellery on him. So anonymous. So discreet. And he looks at me and I swear to God if looks could kill I'd have been vaporised. But he was there.'

Axl didn't say a word, just glared at Niven, 'then went to the far side of the room and sat at a table, then one or two people went to sit with him. Then he announced that he would not go onstage if I was there and I had to leave.'

As a result, Niven was not there for the first three weeks of the Aerosmith tour. He later had the red dice put into Perspex. He still has them today.

As Aerosmith's guitarist, Joe Perry, later recalled, 'Guns N' Roses were different. They had dug down a little deeper into rock's roots. I heard a lot of Aerosmith in them, which meant I also heard a lot of bands that came before us. And I remember being a little jealous, because they were really hitting the nail on the head . . . Part of the thrill was wondering what [Axl] was going to do next.'

Certainly, the supposed ban on the band's 'bad boy behaviour' only applied to the actual tour venues, and even then, as Slash told me at the time, 'We still do what we do, we just stick the booze in plastic cups so it looks like water.' When he came into his dressing room one night after a show, though, and found Aerosmith's singer, Steven Tyler, examining the near-empty bottle of Jack Daniel's on the table, he admitted he was embarrassed. 'Steven looked at me kind of pityingly and said, "Did you drink *all* this before you went onstage?" I had to kind of hide the other bottle of Jack I'd taken onstage with me.'

Doug Goldstein remembers the tour as 'no different to any of the others in terms of having to deal with Axl and Slash'. He describes arriving at one hotel and being told the band's rooms had all been cancelled. 'I told them. "Look, no problem. Just call Vanessa" – the name of the hotel manager – "and tell her we're gonna be pulling the bus up to her house and that twelve of us are going to be sharing her bed with her." So this old gal goes into the back and this big, heavy, Italian-looking guy with a moustache and a tie comes out, and says, "Which one's Goldstein?"

'I'm like, wow, we're really going there? He leans over the counter, he goes, "Look, you're gonna get in your room at three o'clock. You gotta fucking problem with that?" I don't know what it is about my head but when I snap, I snap. So I grab the guy by the tie and I pull him halfway over the counter. He tries to reach for the phone so I tighten up his tie and he's turning purple on me. I go, "You're gonna fucking die before you get a hold of the cops. I suggest you get your fat Guido ass back there and get me my goddamn keys."'

Turning to one of the band's security team, Todd, Doug told him: '"Go put Slash on a luggage trolley and get him up here now." He goes, "What?" I go, "Just fucking do what I said!" So he goes downstairs and he brings Slash, who's obviously passed out, he's literally upside down in that his head's on the luggage bottom and his legs are dangling over the top. But he still has the bottle of Jack in his hand. So Todd rolls him up next to me at the front desk, and there's, like, fifty people waiting to get into their rooms. The general manager of the hotel comes out and he goes, "Hey, he's got to get out of here." I go, "You know what, he's gonna get out of here the second I have a fucking room to put him in. Until then he's your new furniture." Needless to say, I had the keys in about two minutes.

'So I put Slash over my shoulder and we go to the elevator and I'm riding up with about eight guys in business suits and Slash starts urinating down my back. I was like, *motherfucker!* I drop him on the ground and this guy's laughing at me. I turned round and I go, "What?" He goes, "Look, I don't want you to get pissed off at me but I've been watching you since you walked into the hotel. I don't know what they're paying you but it can't even be *remotely* enough for what the hell you have to put up with!" The elevator doors open up and I go, "Yeah, thanks for the observation." I'm literally pulling Slash down the hallway by his hair cos I don't want to have to pick him up by his peed pants.'

Kept abreast of the antics of their support act, but also acutely aware of how many tickets they were helping them sell, Steven Tyler and Joe Perry – the Axl and Slash of Aerosmith, with a shared history of alcohol and drug abuse that far outweighed anything Guns N' Roses had yet come up with – were smart enough to let the circus carry on. One night, Joe came to Slash and told him how 'awesome' his guitar solo in 'Sweet Child' had been that night. When the tour was over, Steven gifted Axl a complete set of specially made silver Halliburton travel cases, costing thousands of dollars. Months later, Steven would also go out of his way to help the band through their drug problems, though only Izzy actually took him up on his offer.

Aerosmith also displayed their class by not causing a scene when *Rolling Stone* arrived on the tour ostensibly to cover both bands and ended up choosing Guns N' Roses for their cover. The Geffen promotional staff were thrilled at the outcome. David Geffen bought Tom Zutaut a Range Rover as a reward for both his hard work – and sheer persistence. Meanwhile, *Appetite for Destruction* officially became America's Number 1 album on 6 August 1988. They got another video, this one for 'Paradise City', in the can, again relatively cheaply, with most of the budget – 80,000 dollars' worth – going, says Niven, 'to Union fees to have six cameras shoot the band onstage in Giants Stadium'. (Something he says he 'mitigated a little bit by taking Vance Burberry with us to Donington armed with a 16mm Bolex'. All of which combined to create another action-packed performance video in an age when most bands were now investing in high-tech video production values to try to please MTV.)

This time when the band flew to England, though, they did so on Concorde. 'The record company went crazy but I just said, fuck it,' Alan Niven says shrugging. 'I felt by then we'd earned the right.'

Indeed. The trip should have been a triumph. Instead, it was a tragedy. One of the worst any of them would face. Looking back years later, some would suggest it was even the beginning of the end of the story of Guns N' Roses. But in truth there were still greater triumphs and tragedies to come.

As Axl yelled into the crowd as the band fled the rain-soaked Donington stage that day: 'Don't kill yourselves!'

But it was already too late.

6

THE MISSING MILLION

Over the course of the summer of 1988, Guns N' Roses had become the biggest rock band in America, and now they were to appear at the Monsters of Rock festival at Donington Park raceway, Europe's most prestigious annual outdoor rock show. They had been booked months beforehand, when *Appetite* had sold no more than a few thousand copies in the UK, and they occupied a place on the bill usually reserved for an up-and-coming act ready to raise the crowd from its early afternoon reverie. With some irony, the show was to be headlined by Iron Maiden, back on home turf, and riding high before a huge crowd that would peak, officially, at nearly 100,000 – though privately estimates put the eventual number at closer to 120,000. The rest of the bill was strong. It was to be opened by Iron Maiden's management stable-mates Helloween, a quirky German 'progressive metal' band. Guns N' Roses would be on next, followed by Metallica off-shoot Megadeth, then David Lee Roth, followed by Kiss – and then Maiden.

The band may not have felt a kinship with Iron Maiden, but they understood the prestige an appearance at Donington conferred on those bands lucky enough to find themselves on the bill. Spirits were high as they arrived in the tented backstage enclosure around noon. I chatted with Alan Niven, who was beguilingly frank about his surprise that *Appetite* had done so well. 'If you had told me before it was released that this album would sell more than about 250,000 copies, I'd have laughed in your face. If you'd told me it would go on to sell a couple of million I'd have thought you were insane.'

In fact, by Donington, *Appetite* had already sold more than three million copies in the US alone, with the 'Sweet Child' single on its way to selling a million on its own. The vibe around the small GN'R caravan enclosure backstage at Donington that year, though, was still determinedly low-key. Very little security, everyone just hanging out. When Lemmy from Motörhead wandered over to say a gruff hello, Duff was besides himself. 'Hey, Lemmy, dude! I fucking love you, man. You're my inspiration!' He burst into a chorus of 'We are the Road Crew', one of Motörhead's classic songs. Even Axl wanted to get his picture taken with a real rock'n'roll outlaw. Slash, meanwhile, had given his top hat to Metallica's Lars Ulrich to wear, before both men snuck off with Megadeth's leader, Dave Mustaine, to grab a little 'taste' of some of that special brown sugar Dave always brought with him to gigs in those younger, stupider days.

The day of the show began blustery and cold, and quickly worsened – traditional Donington weather, one might have said. The first really serious downpour saved itself, with immaculate timing, for the precise moment that Helloween took to the stage at 1 p.m. sharp. A strong wind blew over one of the video screens, which fell harmlessly on some open ground. It was nonetheless a horrible portent of what would come next. The festival site sloped slightly towards the stage, and as the rain lashed down the ground became soaked and slippery, and quickly turned into a mudbath. Donington was a festival that was proud of the 'walk-up' crowd it always attracted – that is, fans who arrive on the day expecting to buy a ticket. So many turned up on the day in 1988, however, that they actually ran out of tickets and the box office staff were having to improvise with make-do scraps of paper.

The crowd grew in size and the mud was churned by thousands of pairs of feet clambering for a good spot from which to watch Guns N' Roses. By the time their set began, at 2 p.m., the rain had eased, but people were still crowding forward towards the stage to catch a glimpse of the band of the moment. Guns began with 'It's So Easy', the sound drifting on the wind, but as they grew into their work through 'Mr Brownstone' and then 'You're Crazy', it became apparent to Axl that those towards the front of the already 50,000-strong crowd were in some difficulty as they were shoved forward on the wet ground by the growing numbers behind them. For once, he was quite right to stop the show. Fans were being dragged out by security. 'Back up! Back up!' he shouted, becoming increasingly panicked by what he could see below him. After what seemed an age Slash began peeling out the riff to 'Paradise City', but bodies were still being pulled from the crowd and Axl stopped the band mid-song a second time.

'Look!' he yelled, 'I'm taking time out from my playing to do this and that's the only fun I get all day.' The situation appeared to ease again and the band edged warily into 'Welcome to the Jungle'. But black clouds reappeared in the sky above the stage and another torrential downpour threatened. They tried to calm the mood by playing a ballad, 'Patience', one of the new acoustic numbers, but the crowd seemed distracted. The intro to 'Sweet Child' received a belated cheer and the band crunched through it as best they could. There was no encore. 'Don't kill yourselves,' offered Axl as he left the stage, unaware of the awful truth that was emerging even as the day unfolded. The sudden surge towards the front of the stage as the band had come on had knocked down dozens of fans, as others slipped in the mud. Two teenagers were trampled in the crush. Alan Dick and Landon Siggers would later die in the emergency tent; Siggers was so badly disfigured his family were only able to identify him through the scorpion and tiger tattoos on his arms.

'I saw the whole thing happen,' the late Maurice Jones, head of the promoters, MCP, told a *Music Week* writer, Jeff Clark Meads. 'The problems were created by idiots, absolute idiots. They were pushing stage right and the crowd compressed. They just couldn't go any further. Then about fifteen feet from the stage, a hole in the crowd opened and people went down. I went down to the front of the stage and I saw First Aid people and the doctors working and I felt so useless . . . I can't describe how it felt. I saw five bodies on the ground and I knew somebody was dead.'

The official statement later issued by Chief Superintendent Dennis Clarke of the West Midlands police division described the crowd at Donington that year as 'otherwise superb' and announced that there had in fact been no arrests, yet reaction in Britain's tabloid press was predictably over the top and some Sunday editions ran wholly inaccurate stories claiming, amongst other things, that the stage had collapsed and that Guns N' Roses had refused to stop playing even after being informed of the plight of the injured fans. 'We even had very well-known and supposedly responsible newspapers saying the stage had collapsed,' Jones complained to Meads. 'The stage didn't collapse and was never in any danger of doing so.'

The coroner's inquest would record an open verdict, concluding there was nothing more that could have been done to guarantee the safety of the crowd. Nonetheless, Northwest Leicestershire District Council placed a crowd limit on all future Donington events of 70,000, and it was two years before promoters were granted another licence.

'We just looked out and it was like, oh, fuck!' said Slash when I later asked him about it. 'You could see that surge when we came on, you could *see* the force . . .' When they were told afterwards that two fans had died, 'It just destroyed the whole thing for me.' Duff seemed even more upset. 'Saw the whole fucking event, man,' he told me. 'I saw it going down. And we stopped, man. We stopped and screamed, "Back the fuck up!" cos we saw the kids going under. "Back the fuck up! Back the fuck up!" And the mud was *this* thick, it was about a foot deep, and we saw the kids go under and then some other people came over them. They couldn't tell they were stepping on people, they thought it was just mud.

'Man, we were like, this is our fault, man . . . I was there and I was watching it and there just seemed like nothing we could do except scream at them. I was ready to jump into the crowd, but I was scared to die myself. Maybe that's chicken shit.' I said I thought it was a brave admission, under the circumstances. But did Duff blame himself personally in any way for the tragedy of the two fans' deaths? 'I tell you, it really crushed us all. It really crushed us all. We went back to the hotel that night and we were watching the fucking news – they didn't know who the kids were yet but one of them had this tattoo. We were just . . .' He drifted into uncomfortable silence. 'At first I felt that it was totally our fault for months and months. I probably will for the rest of my life.'

John Jackson, booking agent for both Guns N' Roses and Iron Maiden, had been standing at the side of the stage when the accident happened. 'You could tell fairly quickly that there was a major problem,' he told me. 'The security guys had spotted something, and they immediately relayed that there was a problem to the crew on the stage, who quickly got a message to the GN'R guys, who were fantastic . . . They couldn't have had any idea what was going on, but they cooled the set down completely. They stopped and did some slow, rambling ad lib bluesy thing to calm the audience down, and in effect ruined their own set. But thank God they did.

'The kids were taken into the St John's Ambulance unit, but my head told me they were dead straight away,' Jackson continued. 'I can't remember exactly when it was confirmed to me that deaths had occurred but it wasn't long after. Very, very few people realised the extent of the tragedy until later, so it wasn't necessarily discussed that the show should be called off. One of the reasons being the crowd had settled and we didn't want to start more trouble. I've got an aerial photo of the audience actually taken around the time of the tragedy and there was loads and loads of room on the site still, plus you could see people still coming up the roads and through the turnstiles. It wasn't a question of a crush; it was a question of people losing their footing because of the mud.'

Shockingly, none of the bands were informed of the tragedy until after Iron Maiden had climbed down from the stage more than eight hours later. The question of whether the festival should have been allowed to continue once the deaths had been made known to the organisers was thus neatly sidestepped. Had Jackson or Jones actually considered cancelling the rest of the show, though? 'I don't think so,' said Jackson. 'It would have been very difficult to tell that many people that the show was cancelled. It could have caused an even greater crowd problem. Over 100,000 people turned up that day, and nearly half of them were still on their way at the time of the tragedy. The previous record attendance had been 66,500 for AC/DC, in 1984. So it was a huge crowd. More than 35,000 people just turned up on the day expecting to buy tickets.'

When Alan Niven broke the news to the band about the deaths of the two fans, 'he was just short of crying,' recalled Slash. 'That changed the whole thing. From such a high to such a low, it was too much. We never felt that carefree again.' Later that night, both Axl and Slash could be found sitting side by side at the bar of their hotel, the scale of the tragedy just too much for them to take in, chatting to their entourage of friends and press pals, but their thoughts clearly elsewhere. As Niven reflected many years later: 'It was heartbreaking, and Slash put it best when he said nothing ever felt quite so carefree after that. It's a little hard to completely dissect that moment.' Right then, the *Rolling Stone* cover line, which had just appeared on newsstands, seemed particularly and horribly appropriate. It read: 'A brutal band for brutal times'.

The deaths of Alan Dick and Landon Siggers cast a pall over the rest of the year. The band played another big festival in September, second on the bill to INXS at the Texas Stadium, but it was a tough date to fulfil so soon afterwards and they considered pulling out. Ten days earlier 'Welcome to the Jungle' had scooped a gong at the MTV Awards. 'Sweet Child', meanwhile, had already overtaken it as the must-see video of the year. Now, suddenly, they were fried, done, just clinging on grimly waiting for the final Aerosmith dates to end and blotting out their worst moments with booze and dope. Both *Appetite* and 'Sweet Child' now sat at Number 1 in the US charts but none of that really mattered any more. As Slash told *Musician* magazine at the time: 'We knew it had to end . . . the thing is, we're burned out.'

The *Appetite for Destruction* tour, now nearly a year and a half old, was not quite over yet, though. There would be a couple of months trying to cool their jets back home in LA, Axl with Erin, Duff with Mandy, and Slash, Izzy and Steven with their various drug dealers and hangers-on. But time was short. In November, Geffen finally issued the mini-album *GN'R Lies* – and rubbed their hands with glee as it quickly rocketed to Number 2, selling more than five million copies along the way. A classic stop-gap to capitalise on a voracious market, the eight-track mini-album comprised the four songs from *Live?!*@ Like A Suicide* and the four acoustic songs they'd recorded with Mike Clink at the start of 1988. The idea had come from an incident backstage at a show in Detroit a few days before the Donington show. As Doug Goldstein was escorting Axl from the backstage area to the band bus, some kid in tears ran up to Axl crying that the bootleggers outside were selling *Live?!*@ Like A Suicide* for $500 a pop and that he couldn't afford it. He asked if Axl had a copy he could let him have. Axl did not, but bummed at being confronted by a genuine fan brought to tears by bootleggers, he was determined to do something.

'Axl said, "Dougie, get his address and send him a copy." So I stop and get the kid's address. We get on the bus and I fire it up, then Axl comes out from the back and he goes, "Dougie, Slash, I need to talk to you." Axl says, "How do we beat the bootleggers?" I said, "Easy." Axl goes, "Oh yeah? How?" I say, "Okay, so *Live?!*@ Like A Suicide* are four, quote-unquote, live tracks. Dude, this is, like, simple arithmetic. Pick, like, your favourite four songs you want to do acoustically. Put out an album and you'll be killing the bootleggers." Because now the [fans] would be getting twice the content for whatever CDs cost back then . . .'

But if, as he insists, *GNR Lies* 'was my idea', Goldstein is equally insistent that he didn't make a penny out of it. If so, he was the only one of the inner circle who didn't. Enticingly packaged in a way that played heavily on the band's growing infamy, the record's original title was *Lies! The Sex, the Drugs, the Violence, the Shocking Truth*, quickly shortened to *GN'R Lies*, and presented in a spoof tabloid newspaper-style sleeve that sent up the growing tranche of stories about their misbehaviour. That should have been it, a simple cut-and-shut that boosted the band's profile, seasoned their music reputation, and made fistfuls of cash for all involved.

And so it would have done but for the record's eighth and final track, Axl's 'One in a Million', which opened its second verse with the lines '*Police and niggers that's right / Get out of my way / Don't need to buy none of your gold chains today*' and its fourth verse with '*Immigrants and faggots / They make no sense to me / They come to our country and think they'll do as they please / Like start some mini-Iran or spread some fucking disease*'.

The general offensiveness of the song was obvious, but within Guns N' Roses it was personally and specifically so. The head of their record label, David Geffen, was gay. Slash's mother, Ola, was black. One of Duff's sisters had an African-American husband and their children were mixed race. What's more, the lines about *'your gold chains'* and *'some fuckin' disease'* were wilfully ignorant and stereotypical, the kind of rubbish you were more likely to hear the KKK spouting than a major rock band.

The song had begun as a throwaway, Axl extemporising as he sat around in his apartment, teasing out the rudimentary riff on the two bottom strings of an acoustic guitar and scat-singing phrases to West Arkeen as the comedian Sam Kinnison ranted on the blaring TV. Coming from the same headspace as 'Used to Love Her', with a decidedly redneck, country twang, it was originally called 'Police and Niggers' and intended entirely as a joke. But Axl worked on the lyric, which returned to one of his favourite themes, the fear and alienation he felt when he first arrived at the Greyhound bus station in North Hollywood. As usual, when backed into a corner, his position became entrenched. The 'mini-Iran' jibe was aimed at a shopkeeper he'd got into a fight with, he said. The use of the term 'nigger' was, he'd explain, used in the same context that John Lennon had used it in his song 'Woman is the Nigger of the World'. Rap bands used the word all the time, so why shouldn't he? He didn't believe in any kind of censorship. On the term 'faggot' he would later tell *Interview* magazine: 'Maybe I have a problem with homophobia . . . Maybe I was two years old and got fucked in the ass by my dad and it's caused a problem ever since. But other than that, I don't know if I have any homophobia.'

Once it became clear that Axl was determined to have the song released on *GN'R Lies*, the band made their objections known; when I saw Slash again in the March of 1989, when the controversy was boiling nicely, he told me: 'There's a line in that song where it says, 'Police and niggers, get out of my way' that I didn't want Axl to sing. But Axl's the kind of person who will sing whatever it is he feels like singing.' He also said that when he'd spoken to his mother on the phone, she'd told him she hadn't yet heard 'One in a Million', but Slash heard via his brother Ash that she had, 'and didn't know what to say to me . . .'

Duff also made his discomfort known. Even Steven made overtures: 'When I first heard "One in a Million" I asked Axl, "What the fuck? Is this necessary?" He just said, "Yeah, it's necessary. I'm letting my feelings out."' Or as Izzy would later tell me: 'That's a song that the whole band says, "Don't put that on there. You're white, you've got red hair, don't use it." You know? "Fuck you! I'm gonna do it cos I'm Axl!" Okay, go ahead, it's your fucking head. Of course, you're guilty by association. [But] what are you gonna do? He's out of control and I'm just the fucking guitar player . . .'

Ultimately, all were rebuffed. The Geffen legal department weren't as easily assuaged. Axl's intransigence resulted in one of the most astonishing – and strangest – solutions in the history of rock'n'roll and its close neighbour, commerce. Axl would write what was essentially an apologia, in tabloid style, to be incorporated into the record's artwork. Printed on the front cover, it ran in full: *'Ever been unjustly hassled by someone with a gun and a badge? Been to a gas station or a convenience store and treated like you don't belong here by an individual who barely speaks English? Hopefully not, but have you ever been attacked by a homosexual? Had some so-called religionist try to con you out of your hard-earned cash? This song is very simple. My apologies to those who may take offence.'*

Axl's only immediate creative ally was Alan Niven, ironically perhaps, given Rose's increasing antagonism towards him. 'I first heard "Million" when Axl sat on his bed and played it for me,' Niven recounts. 'In that moment he shape-shifted into the person he was in that past moment, and instead of someone abrasive, he seemed only vulnerable to me. He was the young soul from Indiana somewhat intimidated by his initial urban experience in LA. There was nothing gratuitous about his intent or performance in that moment and consequently I backed the band doing it. In the moment I didn't think through the effect on Slash and Ola. We don't always make perfect decisions. But then I never really thought of Slash as "black" per se. We used to be less racially divided in England and peoples were just peoples – not African-American or otherwise. Slash was born in Hampstead, for heaven's sake.'

This, though, was another story that wasn't going away. Ever.

By the start of December 1988, Guns N' Roses were back out on the road: five headline shows in Japan, held over from the summer, culminating in a sell-out show at the 14,000-capacity Budokan, in Tokyo. With the exception of Axl, the band were mostly drunk throughout this tour, as they knew they would be unable to score for drugs of any description once inside Japan. As Doug Goldstein says: 'They knew they couldn't take any heroin with them. So on the plane over Izzy takes a handful of sleeping pills and we literally have to carry him through customs – into the van and then up to his room.' Hours later, 'Izzy wakes up and he has literally no fucking clue where in the world he is. So he calls Steven. "Hey, man, where are we?" Steven goes, "We're in fucking Japan." Izzy goes, "No we're not." Steven goes, "I want you to go to the window right now and look outside and if you can see one head of blonde hair I'll suck your dick!"

'Another night, Steven's sleepwalking cos he's fucking drunk out of his mind. Cos that's what they do when they can't get any drugs, they drink their asses off. So Steven walks into his drum tech's room, Tom Mayhew, and pisses in the heater. He thought it was the toilet. He's lifting the seat up . . . oh my god!'

After Japan came three shows in Australia, followed by one in New Zealand. 'Flying from Japan to Australia,' Doug relates, 'Axl is sitting next to Alan Niven. Steven and Tom Mayhew are in the seats in front of them. I am sitting directly across from Steven. I could never sleep on flights so out of boredom I start flicking water onto Steven. It wakes Steven up, who then punches Tom Mayhew as hard as he can. He thought it was Axl. He thought Axl was doing it and he was punching Axl. He hit this poor kid so hard all you heard was eerrrggggghhhhh!! Tom couldn't get his breath cos Steven had just pounded him in the chest.'

And then it was home. Finally. Jetting back to Paradise City five days before Christmas. Where the grass was now greener than ever and the girls so pretty no one could tell the difference any more. 'I think I prefer porn stars,' Slash told me when I passed on a request for a dinner date message from one of the year's *Playboy* Playmates of the Month. 'Less talking . . .'

It would be another two years before Guns N' Roses would set out on tour again. Two years in which *Appetite for Destruction* became one of the biggest-selling albums of the decade, notching up sales worldwide of over 30 million. Two years in which Guns N' Roses went from being everybody's favourite underground band to becoming the biggest, most talked-about band in the world. Even their nearest rivals in the big-and-bad stakes, Metallica, now looked to them for their lead into the Nineties, hiring Mike Clink to make their next album (until it became obvious that they really couldn't follow GN'R) and hanging out with them whenever they were in LA, to the point where Lars Ulrich even had a special white leather jacket made – just like the one Axl wore in the 'Paradise City' video. Or, in the case of Metallica's singer, James Hetfield, hanging out with Slash to score chicks. In his autobiography, Slash recalls 'a girl James wanted to fuck and I let him take her into my bedroom. They were in there for a while and I had to get in there to get something, so I crept in quietly and saw James head-fucking her. He was standing on the bed, ramming her head against the wall, moaning in that thunderous voice of his, just slamming away, and bellowing, "That'll be fine! That'll be fine! Yes! That'll be fine!"'

I was also now spending most of my time in LA and doing a fair bit of hanging out myself with Slash – and Duff and Axl. It was now that I first got a real sense of who each of them might actually be – and how different they all were from each other. Slash was the one I got to know best. A Hollywood sophisticate compared to the others – not least, Axl, whose small-town background was about as far removed from Slash's formative years as it was possible to imagine – he was the most in-control, out-of-control person I'd ever known. Anthony Keids, singer of the Red Hot Chili Peppers, would describe himself to me around this time as 'the buffest junkie you ever saw!' But that said more about his swinging from one extreme to another than it did his ability to somehow 'manage' his drug addiction. Slash seemed to be on a whole other, far more laidback, worldly level. He hated confrontation, yes, something that would prove to be his downfall when it later came to standing up to Axl's increasingly high-stakes demands. But there was something else about him, too. A kind of well-bred insouciance that allowed him to make shooting smack seem like the partaking of a delicacy. That transformed what seemed to the outside world a morbid fascination for handling killer snakes into a kind of benediction. A gypsy's blessing; one for the road, perhaps. Until you or someone like you might show him something better. Should you, or someone like you, be foolish enough to try . . .

I recall going out for dinner with him one night after they'd finished the Aerosmith tour. Slash hunkered down in the dark of a corner booth at the El Compadre restaurant, the cheap Mexican place opposite the Hell House he'd now left far behind. Old habits and old haunts, it seemed, died hard. The shock of curls were the same, but behind them he looked tired, not just road-weary or stoned but bearing the weight of everything that had happened to him – to them – over the past 18 months.

He'd called to suggest dinner and then brought us out here: 'I know this place is kind of sleazy and rundown, but I like it, I feel comfortable,' he said. He told me about the Hell House days and the girls that would give the band blowjobs from under the tables at the El Compadre. But he was in far from his usual hell-raising mood. We spoke about Donington and I asked if he felt in any way to blame. He said not, but talked for a long while about how he'd partition the crowd into separate, safer sections if the band ever played there again, and about how he was agonising over whether or not he should write to the families of Landon Siggers and Alan Dick.

Appetite for Destruction had just passed sales of five million, so we talked about becoming rich and famous and what it meant. 'I'm not gonna take it to the point where I let it have an effect on my personality,' he insisted. 'I'm not going to let it turn me into one of those insecure rock star types who doesn't actually know what the limits of what a fucking pop star means . . .' Yet already the strange kind of rootlessness that overwhelming success can bring was beginning to manifest itself. He was, by his own ad-mission, burned out from touring so hard, and yet 'already bored' by being off the road and back in LA. There were plans to go back into the studio to record a new album – he was recording songs on an eight-track machine at home, he said – which they wouldn't, at least for another two years. There were the endless requests for phone interviews as *Appetite* began to take off across the world, and he was handling most of those because 'Izzy doesn't want to do it, he wants to stay in the shadows. Steven doesn't do a lot of stuff because it's never been his role. Duff likes to do stuff but right now he's at a wedding . . .' And Axl? 'He's very emotional . . . It's not any particular thing . . .'

When I told him that we had an annual sweep at the *Kerrang!* magazine office over which rock stars might snuff it in the forthcoming year and that he was currently top of the list, he laughed and said that Alan Niven had already packed him off to Hawaii once to clean up, 'but I had a girl fly out . . .'

In fact, Niven, who understood that Slash 'was not one for rehab' had, in his words, 'been forced to get inventive when Slash's habit began to completely own him and threaten his very existence'. The first time he put him in his spare bedroom to make him go cold turkey. 'My wife and I took turns to watch over him, wipe the vomit from his mouth and carefully dispense the Valium to take the edge off the process. Sometimes that wasn't enough. He'd refuse the invitation to come to the house.'

Hence the idea of getting Slash out to Hawaii to try to dry out in the sun. 'Hey, Slash, be at the office at noon tomorrow, you've got an interview with *Guitar Magazine* and it's a cover feature,' Niven had told him over the phone. 'When he arrived he was hustled into a limo by Goldstein and driven straight to the LAX airport. There was no such interview scheduled. The two of them flew off to Hawaii . . . totally out of Slash's element and far from his smack sources. He'd have to go cold turkey in the Islands.'

But then Slash had had his 'girl fly out' and when he returned to LA he was as bad as ever. His only real concession to his health, he told me now, was that he'd switched to drinking vodka because the charcoal in Jack Daniel's had begun to stain his tongue and teeth.

A Mexican band started playing loudly in the restaurant, and he got restless. Before we left, he said: 'I've been drinking a lot for a long time and I'm only twenty-three years old and I know that, right? It's not something I'm just so ignorant about that I'm going on this major blowout until all of a sudden something stops me physically. I'm more aware than that, but I'll do it anyway. So if anything does happen, I won't be complaining about it because, you know, *I knew*.'

We parted and I wouldn't see him again for a few months. The momentum behind *Appetite for Destruction* was unstoppable, and began to separate the band from their contemporaries. Guns N' Roses were selling more records than Aerosmith, Mötley Crüe and Poison combined. They would sell more than Bon Jovi, who had just released *New Jersey*, a follow-up to their squillion-selling breakthrough *Slippery When Wet*, from which they would ultimately have five hit singles. They would sell more than Def Leppard, whose two most recent albums had become the first consecutive albums in America to sell more than seven million copies each: *Pyromania* and *Hysteria*.

Guns N' Roses were now entering a place that very few bands had ever visited, and no one had a map of this unknown territory. They were adjusting to new and different lives. They had received their first significant money: each had received a cheque for $850,000, and there was plenty more to come. Axl bought an apartment in Hollywood, on the twelfth floor of a condominium block called Shoreham Towers, behind the Tower Records store on Sunset Boulevard, and a substantial plot of land in Wisconsin. He said he planned to buy a place in New York, too. He toggled between a hotel and the LA home with Erin, and spent some more of his money on a customised Corvette Sting Ray and a black BMW. The LA apartment was decorated in black, with mirrored walls and a display of his gold and platinum records.

Izzy was now holed up with his girlfriend, Desi, 'in the shadows' as Slash put it. Duff was still married and alternately drinking, fighting and making up with his wife. Steven grew so restless he asked Alan Niven if he could go on the road with Great White (the answer was 'no'). Slash had rented an apartment of his own and even, in a bow to his new domesticity, bought a microwave oven. He would soon find a larger house up in the Hills. They

were struggling to get comfortable in their old-new city, seeing
the other, moneyed side of LA for the first time. As Slash would
tell *Rolling Stone* magazine in their cover story of November 1989,
they felt 'like tumbleweed'. And as Izzy would later tell me, sum-
ming up the months of limbo they were about to enter: 'That was
a real dark period for all of us. The drugs and stuff was a big part
of the isolation but it was more than that. It was, like, *self-imposed*
and it got worse . . .'

Guns N' Roses were still conspicuous around LA, but they
were not conspicuously together. Slash and Duff, the good-time
guys, still surfaced at every rat-hole club night party and after-
hours watering hole, but Izzy and Steven were falling deeper into
the claws of heroin, and the messy, chaotic, twilight lifestyle of
closed curtains, phones off the hook and junkie insularity. Axl,
in a new uniform of full beard, shades and backwards baseball
cap, was around, often at the Rainbow or the Cathouse, but he
had his own little retinue now: his amiable half-brother, Stuart,
his faithful chronicler and co-writer, Del James, the photographer
Robert John, a guitar-playing friend from back home named Paul
Huge and another friend from Indiana, David Lank, plus Dana
Gregory, West Arkeen and a revolving cast of others.

The *Rolling Stone* cover story had revealed that Axl had ended
the *Appetite* tour travelling on a separate bus ('First of all, it was
Izzy's idea to get a separate bus,' he said, 'and secondly, after
shows I can't afford to party out like the other guys. There's been
several times when I had to leave the bus because of nerves. It's
impossible to sit there completely straight, listening to someone
who is annihilated go off about something or another').

He was beginning to try to help himself, not least via a diagnosis of clinical manic depression, for which he'd reluctantly
started taking medication (the diagnosis had been made, he explained, after he'd filled in a 500-question form and the only thing
the medication did 'was keep people off my back because they

figure I'm on medication'). Then other times he knew for sure it wasn't him that had the problem, it was the rest of the world. He had an apartment full of weapons, including an Uzi submachine gun that he bought after seeing an advertisement in *Soldier of Fortune* magazine that read: 'When the going gets tough, the tough get an Uzi.' Aside from a three-week period on heroin – an interlude he would often describe in ecstatic terms as 'one of the greatest times of my life' – he and Erin holed up in the apartment, 'listening to Led Zeppelin and fucking'. Yet, with his prescribed medication, he felt he was far cleaner than his bandmates, his iron will stronger than any drug. And having proven himself in LA, left behind his painful upbringing, his belief in himself and his judgement had been justified. Axl was now sure of it.

It was now that the seeds of his eventual takeover of Guns N' Roses were being sown. Not just through his deep need for control, but in the hands-off-the-wheel way in which the others hid themselves from the coming storm. By the time of my next meeting with Slash that March, *Appetite for Destruction* had sold seven million copies and been joined by *GN'R Lies* in the Top 5 albums charts . . . Duff and Steven would appear on the *Howard Stern Show*. Slash and Steven would join Ozzy Osbourne at Irvine Meadows for a blast through the time-honoured 'Paranoid'. Axl would play a low-key show with West Arkeen, running through early versions of 'The Garden' and 'Yesterdays'. Del James would tape another interview with Axl that would appear on the B-side of the 'Patience' single. Axl would hang out with the former Hanoi Rocks singer Michael Monroe on his video set and go to Syracuse, New York, to appear onstage with Tom Petty. Slash would appear onstage with Great White at a show in Montana . . . They would ride out the 'One in a Million' storm (*Billboard*'s editorial had called it 'a piece of racist, gay-bashing garbage') and discover that it barely touched the edges of their fame and success . . .

What ate at them instead were the drugs. Given the band's now seemingly limitless supplies of cash, Slash, who'd already had that unsuccessful stint in Hawaii for rehab, had a new place up in the Hills, playing with his pet snakes, and was 'sinking deeper into my hole'. Izzy spent so much time out of it, he found himself driving down the LA freeway convinced that it was snowing: 'I was staying with this coke dealer and I'd been up for five fucking days, which may have had something to do with it,' he told me. 'I didn't even know I was in trouble until someone pointed it out to me.' He was obsessing over the money he thought the band should be getting while walking around with a cashier cheque for $850,000 crumpled up in his pocket. Steven was 'sitting in some big fucking empty house I'd bought, shooting dope 24/7. I was very naive to the dangers of heroin. The first times I did it were two years apart. It made me so sick. Then the third time I did it, it didn't affect me that way. So I did it every day for a month.' When he cashed his big cheque, 'I was so fucking happy, driving my Mercedes around with my fucking stereo on, and the top down . . . and people just yelling, "Hey, Stevie, what's happening?" That was great.' Now, months later, he was spending most of his days 'never going nowhere, never seeing no one, just out of my fucking mind . . .' Duff wasn't into the permanent midnight of smack, but he was well on his way to alcoholism, and his usually affable nature was being tested by the strain of his marriage to Mandy, which was made more volatile by his endless days back home in LA, with nothing to do but drink, drink, drink . . .

'Patience', the gentlest track from GN'R Lies, replete with Axl whistling over twinkling acoustic guitars, was a hit single that summer, and its sweet melody at least showed that Axl could express his vulnerability in more nuanced ways. But the general vibe was downbeat, best summed up by Slash when I took a trip up into the Hills for an evening at his new home, where we sat surrounded by guitars, amps, three pythons and stacks of books and video cassettes. *King Kong* flickered on the big screen. Now that the tongue and teeth stains had disappeared, he was 'bored' of vodka and back on the Jack and Coke. He was jumpy and jangly. It was way past midnight but the phone never stopped ringing. His guitar tech, Adam, had moved in downstairs. The band were supposed to be 'writing and rehearsing', and he'd written some songs that Axl liked that he was supposed to be showing the rest of the band, but 'I've missed rehearsals with them, they've missed rehearsals with me . . .' He'd even discussed moving in with Axl and maybe Izzy and Duff somewhere that they could work, but the phone kept ringing and he kept getting distracted . . .

It was obvious that he was both out of it and unhappy. 'Now we have a lot of money,' he said, 'we can do whatever we want, except there's nothing I want to do except play. I just want to get back out on the road. I envy all those bands who've got their album done and they're ready to go out.'

LA, once a fantasy playground, had become with fame just another pain in the ass. 'It's actually at a point where I go to a club and end up leaving, totally depressed,' he said. 'It really brings me down. Everybody wants to have your undivided attention, and if you don't give it to them they act like you're an asshole . . . I don't go out much. I don't have that many close friends . . . It gets to be a little bit lonely after a while . . .' We talked for a few hours, and just when I was going to call it quits, Izzy turned up with Billy Squier in tow, looking for a 12-string guitar of Slash's he wanted to borrow. He didn't find it but the party lasted another two days . . .

They did make an attempt to get together over the summer, when Slash, Duff and Steven stayed on Chicago's North Side for a number of weeks working up ideas – among them were the skeletons of parts for 'Civil War', 'Estranged', 'Bad Apples' and 'Garden of Eden'. Mostly, though, they just hung out and got wasted while they waited for Axl and Izzy to join them. Slash could be seen some days riding his BMX bike up and down Clark Street, close to the makeshift porta-studio they had installed above a local venue, the Cabaret Metro. They lived in a split-level brownstone apartment where cocaine was hidden in butter dishes and Italian food was thrown from the balcony at fans below. Girls followed them everywhere – 'Psycho bitches!' Including the daughters of some high-ranking cops. When squad cars showed up the band all ran and hid.

As Slash recalls in his memoir: 'My personal consumption at that point was a half-gallon bottle of Stoli per day, plus whatever I consumed when I was out at night. I'd wake up in the morning and fill a Solo cup eighty-five per cent full with vodka, ice and a bit of cranberry juice. I called it breakfast of champions. Duff was in the same league . . . Some days Duff and I even went to the gym, usually just after our morning vodkas. We'd go to one of those big public YMCAs with our security guard, Earl, to pump iron. We'd be down there in our jeans, doing sets between cigarette breaks – it was invigorating.'

According to Duff's memoir, however, their time in Chicago was largely a washout. 'After two weeks in Chicago, Axl was still a no-show. Slash, Steven and I started to get a little resentful. I mean, what the fuck? Here we were in a city in which we had no interest, no friends – and no singer. . . . I started to drink harder.'

Steven Adler's memoir meanwhile veers somewhere between the two in terms of how he saw his time in Chicago. He recalls the studio they worked in as 'awesome. It had a top-of-the-line PA and a grand piano, and my drums were miked. It was located on the fourth floor of a high-rise building. In the basement of the complex was a popular local nightclub . . . At night, Duff, Slash and I would go downstairs to the nightclub, where we would pick up girls and fuck them right in the club. We rarely took them back to the condo.'

The most telling detail of all though was that Axl didn't arrive until just two days before the band was due to return home to LA. 'Seven weeks and five days later, Axl finally arrived,' Adler writes. 'We have two days left in the studio and were anxious to show him all of the new material. He sat there like we were putting him through some kind of torture. Plain and simple, Axl wasn't interested in our material! He just wanted to record a new song he had been working on called "November Rain".'

Izzy Stradlin, meanwhile, didn't show up at all. Izzy had flown to New York to join up with Axl. Rather than going to Chicago to try to write new material with his band, the singer had decided to fly himself and West Arkeen up to New York, where they checked into the Mayflower Hotel on Central Park West. But when Izzy got there he was treated like an interloper. Like he was the one spoiling the party. Or maybe that was just his paranoia? Izzy was now hitting the cocaine and heroin so hard he didn't trust anybody any more.

'The windows to his apartment were covered in aluminum foil,' recalls Alan Niven. Not just to keep out the daylight, he adds, but because 'It bounced back the government radio spy waves. The door was triple-locked. He never answered the door unless the knock was prearranged and he screened all his calls with a Geiger counter. He was alone with his cocaine and the home porno tapes he had "borrowed" from an unwary and unknowing band member. Messengers and delivery boys brought statements from the accountants, blow from dealers and pizzas from Domino's. The floor was strewn with the wreckage of rock'n'roll paranoia: half-read financials, half-eaten pies and half-gram lines, offered with half-hearted generosity. Izzy had been sucked into a vacuum of paranoia by cocaine. He'd become cold and distant, a chill in his voice . . .'

Just a few weeks before, Izzy had called Alan on the phone late one night and told him in that icy voice: 'I found a million bucks that everyone's forgotten about.' It took Niven a while to realise what Izzy was talking about – and then it hit him. Earlier in the year the deal with the New York-based firm Brockum for them to manufacture and sell official Guns N' Roses merchandise had lapsed.

'Peter Paterno, the band's attorney, called and warned me that Peter Lubin was on his way to my office with the intention of delivering Brockum's new terms,' says Niven. 'You'll be pleased,' said Paterno. 'It's a very good offer.' Yet Niven walked away from the meeting, he says, feeling 'underwhelmed and disappointed. Not for the first, nor the last, time did I have the feeling that the well-being of the band I represented was not necessarily the prime agenda of all those involved. As best I recall, Peter's offer was to advance $500,000 against a royalty rate of eighteen to nineteen per cent.

'My personal opinion was that this was not that good of an offer to make to a band that had now sold in excess of eight million albums in the US alone. Given, however, that the offer was supported and recommended by the band's attorney, I decided I should keep my opinion to myself. Myself and Izzy, that is.'

Niven had phoned Izzy and asked if he'd be interested in taking 'a quiet trip up to see Winterland', Brockum's San Francisco-based rivals, 'and see what they might put up'.

'Sure, Niv,' came the reply. Flights were booked and a rental Corvette was reserved. 'We drove to the old warehouse section of San Francisco, which was home to the massive Winterland facility. Del Furano showed us the print presses and the art departments. Having shown a civil interest we left. Del pressed an envelope into my hand as we parted. As I drove the 'vette south towards the airport I handed the envelope to Izzy. "Better see what he's offered." Iz opened the envelope . . . He was quiet for a while, absorbing the offer. He carefully reread the piece of paper.

"It's pretty good, Niv," he said at last. "Two and a half mill up front and a better royalty rate than Brockum." Once again, independent action had seemed to serve us well . . .'

When, however, Niven informed Brockum of the better offer from Winterland, Peter Lubin offered to match it – and the band went with Brockum again. As Niven says, 'We had, after all, made money together, so the lowball offer Lubin originally made was forgiven. Brockum had been there at the beginning when others weren't.'

There was just one 'wrinkle' to the deal. 'The advance was to be $2.5 million, but only $1.5 would be paid on the signing of the agreement. The remaining million would be placed into an escrow account and released when certain touring criteria were met.' (An escrow account is one controlled by a neutral third party, who if an arrangement is realised will pass the money one way, and if the arrangement is not fulfilled pass it back the other.) 'In this case, a certain number of shows had to be booked, or a certain amount of earnings would be made at retail outlets, before the escrow funds would be released. Either way, there were a million dollars sitting in an escrow account, which could not be disbursed to the band until a tour of some size was booked. Not an unreasonable accommodation. Until, of course, this sum and its disposition became the "missing million" of Izzy's coke-fuelled paranoia later in the year.'

Nevertheless, when Izzy called Niven on 'the missing million' the manager admits he felt 'hurt. I was also scared. I had never seen Izzy so dissolute and uncentered. So unhealthy.' Niven tried explaining, talking Izzy out of his paranoia. But it was not working.

The next he heard Izzy had flown to New York to work with Axl on new material. Perhaps this was a good sign? 'Perhaps he merely substituted one paranoia for another. Perhaps he decided that it was more important to prevent himself from being substituted by Arkeen. Perhaps he was sick of me knocking on his door. Either way, he was on a flight for Kennedy airport.'

But then there was another wrinkle, another damn thing to freak out about – a phone call to Alan Niven from Rich Feldstein, the band's accountant. 'Do you know that Izzy has gone to New York?' Of course, said Niven. 'He's promised to start writing with Ax.' Perhaps a change of environment would help bring about a change of attitude, he said. Then Feldstein dropped the bomb. 'Did you know he took all his money out of the bank?' What the fuck? Feldstein sounded nervous. Told Alan all he knew was that Izzy kept going on about a million dollars being lost. Then he took all his money out of his City National Bank account.

'Oh my God!' said Niven. 'In cash? How much did he have available?'

'It's well over three-quarters of a million,' said Feldstein, 'and it's in a cashier's cheque.' (A banker's draft.)

'Oh shit! You mean, if he loses that cheque he loses three-quarters of a million dollars?'

'That's pretty much the case. We could try to get the bank to cancel it and replace it but there's absolutely no guarantee they will do that. These things are like cash. If he were to lose it, if someone were to take it from him. . . .' Rich's voice trailed off into a despairing silence.

Says Niven now: 'My heart sank. Was he leaving us? Was he putting himself at risk in New York? Was he about to disappear to a Caribbean island? What the hell was he doing?'

A couple of days later Izzy called. Alan took a deep breath before taking the call. 'I did my best to sound unconcerned, un-informed. 'Iz, how's it going? Are you getting any writing done?' "Nah, Niv. I can't deal with writing right now. I can't get into it."'

'Okay,' Niven told him, 'so what are you going to do? Stay in New York for a day or two?' Izzy: 'I dunno. Wanna come and hang out?'

Thinking quickly, Niven suggested 'an alternative plan', that the two of them both take time out and journey instead to New Orleans. Great White were due to headline a show there later that week. 'It was equidistant between New York and Los Angeles, a genuine meeting point for us both. I suggested Izzy join me in the Crescent City. Maybe I could get him to join the White Ones on stage. Maybe a dose of rock'n'roll would make his heart feel good.'

Izzy agreed to meet Niven there the next day at the Omni Royal Hotel. 'As relieved as I was that we could meet and talk, I was very concerned about him travelling with such a huge sum of money. I felt, however, that if I asked him about the cheque he might feel claustrophobic, feel that I was being intrusive and that might be enough to cause him to avoid a meeting.

'I was always pleased to see Iz and no more so than when we sat down to dinner in the hotel restaurant, a huge grill on the ground floor, from where one could see the parade of people partying up and down Royal Street in the French Quarter. The conversation over dinner was stilted. Izzy was still of a suspicious state of mind. I, myself, felt hurt and insulted that he would even think to question my integrity. I tried to explain the function of an escrow account and that all we had to do was book some shows and the money would materialise in a band account. I reminded Izzy I had not taken any commission during the first year that I worked with Guns N' Roses, that I had left every penny I could in the band accounts to enable the development of the band.

'I did, however, feel I could now ask about the $750,000, or more, that Izzy had with him. "I hope you put it in a bank in New York, Iz." "Nah, Niv. I've got it with me." My heart turned to lead. The idea of having over three-quarters of a million, basically in cash, in a New Orleans hotel room, quite frankly freaked the living daylights out of me. I wasn't so sure we could even trust the hotel to put it in their safe. Now *I* was tinged with paranoia and suspicion.'

Niven said he hoped Izzy had at least hidden the cheque well in his room. Izzy just looked at him. 'Actually, Niv, I've got it here.' His head disappeared under the table. He'd hidden it in his sock. He yanked it out and dropped it on the table. 'Wanna take care of it for me and put it back in the bank?' Izzy asked him.

'Part of me was relieved,' he explains now. 'I had his trust again and his money could be put safely back in the bank in Los Angeles – when I got there. Another part of me was frozen with the fearful idea of having the responsibility for so much of his money. God forbid I lose it. When I travel I check my passport, or my wallet, every few minutes. I don't have the insouciance to be casual about such things.'

The night had only just begun, however. Back in his own room, Niven panicked trying to find a spot to hide Izzy's cheque in. 'It felt ridiculous to put three-quarters of a million dollars under the nightstand. It seemed entirely predictable that anyone travelling with nearly a million dollars would tuck it into the back of a picture frame. In the bathroom it could get wet and disintegrate even more.'

He was 'beginning to see the logic of keeping three-quarters of a million dollars in your sock' when the phone rang. It was Izzy: 'Hey, Niv, do you know anywhere we could go at this time of night? Have a drink?'

Pleased to get the opportunity for a bit of bonding over a drink, Niven pulled on his cowboy boots – stuffing Izzy's cheque into his own sock. 'As we strolled into the French Quarter Izzy quietly asked about the well-being of his money. "Don't worry, Iz. It's safe," I replied. "I put it where no one will find it."'

Later that night, they would get into a tussle at a bar called The Dungeon. For which Alan Niven would wreak his own 'GN'R kind of vengeance' by returning the following evening with a bunch of band heavies, demanding an apology and free drinks – or else. (They got both.) And later that week Izzy got up onstage and played a couple of songs with Great White. 'The next day he hopped a plane to Indiana and then took off for Europe. Later that summer, as I travelled through Germany and Scandinavia, I would find music magazines on departure lounge newsstands containing 'off the cuff' interviews Izzy had done on his travels, predicting hellfire and race wars in America. Obviously he was still feeling paranoid. Yet within a couple of years LA burned in the Rodney King riots – never underestimate the intuition of an artist.'

Back in LA, Alan Niven gave Doug Goldstein Izzy's crumpled cashier's cheque and had him re-deposit it at City National Bank. 'I walked with a lighter step once I knew it was there.'

The heaviness returned, though, almost immediately. As by now he knew it always would with GN'R. Alan Niven just didn't know how quickly – or how bad.

7

STUPID JUNKIES

For Izzy Stradlin, things would get worse before they finally got better. On 27 August he was on a flight from Indianapolis, drunk and tired and obnoxious. He 'must have' told a stewardess to 'fuck herself,' he later recalled blurrily, before jumping the queue for the toilet by relieving himself in a bin in the kitchen galley. The pilot put the plane down at the nearest airport, which was Phoenix, and Izzy was arrested for public indecency, a problem because he had a prior for drug possession and could have been jailed for six months. Instead he got another six months' probation and had to keep peeing in cups for urine tests to prove he was clean.

'That was my wake-up call,' Izzy later told me. 'That was the point where I said, this has got to fucking stop. I didn't wanna wind up dead or, worse, in prison.' Instead, Izzy went into rehab and began receiving professional counselling. What really made him stop, though, he thinks now, 'was I *wanted* to. Cos I figured, at some point your heart's just gonna pop, or your mind's gonna snap, right? Eventually, that shit will kill ya, and it does. It kills people all the time. Once I got maybe, like, a week of sobriety, like actually going a whole week without a drink, I thought, oh god, if I can just keep this up . . .' It wasn't easy. 'I'd been straight for a long time before some of the others even noticed. They'd offer me a line. I'd say, "Uh, no thanks, I don't any more, remember?"

But these were, like, the only friends I had. Those first five years we were together, the band was like our little family. Dysfunctional as hell but everybody had each other, you know?'

Two weeks after Izzy's arrest, on 11 September 1989, he and Axl appeared at the MTV VMA Awards at the Universal Amphitheatre in LA. They accepted an award for 'Sweet Child o' Mine' and jammed with Tom Petty, Axl on 'Jailhouse Rock' and both on Petty's timeless 'Free Fallin''. As Izzy walked off stage and handed his guitar to his tech, Mötley Crüe's singer, Vince Neil, jumped out in front of him and punched him in the face, cutting his lip: retribution, Vince would claim, for an unwanted sexual advance from Izzy to the singer's new wife, Sharise, a former mud wrestler from the Tropicana. Depending on whose version you believed, Izzy went down, Vince ran off, Axl chased Vince, Vince offered to fight Axl, Axl told Vince 'to leave my band the fuck alone' – yada, yada, yada, blah, blah, blah and boys will be boys ... Who knew what really went down? Yet the incident, minor though it was, would escalate into a situation that would drag many more people into the mire, me included ...

Before that escalation began, however, Alan Niven found himself in a car with Bill Elson, Guns N' Roses' American booking agent. Elson was driving them from Manhattan to the Meadowlands, in New Jersey, to watch Metallica play. Although Metallica would soon be on an upward curve almost as steep as GN'R's, neither man was particularly interested in the show. Instead, Elson's plan was to 'socialise' (in Niven's description) with Metallica's managers, Cliff Bernstein and Peter Mensch, who, aside from also looking after Metallica *and* Def Leppard, had been asked to 'oversee' the monolithic stadium tour about to be undertaken by the Rolling Stones, still the world's biggest-grossing live act almost three decades after they'd first come to stardom.

The weather was awful, and as Elson drove, he tried to convince Niven that Guns N' Roses should be the support act for the Rolling Stones tour. The offer was $50,000 per show, including the chance to play at the vast, 77,000-capacity LA Coliseum, for which, Elson guessed, lifelong Stones fans like Izzy, Slash and Axl might be prepared to remove their right nuts. The offer had come directly from Mick Jagger's office, Elson mentioned casually.

But if Elson expected Niven to bite his hand off, he was wrong. Niven knew what the band would say (and he was right: 'We've gotta play with the Stones,' Slash and Izzy chorused), but he had a different view. Firstly, in his eyes, the Stones were now a heritage act. Their last tour, he said colourfully, had been 'less than compelling, a sloppy stumble through the material from the obligatory but inconsequential album released for the tour, and a tired thrashing of old chestnuts . . .', while Guns N' Roses were now 'white hot'. Niven was also aware that the Stones had form in buying some relevance by appointing the band *du jour* as their support, a habit that read like a who's who of rock, from Janis Joplin and Santana to Lynyrd Skynyrd and Peter Tosh. In recent times it had included Foreigner, Prince, Southside Johnny . . . happy to offer support spots to anybody with enough current-day cachet to help the Stones sell even more tickets.

Now it was the turn of the new kings of the road, Guns N' Roses – something Alan Niven had no objection to, in principle: credibility by association worked both ways. Any move that helped broaden the public perception of Guns N' Roses, away from the LA metal scene of Mötley Crüe and Poison and more towards the classic rock'n'roll status of the Stones, was most welcome, thank you very much. But at $50,000 a show, when Elson knew better than anyone that Guns N' Roses could now make double that by headlining their own shows – what kind of bullshit was that?

Alan told Bill he'd think about it. Then dug around and discovered that the Stones had already announced two nights at the LA Coliseum and had a further four on hold. Two nights alone represented over 150,000 tickets – with an average seat going at $30, while the best seats were being offered around town by ticket brokers for up to $700 a ticket. Then there was the money that would be rolling in from merchandising sales alone, where as well as the standard $20 T-shirts were such upscale items as a $450 leather jacket and a $190 flight jacket. When a rumour – leaked by persons or parties unknown – that GN'R would support the Stones got out, Niven read the runes, saw what was happening and called Bill to tell him Guns N' Roses would not be doing the shows. Elson was aghast. Nobody turned down the Stones! But when the *LA Times* rang Niven about the rumour, he told them the same thing, citing the age difference between the bands, and pointing to the fact that Guns N' Roses were now the band with all the street credibility.

By this time Slash and Izzy were almost apoplectic. 'Niv, it's the fucking Stones! We've got to do it!' urged Izzy. But Niven stood firm. Finally, Elson called him again.

Said he'd received another call from Mick Jagger's office. There was a new offer: four nights at the LA Coliseum for $500,000. Niven countered that the band's price was now a round million dollars. 'We've already sold him [Jagger] a shitload of tickets,' he told Elson. Once again, Bill was forced to go back to the Stones with bad news. This wasn't how things were supposed to be. It was a gamble, Niven knew, but one worth taking. If the Stones paid up, then Guns N' Roses would earn almost as much for four shows as they would have for an entire tour at $50,000 per night – as well as saving themselves all of the usual costs associated with touring.

There was another element to Niven's thinking, though, that he was not prepared to share with the Stones or anyone else for now but was crucial to his thinking. The fact was, after nearly a year off the road during which all five of them had splintered off into different, sometimes frightening worlds, Guns N' Roses as a working band were in no fit state to go on the road – at least not until four-fifths of them had cleaned up. Apart from the audacity of countering Mick Jagger, whose love of a dollar bill was legendary, it was one of the few cards Niven had to play. When Niven went to watch the Stones play in St Louis he got worried all over again. The show was still a revue, but the Stones were hot again, Keef oozing cool, revivified by a successful solo record and tour, Mick still impossibly athletic and vital. Guns, by contrast, looked near death.

Nevertheless, Niven's gamble had worked. Guns N' Roses would receive a million dollars for their four shows opening for the Rolling Stones, appearing between the opening act, Living Colour, the all-black rock band also then hot-as-a-pistol following the success of their double-platinum debut album, *Vivid*, and the headliners. Now all they had to do was turn up on time. But with a couple of hours to go before the first Stones gig, with 77,000 people already in the venue, Axl Rose was a no-show. The problems had begun a week or so before, at a video shoot for the *Appetite* track 'It's So Easy' at the Cathouse, directed once again by Nigel Dick. 'We always wanted to do a video for that song,' Axl told me. 'We're gonna have a home video at some point, so we wanted to do some videos that were, like, completely no-holds-barred, uncensored type of things. Just live shooting, instead of worrying about whether MTV is gonna play it. Just go out there and do a fucking blown-out live, real risky video.'

The video, which featured sadomasochistic scenes involving Erin, was never officially released. Alan Niven saw to that. 'I get a call from Nigel Dick saying Axl had called Nigel direct, saying, "I want to shoot some footage for this." Nigel's going, "You are going to go fucking ballistic when you see this stuff." He's got her hung from the doorway and slapping her ass, the mouth-gag and so on . . . Lots of fun [but] you don't put it in a fucking video that represents the entire band and put it out there for the whole world to see.' The upshot was that Niven 'wouldn't let the final edit be done and I got the offline copies. The reason for that was I knew he was committing suicide with that bondage shit with Erin. And lo and behold he got divorced. So you know what they would have done with that? I protected the little fuck.'

As if to compound a night of negative energy, David Bowie had shown up to see Slash, and had started talking to Erin Everly, who was appearing in the video. Axl had taken one look at that and started throwing punches Bowie's way before having him thrown off the set. 'Bowie and I had our differences,' Axl shrugged when I asked him about it. 'And then we went out for dinner and talked and went to the China Club and stuff, you know, and when we left I was like, "I wanna thank you. You're the first person that's ever come up and said I'm sorry about the situation." And then I open up *Rolling Stone* the next day and there's a story in there saying I've got no respect for the Godfather of Glam even though I wear make-up and all this bullshit. It's laughable.'

Axl wasn't laughing though when, at the warm-up for the Coliseum shows, a club gig promoted as an *RIP* magazine party, he told Izzy he didn't want to play with the Rolling Stones. Izzy was taken aback but not hugely concerned. Axl was always worried about things to a ludicrous extent. He hadn't wanted to do the Aerosmith tour, then looked back on it as the highlight of the year. Whatever happened, Niv would handle it. Then, at 6 a.m. on 18 October, the morning of the first show, Axl rang Izzy and told him he was quitting Guns N' Roses. Again, however, Izzy was unsure how seriously to take the claim. Axl, by his own admission, 'quit the band every three days', as he'd told Howard Stern in a radio interview just a few weeks before.

This time, though, it was different. With controversy over 'One in a Million' still raging, Living Colour's vocalist, Vernon Reid, had voiced strong concerns in the press. In order to avoid any possible clash at the Coliseum shows, Axl and the band had been allotted their own separate area backstage, on the opposite side from Living Colour's dressing rooms. According to Colleen Combs, Axl's personal assistant, he was already so 'paranoid' about the reaction his first major appearance on stage since the controversy over 'One in a Million' started would provoke, 'he really thought someone was going to take him out. He thought someone was going to kill him.'

When Izzy arrived at the Coliseum that afternoon, he passed the news along to Alan Niven. 'It's gonna be a long four days . . .' he said. Niven, who'd been there before, knew it could go either way: Axl hadn't actually told anyone else he was quitting, just Izzy. Maybe he'd wake up feeling differently. Or he just wouldn't show up and Niven would face the worst day of his professional career. As the hours till show time dragged by, and Axl still failed to arrive, backstage the tension in the GN'R dressing room was such that Doug Goldstein was almost in tears. When Living Colour took to the stage, Niven knew it was time for desperate measures. Once again, he didn't flinch from taking them.

As he says now, Axl not turning up for a show 'was not an altogether novel circumstance and it did not necessarily mean he wouldn't eventually come'. However, his non-appearance at the show in Phoenix the previous year had produced a minor riot with considerable property damage. Now, though, they were playing for much bigger stakes. 'A riot by 77,000 disappointed stadium stoners was quite probable in the event Axl did fail to show. The consequences could be genuinely catastrophic. The tragedy at Donington still haunted my consciousness.'

Niven turned to Stones' production chief Brian Ahern and asked him, 'Brian, do you have a real solid contact in the LAPD? A genuine "no questions" kind of a guy?' Ahern answered, 'I'll send him in.' Without another word, Ahern made the call. 'Cool

and completely without confusion or stress, Brian is an exceptional individual and I will for ever appreciate his calm and his
confidence,' says Niven. 'I spoke with his contact. Within minutes a "black and white", containing a reliable pair of uniformed
cops, pulled up at the Shoreham Towers.' The uniformed cops
raced up to the twelfth floor and began banging on Axl's front
door. 'The startled occupants were herded down to the cruiser.
Sirens wailing and all lights ablaze, the police car sliced through
the evening traffic.' The car drew up at the very foot of the steps
leading to the stage. It was in this manner that Axl arrived in the
Coliseum to appear before 77,000 LA-generates, a mere 25 minutes behind schedule.

As Axl stepped out of the police car he had a face like thunder. When he was then told that Vernon Reid, speaking from the
stage, had given a short speech halfway through Living Colour's
set, to the effect that anybody who called somebody else a nigger
was promoting racism and bigotry, no matter how hard they tried
to explain it away, he was apoplectic. When he was then told that
large sections of the Coliseum crowd had stood on their seats and
applauded loudly, whistling and cheering their approval, he was
ready to kill somebody. 'We went out with a mission,' Reid later
explained. 'I made a statement about "One in a Million" onstage,
and I remember afterward Keith Richards made it a point to
come over to the dressing room and shake my hand.' Ultimately,
he says, 'When I heard that song, I was probably more disappointed than anything, because I liked the band. [But] I thought
the objectification was wack, like I'm somehow standing in the
way of this guy.'

When word got back to the GN'R dressing rooms about Reid's
putdown – and that it had received a standing ovation – concern
over how Axl might react was such that no one could bear to make
eye contact with him. Guns N' Roses took the stage just before
8 p.m. The band was still tuning up, getting ready to blast off,

when Axl grabbed the mike and told the audience, 'Before we start playing, [I want to say] I'm sick of all this publicity about our song.' He then denied he was a racist, but insisted that certain words – against groups of people who offend you – was acceptable, in an artistic context. 'If you still want to call me a racist,' he bellowed, 'you can . . . shove it . . .'

The band cranked into gear and Axl began his manic perambulations around the stage. Now, though, a moment of black comedy was added to the spidery farce. Axl, who had refused to come and view the construction of the Stone's massive stage ahead of the show, found himself blinded by several follow-spots as he attempted to race back from one side of the stage. He ran clear off the stage and plunged into the photographer's pit. 'I stopped breathing,' says Niven. Then slowly a hand holding a microphone emerged from the darkness as, slowly, two security men hoisted Axl back onto the stage. Now, with embarrassment added to his anger and frustration, he went for broke. The second song of the set was 'Mr Brownstone'. Axl stomped to the lip of the stage and told the crowd: 'I just want to say . . . I hate to do this onstage, but I tried it every other fucking way. And unless certain people in this band get their shit together, this will be the last Guns N' Roses show you ever see . . .'

It was a typical piece of Axl grandstanding. The review in the LA Times the next day described it as 'both a troubling and fascinating display – one that will probably go down as a storied moment in LA rock. Rose has the potential to be one of the most compelling figures in American rock since the late Jim Morrison.' But below the surface it was another case of events in his life conspiring to send Axl Rose into a tailspin. Not only were the band rusty and drugged out – Slash's heroin dealer had a backstage pass – and not only had he discovered David Bowie hitting on his girlfriend, but a few days before the shows he had been contacted indirectly by William Rose's brother, who'd told Stuart that William Rose was dead. 'Great family,' Axl told me with a mournful shrug. 'I don't even know how he died. And I don't care . . .'

Axl had been referring onstage specifically to Slash and Steven. Slash, whose mother, Ola, was at the show, told me afterwards that he had thought about walking off when Axl made his shocking little speech. However, there was no denying that he was, as he put it, going through another 'really bad phase'. Nevertheless, he admitted he'd avoided meeting any of the Stones because he was so 'high out of my gourd . . . That was during my real wasted days, and basically when you are high like that you don't care who it is; nothing was more important than getting on with what I had to get on with.'

Steven, who was now shooting up smack on a daily basis, had been even more appalled. '[Axl] said to me, "Just start playing 'Brownstone',"' he recounts. 'So I'm playing "Brownstone" and he comes out and says everybody's fucked up on dope. He was so gone that I'm hiding there behind the drums thinking, I don't know this guy . . .'

According to Duff, everyone 'was pissed off at [Axl] for that. But I can say I was pissed off with Axl for doing that because I was not one of the guys that he was talking about. I mean, I just walked into that thing. So I was furious, of course. But the next day we were on the phone together, and, you know, it was okay, he explained his reasons for doing it. [Axl] was blowing off a lot of steam about a lot of shit. A *lot* of shit . . . That's what happens with this band, we don't bottle shit up. We just let it out.'

According to Alan Niven, at the end of the set Axl had raced off the stage, 'head down and radiating an intense glower, warning all and everyone not to approach him'. As he headed for the dressing rooms, David Geffen himself approached from the top of the stairs.

'Great show, Axl,' said David.

'Hope you liked it, fucker,' Axl nearly spat. 'Because it's the last one you'll ever get.'

Niven, who was behind Axl, recalled how Geffen looked stunned. 'Leave it, David. I'll fix it,' he told Geffen. Though, 'God knows how, I thought to myself.'

Early the next day, both Alan Niven and Doug Goldstein drove to Shoreham Towers to check on Axl, see if perhaps he'd cooled down and changed his mind about – yet again – leaving the band.

'Axl was in bed and he was not going to leave it,' Niven later wrote. 'Not for anything or anyone. On his way to the apartment I had suggested Dougie stop and get a bag of donuts, a very, very large one.'

Axl sat in bed and complained about Slash. He complained about Steven. He complained about Duff. He complained about everyone and everything but his worst vitriol was reserved for Slash. He didn't care if he had a show. He did not care that it was with the Stones, in front of 77,000 more people. He hated Slash. He wasn't going to go on a stage with him ever again.

'All Doug and I could do was to listen and listen and listen and keep him talking. And feed him donuts. As the morning wore on into the afternoon the sugar began to build in his bloodstream – a tsunami sugar rush was developing. Axl began to get animated. His legs began to jerk fitfully under the sheets. Energy was building with nowhere for it to go. It was just enough for us to be able to persuade Axl that if, and that would be a big "if", we could get Slash to apologize to Axl, for his heroin use, for whatever, and in public, then maybe, possibly, perhaps, he *might* think about doing the show.

'I quietly slipped into the living room. I got on the phone with Slash. "I don't want to hear anything but a groveling apology, Slash," I growled into the phone. "I don't care how you feel or whether it's justified in any way shape or form. It's the only

chance we have to get him on stage today and that's all that matters right now."'

Whether Slash would comply with such demands was moot.
As Niven so elegantly put it: 'Anyone who is not sharing the
needle will have, at the least, some degree of resentment about
those who are – there's almost nothing quite as selfish, detached
or destructive as a smack habit. Addicts, of course, always have
the arrogance of their superior and totally misplaced belief that
they have control of their usage.'

Axl, though, 'surely had grounds to be pissed, but his method
of dealing with the situation had the selfishness of the narcissis-
tic sociopath. Axl wasn't that concerned with Slash's condition as
much as he was mad that Slash was not demonstrating a dutiful
compliance to Axl's whim and will . . .'

In the end, Slash went along with it. Partly because it suddenly felt like if he didn't it was he who would be blamed for
the band fucking up their biggest engagement yet. Partly, perhaps, because he knew Axl had a point. As well as the aborted trip
to Hawaii, Doug Goldstein had taken Slash into his Hollywood
home to try to detox. But again with less than satisfactory results.
As he describes: 'It was prior to my being married but my soon-
to-be first wife was with me.' For ten days, they put up with Slash
'crawling on my floors, vomiting, defecating, urinating . . . And
I'm cleaning it up.' When Goldstein had to leave for a couple of
days to go on tour with Great White, he says, he came home to
stories of Slash waking up his flatmate, Ross Goza, in the middle
of the night screaming for drugs. Goza was a music director for
LA's biggest rock radio station, KNAC. 'He was woken up with
Slash choking him, saying, "You're gonna drive me to fucking
Los Angeles! [To score.] And you'll never tell Doug or I'll fucking
kill you!" And Ross is like, "Okay." So Slash wrote him a cheque,
which Ross still has . . .'

Even before the Stones shows, 'I was tired of taking him to rehab facilities that he would check himself out of the first night,' says Goldstein. He had even taken to paying people to spy on him. 'Slash used to score at a magazine stand. So there was this guy in the office building across the way, and I was paying him, and he would call me and say, "Oh, yeah, your guy was by today. Twice!"' In that long, dark period after they came off the road from the AFD tour, trying to keep track of them 'was crazy'.

Whatever his reasons, in the end Slash swallowed his pride and made an apology to Axl. 'With great reluctance he said he would consider repeating it onstage,' Niven remembers. 'Axl, in turn, halfheartedly agreed to consider coming to the show.' Slash duly made his own announcement from the stage that second night vowing to quit his evil ways. '. . . Last night I was up here and didn't even know it,' Slash told the crowd. 'Smack isn't what it's all about. No one in this band advocates heroin. We're not going to be one of those weak bands that fall apart over it.' Or as Alan Niven puts it: 'Bless his heart, Slash took the bullet for the team.' As for Axl, says Niven, 'He had proven that he could make almost everyone bend to him. His future power grabs, his demand for control and ownership of the name, started to become clear in his mind. Perhaps it was at that very moment, full of donuts and angry at being hauled to a show in a police car, under threat of being handcuffed, that he decided what he wished the future of the band to be.'

When, a few weeks later, I asked Axl about it, he was still adamant he'd done the right thing. 'That was definite and that was serious. I mean, I offered to go completely broke and back on the streets, cos it would have cost, like, an estimated $1.5 million to cancel the shows, okay? That means Axl's broke, okay? Except [for] what I've got tied up in Guns N' Roses' interests or whatever. But I didn't want to do that because I wouldn't want the band to have to pay for me cancelling the shows. I don't want Duff to lose his house cos Axl cancelled the shows. I couldn't live with that. But at the same time I'm not gonna be a part of watching them kill each other, just killing themselves off. It's like, we tried every other angle of getting our shit back together and in the end it had to be done live. You know, everybody else was pissed at me but afterwards Slash's mom came and shook my hand and so did his brother.'

He said that Elton John had actually sent flowers to his dressing room after the first show with the Stones. 'Yeah, it was great. He sent these flowers and a note. He didn't mean it against the Stones. It was meant towards the press and anybody else who was against Guns N' Roses. It said: "Don't let the bastards grind you down! I hate them all too . . . Sincerely, Elton John." That was just the greatest.'

Had it worked, though, this public shaming of his bandmates? Axl grinned. 'It way worked, man! Cos Slash is fucking on like a motherfucker right now. And the songs are coming together, they're coming together real heavy.'

Within a week of finishing the Stones shows Doug Goldstein had taken Steven Adler and Slash to detox in Arizona, this time at an exclusive golfing resort. Turning up unannounced at Slash's house was now a familiar ritual. Goldstein would tell him, 'Okay, you need a pair of shorts and a pair of shoes. I'm gonna have to look inside your shoes first though. And I'm buying the smokes. Because what they used to do was hide little heroin balloons in the bottom of a pack of Marlboro. Towards the end it was, basically, I'm picking you up and you're gonna be naked – *and* I'm gonna do a rectal search!'

This time, though, with the trip to Arizona, Goldstein would have Slash *and* Steven to try to deal with. 'I'm supposed to monitor them while they get clean,' he recalls. 'So I got my sleeping pills and I'm going to administer to them. I pick up Steven and

I go to Slash's house and somebody had tipped him off, right? So he's in the wind – nowhere to be found – but I said, "Fuck it, Steven, we're going."

'We get on a plane and we're out there for about four days and Stevie's sleeping till, like, three in the afternoon. So I said, "Look, I'm gonna go golf in the morning." Steven goes, "Yeah, yeah, I'll just sleep in." So I leave the hotel at, like, five thirty in the morning and it's about maybe eight and I make my first birdie of the day. It's hole nine, and this marshal pulls up and says, "Is there a Goldstein in the group? You need to call your office." I call the office and Niv picks up. He goes, "Where the fuck are you?" I go, "I'm golfing, why?" "Slash is on his way to jail!" I go, "You're in LA, go fucking bail him out." He goes, "He's in fucking Arizona at your hotel, you dumbass."'

Unbeknownst to Doug Goldstein, Steven, unable to bear the gnawing pangs of heroin withdrawal any longer, had phoned Slash in LA the night before, begging him to 'bring some junk and come out and we'll party here'. Panicked, Goldstein jumped into his golf cart and drove as fast as he could back to the hotel. When he pulled up, he says, 'There's maybe ten cop cars, an ambulance, a fire engine and about 200 people all in a circle.'

Wading his way through the crowd, he saw Slash, 'standing there stark naked and bloody. I'm like, oh no, this ain't good! Slash goes, "Dougie, I was in the shower, right? I looked through the keyhole and these guys were shooting guns at me. But they don't shoot bullets. They're shooting arrows! The arrows are going, like, ping bang ping!"

'I was like, oh my god . . . One of the cops who is standing next to him goes, "Hey, Slash, give him a physical description." Slash goes, "Okay, so, the tall one, he was, like, four feet eight inches and he's wearing an AC/DC T-shirt." He saw that through the keyhole of course, right? I look at Earl Gabbidon, Axl's bodyguard, and go, "Do me a favour, here's my room key, go get the briefcase." I used to carry a briefcase with $50,000 everywhere I went for situations just like this. I say to Slash, "Tell me what happened?" He goes, "So they're shooting arrows at me so I said fuck it, I'm gonna kick their asses! So I broke through the shower door. Broke through the bathroom door then started counting the arrows in my head. Then these fuckers outran me but then some bitch comes up to me speaking in tongues so I fucking knocked her out and threw her on the ground . . ."

'It was the *maid*. She was speaking Spanish! Now I've got my briefcase in my hand and I see this guy in the crowd and his shirt is bloody. I pull him to one side and I go, "Let me ask you a question. What did you see?" "I saw everything." "You saw him hit the maid?" "Yep, I saw him hit the maid." I said, "You know, I can't help noticing you're wearing a monogrammed shirt." He's like, "No, no, no. My wife bought it at, like, a bargain place." I said, "Look, I know what I'm doing. Don't tell me. That's a fucking monogrammed shirt. That's a $2000 shirt, right?" So I give the guy two grand. "So tell me again, what did you see?" He goes, "Oh, ho, ho, ho! *Got it!* I didn't see shit . . ."

'So he walks away. Then I go, "Where's the manager on duty?" This guy goes, "That's me." I go, "Have you looked at the room yet?" He goes, "Yeah." I go, "Any idea of the damage yet?" He goes, "Yeah. The room's gonna be out of commission for two days while we repair it. It's not that bad a damage really. You're probably looking at, I don't know, two grand." I go, "I'm sorry, did you say five grand?" So I give him five grand for that.

'I ask him, "How about the maid? What does she make?" He says, "Maybe $600 a month." I go, "So three grand will cover her?" He goes, "Absolutely!" Meanwhile, the cops are cracking up, cos they totally see what I am doing. I look at the cops, I go, "Hey, guys. I got a feeling if you look around the crowd you're not gonna find anybody who wants to testify against this guy any more." They go, "You know what, get him out of here right now or we'll be back to do it for you."

'And the whole time, Steven is standing on his balcony, yelling: "Stupid junky! Stupid junky!" I'm like, "Get the fuck back in your room and shut up!"'

When Slash arrived back in LA, though, the nightmare continued. Duff, his mother, Ola, and brother, Ash, were waiting for him to stage an intervention. Too exhausted and embarrassed to argue, Slash caved in and promised them he'd go to rehab. This time Doug Goldstein flew him to a well-known professional rehab joint in Sierra Tucson. 'After three or four days,' Slash said, 'I decided, "Fuck this . . ." He called his heroin dealer from the airport and flew home to LA.'

Niven and Goldstein had a little more success when a few weeks later they managed to persuade Steven to take the trip to Tucson. Truly, this was last-resort time. The golf resort 'cure' had been the first time Steven had even considered any kind of managed withdrawal. They had tried the same trick of essentially kidnapping him and flying to Hawaii that had nearly worked with Slash, but as soon as he and Goldstein were in their seats in first class Steven had begun to scream blue murder. 'He knew what was coming,' Niven recalls. 'The aircrew were not happy. "It's gonna crash, its gonna go down!" he yelled. "The fucking plane's gonna crash!"' He tried to climb out of, and over the back of, his seat as Doug struggled to fasten his seatbelt. 'The fucking plane's gonna go down in flames, let me off it!' he howled.

Steven and Dougie were hastily shown off the plane. Now, though, in the wake of Axl's ultimatum onstage at the Coliseum, he simply had no choice. Not if he wanted to keep safe his gig in Guns N' Roses. 'Doug and I came to know the rehab centres of America as well as we knew the concert venues,' Niven sighs.

Steven would stick it out in Tucson for longer than Slash. But only just. The detox didn't take and within weeks he was back where he'd started. Doug Goldstein got some insight into why that might be, he says now, when he took it upon himself to visit Steven's parents. 'I drive out to the valley and they're showing me pictures of Steven . . . big-time Jewish family sitting around eating potato knish.' Goldstein told them where their son Steven was, that he needed their help. He was trying to get their son sober. Could they tell him what had happened in his life to make him that way?

'The dad starts talking. "Hey, Doug, Deanna, she's throwing a Tupperware party, so Steven's out with his friends, he's getting drunk, he's twelve years old, and he comes home and in front of all the ladies he starts throwing up." He goes, "You're from a good Jewish family, what does a good Jewish family do? Throw him out of the fucking house!" I go, "Really? I know a lot of Jewish families. I'm from a good Jewish family and my family would have hugged me and found out what the hell's wrong. You threw him out of the house at age 12? Where the fuck did he live?" "Well, we don't really know that."

'Well, I do. He lived on the roof of his school for three months until his grandmother found him and brought him in. So when people go, "Stevie's so cute, he's like a little kid", well, no shit. Here's maturation pretty much stopped at age twelve. Pretty sad, man . . . Very sad.'

He continues his theme. 'That kid would stick around until four a.m. to sign all the autographs. He was the face of GN'R to the fans, at the local venues, he was a sweetheart – without the drugs.' The problem was, where the others would find ways to function – or at least, maintain – on dope, Steven was like a downhill racer without brakes. 'I'm telling you: as tough as Slash was, Steven was harder. Whenever it was kind of go-time, Slash kind of – I don't know how to put it, he just kind of knew when to back off the partying. Steven kind of never really got that.'

Or, at least, not until it was too late. 'I tried every different thing I could think of to try and get Steven sober and it just . . . at the end of the day, if somebody's not willing to go through those steps then it's just not gonna happen.'

Despite the up-and-down nature of their four shows with the Stones, Mick Jagger had been alive to the impact the headlines generated by Axl's onstage outbursts had on ticket sales. All four Coliseum shows had been massive sell-outs. For a band on its first major US tour for nearly a decade this was good news indeed. When the Stones then announced a special show they would be doing in Atlantic City, on 19 December, that would also be available to see on TV via a pay-per-view deal similar to that more usually arranged around heavyweight boxing champion-ship world titles, Jagger had no doubt over who would add the icing to that delicious pay-per-view cake: W. Axl Rose and Izzy Stradlin – the Jagger and Richards, no less, of Guns N' Roses. 'He ignored Slash,' says Alan Niven, 'as he would decades later in Los Angeles when inviting guests onto the stage at the Staples Center during their latest "Last Time" tour.'

The idea was simply that Axl and Izzy would come up onstage and join the Stones for one number. When the Stones' office sent word that Axl and Izzy could pick which Stones song they would like to help sing and play, neither of them knew what to say. 'I dunno,' Axl told Niven. 'There's so many. How do you pick one? Ask Iz.'

'Tell the Stones what to play? I dunno,' echoed Izzy when Niven called for his input. Niven decided to take the matter in hand and choose for them. 'I called Jagger's office and told them they would just love to perform "Salt of the Earth". Apparently that threw everyone into a bit of a tizzy since the band had never played the song live before. But I could not think of a more rel-evant statement, or a better treat for Stones fans, of which I was still one.'

Staged six days before Christmas, the final show of three at the East Coast gambling capital, this was to be the glorious finale to the Stones' *Steel Wheels* tour. As well as Axl and Izzy, Eric Clapton would also be putting in an onstage appearance (on 'Little Red Rooster'), as would John Lee Hooker (on 'Boogie Chillen'). With the 16,000 tickets for the show selling for anything between $40 and $240 a go, and the pay-per-view slots going for a 'suggested retail' price of $24.95, this was another giant payday for the Stones for which nothing must be allowed to go wrong. That was the plan anyway.

But as Alan Niven would chokingly recall: 'In Atlantic City, Axl was late to arrive to the hotel, late for rehearsal and late for the stage. He ordered me to go tell the Stones he would be present for rehearsal an hour or so later than scheduled. When he told me to do that, it was literally, "You're fucking joking, Axl. Get in the shower. I'll wait in my room."' Knowing that would hardly work, 'I prevailed on Izzy to go to the rehearsal and buy Axl a few minutes while he composed himself.'

But when a forlorn Izzy sidled up onstage at the sound check, Keith Richards let him have it. 'Where's your fucking singer?' Izzy mumbled an apology. Then did his best to fill in for as long as he could as the band worked their way fitfully through the unfamiliar 'Salt of the Earth'. When Axl showed up an hour later, Keith confronted him. According to Izzy, says Niven, 'Axl made some excuse about partying, missing a flight, whatever, Ax always had some lame excuse.'

'Well, I slept in a fucking chandelier last night,' growled Keith, 'but I'm on time.'

But Alan Niven wasn't around to see that. Axl had been so furious with his refusal to tell Jagger and Richards they would have to wait for him, he had effectively banned his own manager from the show. Niven, equally furious, was happy to leave. He says that 'a very embarrassed Brian Ahern came to the room and told me, "I hate to tell you this, but Axl says he's not going to go to rehearsal unless you're out of the building." I went, "Fine." I wrote a little note to Axl telling him he was behaving really badly. He had good people who cared about and loved him. Then I went home and did what everybody else was gonna do and watched it in the comfort of my own home on pay-per-view.'

Yet when he did, he says now, he couldn't help but note how, as he put it, 'Axl's passion and conviction would utterly outshine Jagger's languid indifference when they performed "Salt of the Earth". Urchin Axl truly connected to the sentiment of the song. Back in the day, when the little fucker was "on", fired up by contention, conflict or competition, he was simply brilliant.' On a wall in his office these days he has a framed photograph of Izzy Stradlin, Keith Richards and Ronnie Wood onstage together in Atlantic City. 'It's like watching three gems being put on the same cushion in front of you.'

Axl would also share happier memories with me of Atlantic City. Whatever tensions his late arrival had aroused with Keith Richards, he said, Mick Jagger had been quick to be emollient. He related how Jagger and Eric Clapton had 'cornered' him about David Bowie at the sound check. 'I'm sitting on this amp and all of a sudden they're both right there in front of me. And Jagger doesn't really talk a lot, right? He's just real serious about everything. And all of a sudden he was like', doing a cockney accent, '"So you got in a fight with Bowie, didja?" I told him the story real quick and him and Clapton are going off about Bowie in their own little world, talking about things from years of knowing each other. They were saying that when Bowie gets drunk he turns into the Devil from Bromley! I mean, I'm not even *in* this conversation. I'm just sitting there and every now and then they would ask me a couple more facts about what happened, and then they would go back to bitching like crazy about Bowie. I was just sitting there going, wow . . .'

*

Back in LA at the start of 1990, disorientated by the fame and the money and the madness inherent in having everything they'd dreamed of come true, they drifted. Slash and Duff showed up at the American Music Awards, drunk and coked, slurring and swearing . . . Axl and Slash jammed with Aerosmith at the Forum . . . Slash and Duff guested on an Iggy Pop record . . . Duff got divorced from Mandy, who he'd had a big fight with on New Year's Eve . . . then, in April, the band played Farm Aid in Indianapolis, a televised gig that showed Steven in his worst possible light . . . Axl got married to Erin Everly in Las Vegas, after threatening to shoot himself if she refused . . . Slash jammed with The Black Crowes in New York . . . the days and nights rolled by, end on end. Every time I spoke to Slash – or Axl, or Duff, all of whom now came to me with different stories, crazy concerns, out-there insights and bad craziness – it was the same but different. Something new that had happened that made the rest of us feel old. You feared for them but at the same time you wondered at them, too. Wasn't this what the real rock'n'roll lifestyle was supposed to be about?

When the *LA Times* ran a story about Axl winning 'a temporary restraining order against the West Hollywood neighbor he is accused of hitting over the head with a wine bottle', it made headlines in every music magazine, radio station and music TV channel in the world. Yet nobody who'd ever had the remotest dealings with Guns N' Roses was the least bit surprised by the story. Gabriella Kantor, who lived along the corridor from Axl at Shoreham Towers, had called the cops, claiming Axl had hit her with a bottle after 'an altercation'. Though no charges were filed, the band's lawyers had got a judge to place the restraining order on Kantor, whom they described as 'a potentially dangerous rock 'n' roll groupie . . . upset that she is not a part of [Rose's] social and or professional life'.

In order to try to keep a cap on things, Doug Goldstein was now paying $1000 a week to another occupant 'just to tell me the goings on. He was a Middle Eastern guy, cute as hell. He calls me one day, absolutely out of his mind. "He's fucking crazy! I don't want your money! Fuck you!" I go, "Slow down, what happened?" "He crazy!" I go, "Yeah, I know. But what happened?"

'What happened was Axl had taken Erin's Halliburton suitcase and thrown it off the twenty-fourth floor and almost hit this guy.' He laughs. 'He'd have killed him if that had hit him. Are you kidding? No question, but very funny, actually. Another time, I got a phone call saying you better come up here. Axl shoved a piano out of the front window of his apartment. I mean, this shit, I wasn't trained in this! Like, I'm calling crane companies, right? To come get this piano out of the fucking weeds down below the home. It was brilliant, man! I'll tell ya, every day it was a different challenge. And it was okay because it was kind of fun. It was like, okay, never dealt with this one before.'

Axl moved out of his apartment for a while, to stay at the Sunset Marquis, where another scuffle took place in the dining room one morning – but which the hotel management, famed for their tolerance of the 'unconventional' ways of famous entertainers, were happy not to make a big deal of. This was Axl Rose, after all, now the most famous rock star in the world. Who would be dumb enough to fuck up that relationship?

Then four months after the shows at the Coliseum, the spat between Izzy, Axl and Vince Neil at the MTV Awards began to send out its shockwaves. None of us could have guessed then how far they would spread. It was January 1990. I was staying at the home of the band's PR, Arlett Vereeke. Late one night the phone went. It was Axl, calling to rant about something or other he'd just read in *Kerrang!* Arlett told Axl I was there, and she handed over the phone to see if I could help. He told me to come to the

Shoreham Towers apartment right away, where he would make some sort of 'statement'. He 'was in the mood to talk'. Arlett drove me over, and sat in on the whole interview, which made it more disconcerting when Axl tried to claim later I had made parts of it up – and Arlett dutifully backed him. But then, having once been a rock PR myself, I knew that that's what good PRs do: back their clients to the hilt, right or wrong. It's not the writer who's paying their bills.

Axl answered the door and immediately turned his back on us, stomping down the corridor and launching straight into the 'statement'. Standing there in crumpled T-shirt and jeans, his big red beard covering most of his face, he began raging about Vince Neil, who had been 'saying some shit' in *Kerrang!* – specifically, Neil's claim to have punched out GN'R guitarist Izzy Stradlin for 'messing' with Vince's wife, Sharise.

What came next was pure Axl Rose circa 1990, part hubris, part passion, part pain, and part ludicrous hyperbole. The whole incident was 'bullshit', he ranted. 'Guns or knives, motherfucker . . . I don't care. I just wanna smash his plastic face' – this last a sarcastic reference to Vince's then recent, supposedly hush-hush cosmetic surgery.

'I can't believe this shit I just read in *Kerrang!*' he snarled, holding up a copy of *Kerrang!* dated 4 November 1989 and yanked open at a page from Jon Hotten's interview with Mötley Crüe. 'The interviewer asks Vince Neil about him throwing a punch at Izzy backstage at the MTV awards last year, and Vince replies . . .' Reading aloud sarcastically: '"I just punched that dick and broke his fucking nose! Anybody who beats up on a woman deserves to get the shit kicked out of them. Izzy hit my wife, a year before I hit him." Well, that's just a crock of shit! Izzy never touched that chick! If anybody tried to hit on anything, it was her trying to hit on Izzy when Vince wasn't around. Only Izzy didn't buy it. So that's what that's all about . . .'

He continued ranting as I set up the tape recorder. '. . . Vince's wife has got a bug up her ass about Izzy. Izzy doesn't know what's going on, Izzy doesn't fucking care. But anyway, Izzy's just walked offstage. He's momentarily blinded, as always happens when you come offstage, by coming from the stage lights straight into total darkness.' Which was when he said Vince came out of nowhere and hit Izzy. 'Tom Petty's security people jump on him and ask Alan Niven, our manager, who had his arm round Izzy's shoulders when Vince bopped him, if he wants to press charges. He asks Izzy and Izzy says, "Naw, it was only like being hit by a girl" and they let him go.

'Meantime . . . I'm walking way up ahead of everybody else, and the next thing I know Vince Neil comes flying past me like his ass is on fire or something. All I saw was a blur of cheekbones!' He carried on like this, about how he wanted to 'see that plastic face of his cave in when I hit him'.

'Are you serious about this?' I asked him. He said he was. 'There's only one way out for that fucker now and that's if he apologises in public, to the press, to *Kerrang!* and its readers, and admits he was lying when he said those things in that interview. Personally, I don't think he has the balls. But that's the gauntlet, and I'm throwing it down . . .'

We sat down in the only two available chairs not smothered in magazines, ashtrays, Coke cans, barf-balls, more ashtrays . . . Axl sat perched in the balcony window overlooking the pulsing neon ooze of the Hollywood hills below. He lit another cigarette and waited for me to begin.

Axl didn't really believe Vince Neil would take up that gauntlet and arrange to fight it out with him, surely? Still reluctant to make eye contact, he stared into space as he spoke.

'I've no idea what he will do. I mean, he could wait until I'm drunk in the Troubadour one night and come in because he got a phone call saying I'm there and hit me with a beer bottle. But it's like, I don't care. Hit me with a beer bottle, dude. Do whatever you wanna do but I'm gonna take you out . . . I don't care what he does. Unless he sniper-shoots me – unless he gets me like that without me knowing it – I'm taking him with me and that's about all there is to it.'

What if Vince were to apologise?

'That'd be radical! Personally, I don't think he has the balls. I don't think he has the balls to admit he's been lying out of his ass. That'd be great if he did though, and then I wouldn't have to be a dick from then on.'

It was so insanely ridiculous, so marvellously over the top I had to stop myself from laughing out loud. The biggest rock star in the world was offering a private audience in his own home and threatening to fight one of the other biggest rock stars in the city. Yet when the interview was published three months later, things became a whole lot less amusing.

The first hint of trouble I had was when Arlett tried to obtain the interview tape by telling me the band wanted to run it on 'a special GN'R phone-line'. I asked for the number of this 'special phone-line'. That's when the mumbling and back-pedalling began. She said she'd get back to me. She did, a few days later. This time, though, the approach was more direct. Axl would 'really like' a copy of the tape, because – well, how could she put this? – 'He doesn't think he really speaks that way.' What? 'You know, that he would . . . say . . . those things.' I still didn't quite get it. 'Axl doesn't believe he said those things. Huh? What does he think happened then – I made them up?'

Silence.

'But you were there . . .'

'Yes,' she said, hesitantly.

'I even checked with him first,' I said, remembering how I had read some of the most inflammatory quotes back to Axl over the phone – Arlett's phone – a few weeks later, in order to give Axl the chance to retract or reword them. And how he had told me: 'I stand by every fucking word, man . . .'

'Yes,' she said again, 'I know. But if you could just send him the tape . . .'

I refused. Not because I felt I had anything to hide. I had been writing about Guns N' Roses for three years. Of all the bands I had built long-term relationships with in those days – Metallica, Ozzy Osbourne, Led Zeppelin, Iron Maiden, Def Leppard, to name a few – I had always felt I enjoyed a particularly close bond with Guns N' Roses. There had been several occasions when I had deliberately not printed certain stories, in order to underline the trust we shared. Now this. What was Axl thinking? I felt insulted, let down and very angry. I decided to wait for the whole thing to blow over. Axl was always in a shit fit about something. Tomorrow it would be somebody else's turn.

What I didn't know then, though, was that Vince Neil had read the interview, and contacted Axl through various intermediaries to let him know he'd be only too willing to settle their score whenever and wherever Axl wanted. That was no surprise. Vince was a tough Mexican kid who'd grown up in a rough part of LA and was more than able to look after himself. As he related in Mötley Crüe's 2001 autobiography, *The Dirt*: 'The only thing that would have given me more pleasure than a number one record was breaking Axl Rose's nose . . . I wanted to beat the shit out of that little punk and shut him up for good. But I never heard from him: not that day, not that month, not that year, not that century. But the offer still stands.'

Doug Goldstein tells me now that the fight offer had been so serious, the boxing promoter Don King had got wind of it and offered to stage it anywhere the pair wanted. His answer, rather than 'guns or knives motherfucker', was to say that he hadn't said it at all. We wouldn't meet again for another year, at which point the situation would worsen further.

Meanwhile, for all of Guns N' Roses, their lives would continue to shift at bewildering speed, the madness barely easing.
And as the months shot by like the lights of a speeding train, the
one thing nobody seemed willing – or able – to talk about seriously was when – and if – there would be a new Guns N' Roses
album.

'It was so splintered and such a struggle but I remember we
finally got together after just a major rollercoaster ride of ups and
downs,' Slash recalled years later. 'It was at my house on Walnut
Drive in the Laurel Canyon hills. We compiled thirty fucking
songs, more than thirty songs, in one evening. That was the one
time in all of it that I remember that the band felt like itself. Just
the guys like I was always used to – Izzy, Duff and Axl. We managed to put a focus on thirty-six songs. That was the only group
writing session we had where we were all together in one room.'

Slash had offered up another long song, called 'Coma', which
he had written 'while I was completely stoned'. Izzy, the cool-
as-fuck riff-king, had a slate of them: 'Pretty Tied Up', 'Double
Talkin' Jive', 'You ain't the First', '14 Years'. Duff brought along
'So Fine' and 'Dust n' Bones'. Plus another Sid Vicious pastiche
he had first sung for me in the kitchen called 'Why Do You Look
at Me When You Hate Me?'

And Axl had more, too: songs on which he'd collaborated with
his most trusted friends, Del James and West Arkeen. West already had a co-credit on 'It's So Easy', of course, from the *Appetite*
days, but would now also add his name to the new songs 'Bad
Obsession', 'Yesterdays' and 'The Garden'. James shared credits
on the latter two as well. At the time it suited Slash's purpose.
'West and Axl and Del and Duff, that was more what that was
like,' he said. 'I didn't mind. As long as the song was good and
I could do something with it. I remember "It's So Easy" being
one of those songs that when I first heard it in its original form
I was like, whatever, but then I got to it and changed it to what

it sounds more like now. I remember "The Garden" being really good. But, no, I didn't mind too much. I was usually too preoccupied doing whatever debauched shit I was doing. If everybody was busy doing that, nobody was looking over my shoulder while I was doing what I was doing.'

Looking back now, though, Slash acknowledged that the evening on Walnut Drive was, in retrospect, the end of something, one of the last times they were all together. 'That was a very poignant moment,' he said. 'And the next thing you know we were looking for drummers . . .'

8

FLYING LIKE A SPACE BRAIN

We had all seen in the New Year in 1989/90 by joining in with the chimes on MTV . . . 8, 7, 6, 5 . . . That is, myself, Slash, Duff, Arlett and several other Hollywood hound dogs, rising high on champagne, weed and whatever else our happy gang of over-entitled sun dogs it felt right to be doing round about that time and place . . . 4, 3, 2 . . . HOORAY!

It felt like a good time to be alive. And yet the next couple of months would give me a startlingly contrasting view of just how upside-down life in LA could be, the twin faces of comedy and tragedy combining to – though I didn't know it then – shred my career into confetti. I would recover. Everyone who went through the demented excesses of the 1980s would have to find a way to recover eventually or simply never be seen again. But it still amazes me how quickly the highs turned to lows. But then it still amazes everybody I've spoken to who ever had anything to do with Guns N' Roses in their full toxic bloom how suddenly shit turned to gold and then platinum – and then back to shit again. Haunting all of us for the rest of our professional days.

What follows are two interviews I did, first with Slash and Duff, then the more sensible parts of the Vince Neil-related interview I did with Axl, over the days that followed that New Year's Eve party. The first, intended for broadcast on a show I presented in those days for Capital Radio in London, captures the spirit of

Guns N' Roses in the late-late-show era of the big-haired Eighties better than anything else I probably did with them. It's not clever but it is funny. The second, conducted in those twilight hours Axl has always preferred to do his business in, now weighs heavy with portent – with the things that troubled Axl then, and several clues as to the things that would continue to trouble him in all his days to come.

I set them out here as clear and unvarnished as I am able.

The Capital Radio interview between myself and Slash and Duff, which was conducted in West Hollywood one drunken evening on the second day of January 1990, was never eventually broadcast, for obvious reasons, as you will see. But it is presented here in its full, inglorious glory.

It begins with the sound of a very drunk Duff singing: 'Doe, a deer, a female deer . . .' Then my voice, in radio presenter mode, explaining to them that although we are prerecording the interview the show itself will go out live. 'So you can say or do whatever you like, but . . .'

Slash: Can we say 'fuck' in it?

Mick: If you must, but try and keep it to a minimum, okay?

S: Oh, cool. Okay.

M: So, imagine it's a Saturday night in London.

S: Is it raining? Most likely . . .

M: Just follow me, okay? I'm gonna start. Right. Slash. Duff. Thank you both for coming on the show . . .

S: Well, thank you for letting us watch you come. [Much sniggering.]

M: [starting again]: Okay, here on Capital FM I'm talking to Slash and Duff from Guns N' Roses. It's the day after New Year's Day . . . Did you both have a good time over Christmas and New Year?

Duff: Oh, yes! Oh, yes!

S: Fucking wonderful . . .

D: Oh, yes! We're gonna go and do our record pretty, uh . . . like, in two weeks.

S: Yeah, so anybody who's been wondering, it will happen.

M: That's good, because you know what people have been saying in England – that you're never gonna make another record because you're such bad boys you'll never get it together . . .

D [blowing a huge raspberry]: AAHHH! PUUHHHSSSST-TTTT!! They're WRONG!

M: Do you have anything to add to that, Slash?

S: Yeah! Fuck YOU . . . Ha, ha! No. We're gonna make another record. We've just been through a lot of shit, you know. It'll be fine. Just relax. It's gonna be a really good one, too. It's gonna be very . . .

D [interrupting]: Imagine, like, riding on the Tube. Getting, like, one of those Tube tickets and riding on the Tube and then, like, getting lost on the Piccadilly Tube, and then you go to the Thames Tube and then it's like, you get on another Tube and you get lost and lost and lost . . .That's what happened to our band, kind of, like, in the fucking . . . broad scale of things. And we ended up on the Thames River in the rain. That's, basically, what happened . . .

M: . . . the band were on the River Thames in the rain and that's why the new album didn't get made last year?

S [nodding enthusiastically]: We were drunk, we were lost and we had nowhere to go . . . And my top hat got fucking ruined . . .

D: And now we're back dry in the, er . . . somewhere dry.

S: No, no, the thing is, it's not like we're . . . um . . . I won't mention any names. But we're not like some bands who make records like jerking off . . .

D: POISON?

S: No, no . . . It just means a lot to us, so we're just taking our time with it and . . .

Slash (3rd row, 2nd
from left) in his 6th
grade class photo from
Third Street School in
1977 in Los Angeles.
(Getty Images)

Slash plays with his first
band Tidus Sloan during
lunchtime at Fairfax High
School on 4 June 1982.
(Getty Images)

Duff McKagan, Izzy Stradlin, W. Axl Rose, Steven Adler and Slash pose for an early group shot in a booth at Canter's Deli in June 1985. (Getty Images)

Above left Steve Darrow (left), W. Axl Rose and Slash of the rock group 'Hollywood Rose' perform at Madame Wong's on 16 June 1984. (Getty Images)

Left Axl and Slash backstage at the Stardust Ballroom in LA on 28 June 1985. (Getty Images)

Left Slash with his English father
Tony Hudson backstage at the Roxy
Theatre, LA, on 31 August 1985.
(Getty Images)

Below left Guns N' Roses onstage
at the LA Street Scene on 28
September 1985. (Getty Images)

Right Pam Manning dancing with
Axl onstage at the Whisky-A-Go-Go
on 5 April 1986. (Getty Images)

Below Izzy in Tokyo, 1988,
holding his award for the *Music
Life* 'Popularity Vote' and a
bottle of saké. (Getty Images)

Backstage at the Santa Monica Civic Auditorium after opening for Ted Nugent on 30 August 1986.
Centre: Geffen A&R rep Teresa Ensenat and Tom Zutaut, who signed the band to Geffen.
(Getty Images)

Axl onstage at the Castle Donington festival, England, 1988. Two fans died during their set. (Getty Images)

Axl and Slash onstage at Rock In Rio II on 15 January 1991. (Getty Images)

Axl shares the stage with Mick Jagger at the Rolling Stones show in Atlanta, December 1989, performing 'Salt Of The Earth' – suggested by GN'R manager Alan Niven, who Axl then banned from the show. (Getty Images)

Axl with would-be second wife, Stephanie Seymour. The model would later claim in court that after one fight the singer had grabbed her by the throat and dragged her barefoot through broken glass. (Getty Images)

D: WARRANT?

S: Sshhh . . .

D: BRITNEY FOX?

S [giggling]: It'll come back to haunt you, I promise you.

D: No, I'm just kidding. No, what happened was . . . the album went wuuhhh! And then we went wuuhhh!

S: No one expected . . . I thought – no offence to Lemmy or any of those guys – but I thought it would be like a Motörhead album, it would just come out and, you know, no big deal . . . Yeah, right.

D: We went through a lot of stuff and then, after that, it took us a while to recoup and deal with our own lives.

S: You get places to live . . .

D: And deal with our own lives.

S: And girlfriends . . .

D: And deal with our own lives.

S: Oh! That's true! We all broke up with our old ladies today.

D: Divorce!

M: This is an official announcement, is it?

D: Okay, this is in England – that's many area codes away, right? Well, I got divorced, girls . . .

M: Okay, before we get any further . . .

D: No, let's get much further!

S: No, this is deep! This is deep!

M: We're gonna go much further, but first we're gonna play a Guns N' Roses track. Which track shall we hear?

D: 'Nightrain'!

S: No! No, no, no, no, no, no, no . . . 'You're Crazy'.

D: *You're* crazy . . .

S: I'm nuts, but no, play 'You're Crazy' . . .

D: Okay, 'You're Crazy'.

S: No, no, no, no, no, no, no, no! Fuck, I can't remember the name of it . . .

D: 'NIGHTRAIN'!

S: No! Everybody plays 'Nightrain' . . . Um . . . [starts snapping fingers] . . . um . . .

D: Are you going down?

S: No, no, no, no, no! Um . . .

D: We don't even remember our own record . . . 'It's So Easy'?

S: No, the one . . . ' . . . pulls up her skirt'. The song we never play any more? [Both start humming two completely different riffs loudly. The interview has already descended into full-blown Spinal Tap absurdity.]

D [looking at me]: You know the song we're talking about . . . [starts humming again].

S: No, wait, wait! We have to figure this one out. [Both start singing and humming and clicking fingers etc.]

S: God, this is horrible . . . Um . . . 'My way, you're way . . .'

D: 'ANYTHING GOES'!

S: 'Anything Goes'!

M [jolly radio voice]: Okay, this is 'Anything Goes' . . .

D: By us, yes!

[I back-announce the record and we get back into interview mode. Sort of.]

M: What were we talking about?

S: Nothing in particular . . . We got rid of our girlfriends, that was major.

D: That was major! And both on the same day!

S: On the same day! It was serious . . .

M: Okay, let's talk about the girlfriends . . .

D: No. Let's talk about music.

S: Yeah, sure. It'd be more . . .

D: I don't, uh . . . naw.

S: We already got good new ones!

D [whispering]: I can't talk about this. I got lawsuits and shit . . .

S: Yeah, okay, okay, okay, okay. All right, never mind. Yeah.

No. I have a new girlfriend. He's . . . he doesn't really have a new girlfriend, because he's still married . . .

D: No, I'm not! I just can't talk about it . . . Mick, let's talk about you for a second.

S: That's a cool shirt.

D: What's going on with you, back home? Do you have a girlfriend back there?

S [nudging him]: She's here! Her name's . . .

D: That's right! Oh, she's beautiful! You did good! You guys over in England, Mick is fucking happening. He's got a fucking happening girlfriend . . .

M [fumbling]: That's very nice of you to say so, but getting back to the interview . . .

D: Me and Slash both have Corvettes now. Can you believe that shit?

M: . . . the question everybody wants answered is, what have you been doing this year, why hasn't your album come out, and when will it come out?

S [shaking his head]: We've been adjusting . . .

D: But we have thirty-five songs!

S: We have thirty-five new songs. But we've had to . . . Let me put it this way . . .

D: Put it some fucking way, please. I tried to earlier.

S: The first fucking time we . . . Can I say that?

D: Yeah, do.

S: . . .The first fucking time we came to England, we like, we were just like . . . like . . . just . . . here's the plane ticket, everybody go, and we're all wuh-ooh-uh! And we get drunk and fucked up and sick in the street and stuff. Things changed . . . [Both start talking at once.]

D: We just sat in the street across from the Marquee and just drank. We didn't know. We thought we'd just be, like, some opening band and stuff, and we got there and the place was sold out!

S: We thought it was the greatest thing ever. Now we have homes . . .

D: But fuck that, England was like our homecoming ground . . .

S: No, no, no, but the changing thing, that's what's important.

D: That's what's been happening this year, yeah. But the transformation from England to, like, now is . . .

S: But we haven't changed.

D: No, we haven't changed.

M: Well, you're still drunk, anyway.

S: It's the day after New Year's. YOU'RE drunk, too!

D [laughing]: Mick, are you going to be able to use this interview?

M: I'm gonna give it a shot.

S: We're not built for rock star shit.

D: We aren't! We aren't! [Goes into long incoherent rant about a fight he got into at a club on New Year's Eve] . . . and the guy was bigger than I was, but I just went CAH-BOOOM! And . . . his eyes crossed, like you see in the cartoons, like that? And he went down. And then everybody dragged him back and dragged me back, but they were dragging him past me and I fucking biffed him three more times in the head! They said I broke his jaw . . .

S: Nasty [Suicide – former Hanoi Rocks guitarist] stuck his arm in through the crowd and got one in there, too!

D: So we go through this shit all the time, people trying to fuck with us. I was telling you earlier, if anybody fucks with my homeboy here, Slash – and it's happened before, like if a big guy was gonna hit him – I've stepped right in front of him.

S: Sure, and I can hide in the crook of his knee . . .

D: I beat up a guy for him once. And he'd do that for me.

S: But not to sound stupid, because we're starting to sound stupid . . .

D: Because we're drunk! We're drunk! Of course we're gonna sound stupid.

S: No, but we're a fucking band . . .

D: Yeah . . . that's what it comes down to.

M: All right, let's play some more music. What this time? It doesn't have to be Guns N' Roses . . .

[Both simultaneously.]

D: 'SCARRED FOR LIFE'! ROSE TATTOO!

S: 'Scarred for Life'. Rose Tattoo . . . [Duff goes into invisible guitar routine, singing at the top of his voice. We come back from the record.]

D: Oh, I fucked up . . .

S: We are intelligent, though.

D: We're not right now, though. Mick, you got me drunk!

S: We just like to have fun. Go out there and jam. It's like this, to put it bluntly, we go out there and we play, and we're very conscientious about our music, and we're sick of fucking talking about it.

D: Yeah, that's a good point.

S: It's true.

D: That's a good point.

S: It's like, it's old . . .

D: We don't mind talking to you because you know what it's all about. But most people go, 'So what's it like being – a – ROCK – STAR?' Like, what? What is a rock star?

S: It's a hard stone that shines. Ha ha ha!

M [deciding enough is enough]: So let's clear it up for everybody . . .

S: In England? We love you guys.

D: We really do love you guys.

S: We fucking kicked ass in London, that first time.

D: I love the Marquee. I love London.

S: We did suck in a couple of places, though . . .

D: When we go back we're gonna do the Marquee . . .

S: No, man, it's gone.

D: Oh yeah, it's that new place.

S: I think we're gonna do Wembley.

D: No, let's do that biker club! Let's do that biker club! I don't wanna do Donington again.

S: Not Donington, Wembley . . . [Much discussion ensues over the pros and cons of Wembley Stadium versus Donington Park, with everybody talking at once.]

S: Do two bands, that's cool. Five bands on the bill, all day long . . . it's just . . .

D: No way. No Donington.

M: Well, wherever it is, I know you're both looking forward to playing live again as much as your fans are.

S [pulling face]: Man, we have to get out. When we get this record done, we'll go.

D: Hear this? Hear this? Hear this? [Duff grabs the sides of the table and bangs his head with an audible thump against it.]

S [disdainfully]: What was that?

D: Oh, you do it, too? Okay, together . . . one, two, three, four! [Both lean over and, as one, head-butt the table together, making an even more audible THUMP on the tape.]

M [desperately trying to wrap it up now]: You heard it live and exclusive on Capital Radio . . . I'd like to thank Duff and Slash for joining me this evening . . . [Much braying of laughter in the background.]

S: Anybody who stayed tuned, thank you for listening . . . Ha ha ha!

D: Yeah! I thank you! Because, uh . . . hah . . .

M: What are we going out on? [Long pause.]

S: 'We are the Road Crew' by Motörhead?

D: YES! [Singing] We are the ROAD CREW . . . da-nah-nah-nah-nah-naaaawww . . .

S [above the noise]: We had a band called Road Crew once. 'Rocket Queen' came from that track . . .

D: Right! Lemmy, hi! From Duff and Slash! And the rest of you boys, 'Philthy' and all you guys . . .

S: Hello!

D: Lemmy, you rock!

[We say our 'radio' goodbyes . . .]

D: SEE YA! We'll see ya soon!

S: Mick, thank you for holding the mic for so long. I couldn't even hold my dick that long . . .

D: I've seen you do it! Remember, when we were on the road, and I pretended I was, like, asleep and you talked to your girl-friend on the fucking phone and you'd have your little rag and you'd go, 'Get the Coke bottle, baby.' I was pretending to go to sleep and he's there beating off, and shit.

M: And on that happy note . . .

D: . . . I'd be trying to get to sleep and he'd be like, 'Oh, baby. I'm saving a load of come in my rag for you . . .'

TAPE ENDS ABRUPTLY.

It was a very different mood, of course, when I went to Axl's place to interview him just a few nights later. He didn't even say hello when he answered the door, just went straight into it. Trying to move the conversation on from his invitation to Vince Neil for a dual, I asked Axl about his run-in with David Bowie before the Stones shows. I'd been told the two of them were now the best of buddies, was that right?

'Well, I don't know about "best buddies". But I like him a lot, yeah. We had a long talk about the business and stuff and I never met anybody so cool and so into it and so whacked out and so sick in my life. I remember looking over at Slash and going, "Man, we're in fucking deep trouble", and he goes, "Why?" I go, "Be-cause I got a lot in common with this guy. I mean, I'm pretty sick but this guy's just fucking ill!" And Bowie's sitting there laughing and talking about "One side of me is experimental and the other side of me wants to make something that people can get into, *and I don't know fucking why! Why am I like this?*" And I'm sitting there thinking, I've got twenty more years of . . . *that* to look forward to? I'm already like that . . . twenty more years? What am I gonna do?'

He laughed. Suddenly we were getting on fine again. I decided to ask about some of the more serious, close-to-home rifts he'd recently become part of. Primarily, the speech he'd given onstage about Slash and Steve dancing with Mr Brownstone. The bit where he'd announced he was leaving the band. Was that also his job now, to be the guy in the band who lays down the law – the dictator of the band?

'Depends who you ask and on which day. We got into fights in Chicago, when we went there last year to escape LA and try and get some writing done. Everybody's schedules were weird and we were all showing up at different times. But when I would show up I was like, "Okay, let's do this, let's do that, let's do this one of yours, Slash. Okay, now let's hear that one Duff's got . . ." And that's when everybody would decide I was a dictator. Suddenly I'm a total dictator, a completely selfish dick, you know? But fuck, man, as far as I was concerned we were on a roll. Slash is complaining we're getting nothing done and I'm like, "What do you mean? We just put down six new parts for songs!" We've got all this stuff done in, like, a couple of weeks. So suddenly, like, everything's a bummer and it's all my fault.

'And he was like, "Yeah, but I've been sitting here a month on my ass waiting for you to show up." I'd driven cross-country in my truck to Chicago from LA and it had taken me weeks. So suddenly, like, everything's a bummer and it's all my fault. But after working with Jagger it was like, 'Don't anybody ever call me a dictator again. You go work for the Stones and you'll find out the hard way what working for a real dictator is like!"'

Had he had a chance to 'hang' with Jagger or any of the Rolling Stones when the band had supported them?

'Not really. Not Jagger, anyway. That guy walks offstage and goes and does paperwork. He checks everything. That guy is involved in every little aspect of the show, from what the backing singers are getting paid to what a particular part of the PA costs to buy or hire. He is on top of all of it. Him and his lawyer and a couple of guys that he hangs with. But, basically, it's all him. And this is where I sympathise. I mean, I don't sit around checking the gate receipts at the end of every show, but sometimes the frontman . . . I don't know. You don't plan on that job when you join the band. You don't want that job. You don't wanna be that guy to the guys in your band that you hang with and you look up to. But somebody's got to do it. And the guitar player can't do it because he is not the guy who has to be communicating directly with the audience with eye contact and body movements. He can go back, hang his hair down in his face and stand by the amps and just get into his guitar part . . .'

He talked about how the shows at the Coliseum taught him how to perform on a stadium stage.

'You have to learn how, but it can be done. You know, like someone goes, "You're gonna have this huge arena tour next year, dude!" And I go, "I know, but that's the problem. I can work a *stadium* now." And I can. And if I can work it, then that's what I wanna do. It's just bigger and more fun.'

I asked Axl what he could tell me about how the next Guns N' Roses album was shaping up.

'It's coming together just great,' he enthused. 'I've written all these ballads and Slash has written all these really heavy crunch rockers. It makes for a real interesting kinda confusion . . .'

Writing for this next album was a universe away, though, from the way the material for the first album came about, he explained. 'One reason things have been so hard in a way is this. The first album was basically written with Axl coming up with maybe one line and maybe a melody for that line, or how I'm gonna say it or yell it or whatever. And the band would build a song around it. This time around, Izzy's brought in eight songs, at least, okay? Slash has brought in an album. And Duff's brought in a song. Duff's said it all in one song. It's called "Why Do You Look at Me When You Hate Me" and it's just bad-assed! But none of this ever happened before. I mean, before the first album I think Izzy had written one song in his entire life, you know? But they're coming now. And Izzy has this, like, very wry sense of humour, man. He's got this song about . . .' He half sang the lyrics: ' . . . "*She lost her mind today / Got splattered out on the highway / I say that's okay . . .*"' He laughed. 'It's called "Dust and Bones", I think, and it's great. The rhythm reminds me of something like "Cherokee People" by Paul Revere and the Raiders, only really weird and rocked out. It's a weird song. But then it is by Izzy, what can I tell you?'

He obviously enjoyed working in the recording studio, I remarked. More than playing a show?

'Yeah, I do. I prefer recording to doing a live gig, unless I'm psyched for the gig. Before the gig I always don't wanna do the fucking show, and nine times out of ten I hate it. If I'm psyched it's like, let's go! But most of the time I'm mad about something, or something's going fucking wrong . . . I don't enjoy most of it at all.'

Wasn't that partly his own fault, though? Some people had accused him of having a very belligerent attitude.

'I don't know exactly . . . Something always fucking happens before a show. Something always happens and I react like a motherfucker to it. I don't like to have this pot-smoking mentality of just letting things go by. I feel like Lenny Kravitz: like, peace and love, man, for sure, or you're gonna fucking die! I'm gonna kick your ass if you mess with my garden, you know? That's always been my attitude.'

Had that attitude hardened, though, with the onset of fame?

'Meaning what exactly?'

Did he behave that way because his fame and notoriety almost forced him to? Now he did look at me.

'I've always been that way, but now I'm in a position to just be myself more. And the thing is, people do allow me to do it, whether they like it or not. It's weird.'

Did he ever take unfair advantage of that, though? Long pause.

'. . . No. No, usually I'm just an emotionally unbalanced person,' he said, smiling. 'No, really. I'm usually an emotional wreck before a show because of something else that's going on in my life. I mean, as I say, something weird just always happens to me two seconds before I'm supposed to go onstage, you know? Like I found William Rose . . . Turns out, he was murdered in '84 and buried somewhere in Illinois, and I found that out, like, two days before a show and I was fucking whacked! I mean, I've been trying to uncover this mystery since I was a little kid. I didn't even know he existed until I was a teenager, you know? Cos I was told it was the Devil that made me know what the inside of a house looked like that I'd supposedly never lived in. So I've been trying to track down this William Rose guy. Not like, I love this guy, he's my father. I just wanna know something about my heritage – weird shit like am I going to have an elbow that bugs the shit out of me when I get to forty cos of some hereditary trait? Weird shit ordinary families take for granted.'

His real father was murdered?

'Yeah, he was killed. It was probably, like, at close range, too, man. Wonderful family . . .'

I asked about the intense criticism he'd received personally over 'One in a Million'. Did he feel that his harshest critics simply missed a lot of the humour in his songs?

'To appreciate the humour in our work you gotta be able to relate to a lot of different things. And not everybody does. Not everybody can. With "One in a Million" I used a word ['nigger']. It's part of the English language whether it's a good word or not. It's a derogatory word, it's a negative word. It's not meant to sum up the entire black race, but it was directed towards black people in those situations. I was robbed, I was ripped off, I had my life threatened. And it's like, I described it in one word. And not only that, but I wanted to see the effect of a racial joke. I wanted to see what effect that would have on the world. Slash was into it . . . I mean, the song says: "Don't wanna buy none of your gold chains today". Now a black person on the Oprah Winfrey show who goes, "Oh, they're putting down black people" is going to fucking take one of these guys at the bus stop home and feed him and take care of him and let him babysit the kids? They ain't gonna be near the guy!

'I don't think every black person is a nigger. I don't care. I consider myself kinda green and from another planet or something, you know? I've never felt I fit into any group, so to speak. A black person has this 300 years of whatever on his shoulders. Okay. But I ain't got nothing to do with that. It bores me, too. There's such a thing as too sensitive. You can watch a movie about someone blowing the crap outta all these people, but you could be the most anti-violent person in the world. But you get off on this movie like, yeah! He deserved it, the bad guy got shot . . .

'Something I've noticed that's really weird about "One in a Million" is the whole song coming together took me by surprise. I wrote the song as a joke. West [Arkeen] just got robbed by two black guys on Christmas night, a few years back. He went out to play guitar on Hollywood Boulevard and he's standing there playing in front of the band and he gets robbed at knifepoint for seventy-eight cents. Couple of days later we're all sitting around watching TV – there's Duff and West and a couple other guys – and we're all bummed out, hungover and this and that. And I'm sitting' there with no money, no job, feeling guilty for being at West's house all the time sucking up the oxygen, you know? And I picked up this guitar, and I can only play, like, the top two strings, and I ended up fucking around with this little riff. It was the only thing I could play on the guitar at the time. And then I started ad-libbing some words to it as a joke. And we had just watched Sam Kinison or something on the video, you know, and I guess the humour was just sort of leaning that way or something. I don't know. But we just started writing this thing, and when I sang "*Police and niggers / That's right . . .*" that was to fuck with West's head, cos he couldn't believe I would write that. And it came out like that.

'Then the chorus came about because I like getting really far away, like "Rocket Man", Elton John. I was thinking about friends and family in Indiana, and I realised those people have no concept of who I am any more. Even the ones I was close to. Since then I've flown people out, had 'em hang out here, I've paid for everything. But there was no joy in it for them. I was smash-ing shit, going fucking nuts. And yet, trying to work. And they were going, "Man, I don't wanna be a rocker any more, not if you go through this." But at the same time, I brought 'em out here, you know, and we just hung out for a couple months – wrote songs together. Had serious talks, it was almost like being on acid cos we'd talk about the family and life and stuff, and we'd get really heavy and get to know each all over again. It's hard to try and replace eight years of knowing each other every day, and then all of a sudden I'm in this new world. Back there I was a street kid with a skateboard and no money dreaming about being in a rock band, and now all of a sudden I'm here. And it's weird for them to see their friends putting up Axl posters, you know? And it's weird for me too. So anyway, all of a sudden I came up with this chorus,

"You're one in a million", you know, and "We tried to reach you but you were much too high . . ."'

I asked about the fact that so many of his lyrics were littered with drug analogies. My point was that back in the Sixties and Seventies this would have been par for the course. But in the all-new, more hypocritical atmosphere of the uptight Eighties, such things now tended to mark the band out as different from the rest. Was that the real point, or were they all just hyper-autobiographical?

'Everybody was into dope then and those analogies are great in rock songs – Aerosmith done proved that on their old stuff, and the Stones. And drug analogies . . . the language is always, like, the hippest language. A lot of hip hop and stuff, even the stuff that's anti-drugs, a lot of the terms come directly from drug street raps. Cos they're always on top of stuff, cos they gotta change the language all the time so people don't know what they're saying, so they can keep dealing. Plus they're trying to be the hippest, coolest, baddest thing out there. It happens. So that's like, "We tried to reach you but you were much too high" – I was picturing 'em trying to call me if, like, I disappeared or died or something. And "You're one in a million" – someone said that to me real sarcastically, it wasn't, like, an ego thing. But that's the good thing, you use that "I'm one in a million" positively to make yourself get things done. But originally it was kinda like someone went, "Yeah, you're just fucking one in a million, aren't ya?" And it stuck with me.

'Then we go in the studio, and Duff plays the guitar much more aggressively than I did. Slash made it too tight and concise, and I wanted it a bit rawer. Then Izzy comes up with this electric-guitar thing. I was pushing him to come up with a cool tone, and all of a sudden he's coming up with this aggressive thing. It just happened. So suddenly it didn't work to sing the song in a low funny voice any more. We tried and it didn't work, didn't sound right, it didn't fit. And the guitar parts were so cool I had to sing it like, HURRHHHH! So that I sound like I'm totally into this.'

It certainly didn't sound like he was faking it on the record, I said.

'No, but this is just one point of view out of hundreds that I have on the situation. When I meet a black person, I deal with each situation differently. Like I deal with every person I meet, it doesn't matter.'

Had he taken any abuse personally from black people since the controversy over the song first broke?

'No, not actually. Actually, I meet a lot of black people that come up and just wanna talk about it, discuss it with me because they find it interesting. Like a black chick came up to me in Chicago and goes, "You know, I hated you cos of 'One in a Million'." And I'm like, "Oh great, here we go." Then she goes, "But I ride the subway . . ." All of a sudden she gets real serious. She says, "And I looked around one day and I know what you're talking about. So you're all right." I've got a lot of that . . .'

What about from other musicians?

'I had a big heavy conversation with Ice Cube,' he mentioned casually. One of the five-man team of rappers known as NWA [aka Niggerz Wit Attitudes] whose track "Fuck tha Police" had caused so much heat it had every cop in LA gunning for them, with Ice Cube coming up with key lines like *"I don't know if they fags or what / Search a nigga down, and grabbing his nuts . . ."*

According to Axl, Cube had written him a letter, 'wanting to work on "Welcome to the Jungle" cos he'd heard I was interested in turning it into a rap thing. He wanted to be part of it. Anyway, we ended up having this big heavy conversation about "One in a Million", and he could see where I was coming from all right. And he knows more about that shit than most.'

Finally, we let the gnarly topic of 'One in a Million' go. Axl lit another cigarette, opened another can of Coke, and we steered the conversation back to the next Guns N' Roses album. 'There's, like, seven [finished] songs right now,' he said, 'but I know by the end of the record there'll be forty-two to forty-five and I want thirty of them down.'

Was he thinking of making it a double album then?

'Well, a double album or a single, seventy-six minutes or something like that. Then I want four or five B-sides – people never listen to B-sides any more – and that'll be the back of another EP. We'll say it's B-sides, you know. Plus there should be four other songs for an EP, if we pull this off. So that's the next record and then there's the live record from the tour. If we do this right, we won't have to make another album for five years,' he added with a crooked grin.

Five years? Seriously? Why would he want to wait that long?

'It's not so much like five years to sit on our asses,' he said. 'It's, like, five years to figure out what we're gonna say next, you know? After the crowd and the people figure out how they're gonna react to this album.'

What kind of musical direction does he see the band taking on this next album then? (This was not a question one would have asked, say, Mötley Crüe or Bon Jovi, but it was clear even then that Axl always had bigger things in mind for Guns N' Roses.)

'This record will show we've grown a lot,' he said with a straight face. 'But there'll be some childish, you know, arrogant, male, false-bravado crap on there, too. But there'll also be some really heavy serious stuff.'

It had been such a long time since *Appetite for Destruction* first came out, though – nearly three years at that point – wasn't there the possibility of a backlash building up in time for the new album?

'It doesn't fucking matter. This doesn't matter, man. It's too late. If we record this album the way we wanna record this album, it could bomb, sure. But five years from now, there'll be a lot of

kids into it in Hollywood. Ten years from now, it'll be an underground thing like Aerosmith and Hanoi Rocks. The material
has strong enough lyric content and strong enough guitar parts,
you'll have no choice. It'll permeate into people's brains one way
or another. If the album doesn't sell and be successful, some day
in ten years from now someone's gonna write a record and we're
gonna be one of their main influences, and so the message is still
gonna get through. Whatever we're trying to say and the way in
which we try to say it, we pay attention to that. If we get that right,
the rest just takes care of itself. There is an audience for what
we're saying that's going through the same things we are, and, in
a way, we are leading.'

How conscious was he of their perceived role as 'leaders'?

'It's been . . . shown to me in a lot of ways. I didn't want to
accept the responsibility of it really, even though I was trying,
but I still was reluctant. Now I'm kind of into it. Because it's like,
you have a choice, man, you can grow or die. We have to do it –
we have to grow. If we don't grow, we die. We can't do the same
sludge, I'm not Paul Stanley, man! I can't fucking play sludge,
man, for fucking thirty years. Sludge, man. It's sludge rock.

'That's one of the reasons why 1989 kinda got written off.
We had to find a whole new way of working together. Everybody
got successful and it changed things, of course it did. Everybody
had the dream, when they got successful they could do what they
want, right? That turns into Slash bringing in eight songs! It's
never been done before, Slash bringing in a song first and me
writing words to it. I've done it twice with him before and we
didn't use either of those songs, out of Slash's choice. Now he's
got eight of 'em that I gotta write words to! They're bad-assed
songs, too.

'I was working on, like, writing these ballads that I feel have
really rich tapestries and stuff, and making sure each note, each
effect, is right. Cos whether I'm using a lot of instrumentation

and stuff or not, I'll still write with minimalism. But it has to be right; it has to be the right note and it has to be held the right way and it has to have the right effect, do you know what I mean?'

Actually, I was taken aback. I hadn't realised that the man who'd written 'You're Crazy' and 'Out ta Get Me' was such a perfectionist. 'What people don't understand is there was a perfectionist attitude to *Appetite*. There was a definite plan to that. We could have made it all smooth and polished. We went and did test tracks with different people and they came out smooth and polished. We did some stuff with Spencer Proffer and Geffen Records said it was too fucking radio. That's why we went with Mike Clink. We went for a raw sound because it just didn't gel having it too tight and concise.

'We knew what we were doing, and we knew this: we know the way we are onstage, and the only way to capture that energy on the record, okay, is by making it somewhat live. Doing the bass, the drums, the rhythm guitar at the same time. Getting the best track, having it a bit faster than you play it live, so that brings some energy into it. Then adding lots of vocal parts and overdubs with the guitars. Adding more music to capture ... because Guns N' Roses onstage, man, can be out to lunch! But it's like, you know, visually we're all over the place and you don't know what to expect. How do you get that on a record? That's the thing.

'That's why recording is my favourite thing, because it's like painting a picture. You start out with a shadow, or an idea, and you come up with something and it's a shadow of that. You might like it better. It's still not exactly what you pictured in your head. But you go into the studio and add all these things and you come up with something you didn't even expect. Slash will do, like, one slow little guitar fill that adds a whole different mood that you didn't expect. That's what I love. It's like you're doing a painting and you go away and come back and it's different. You allow different shading to creep in and then you go, "Wow, I got a whole different effect on this that's even heavier than what I pictured. I don't know quite what I'm on to, but I'm on it", you know?'

I noted that they were using Clink again to produce the new album. Axl was insistent, though, that they would also be bringing in extra elements to their sound that simply weren't available to them first time around.

'We're trying to find Jeff Lynne,' he said. Jeff Lynne? The mastermind behind the Electric Light Orchestra and, more recently, the Traveling Wilburys? I struggled to picture Jeff Lynne working with Guns N' Roses. Not Axl, though. Turned out he'd been an ELO fan throughout his teens.

'I want him to work on "November Rain", and there's, like, three or four possible other songs that if it works out I'd maybe like him to look at.' As an additional producer to Clink? Or to contribute some string arrangements? 'Maybe some strings, I don't know. Cos this record will be produced by Guns N' Roses and Mike Clink. I might be using synthesiser – but I'm gonna say I'm using synthesiser and what I programmed. It's not gonna be like, "Oh, you know, we do all our shows live", and then it's on tape. That's not gonna be the thing. I mean, I took electronics in school. It's like, I don't know shit about synthesisers but I can take a fucking patch-chord and shape my own waveforms and shit, you know? So now I wanna . . . you know, jump into today. I've never had the money to do it before. Maybe someone like Jeff Lynne can help me. It's a thought.'

Of course, as we know now, using synthesisers and 'jumping into today' was to become a thought that grew in Axl's mind to the exclusion of almost all others in the 1990s. For now, though, it was all about enhancing the band rather than going all the way back to the drawing board. Axl had recently told another magazine writer that if 'November Rain' wasn't recorded to his complete satisfaction he would actually quit the music business. 'That was then,' he shrugged. 'At that time it was the most important song to me.'

Had he been serious, though, about quitting the biz? 'Yeah, that's the fucking truth, all right. But the worse part of that is, like, if you wanna look at it in a negative way, I've got four of those motherfuckers now, man! I don't know how I wrote these, but I like them *better* than "November Rain"! And I'm gonna crush that motherfucking song, man! But now I've got four of them I gotta do, and they're all big songs. We play them and we get chills. It started when I came in one day with this heavy piano part, it's, like, real big, and it fits this bluesy gospel thing that was supposed to be a blues-rocker like "Buy Me a Chevrolet" by Foghat or something. Now it's turned into this thing, like "Take Another Piece of Heart" [by Janis Joplin] or something . . .'

My head was still swimming over the notion of Guns N' Roses, the most dangerous band in the world, working with Jeff Lynne, the most anonymous rock star in the world. Why him? Was Axl a closet ELO fan?

'Oh yeah, I'm an ELO fanatic! I like old ELO, *Out of the Blue*, that period. I went to see them play when they came to town when I was a kid and shit like that. I respect Jeff Lynne for being Jeff Lynne. I mean, *Out of the Blue* is an awesome album. So, one: he's got stamina. And two: he's used to working with a lot of different material. Three: he's used to working with all kinds of instrumentation for all kinds of different styles of music. Four: he wrote all his own material. Five: he produced it! That's a lot of concentration, and a lot of energy needed. Hopefully, I would like, if he's available, to have him. He's the best. But I don't know if we can get him or not.'

Intrigued as to what other artists he'd been influenced by, I asked him for his three favourite songs from his youngest days, the ones that still burned large in his musical memory. I'd become so used to Slash and Duff citing bands like Aerosmith,

Motörhead and the Sex Pistols, it hadn't occurred to me until right then that Axl might have a much broader range of inspiration to draw from.

The first song he picked was by Led Zeppelin. Very Guns N' Roses, actually, you might say. Except that the track he picked was one of Zeppelin's least acclaimed; indeed, one of the tracks they were originally lampooned for: 'D'Yer Maker', from their *Houses of the Holy* album – and a minor US hit single in the summer of 1973. Only Axl pronounced it *Dyer* Maker – until I explained that it was actually a play on the word 'Jamaica', said with an English accent, based on the song's self-conscious reggae-feel.

He stared at me. 'Wow. I never knew that. When I was in grade school I used to write down the names of, like, all the novelty songs. Like "Spiders and Snakes" [by Terry Jacks] and stuff like that. Then I heard "D'Yer Maker" and I made fun of it like crazy. I was telling everybody about this weird song I'd heard on the radio. So I'm laughing at it and this and that, but by recess in the afternoon I'm sitting in the corner with my pocket radio and I just had to hear that song again. I mean, I *had* to hear it. That was, like, the first case of "*I have to hear that song.*" I had it going through my head and I had to hear it.'

It was his belated discovery of Zeppelin's music, he said, that 'got me into hard rock'. Axl was just 11 at the time and had never heard of them before. 'I heard that and then I was hooked. After that I was Led Zeppelin all the way. That song just blew my mind. I thought, how does he write like this? How does he feel like this? I mean, cos everything around me was, like, religious and strict. Even though we were in a city we went to a country church and stuff. I mean, the language was so much different. There was no, whoa, cool vibe and stuff, like in that Zeppelin song. It was like, how did he think like that, you know?'

Axl's expression darkened, however, as he recalled how it was while trying to learn the chords to 'D'Yer Maker' on the family piano that he first got 'knocked right off the piano bench' by his stepfather. 'I would play and then I would do the drum-break on the top and just beat the shit out of the piano. Then get knocked right off. Pow!'

The second track that had influenced him most back then, he said, was 'Benny and the Jets' from the 1973 Elton John double album, *Goodbye Yellow Brick Road*. Axl said he was also a great fan of Elton John's lyricist, Bernie Taupin. So much so, he said he'd love to be able to interview Taupin about his lyrics. (Interestingly, when Taupin was later asked for his opinion of Axl's own lyrics, he claimed he was 'an admirer', particularly of the lyrics to 'Sweet Child o' Mine'.)

'Elton John is just the baddest!' Axl said grinning. 'There's nobody badder when it comes to attacking the piano and using it in a rock sense. I mean, you're gonna tell me that "Saturday Night's Alright for Fighting", or "Grow Some Funk of Your Own", or, like, "Ballad of a Well-Known Gun" or "Somebody Saved My Life Tonight" and things like that, ain't heavy songs? There's no way! Those guys wrote seven number one albums in the US from, like, '72 to '75. Bernie Taupin was twenty-five years old, writing off the top of his head, writing albums in two hours! And the guy's vocabulary and education . . .' He shook his head in awe.

'It was so amazing they decided to go rock'n'roll rather than go classical or whatever. And they blended all these different styles – amazing! And "Benny and the Jets", with the ambience and the sound and the way it's recorded, made me *want* the stage. That's the song that made me want the stage, cos it made me think about a concert and being on a stage and the way it would sound in a room . . . Plus, it just reminded me of the glam scene that was going on then around America and the clubs that I would read about in the old *Creem* magazine . . . Elton John's singing is amazing and that piano solo can't be touched. It's an amazing record. Then when I got the piano book and was trying to learn the song, I discovered the guy's playing ten fingers of the weirdest chords in the world, you know? It's like, what made him think to hit this combination of five notes that makes the initial bomp-bomp-bomp? It's not just, like, a major note, it's all these weird combinations. He just pulls stuff off that nobody else does.'

Along with Billy Joel, he said, Elton John was the major influence on his own songwriting style. 'I've played piano in a style influenced by Elton John and Billy Joel. But it's minimalistic [sic]. I know what I can and what I can't do, so I aim it real carefully. But it's basically influenced off Elton John's attack – and his singing. If you want to learn how to sing all different styles, try singing like Elton John – anything from the blues on. It amazes me that radio in America doesn't give Elton John the space that they give Led Zeppelin, the Beatles and the Stones. You know, you don't have the Elton John Hour, yet you can have 400,000 people going to Central Park to see Elton John, and you're gonna have sold-out tours all over the country. I don't understand it . . . I haven't met a group of people that after you've played everything all night and you put on an Elton John record, that don't go, "Cool . . ." and kick back, and like it that the album's on. Any of the first seven or eight albums, you put one of those on and everyone just relaxes . . . It makes you feel good cos of the vibrations in the styles of the songs, the styles of writing. And the way they take you so many different places on, like, one album.'

Axl's third and last choice of track that most influenced him from his childhood was the most surprising: 'I'm Not in Love', a Number 1 single in 1974, in both Britain and America, for 10cc. 'For me,' he said, 'that song goes back and forth along with "Layla" by Derek and the Dominoes and Metallica's "Fade to Black". As weird a cross as it may seem, those three songs are my favourite songs of all time. But we were talking about when I was young. "Layla" I didn't get into till I was a bit older.'

The fascination for 10cc had begun, he said, at a drugstore he used to stop in on his way to piano lessons as a teenager. 'It was very nice and conservative but had this liquor section that you weren't allowed into unless you were twenty-one – they had magazines like *Playboy* and stuff like that. So I would go there early and I'd hang out for hours in this drugstore. Like, steal a look at these magazines. I was really into *Oui* magazine. The photography was amazing. And I'm just discovering girls and stuff like that and I'm, like, going with the girls in my school and stuff, in my class. But they're boring. But in these magazines, like, these are women and they're great, you know? All right!

'Well, "I'm Not in Love" was always on in this place. And the production is so amazing. It's this guy who is in love, but yeah, doesn't want to be in love, or whatever. Doesn't want to deal with it. He's contradicting himself all the way through the record. Plus, it's, like, the coolest attitude. It's, like . . .' He began to sing softly: 'I keep your picture . . . on the wall . . . It hides a nasty stain . . . that's lying there . . .' He stopped, came back down again. 'That's so, like, nonchalant, so cool. But the production and the song has always stuck. Whenever I'm having a heavy emotional situation, or meeting someone, it's like, I'll get in the car and I'll just turn on the ignition and that song will always be on the radio! I mean, that song messes with my life, man.'

We settled back again, listening to the tape Axl had been playing in the background while we talked. The volume was low, I couldn't make out who it was, but I recognised the buzz. 'Cheap Trick,' Axl said. '*In Colour*, featuring Rick "The Dick" Nielsen. What a fucking asshole! I love Cheap Trick, too. It's kinda funny now, cos I listen to it and just laugh at him.'

Why? What had happened?

'There was a thing in *Rolling Stone* where he said he fucking decked Slash! He didn't deck Slash! Do you think anyone is gonna fucking deck Slash when Doug Goldstein is standing right there between them? It's not gonna happen.'

It was like we were back to Vince Neil again. Why did everyone want to tell the world they'd punched one of Guns N' Roses?

'Because Guns N' Roses has this reputation for being bad, you know, the new bad boys in town, and so, like, hey, man, it perpetuates down to fucking Rick Nielsen wanting to get back in good with the youth market by claiming he's badder than Guns N' Roses, you know? If he had any real balls, he'd apologise to Slash in the press. Not in person, he can come up to me and say he's sorry all he wants, it doesn't mean shit till he says it in the press.

'Now, Bowie's a different situation, because Bowie hasn't talked to the press about our bust-up. So Bowie can apologise to me, and then when they see photos of me and him together they'll go, "Fuck, we tried to start a war and look at these guys, they're hangin' out!" Ha! That's cool, you know? Like Jagger was supposed to have told me off and the next thing you know I'm on-stage singing with him – that fucked with a lot of 'em. I mean, it's either somebody kicked our ass or it's how some chick is scared I'm gonna come kill her cat. I mean, I could make a joke about it, but . . .'

I didn't want to lose the good feeling we'd established so I pushed him for some funny stories about other old rock stars he'd met. Keith Richards?

'I asked him about Billy Idol ripping the idea off for the *Rebel Yell* album off him, kinda joking. And he goes' – adopts the tie-dyed Cockney again – "Stole it off my fucking night-table, he did!" I thought that was great.'

Unprompted this time he went into a story about meeting John Entwistle of The Who. 'I said I'd always wondered about these rumours about "Baba O'Riley", you know. Like for the keyboard parts they went and got brainwaves and then programmed them through a computer, you know? So I asked Entwistle, and

Entwistle's annihilated out of his mind, right? He's in his own little world, and he looks at me and goes, "Brainwaves? What fucking brainwaves? Townshend's got no fucking brainwaves!"' He sniggered. 'Then I asked him about the time he was supposed to have shot up all his gold records, and he said, "I'll let you in on a secret, mate. Those were all Connie Francis's gold records. I fucking stole 'em!" I said, "Wow, okay, I've had enough of this guy. I can't deal with him any more!" He was just fucking lit and ready to go . . .'

It was now near dawn. Nearly time to leave, surely. As a parting shot I told Axl how – this spat with Vince Neil notwithstanding – relaxed he seemed right now, not a bit like his image. 'I'm happy to kick back tonight and sit around jawing,' he said, 'because today everything is under control. Tomorrow – wait and see – it's fucking over! Something will come up.'

He went on: 'There's only one thing left, and that's this damn album, man. That's it. I mean, we may do another record but it's like, Guns N' Roses doesn't fully function, nothing ever really happens, to its utmost potential, unless it's a kamikaze run. Unless it's like, this is it, man! Like, fuck it, let's go down in fucking flames with this motherfucker! That's how we are about the record, everybody's like, we're just gonna do this son of a bitch . . .'

And then what? What was the grand plan after that?

'The main thing about the next record is this is our dream, to get these songs out there into the public. Then once we get out there we'll fight for them with the business side and stuff. But at this point that's not what's important. What's important is the recording of the songs. If the business comes down really hard on us in a weird way, then we'll make our choices – do we wanna deal with this, or do we not wanna fucking deal with this?

'The record will sell a certain amount of copies the minute it comes out anyway, and we could live off that for the rest of our lives and record our records on small independent labels, it doesn't matter. I mean, that's not in the plans, but, ultimately, it just doesn't matter, you know? It's all down to what we want to deal with. Do we wanna be giving everything that we feel we have inside of ourselves, to do the shows, to our top potential? Yes, we do. But I don't choreograph things. I don't know when I'm gonna slam down on my knees or whatever. It's like, you have to ask yourself, do I wanna give all that, and have someone fucking spitting in my face? Does it mean that much to me? No! I dig the songs. If you don't want them, fine. I don't have to give them to you.'

He so often threatened to walk away from Guns N' Roses, though, it was becoming like the boy who cried wolf. Could he ever really leave all this behind?

'If I wanted to badly enough, sure. This is all right, in bits and pieces, but whether it'll take up all the chapters in the book of my life, I don't know. I would like to record for a long time . . . I have to make this album. Then it doesn't matter. This album is the album I've always been waiting on. Our second album is the album I've been waiting on since before we got signed. We were planning out the second album before we started work on the first one. But as much as it means to me, if it bombs, if that happens, yeah, I'm sure I'll be bummed business-wise and let down or whatever, but at the same time it doesn't matter. It's like, I got it out there. That's the artistic thing taken care of. Then I could walk away . . .'

What about the money, could he walk away from that?

'I'd like to make the cash off the touring, and then I'd like to walk away knowing that I can support my kids, for whatever they want, for the rest of my life, you know? And that I can still donate to charities. I'd like to have that security. I've never known any security in my whole life. The financial aspect is just to get that security. If I have that in the bank I can live off the interest and still have money to spend on whatever – including, top of the list, the welfare of my own immediate and future family.'

As for the next album, he said, 'I just hope the people are into it, you know? I think that the audience will have grown enough, though. It's been three years – they've gone through three years of shit too, so hopefully they'll be ready to relate to some new things. When you're writing about real life, not fantasy, you have to take time to live your own life first and allow yourself to go through different phases. Now I think there's enough different sides of Guns N' Roses that when the album is finally released no one will know what to think, let alone us! Like, what are they trying' to say? Sometimes even I don't fucking know . . .'

9

THIS CLOSE TO HEAVEN

Tuesday, 17 September 1991. The clock was edging towards midnight in New York as Donald Trump sat in his limousine, accompanied by five young women, apparently models. He liked to travel in style although his business empire had just hit a bump in the road and he'd recently had to sell his 282-foot superyacht, the *Trump Princess*, to a member of the Saudi royal family, for a reported $110 million. Hearts bled for him. The limo was headed for Tower Records on the corner of East 4th and Broadway. Outside the store, lines had begun to form – but not to gawp at Trump. He, like all of the others who'd gathered, was there to take part in an American phenomenon: the simultaneous release of two studio albums by Guns N' Roses. The Donald, as usual, was in the business of putting himself where it was at, and where it was at in America right then was buying the new records by Guns N' Roses. If there was a single symbolic moment that illustrated best how far the band had come and how quickly, it was the shift in circumstances between the emergence of *Appetite for Destruction* – number 182 with an anchor on the *Billboard* chart in the week it came out – and *Use Your Illusion*, volumes I and II, which were not so much albums as a cultural phenomenon, one for the billionaires and future presidential candidates as well as the kids on the street.

On the opposite coast, Slash was dreaming of escape. What should have been a moment of triumph had been darkened by the preceding months. He had booked a safari holiday to Tanzania, leaving on 17 September from LAX. 'On the way to the airport, I stopped by Tower Records at midnight, stopped by the back door to see people on the stroke of midnight file in to buy the record, just to witness the reality of where the band was at,' he told the writer Jon Hotten in 2011. 'Suddenly I was a member of a group that had become the very thing I was a fan of since I was fourteen or fifteen years old . . . We had become all of that and more. I was watching people buy the record through the two-way mirror that I myself had been arrested from for stealing cassettes years prior, so it was really a magic little moment. Then I took off and went to Africa and got away from it. I went out to the Masai Mara for a couple of weeks, and that's about as far removed from rock star as you can get.'

When he returned from Africa, *Use Your Illusion II* had been purchased 770,000 times and stood at Number 1 on the Billboard Chart. *Use Your Illusion I* had sold 685,000 and occupied the Number 2 position. Guns N' Roses were the biggest band in the world, standing on a summit that every kid in every band across the globe wanted to climb. 'Answered prayers cause more tears than those that remain unanswered,' Truman Capote had once said. Guns N' Roses were about to find out why.

The simultaneous release of the *Use Your Illusion* albums was a moment – perhaps *the* moment – not just for Guns N' Roses but for the Los Angeles scene of the 1980s and early 1990s. There was little to compare it to. Of the city's most famous and significant rock'n'roll bands, Van Halen's second album, *Van Halen II*, had been recorded and released within 14 months of their debut, peaked at Number 6 on the Billboard 100 and was followed a year later by *Women and Children First*. They would not register a Number 1 album until their seventh album, *5150*, made it in 1986. Mötley Crüe, almost as influential, saw their second record, 1985's *Shout at the Devil*, just about break the Billboard Top 20. *Dr Feelgood*, their fifth studio album, was their first Number 1 album, in the October of 1989, by which time *Appetite for Destruction* had already enjoyed a couple of stints at the summit. In a way, the entire LA rock scene seemed to have been building towards something like *Use Your Illusion*, a peak cultural event that encapsulated all of the hedonistic madness and lust for immortality that fuelled the era; an event that would stick it to all of the sniffy critics and guardians of taste who had dismissed this kind of rock as second-rate, the airport novel of the music world, simply by its sheer scale.

'The momentum you try and create then creates its own momentum,' says Alan Niven of the process. 'If you're Sisyphus and you're rolling the rock up the side of the mountain it's hard freaking work. Then you get the rock to the peak of the mountain and suddenly the damn thing rolls away from you. Your labour turns into lost control.'

Niven had been shrewd enough to realise how difficult following *Appetite* would be. The record was a phenomenon, an unrepeatable statement of intent. *GN'R Lies* had been a clever stopgap and had bought them some time, but now Niven had a laundry list of concerns and worries, at the top of which was the physical condition of his charges. The press had taken to calling them 'the most dangerous band in the world', a sobriquet that the fans lapped up but that Niven knew was close to becoming a terrible reality. 'One of the things I'm proud of is that at least none of the band members died on my watch,' he reflects. 'That took a lot of effort. The bottom line is, you have to help them fight the battle, but only they can win the war . . .'

Slash was equally candid: 'I went from a basic gypsy troubadour-type kid without anything through years of touring with Guns and all those experiences just basically living on the road and never really living anywhere else, and then just sort of thrown into superstardom and not knowing how to handle that, and not knowing . . . not having any domestic skills for living at home. Just not knowing which way to turn and not necessarily knowing whether I was happy or not. And then pulling into a major drug depression and having to get it all back together to go in and make the record and being completely disjointed.'

The sense of dislocation was palpable, the dream so real . . . now Los Angeles was turning a new face towards them. 'We all bought our houses and we all had our friends, and our friends would be saying, "*You're* the glue that holds the band together,"' said Duff McKagan. 'And we're all getting that. You don't know what to think. It's never happened to you before. The record finally broke in the States a year after everywhere else. All of a sudden we came back to LA, and everyone in the clubs, they're all dressed like us. Imagine coming back and you're a cultural phenomenon. People are dressing like you. Your music is being played on the radio all the time. You walk into a grocery store and you're on the cover of *Rolling Stone*, and people see that magazine cover and they see you and they're freaking out. This is in the grocery store I've always gone in . . .'

By the start of 1990 they were in varying states of physical and spiritual disrepair. Worst hit was Steven, whose sunny SoCal exterior hid anxiety and pain that even the industrial amounts of narcotics he was now taking could not quell. 'He was suffering the worst and couldn't pull it back,' said Duff. 'We had this unwritten sort of code – pull it back when it's sensible, when it's time to record or time to play a show. Pull it back. Check yourself. There had been a few times where we'd check each other. You know, "Hey, dude . . ." And that's all you'd have to say. It was a sort of honour amongst thieves. But Steven wasn't able to pull it back time and time again. Slash and I told him quite a few times,

"Dude, it's us talking to you. If we're telling you you're getting too fucked up, you're getting too fucked up. Look who's talking to you. We're worried about you. We're the guys that everyone else is worried about, and we're worried about you." It was really heartbreaking.'

During the early weeks of 1990 word was Steven had actually been fired, for his failure to comply with Axl's onstage demands at the Stones show to quit 'dancing with Mr Brownstone'. Then, the last time I spoke to Axl – the day I phoned to check he was still okay with me going ahead and publishing his broadside against Vince Neil – I took the opportunity to ask about Steven. First he's out of the band, then he's back again . . . What's the story right now, I asked? 'He is back in the band,' said Axl. 'He was definitely out of the band. He wasn't necessarily fired, we worked with Adam Maples [of the Sea Hags], we worked with Martin Chambers [of The Pretenders], and Steven did the Guns N' Roses thing and got his shit together. And it worked, and he did it, and he plays the songs better than any of 'em, just bad-assed, and he's GN'R. And so if he doesn't blow it, we're going to try the album with him, and the tour and, you know, we've worked out a contract with him . . .'

A contract? Stipulating that he had to stop taking drugs or he was out of the band? 'Yeah, exactly. But, you know, it's worked out. It's finally back on and we're hoping it continues. It's only been a few days so far. It's only been since Thursday last week, and he's doing great. We're all just hoping it continues.'

A few weeks later, on 7 April, Guns N' Roses appeared at Farm Aid, the now annual benefit concert to raise money for family farmers in the US, spurred on by Bob Dylan's comments at Live Aid in 1985 saying he hoped some of the money would help American farmers in danger of losing their farms through mortgage debt. Hosted by Willie Nelson, the 1990 show was televised live from Indianapolis in Indiana, an hour's drive from Axl's home town of Lafayette. It was important to Axl to make this a good one. Coming onstage in a cowboy hat and shades, Axl began by telling the crowd: 'I'd like to dedicate this performance to my Uncle Bob Rose . . .'

But the 13-minute set was a shambles. The band hadn't played live since opening for the Stones six months before. They hadn't rehearsed either. Steven Adler, who was clearly having trouble, later claimed the band had deliberately sabotaged his performance, in order to have a reason to fire him permanently.

'They weren't clueing me into new songs or even telling me what they were playing.' Steven had made a theatrical dive for his drum riser at the start of the show – and missed it by four feet. The band started with one of their best new numbers, 'Civil War', written by Axl, Slash and Duff, which Steven had been struggling with in the studio and had never played all in one go with the band. It provided for a very shaky start. Things got even worse, though, with the second number, a cover of the UK Subs' 'Down on the Farm', which Steven later claimed he had never even *heard* before. At the end of the short set, Axl yelled, 'Good fucking night!' threw the mike to the ground and strode off, clearly unhappy.

Steven Adler was officially fired from Guns N' Roses in July 1990.

If the best rock'n'roll bands are like gangs – us against the world – then this one was about to break up, losing something that, once gone, could not be recovered. In a gang that traded on its dangerous reputation, Steven Adler had become too big a risk. Axl had once said, 'We're a bad-boy band. We're not afraid to go to excess with substances, sexually and everything else. A lot of people are afraid to be that way. We are not.' But even bad-boy bands had their limits, and the arrival of smack as their drug of choice was the end of any kind of innocence. Their decadence was now of the darkest kind. 'The lifestyle was a huge part of it,' Adler explained. 'It's like, sex and rock'n'roll, that was the lifestyle

I was living, right from the start. It was never heavy drugs at first. The heroin thing didn't come until after we were successful. I was a big pothead. That's what I liked, the three Ps, man – Pot, Pussy and Percussion . . . We had waaay more fun before we got success than after.

'Heroin, that was something that Slash was doing,' Adler went on, 'because we came off this huge tour – 20,000 to 30,000 people per night – and we were waiting to go into the studio, and Axl kept delaying it . . . It was just something people were doing. I don't blame my decision to try it on Slash, I just wanted to try it, even though I'd never really liked drugs. Izzy was doing it, and Slash, and I thought, well, let me try it. And the thing is, the first two times I tried it, I never used a needle. I was like, "No way", and they said, "You don't need to use a needle, you can just smoke it . . ."

'The first two times, I was so sick, and as sick as it sounds, I did it again. I was waking up every day, and not having something wonderful and exciting like a gig to do, I started to get down, a real depression, like a Valium down. And time flies when you get on [heroin] . . . that's why I got into it. I kind of took it to make the time go by. Getting addicted,' he somewhat naively insisted, 'was the last thing I expected to happen.'

'It was totally regrettable,' said Slash. 'But the band finally got to the place where we wanted to make a record, which was a hard enough place to get to . . . we're talking about the span of about a year, which to us was like a lifetime, and Steven . . . we could not get him back to front. We were resigned to the fact that he wasn't going to be able to do it in the time frame that we needed to get going, because we might miss the bus. We might fall apart again and take another year to get it together.'

Every time Steven now sat at a drum kit, it seemed as though he blew it. He was too out of it to function, even in the louche, loose style that he'd always played in. Slash, Duff and their producer, Mike Clink, found themselves on the sharp end, stuck in the studio trying to work on the nuts and bolts of getting basic tracks for the songs down with a drummer who could no longer perform. The clock was running and the bills were growing.

'Steven is not the world's best drummer by any stretch,' Alan Niven conceded. 'But he had a quality that he brought to the band that anybody would accept as being part of the magic. He had such an enthusiasm for what he was doing. Duff even had to show him what to play sometimes. Let's be real – Steven's not going to be sitting in with Chick Corea any time soon, but exuberance is just the right word for him. So did we want Steven to go? Fuck no. Replacing people in bands is a pain in the ass. It changes the dynamic personally and musically. We tried for the longest time to give Steven a vision and a function. There was a combination of factors going on. One was that he could just not connect to the kind of material that Axl was writing. "Coma", "Estranged" . . . he'd just roll his eyes. And, of course, the fact that he had no control over his heroin habit.'

Adler's recollections of the time are harrowing enough, even through the haze with which he recalled them: 'Man, I was fucked up, and I have never denied that, I couldn't really deny it because it was pretty fucking obvious . . . But I wasn't the only one. I remember one day Slash called me to go to the studio and play "Civil War", I think it was. I'd been given an opiate blocker by a doctor. I still had opiates in my system and it made me so sick. I must have tried, like, twenty times to play it, but I couldn't. I was very weak and I didn't have my timing. Slash and Duff were shouting at me and telling me I was fucked up.'

The band had one card left to play. A legal document was drawn up – the contract Axl had mentioned to me – that put him on a 30-day probation designed to allow him time to kick his heroin habit. Failure to do so would result in his sacking. Steven Adler signed it on 28 March 1990. 'We were like, what do we do?'

recalled Duff. 'We had a band lawyer, and it was like, okay, you've got to warn him formally. This will scare him. You're gonna get six months and you've got to do this and that. The lawyer's like, okay, we'll try that. We really thought that he'd pull it back and he didn't. All the way up to getting Matt Sorum to play on the record, we thought that would get Steven back. Then we realised, it's just not going to happen. It's just not. I wouldn't be being honest if I told you I knew exactly the point. I don't remember exactly when it was but it was right in there. I just thought for a while, he's going to come through this cycle. I'm not sitting here twenty years later in judgement. We all had our battles.'

'In no way was it minor,' says Alan Niven of the decision to put Adler on probation, and of the drummer's inability to recognise the threat. 'It was incredibly painful and frustrating. I've got to confess I'm still capable of a flash of red-hot anger with Steven at that. I have an understanding of why and what happened to him. But it was survivable. We spent a lot of time with Steven trying to get him through it and I resent the fact that he plays the victim, I think that's bullshit. You know, own up, Steven. Be responsible for your own decisions and actions. You let us down, all of us. And we got to the point where putting him on probation didn't work. This whole cockamamie thing about "they didn't pay me my royalties" is bullshit. He was paid his royalties and in fact he was paid composer royalties that he didn't deserve. That was a courtesy bestowed on him by the rest of the band in a sense of all for one and one for all. If everybody's sharing the writing credits, nobody is going to be trying to foist bad ideas on another person. You can hold that creative magic together and not let that kind of argument undo it. When you start with a band, two things are going to fuck you up, and the first is fighting over composer royalties – mechanicals, as they're known. The other is your girlfriends and wives. They'll fuck you up worse than drugs.'

By July the situation had become untenable, not that Adler seemed to have grasped the fact. 'I got a call a few weeks after that and I had to go to the office and there was all these stacks of papers, contracts, for me to sign, and I realised that I was being fired . . .'

For many years, Adler's departure has been linked to a dark rumour concerning Erin Everly, who had wed Axl on 28 April. (Everly would claim in a 1994 interview with *People* magazine that the proposal had been somewhat unconventional – Rose arrived at her apartment at 4 a.m. with a gun in his car and threatened to kill himself unless she married him. They drove to Las Vegas that same night.) Adler is said to have found himself in the middle of this volatile relationship when Everly overdosed at his house (an event he acknowledged in his 2010 autobiography).

Axl confirmed in a 1992 interview with Del James that Everly had been found 'naked', and been taken to the emergency room. 'I had to spend a night with her in an intensive-care unit because her heart had stopped thanks to Steven,' Axl told James. 'She was hysterical, and he shot her up with a speedball. She had never done jack shit as far as drugs go, and he shoots her up with a mixture of heroin and cocaine? I kept myself from doing anything to him. I kept the man from being killed by members of her family. I saved him from having to go to court, because her mother wanted him held responsible for his actions.'

Two decades later, Alan Niven addressed the full extent of the rumour directly: 'Axl was fucking convinced that Erin had been overdosed and raped,' he said. 'Well, that's going to go down well, isn't it? That was a really clever choice that you made there, Steven, and it really helped everybody. Is it any surprise we got to the point that we had to seriously consider getting someone else? Did we have any choice?'

Whatever the full extent of the story, the incident further loosened the bonds that had kept the original five together. Axl's marriage would not survive the year. Erin claimed that he first threatened divorce a month after the wedding, and then two months after that, she alleged that the singer beat her so badly she was hospitalised. In September she fell pregnant – 'I thought it could have been a cure for Axl' – but she miscarried and, she said, had to sell her Jeep to play her medical bills. The marriage was annulled in January 1991.

Izzy Stradlin was the first to realise what the band had lost musically with Steven Adler's sacking. '[It was] a big difference,' he said in a 1992 interview. 'The first time I realised what Steve did for the band was when he broke his hand in Michigan [in 1987]. Tried to punch through a wall and busted his hand. So we had Fred Coury come in from Cinderella for the Houston show. Fred played technically good and steady, but the songs sounded just awful. They were written with Steve playing the drums and his sense of swing was the push and pull that give the songs their feel. When that was gone, it was just . . . unbelievable, weird. Nothing worked. I would have preferred to continue with Steve, but we'd had two years off and we couldn't wait any longer. It just didn't work for Slash to be telling Steve to straighten out. He wasn't ready to clean up.'

Nonetheless it was Slash who found Adler's replacement, the hard-hitting, 29-year-old Californian Matt Sorum, who got his break drumming on Tori Amos's debut record, *Y Kant Tori Read* (a foray into soft rock that Amos has subsequently requested not be reissued), which in turn led to a spell with The Cult, then in the midst of their reinvention from self-consciously mystical North of England Goths to balls-out arena rockers with a sound so monolithic it made AC/DC sound like Madonna. Sorum was a rocker through and through, a good fit temperamentally, who grew up admiring 'Keith Moon and Roger Taylor – guys who drove around in Rolls-Royces with bimbos, drinking champagne and driving their cars into swimming pools. That's my idea of a rock star; that's why I did it. I grew up idolizing rock'n'roll debauchery, sex, drugs and rock'n'roll party.'

'I remembered seeing Matt with The Cult and thinking that he was the only good drummer [I'd heard], and calling him and having him come down,' Slash said. 'We started rehearsing this material and next thing you know we're in the studio. Getting the basic tracks together so that we could play them front to back actually happened really quickly. But that's a hell of a lot of material and it was an epic journey.' Alan Niven took a different view. 'Matt is a competent drummer but he couldn't replicate Steven. He has a great consistency but he also has a heavy hand. He cannot match the feel that Steven had.'

As Izzy had predicted, the pulse of the band changed with Sorum's arrival, and yet he fitted in in more ways than one – 'Here I was replacing the drug addict drummer, right? But he did heroin and I had cocaine' – and he offered momentum at a time when things had stalled badly. 'That was one of the reasons why it was okay to let Steven go, because I'd been through so much in such a short amount of time in order to get to the point where it was time to go into the studio,' said Slash. 'I had to clean my act up and I was ready to go. That's really my whole purpose in life, to play and record and to tour. I was 200 per cent locked into it.'

Yet the doubts and the cracks were growing. 'We make choices every day,' Alan Niven told Jon Hotten in 2011. 'With *Use Your Illusion*, Slash made a choice and I totally understood it, and to this day I don't agree with it.' Speaking now, he recalls an event that made him understand that the politics of the band had shifted irrevocably from the original one-for-all gang mentality. One Friday night when he and Slash went to see Albert Collins, the blues guitarist, play, 'and I came crawling home on the Sunday afternoon so jagged on coke I had to take an X [ecstasy pill] to get down.'

At one point on that lost weekend they were sitting alone

together in Slash's Laurel Canyon house. 'Here's the thing,' says Niven, 'you can never remember a single conversation you have on coke. But I remember very clearly what Slash and I talked about. The main thrust was he was really upset about how things were going with *Use Your Illusion*. He felt that one song of that kind of epic style might be appropriate, but so many? I was trying to persuade him that he really needed to articulate that to Axl. He looked at me and he said, "My dad has got a cupboard full of gold and platinum records and he doesn't have a pot to piss in. I'll do what I have to do to get the cheque. I'll compromise." And that's where he folded. From then on, Axl was in charge.'

At the same time, the distance between Alan Niven and Axl Rose was growing, too, something exacerbated by the fact that Doug Goldstein's relationship with Axl was drawing closer. Slash could see that another power struggle was developing. 'That was a volatile situation that was going to explode at some point,' he said. 'Alan wasn't going to take Axl's shit and Axl could not stand that, so it was a battle. I think in hindsight, although it wouldn't have been any fun, but all we could have done differently was just to refuse Axl everything that he ever wanted. I don't think it would have been very productive, but, all things considered, what we ended up doing was going along with a lot of stuff just in order to be able to continue on, which built a monster.'

At first, with Sorum in for Adler, the speed that the material began to come together covered over any cracks. Although the entire process would take nearly two years and seven recording studios, one of the most remarkable elements of *Use Your Illusion* is how quickly the basic tracks were laid down. But then the different visions for how the album should sound became manifest. 'With a new drummer we did thirty-six songs in thirty-six days so we weren't fucking around,' Slash recalled. 'After the basic tracks were done, I'd spend three weeks doing guitars, which for thirty songs was actually pretty fast. I was sometimes doing two songs in one day. But everything hit a brick wall when it came to doing the synthesiser stuff, and I never agreed with doing the synthesiser stuff anyway. Although I think some of it is brilliant, it was part of the new way, which was the beginning of the end. That was the beginning of the whole process taking for ever. It was like a lot of days were not working, some days it was working, and most of the record was finished. It didn't really need all the rest of it. That was the biggest disagreement for me.'

Izzy exiled himself, also distanced by the scale of the recording. 'I did the basic tracks, then he [Slash] did his tracks, like a month or two by himself. Then came Axl's vocal parts. I went back to Indiana . . .' Axl was fixating on 'November Rain' and 'Don't Cry', big songs into which he'd poured some of his deepest feelings. 'Axl had this vision he was going to create,' said Matt Sorum. 'We'd start at noon, the work ethic was cool. There was a lot of alcohol around, but the heroin thing had definitely subsided at that point – Slash had quit, Izzy had quit. We were dabbling in cocaine and partying rituals. It was candlelight in the studio. You'd look and there's Sean Penn and Bruce Springsteen hanging out, and supermodels like Naomi Campbell and Elle McPherson. It was like a Fellini movie! But it was never really cool to do a lot of drugs in front of Axl. Even though he'd be on some pills, like, "Yeah, man, I just took a bunch of Halcion." I did some coke with him once and he talked for about fucking ten hours! I never did coke with him again . . .' But the sessions became more drawn out as Axl strived to match the music with the versions in his head: 'It was later nights. We'd start at six or seven. Axl would want to do "November Rain" and "Don't Cry", his songs.'

'Axl's a perfectionist, that's what makes him great. The end product's great, but it gets maddening to work with that person,' Duff McKagan said of those apparently endless studio nights. 'There's no hashing out with them. "November Rain", in particular, the song was torturing him. He was happy he was finally finished with it. It wasn't really characteristic of the band.'

In fact, as Axl had suggested in our interview, 'November Rain', a long piano ballad with a tender lyric that would go on to be a Number 2 hit single, was set up to be the keynote track of the entire album. While it sounded like the kind of tune that a band with the commercial leeway to indulge their artistic whims would cut, Axl in fact had a fairly final version of it as far back as 1983. Tracii Guns remembered the song well: 'When we were doing that EP for LA Guns, like '83 . . . He was playing "November Rain" – and it was called "November Rain" – way back then. It was the only thing he knew how to play, but it was his. He'd go, "Someday this song is gonna be really cool." And I'd go, "It's cool now." "But it's not done" . . . And, like, anytime we'd be at a hotel or anywhere there'd be a piano, he'd just kinda play that music. And I'd go, "When are you gonna finish that already, you know?" And he'd go, "I don't know what to do with it."' While according to Slash, there was a 20-minute version of the song that went back to their pre-*Appetite* days when Nazareth's guitarist, Manny Charlton, produced a demo for them. 'It was on acoustic guitar and piano,' Slash recollected. 'It was really epic.'

It is tempting to look back at the *Use Your Illusion* material now through the prism of what came next and see Axl Rose taking control via the grandeur of his songs, living out all of the rock star fantasies he had as a boy in Indiana, ambition vividly drawn through every overblown moment. If *Appetite* was a record made by hungry street hustlers, *Use Your Illusion* was a dispatch from high in the Hollywood Hills, with all the decadence of the mansions that clung to the canyon edges, way out of reach of the kids on the Strip.

Alan Niven had some insight into where Axl's urge to reshape the band was coming from: 'When he was younger, he played piano and composed on piano. I'd lay a bet that a record like

Goodbye Yellow Brick Road [by Elton John] had a huge impact on him. He aspired to that level, and anybody who has a hero and aspires to match a hero also in their heart hopes to exceed their hero and validate their presence. So I think he always had that in his bloodstream. The big construction was something he always wanted to do, but I think it's ill-advised to do an album that's over-weighted with material like that unless you're going to do it utterly seamlessly, as someone like David Gilmour does.'

'November Rain' and 'Estranged' came from that place: big, ambitious pieces with themes that hinted at Axl's obsessive nature: '"November Rain" is a song about having to deal with unrequited love,' he explained. '"Estranged" is acknowledging it and being there. And having to figure out what to fucking do, it's like being catapulted out into the universe and having no choice about it and having to figure out what the fuck are you gonna do because the things you wanted and worked for just cannot happen.'

The white-hot anger so apparent on *Appetite* and onstage was still there too, a rage which he didn't seem to be able to contain artistically. Alongside 'November Rain' and 'Estranged' and 'Don't Cry' came 'Get in the Ring' (which targeted by name this writer, plus the American music journalists Andy Secher and Bob Guccione Jr), 'Right Next Door to Hell' (inspired by Axl's neighbour Gabriella Kantor) and 'Back Off Bitch' (which went all the way back to his days with his former girlfriend Gina Siler), songs that sought to settle explicit scores from a public platform from which their subjects couldn't possibly respond. It was an area in which he already had form.

'I thought they were tiresome, small-minded and mean,' says Alan Niven. 'I'd already been through "One in a Million" with him. I'd backed him on that because I accepted his motivation was a sincere representation of his mind-set at the time he was arriving [in LA]. But with the meanness and the vitriol – if you're going to apply it, apply it to something big. He'd make his attacks on his next-door neighbour or journalists, and I'm thinking, "Axl, this is the scope of your world?" There was a schizophrenia . . . And I had a band here of prodigious skill, spirit and intelligence. When Axl played "Civil War" for me, I was absolutely over the moon. The simple cleverness of saying, what's so civil about war? Clarity of expression. Great song. Then he plays me "Right Next Door to Hell" . . .'

Axl spoke about the motivation for writing so directly a year after the album's release: '"Back Off Bitch" is a ten-year-old song. I've been doing a lot of work and found out I've had a lot of hatred for women. Basically, I've been rejected by my mother since I was a baby. She's picked my stepfather over me ever since he was around and watched me get beaten by him. She stood back most of the time. Unless it got too bad, and then she'd come and hold you afterward. She wasn't there for me. My grandmother had a problem with men. I've gone back and done the work and found out I overheard my grandma going off on men when I was four. And I've had problems with my own masculinity because of that. I was pissed off at my grandmother for her problem with men and how it made me feel about being a man. So I wrote about my feelings in the songs.'

Other titles included Duff's 'Why Do You Look at Me When You Hate Me' – about to be transmogrified at the last minute into the blistering 'Get in the Ring' – and 'So Fine', Duff's 'ode to Johnny Thunders', which he sang lead on à la Sid Vicious; Axl's beloved epic, 'November Rain'; another Elton John-style, autobiographical Axl ballad called 'Estranged'; the swaggering, Stonesy 'Shotgun Blues', allegedly about Vince Neil; and another ten-minute Axl-penned epic co-written with Slash about a real-life overdose, called 'Coma', replete with the sound of a defibrillator, hired in for the occasion, and some authentic ECG beeps; Izzy's self-explanatory 'You Ain't the First' and 'Pretty Tied Up', about a real-life dominatrix he knew 'down on Melrose', plus 'Dust and Bones' and 'Double Talkin' Jive' (both featuring lead vocals from the guitarist); Slash and Izzy's 'Perfect Crime' and a clutch of sneering Izzy and Axl rockers, 'You Could be Mine', originally from the *Appetite* sessions, its bitter little couplet '*With your bitch-slap rapping and your cocaine tongue / you get nothing done*' appearing in the *Appetite* inner sleeve artwork (an indication of how close it came to making the cut) and '14 Years' (again, featuring Izzy on vocals). Then there were the more full-on Slash and Axl tracks like 'Don't Damn Me' (also featuring some lyrics by Axl's old Lafayette pal David Lank), 'Garden of Eden' (Axl's tirade against organised religions that made 'a mockery of humanity') and the Zeppelin-esque 'Locomotive'; plus a handful of 'joke songs' in the 'One in a Million' mould: 'Be Obsession' ('*I call my mother / She's just a cunt now . . .*') and 'The Garden' – the latter co-written by Axl, West Arkeen and Del James and featuring the duet between Axl and Alice Cooper. 'I did my bit maybe three times, but Axl was a perfectionist,' Cooper relates, 'almost to the point where you want to say, "At some point, Axl, it's gotta be good enough."'

There were also two new versions of 'Don't Cry', the maudlin Axl and Izzy ballad from the demo tape Tom Zutaut first heard – now featuring on backing vocals another Indiana escapee, named Shannon Hoon, younger brother of Axl's old high-school friend Anna, and soon to become famous in his own right in Blind Melon. Axl remembered it as the first song he and Izzy wrote together, a song about a girlfriend of Izzy's: 'I was really attracted to her. They split and I was sitting outside the Roxy, and, you know, I was, like, really in love with this person, and she was realising this wasn't going to work, she was telling me goodbye. We wrote it in about five minutes,' he said. Plus an updating of a West Arkeen tune called 'Yesterdays' (with additional lyrics by Del James). Musically, the tracks certainly roamed widely across the borders of the rock and pop spectrum, from Axl's intricate piano-led balladry to the jaunty banjo with which Slash introduces one track, to the remarkably adept sitar playing Izzy's utilises in the intro to another, going even further forward with the self-consciously futuristic synthesisers and electronica Axl fiddles with on the track that would provide the esoteric finale to the collection, 'My World'.

Steven Adler only appeared on one track – ironically, the track he had such difficulty recording it led indirectly to his sacking: 'Civil War'. It was an early version of 'Civil War' – the most ironic flag-waver since Hendrix's wilfully misshapen 'Star Spangled Banner' 20 years before – to appear on the *Nobody's Angel* compilation album, a fundraiser organised under the aegis of George Harrison, with all proceeds going to the Romanian Angel Appeal, a charity set up to aid those children left orphaned by the Romanian Uprising of December 1989. An earlier version of another track reheated for the *Use Your Illusion* set, their cover of Dylan's 'Knockin' on Heaven's Door', had also been included on the soundtrack album to the 1990 movie *Days of Thunder* – or *Top Gun* on wheels as its producer, Jerry Bruckheimer, called it. The resultant video – itself an out-take of a performance filmed at The Ritz club in New York in 1988 – quickly shot to Number 1 on the MTV most-requested charts, despite Axl's repeated swearing throughout the song being bleeped out.

Of the nearly 40 different tracks that would be recorded – aside from the new originals and various covers there were also some older songs that had been re-recorded but didn't make the cut, rubies lying in the dust like the anthemic 'Ain't Goin' Down' and the more throwaway 'Just Another Sunday' – 30 would make the finished track-listing. The problem was how to present them. Double album? Triple album? Or cut them right back to the bone and make one ton-up single album?

As Axl told me: 'When you're writing off your life and not fantasy you have to, like, have gone through these different phases. And now I think there's enough different sides of Guns N' Roses that, like, no one will know what to think, let alone us. Like, what are they trying to say? I don't fucking know!'

Axl said the band was still writing even as recording was taking place. 'It's like, I wrote this thing . . .' He closed his eyes and began to recite. 'It goes, ah, "*Call us violent / I say we're a product of our environment / Call us hostile / Babe, we gotta survive / You call us heartless / Before we had the money nobody gave a damn / You call us deadly / All my life you been killing me . . .*"' He opened his eyes again. 'So the mean stuff is there at the same time as the ballads are now. And then Izzy's got his sense of humour in there, too. Like, "*There were lots of other lovers / Honey, you weren't the first*", then something, something, then, "*But you were the worst / Yes, you were the worst*" . . .' He laughed. 'I'm gonna try to get him to sing that one cos Izzy sings it the best. But, like, there'll also be West playing on "The Garden", because West plays that song the best. And Slash wants to do the solo. He's like, "I'm gonna nail that motherfucker this time!" He's been trying to nail the solo for "The Garden" for the last three years . . .'

Axl's thing, he said, was 'to give a broader picture of Guns N' Roses'. For him, all this new material, however it came out, would essentially form 'like a trilogy – *Appetite*, *GN'R Lies* and this, okay? That those three albums were kind of like, Guns N' Roses can do whatever the fuck they want. It might not sell, but, like, it will break our boundaries. The only boundary we're keeping is hard rock. We know that's a limitation, in a way. But we want to keep that because we don't want it to die, you know? And we're watching it die. At least we were before Guns N' Roses formed. We were watching it just kind of being obliterated. By radio – by, like, all the stations not playing heavy metal any more, and all this crap. And so we decided, okay, we like a lot of guitars, we wanna keep it.'

*

With so many songs and different styles, *Use Your Illusion* was never going to be a completely coherent artistic statement. Bob Clearmountain, who had worked as engineer and producer with everyone from The Who to the Rolling Stones, was brought in to mix the songs and try to make the thing a whole. Alan Niven kept seeing Bob's name credited 'on all of these records that are blowing my ass off. I thought, he must be a genius. He's wonderful!' But Clearmountain's efforts were made fraught by the ever-watchful presence of Axl. 'Poor fucking Bob. Axl moved into the Record Plant. He ate, slept and shat there. He was there all the time, breathing down Bob's neck. And finally we're informed that they're done. God knows how they ever got through all that stuff with Axl with his myopia.'

Tom Zutaut and Alan Niven received their copies of the mixes at the same time. When Niven listened to the DATs in his music room. 'My heart just went into my boots.' He called Zoots and asked him to come to his house, where the two men sat in Niven's music room and started to play the mixes again. 'Then we just turned them off,' says Niven. 'They had no vitality. No punch. They were overworked. There was no spontaneity. There was nothing vital in them whatsoever.' At which point, says Niven, 'Tom and I started to foment *a wicked idea*. We looked at each other and said, he's such a fucker to us all, let's put this record out as it is. And let everybody know that he oversaw the mixes. The idea was so giddy to us we sat there and started laughing until we cried at the prospect of doing it. We were looking each other in the eye going, "Let's let the fucker swing . . ." We were so tired of him at that point.'

Once they'd stopped laughing, they decided they had to take drastic action. In an effort to try to save the day, they turned to the British production wizard Bill Price, whose brilliant work in the past with tendentious English rock acts like the Sex Pistols, Roxy

Music and The Pretenders would, they gambled, make him the best man to try to bring the best out of the sprawl of new GN'R material. Bill, says Niven, was great at 'bright and sparkly. And, thank god, Bill did a *huge* job and saved what was saveable on there.' Price delivered a 'loud, in-your-face, heavily compressed' mix of 'Right Next Door to Hell' to show how he felt the band should sound. 'It was a very long process,' Price recalled. 'The last half a dozen songs were recorded, overdubbed, vocal-ed and guitar-ed, what have you-ed, in random recording studios dotted about America when they had a day off between gigs because the tour had already started. My mixing mode then switched into flying around America with pocketfuls of DATs, playing it to the band backstage.' Price somehow got the job done, and the Clearmountain mixes were, Alan Niven said, destroyed out of respect for the producer.

The amount of songs that the band wanted to release, however, presented a commercial problem for Niven and Geffen Records. With 30 tracks and a combined running time of over two and a half hours, a vinyl version would, in effect, be akin to a quadruple album. Even with CD technology allowing for a much-expanded running time per disc, it would take two CDs to launch all 30 songs as one album. At first, though, that's what they decided to do: 30 tracks spread over two CDs presented as one coherent album. Certainly, such grandiosity sat well with Axl's idea of the band's monumental destiny – instantly propelling *Use Your Illusion* into the exalted realms of a modern-day *Tommy* or *The Wall*.

Tom Zutaut suggested they release a double album, followed a year later – halfway through what already promised to be a two-year world tour – by a more conventional single album, with the added prospect of at least one EP – or mini-album, à la *GN'R Lies* – of the various cover versions Axl was also now insisting the band record – including 'Down on the Farm', 'New Rose' by The Damned (with lead vocals from Duff), 'Don't Care about You' by

Fear, 'Attitude' by the Misfits, 'Jumpin' Jack Flash' by the Stones, 'Black Leather' by the Sex Pistols (featuring the Pistols' guitarist, Steve Jones) and, most surprisingly of all perhaps, a heavyweight version of 'Live and Let Die', Paul McCartney's hit theme tune to the 1974 James Bond movie of the same name. Slash told me there was even talk of a series of EPs – one punk-themed, one funk, one rap, one rock – and the probability of a live album at the end of the tour too.

But in what would prove to be his last significant commercial decision for Guns N' Roses, Alan Niven had a better idea. 'As the material was growing, I was getting more and more apprehensive about it being a double CD, and I was getting more apprehensive about it selling as a double CD, which made it much more expensive for the individual. The last thing I wanted to develop was the reaction from the fans that now they've become excessive and there are these long meandering songs, and it's a thick double record that's hard to get into. I persuaded Axl that from a fan's economic point of view to be able to go and buy one album one week and one album the next was less onerous.

'The other aspect was that I looked at it and said financially you get a better return on two separate albums than you do on a double, you earn more in royalties. And it hadn't been done before [in the new CD era].' He recalled how the 1968 Jimi Hendrix double album, *Electric Ladyland*, had originally been sold as two separate LPs. 'There was some sort of sense of precedent and it could be viewed as critically valid. We had a huge cloud to get out from under and that was the incredible sales of *Appetite*. I was very nervous of a situation where we might sell two million double albums, having sold at that point something like 12 million of *Appetite*.

'I had a meeting with Rosenblatt, and he pushed a pencil and a piece of paper at me and said, write down what you think we're going to do. Believe it or not, I wrote down that I thought we'd do four million of each single album, which meant we could say we'd sold eight million albums. That, I thought, would have a sense of continuity as opposed to drop-off. Rosenblatt loved it because fiscally it worked better for Geffen than a double album. He could absolutely see the intelligence behind it.'

There would eventually be two albums: *Use Your Illusion I* and *Use Your Illusion II* – the title lifted from a Mark Kostabi artwork of the same name that Axl had recently become fascinated by. Nevertheless, Niven admits, he was 'fucking terrified' when he broached the idea with Axl. 'Can you imagine what a retail disaster that would have been if that had been a fucking double album priced at fucking $29? We'd have done one and a half million if we'd been lucky, and we were coming off eight [of *Appetite*]. It would have been a fucking nightmare. I sat Axl down and said, "We've got a working-class following. You wanna charge them thirty bucks in one go? If we do it as two separate albums they can buy one, one week, and one the next. And you're not digging into their fucking grocery money, Axl." And he bought it! He bought it.'

So, ultimately, did everyone else. Doug Goldstein says the only argument he can remember having with Axl in those days was over how to release the two *Use Your Illusion* albums. 'My argument was let's release two really strong albums away from each other, which will lengthen the arc of tour cycle time. But Axl was stuck on the fact that nobody had ever entered the charts at 1 and 2 at the same time, and he wanted to do that. And in fact he did.' Indeed, within a week of release, *Use Your Illusion II* had gone straight into the US charts at Number 1, with *Use Your Illusion I* right behind it at Number 2. This was now about more than just success. This had become a cultural signifier, a piece of living history, the last great event of the vinyl and CD era.

Axl had also insisted on wrapping both CDs in a facsimile of Kostabi's original painting: a detail from *The School of Athens*, one of the most famous frescos by the sixteenth-century Italian

High Renaissance painter Raphael – with *Use Your Illusion I* coloured yellow and red, while *Use Your Illusion II* came in purple and blue. A young Estonian-American artist who first came to the attention of the New York art scene in the Eighties, Kostabi's work was a kind of Warholian expression of designer chic (a Bloomingdale's shopping bag) and curation (his NY studio, dubbed Kostabi World, employed a number of 'painting assistants' and 'ideas people'). For Alan Niven, Kostabi was 'an art scavenger deeply [that] didn't do anything except sign his name to stuff that he had people put together. And he'd scavenge images from historical pieces.'

Nevertheless, Axl was happy to pay Kostabi $85,000 for the painting so that he could use it for the covers. Niven now maintains, however, 'We could have used that painting for the artwork and Kostabi couldn't have done nothing about it because he was using public domain images.' He goes on: 'While I'm looking at it and thinking, great when it comes to the merchandising, we don't have to pay Kostabi or anybody else a dime, it always made me smile to think of Axl writing a huge cheque to this guy when he could have had Del James paint similar backgrounds, cut out the same image, stick it on and give Del a six-pack.'

Despite the over-elaboration of the packaging, the overselling of the importance of the music, the bent-over-backwards desire to do something that was simpler bigger and better than anything so far produced in a time and place that thrived on believing it was the biggest and best at everything, the end product would be an impossible-to-swallow-whole maze of musical journeys that crisscrossed and overlapped, collided spectacularly and, in some cases, seemed to lead nowhere, before taking off again on another wondrous musical expedition. Ultimately, where *Appetite for Destruction* had expressed a single vision – a compelling and irresistible one-note howl of angst and ambition – *Use Your Illusion* would see the personalities and artistic aspirations of the band shatter into their component parts. Everyone seemingly alone out there spinning around in space, moving at the speed of light from one tripped-out farscape to another without once looking down for fear of falling, falling, falling . . .

'When it comes to *Use Your Illusion*, somewhere in there is one perfect album, no longer than fifty to sixty minutes,' reckoned Alan Niven, looking back. Yet it was the sheer audacity of releasing so much material in one go that said the most about them. *Use Your Illusion I* and *II* became albums that said plenty about their time. They are indulgent, bloated by lengthy cover versions and created by men who weren't hearing the word 'no' too often. And yet they are also unafraid and unapologetic, and they contain some of the best work Guns N' Roses ever produced. Interestingly, too, they lend perspective to the band's two other major releases: a clear line can be drawn through them from *Appetite for Destruction* to *Chinese Democracy*. 'When I look back on it, it was a monumental achievement,' said Slash, years later. 'The first thing I think of when I think of those albums is that it was such a whirlwind of shit was happening at that particular time, but it was a huge accomplishment. I think the *Use Your Illusion* records, if you know the back-story, were very victorious. After all of it, we came through.'

'That record polarised people. I've come to understand that, and I've come to be at peace with the whole thing,' said Duff McKagan in 2011. 'I only figured this out recently. "When are you guys gonna get back together?" Well, none of us guys have said we're going to. I wonder if some people – not all – if some people think if we got back together, they'd get their teenage years back? Are they asking us to get back together so that they can get their youth back, even for a minute? The title of the record, it's fucking appropriate, when you think about it . . .'

They would also provide a commercial peak that no one would enjoy again. 'Most people go through life saying, "I wonder what it's like to get to the apex of your occupation,"' Alan Niven con-cluded. 'A lot of people spend their lives worrying about anonym-ity. But when you get to the apex of your occupation, you find out it's a fucking illusion, it doesn't exist. And when your anonym-ity is compromised, you find out its value. The toll came later and when it did come it hit hard. I went through the severest depression you can go into, the bottom of the black pit. I felt that everything I loved and believed in had proved itself worthless and all the relationships I'd put stock into had realised a betrayal.'

With Niven and Adler gone, with Izzy on the brink, with Slash and Duff blindsided by their drug habits and their desire for a hassle-free, rich-rock-star life, with Doug Goldstein in place and Axl in control, with the money rolling in and fans across the world ready to pack stadiums in which to watch them play, the scene was set for a takeover, and that was exactly what was going to happen.

PART TWO

Real's a Dream

'The junk merchant doesn't sell his product to the consumer, he sells the consumer to his product. He does not improve and simplify his merchandise. He degrades and simplifies the client.'

William S. Burroughs, Naked Lunch

10

THIS SIDE OF HELL

Slash shook his head and smiled that crooked smile. 'It's like, I thought, once we get out of LA and back on the road, everything will work itself out again,' he said. 'But, like, that's when everything got *really* crazy. I mean, out of control! Like, we went out on tour again after all this time and . . . like . . . never came back . . .'

Things had been strange for a long time. Now, in Brazil, in January 1991, where Guns N' Roses were booked to appear for two nights at the Rock in Rio festival, things got seriously weird. They'd almost finished *Use Your Illusion*, and Alan Niven had booked them their first full-length live shows since the LA Coliseum gigs with the Rolling Stones in October '89. Only snag: Axl, via Doug Goldstein, had informed Niven that he would not be welcome in Rio. The festival itself – the second of its kind after a money-grab debut in 1985 – was a fortnight-long bacchanal that saw half of the rock world decamping to three hotels in the city: bands, crews, broadcasters, record company types, press, wives, girlfriends, groupies, hangers-on and anyone else who could lay their hands on a laminate and the price of an air fare, all sequestered at either the Rio Palace or Copacabana Place hotels on Copa beach. Or, in the case of Guns N' Roses and their entourage, a few miles away at the even more exclusive Intercontinental hotel, high on a cliff overlooking Ipanema beach.

The shows themselves were to take place at Brazil's most famous football stadium, the Maracana, and would run for nine nights. Guns N' Roses and the other headline acts, Prince and George Michael, were booked to headline two shows apiece, with A-Ha, New Kids On The Block and INXS taking care of the others. All sorts of support acts were there, too, from the teenybopper Disney queen Debbie Gibson to Woodstock veterans Carlos Santana and Joe Cocker, plus battle-hardened hell-raisers the Happy Mondays and Billy Idol, and experienced stadium rockers like Judas Priest, Queensrÿche and Faith No More.

Guns N' Roses had rehearsed at Long Beach before flying to Rio three days before their first show and rehearsing again at a small facility in the city. Along with the new material, the shows would be the first for Matt Sorum and new keyboardist Dizzy Reed, so there was already a different vibe around. I was in Rio to write about the whole demented circus and the creeping paranoia and the sense of change were right there, too, and I could feel both like a cold wind on the back of my neck. It had the Vince Neil interview at its root, a story that had rotted away in Axl's head, a supposed injustice that spelled doom not just for this writer but for any others that now put in requests for interviews. From now on journalists and photographers would be required to sign written agreements, essentially forfeiting control of their own material: Axl's latest attempt to try to control every aspect of his environment.

A two-page document giving the band copyright ownership and approval rights, on pain of a $200,000 damages claim if violated, though impossible to enforce in practical terms, naturally proved immensely unpopular with all sections of the media in Rio. A host of important magazines refused to sign the contracts, including *Playboy, Rolling Stone*, the *Los Angeles Times, Spin* and *Penthouse*. Axl, though, merely shrugged. As Geffen Records' publicity chief, Bryn Bridenthal, commented: 'In twenty-five years of doing publicity I've never dealt with a press contract before, but when you deal with this band, you deal with a lot of firsts.' Although the contracts would later be revised, dropping the $200,000 penalty, they would become a source of ill-will throughout the forthcoming world tour.

Had we all taken a step back at that moment, however, we would have seen the dimensions of their universe, the Big Bang expansion that they were living through. The *Appetite for Destruction* tour had begun at the Marquee in Wardour Street with the band holed up together at a cheap rental flat in Kensington. The *Use Your Illusion* tour began when they travelled to Rio de Janeiro on a Boeing 727 leased from the MGM Grand hotel in Las Vegas. 'It was a great crash pad,' recalled Slash. 'It was pretty ornate: it had all of these little private lounges and bedrooms.'

They liked the 727 so much they hired it for the rest of the tour. And while the jet was bigger than the apartment they'd stayed in for the Marquee shows, they'd been a gang back then, tight and inseparable. Now, Steven was gone, and the gaps between them were widening. 'We got the gigs supporting the Rolling Stones,' remembered Duff in 2011. 'We're massive Stones fans, so that was great for us. We got down there and the Stones each had their own limo, their own trailer, their own *lawyer* – you know, Mick has one, Keith has one, Charlie has one . . . I remember turning around to Izzy and saying, "Man, we'll never be like that." Of course, six months later, that was us . . .'

While they were in LA the divisions had been easier to hide, or at least to ignore. Thrown together on the road, in the plane and at the hotel and the sound check and the gig and the inevitable party afterwards, it was easy to spot that Guns N' Roses had split into three camps. There was the party-hardy duo of Slash and Duff, who were quickly joined by Matt Sorum; there was Axl, who had the constant worry about keeping his voice in shape and who was consciously isolating himself from the worst excesses of drugs and booze; and there was Izzy, still clinging to sobriety but whose doubts about his future in the band were mounting by the day as the tour stretched out before him, apparently endless. As Slash would write in his memoir: 'Duff and I had our new party buddy Matt and no matter how many days we'd stay up, we could always play the gig. We just felt like we were kings of the world; we had a good time with everything and we always did our job. Izzy, unfortunately, was shell-shocked; he was trying his best to keep away from our whole partying scene, so the tour from the start wasn't as much fun for him. And Axl; well I won't pretend to know what was going on with him, then, now or ever.'

It was a key admission. The world may have seen Axl and Slash as the natural successors to Mick and Keef, the self-styled Glimmer Twins embodying the look, sound and lifestyle of their band, but it was miles from the truth. Axl and Slash had never been that close on a personal level, happy to write together and play together on stage, but equally happy to leave each other the fuck alone off it. Like much else about Guns N' Roses by the early Nineties, 'Axl and Slash' was already an illusion, existing mainly in the minds of the fans who wanted it to be true. The Rock in Rio shows, it was hoped, would re-announce and redefine Guns N' Roses as a viable entity. Live like a suicide! This would be bigger, brasher and more spectacular than before, widescreen entertainment for the new masses of fans – 130,000 per night in Rio. But without Steven and with the additional keyboards of Dizzy Reed, it sounded different. On huge stages with a vast production, the band looked different, too, marionettes dancing in the mid-distance. The set lists were unfamiliar, as 'Civil War', 'Estranged', 'Double Talkin' Jive' and 'Pretty Tied Up' were tucked amongst the *Appetite* hits, along with Slash's 'Godfather Theme' solo, a Matt Sorum drum solo and a snippet of Alice Cooper's 'Only Women Bleed'.

When at the end of the festival they flew back to LA to finish working on the *Use Your Illusion* material and to begin production rehearsals for the tour proper, no one knew that the lollapalooza of endeavour and excess that had begun in Brazil would run, in all, for two and a half years, a labour of love and blood that would change the lives of almost everyone who took part. 'The expanding gap between Axl and me and between Axl and the rest of us got pretty wide while we were having the records mixed,' admitted Slash. Tapes were being couriered from the studio to Axl's house, a situation the guitarist felt was merely 'tolerable'.

It was to be an interview given by Slash to *Rolling Stone* soon after Rock in Rio that became the next bump in the road. In it, Slash likened his relationship with Axl to 'two fucking Japanese fighting fish in the same bowl. We've always been the same. We have our ups and downs, and we butt heads. As long as I've known Axl, we've had so many differences that have been like the end of the line as far as we were concerned. I think that happens with most singers and guitar players, or whatever that cliché is. It might look a little intense on the outside, seeing all this shit that we're going through, but it makes for a tension that's – in a morbid kind of way – really conducive to the music we collaborate on. But as far as Axl goes, he is the best singer-lyricist around.'

The magazine ran the piece as their cover story at the end of January, and 'from what I understand Axl was cool with it,' said Slash, 'or at least didn't see anything wrong with it at first'. But when the guitarist arrived at Long Beach Arena for production rehearsals for the tour just days after the magazine had been published, he found the straitjacket he'd bought as a Christmas gift for Axl left on his guitar amp for him to discover as he walked onstage. 'It was exactly the sort of eggshell walking the band had become,' Slash said of the days of silent treatment that followed. It was a classic pattern that many would recognise from a bad marriage; the non-communication, the feeling that any small incident could set off another uncivil war.

'I think he and I are just completely different people,' Slash later reflected. 'In the early years I worked really hard to understand him so that we could be close, and I would feel that there was a point where there was an understanding and then he would turn around and any number of things would happen where I would feel completely deceived, and that builds up such a distance. When we were touring we were never in the same room except when we were onstage, and that kind of lack of communication is what builds animosity in a volatile situation – with two within the group of powerful people working in tandem but really completely far apart.'

It wasn't just Axl and Slash who were now locked in a battle for ultimate control of Guns N' Roses. It was Alan Niven and Doug Goldstein. In a 2011 interview, Niven recalled how, in March of 1991, just as Bill Price had completed his mixes, he was at a Great White show at the Meadowlands in New York when he got a phone call from Axl, who told him that they could no longer work together. 'I said, "Well, I'll be back in LA in a couple of days, let's have dinner and talk about it", and that was the last time I ever spoke to him. He agreed we'd have dinner. My perception was, maybe this is permanent, maybe it's not. Obviously he had his agenda.'

Niven maintained that 'One of the factors is that [Axl] didn't feel he had total control of me. Because I had other responsibilities and other interests, he couldn't control me exclusively. I don't think that sat very well with him. That was slightly ungrateful because there were moments in the development of GN'R where Great White were a hello for them and that's never been acknowledged and appreciated.' He pointed out that the 'Welcome to the Jungle' video 'wouldn't have happened without Great White. And Great White broke before Guns N' Roses did. They went gold in the November of '87 and that gave me a little bit of leverage

I could use with GN'R. Obviously if a manager's got one band breaking and all over radio, you tend to hook the other band on and go, yeah, look at this one, too.'

According to Doug Goldstein, however, the division between Alan and Axl had existed a long time and had only grown deeper in recent months. Speaking now, Goldstein says he feels 'the only reason that Niven had brought me in was because he hated Axl and Axl hated him'. He recalls a telling incident when he was sitting with Axl at the back of the tour bus 'just after I had started with the band as their tour manager . . . Niven walks [up] with a piece of paper and hands it to Axl. And Axl goes, "What's this?" Niven goes, "Lyrics." Axl goes, "Are you fucking kidding me? You're my manager. You're not my co-writer. I don't know if you think you're Bernie Taupin or what but you'll never fill that role with me. This isn't Great White." Then he opened the bus vent and let it fly. I was like, these guys just don't like each other.'

But while Niven acknowledges that his relationship with Axl was bruising – 'There would be a blast and a silence and a blast and a silence,' he says now. 'The silences were the worst because you knew there was a blast coming. Something to complain about, some issue, something you weren't doing right. Usually a phone call. Or [Doug] would relay the message' – he is convinced Goldstein was an opportunist with an eye for the main chance. 'He let the dark side take over,' he says simply.

According to Goldstein, though, 'the reality is, for two and a half years Axl tried to terminate him and I told him, fuck you, you can't he's my partner'. He insists that at the time Niven was fired 'Axl hadn't spoken to Niven in about nine months. So Alan was doing the Great White stuff. I was doing the GN'R stuff. And Slash and I used to save him for about two and a half years. Axl would call and say, "He's fired." And I'd say, "You can't fire him. He's my partner." Then I'd enlist Slash's aid and he'd call Axl and say, "No, you're not gonna fire him, he's our manager." So we kept him involved for, like, two and a half years when he should have been fired in the first place.'

Goldstein recalls the clinching incident that in his view triggered the end. 'Axl has his annulment come through with Erin Everly, and he's obviously excited about it. So he calls me and says, "Oh my god, you know what came through?" I said, "Good for you. I know that's been weighing heavy on your head. What do you say you go to a restaurant with your girlfriend and I'll buy you guys a bottle of champagne?" He says, "Wow, Doug, thank you, that's great."

'So he goes, "Can I talk to Alan?" I thought, oh shit, right? So then I thought, you know, maybe this is Alan's way back in. So I go to Alan's office, which was in the back and I said, "Alan, Axl's on the phone", and I said, "Look, his annulment just came through, he's excited . . ." He goes, "Dougie, I know how to handle it." He picks up the phone and Axl tells him whatever it is he tells him and Alan goes, "Really? How sad for you. Yet one other thing you failed at." I was like, "Are you fucking kidding me?"'

'My phone rings. It's Axl. He says, "You heard that?" I go, "Yeah, I heard that." He goes, "You know what, Doug? I'm tired of you and Slash saying I have to work with him. Fuck him. I'm never working with him again. I'm getting in my car." He had this little convertible BMW. He says, "Wherever it runs out of gas I'll be getting a job there at the local gas station. You and Slash can find me. I suggest you work this out."

'So I called Slash, which was my normal MO, and I said, "Look, Axl's trying to fire Alan again." And Slash says, "Doug, I'm tired of this guy . . ."' Goldstein goes on to make an allegation against Niven that the latter bitterly refutes. To do with a dinner Alan had given for Slash and his then fiancée, Renee Suran. Says Niven: 'Slash and Renee left before the first glass of wine had been broached. He said she wasn't feeling well.' More significantly, he remembers, this was just a few days after another dinner he had given to celebrate Axl's twenty-ninth birthday, 'which he failed to attend – and at which Zutaut, who had been at Axl's with Doug, leaned into my ear and whispered, "Doug is not your friend" . . . As I recall, I wanted to get a sense of where the land lay with [Slash] . . . I guess I found out.'

The upshot was that Doug Goldstein would take over as the manager of Guns N' Roses, forming his own newly named Big FD [Fucking Deal] management company. When asked in 2011 about what went down when Niven was fired, Slash said this: 'I backed Alan all the way up to a certain point and then he did actually do something that set me off and I said, I can't fight for you any more.' Though he quickly added: 'But that was a volatile situation that was going to explode at some point. In other words, I can't see how it would have turned out had we done it differently. All I can see happening is that nothing would have happened, because it would have been at a standstill. I think we probably would have broken up a lot sooner.' He was insistent, though, that his feelings were always conflicted about appointing Goldstein as Niven's successor. Slash in 2011 to Jon Hotten: 'Alan was somebody that I trusted, whereas I knew Doug was somebody that played both sides against the middle. In other words, he's telling me one thing, telling Axl another and appeasing Axl all the time. It became sort of, like . . . divide and conquer. And I was aware of it, but, at the same time, as long as shit was getting done I was okay. As long as we kept booking tours and I was sort of kept in the mix as far as the mechanics, that's how we managed to get from 1990 to 1990-whatever.'

Again, though, Goldstein has a somewhat different version of events. 'Slash used to come to me and say, "Doug, we are *so* happy that you're working with us because all Alan does is get drunk and do blow with us." I'd come back to Alan and say, "Look, they don't want you partying with them." And he'd say, "Fuck off. You need to be one of them." And I'd say, "You're out of your mind.

No, they *don't* want that." No matter how hard I tried to beat that into his head he just never got that.'

'I don't know what you've heard but I was actually very careful about preserving my sense of responsibility,' says Alan Niven. 'I'd get high with Izzy. Now and then with Slash. But that was it.' The fat had been in the fire, he points out, since 'Axl's demand that I not go to Rio . . . What I did know is that the band would bend to anything from Axl to just get as much of the tour done as possible.'

For some objectivity I asked Stephanie Fanning for her views on why the relationship between Alan Niven and Doug Goldstein ended so bitterly. Speaking down the line from her home in Malibu, she recalls: 'During and after the *Illusion* records were done and they were gearing up for that tour and everything, Alan got along great with all of the band. He was the guy who would maybe have fun with them a little bit, party or whatever. But he was also the business guy and they respected and loved him.

'But Alan and Axl would clash . . . That was no secret. Alan stands his ground. Alan doesn't really kiss anybody's ass. He doesn't really say what you want to hear. He says what *should* be heard. It came to a point where Axl had really had enough of Alan. I think maybe Doug sat back at that time and said maybe I want to be the guy in charge. Maybe I want to be the one with all the power. Maybe I want to be the one making all the money . . . and Axl was also close to being done with Alan. Then Doug stepped in and kind of went with it.'

She sighs. 'I mean, what would all of us do at that time in our lives, at that age? They were getting ready to do one of the biggest tours of all time with one of the biggest records of all time. I don't know what all of us would do if you put us in that position. Cos Axl was saying, "He's done. I want him out." And he knows Doug couldn't fight back.'

*

Doug Goldstein took over as Guns N' Roses' manager just as the *Use Your Illusion* tour was about to begin with three warm-up shows in San Francisco, Los Angeles and New York, and the dynamic of the band shifted once more. Slash was in no doubt that Doug was Axl's man. Yet the world from Axl's point of view looked very different. Slash, Duff and Matt were locked into their party-hearty lives and they weren't planning on pulling back – hedonism and decadence were perks of the job. Izzy, meanwhile, had kicked his coke and heroin habits and was now having serious doubts about the whole escapade. And Axl knew that he had to stay pretty straight in order to sing for two hours a night: 'I have a different physical constitution and different mind-set about drugs than anybody I've known in Hollywood, because I don't abstain from doing drugs, but I won't allow myself to have a fucking habit. I won't allow it,' he told Del James.

There was also all the small stuff to be sweated. Doug Goldstein recalls one such incident he feared would derail the tour before it had even begun, involving Axl's pets, two longhaired Maltese dogs named Porsche and Geneva. 'Like the dogs Zsa Zsa Gabor used to have,' explains Doug. Axl 'used to fawn over these dogs. They basically ruled the home.' When the singer left for a short vacation ahead of the *Illusion* tour beginning in earnest, he asked Goldstein if he'd look after them for him. 'I was renting a home at the time in LA. We had a backyard. So no problem.'

Staying with Goldstein was the band's production manager, Dale Skjerseth, aka 'Opie' for his resemblance to the Opie Taylor character from the American Sixties sitcom *The Andy Griffith Show*. Halfway through Axl's vacation, Opie called Doug at the office one day. 'He says, "Oh-oh. We're in big time trouble."' Opie had let the dogs outside and when they came back inside they were covered in crap, their fur thick with detritus. 'He said, "So I took them to the groomers and said please get the stickers out of them, and I came back two hours later and they had shaved them bald!" I'm going, "Fuck me!"

'We were gearing up for the *Use Your Illusion* tour and so all of us are on pins and needles, don't do anything to frustrate Axl at this time. Otherwise we're all fucking going home. In the end I said, "You know what, I'm gonna take my dick in my hands and fucking raise the courage and call Axl and tell him what happened." I was dejected as hell. I was like, we're two seconds away from the whole thing being pulled. What am I gonna tell the band, it's over two fucking bald dogs?

'So I get Axl on the line and I go, "Hey, bud, how's your trip?" He goes, "Yeah, really good." I go, ". . . Um. Need to share something with you." He goes, "What's up?" I go, "It's about Porsche and Geneva." He goes, "Are they okay?" I go, "Yeah, yeah . . . they're doing okay." He goes, "Doug, what's going on?" I go, "Well, um . . . we've had a haircut. They kind of got in the backyard and all these stickers in their fur so Opie and I thought, you know, rather than hand you back dogs that were full of stickers, we'd do ahead and get them cut a little bit." He goes, "What's a little bit?" I go, "Well, they're kind of shaved." He starts laughing. He goes, "Don't worry about it. We do that with them all the time." I'm like, *thank God!* I mean my heart was pounding. I thought, I've got to call all the promoters . . . It's not like one of the guitar players died. It's two bald dogs.'

Other times things could still be fun. When Tom Zutaut called Doug Goldstein one day and told him that Arnold Schwarzenegger wanted to put 'Welcome to the Jungle' in his new movie, *Terminator II: Judgment Day,* Goldstein laughed and said, 'Are you fucking high? Tom, we're currently recording *Use Your Illusion I* and *II,* why in fuck would we go after a song that's now four years old? This is the perfect opportunity to put together our lead track from [the new] record. What better situation could we have?' So he pitched Arnold "You Could be Mine" . . .'

Schwarzenegger loved the track so much he came back and told them he wanted to be in the video! The result was one of the iconic videos of the early Nineties, a head-rush confection of live band action and spectacular scenes from what was about to become the biggest hit movie of the year.

Goldstein remembers the meeting at Schwarzenegger's Hollywood home where the idea was first discussed. 'We all went to Arnold's house and that guy is the best salesperson I've ever seen in my life. Oh my god, the band was salivating at his every word. He knew what every guy liked. He knew that Niven was the port and Cuban cigar guy. He knew that I was a Diet Pepsi drinker. He knew that Slash was a Jack Daniel's guy. He knew that Axl was a Dom Perignon guy. He knew that Duff was a Stoli guy . . . The thing that I loved is that *he* decided to put himself in the video, which was brilliant!

'Another thing he did, he has [his wife] Maria in the kitchen cooking. Tell me that normally they don't have house staff there? They made sure that they were all gone when we showed up though. So the appearance was, hey, it's me and poor Maria, living in this big home and doing it on her own. He was so fucking calculated it was incredible! Charming and alluring and oh my god, *I* wanted to sleep with the guy!' He laughs. As for Axl, 'He loved him! He absolutely fucking oh my god *loved* him!'

Out on the road, at first everything was cool, magical even. Whatever the problems offstage the chemistry was still there, especially between Axl and Slash. Axl was singing brilliantly well, absolutely at the peak of his powers. There was an almost electric charge to headlining their own arena tour – thousands upon thousands of people there not to see a festival bill as they had been in the past, but buying tickets to see the biggest, baddest rock'n'roll band on the planet. They kept the set list loose and interesting: they had at least 30 songs in the repertoire. They'd open with one of 'It's So Easy', 'Nightrain', 'Welcome to the Jungle' or 'Perfect

Crime'. 'Mr Brownstone' and 'Live and Let Die' were mid-set reg-
ulars. 'November Rain' was Axl's baby, played at a piano that rose
up through the stage on a specially constructed platform. Slash
had his Godfather solo spot and Matt played a drum solo. 'Paradise City' would close the show. Around them, they dotted the
best of *Appetite* and *GN'R Lies*, plus some fierce takes on the *Use
Your Illusion* highlights. As the tour ran on and the albums were
released, the crowds became more familiar with the new records
and the likes of 'Civil War' and 'Estranged' became mesmerizing
moments too. 'We were an unreal band with an unreal singer,'
remembered Slash. 'Axl was amazing . . .'

It didn't last.

Alan Niven's last significant act as the manager of Guns N'
Roses had been to instigate a renegotiation of the band's contract
with Geffen Records. Any other label might have initiated its own
renegotiation talks with an act that had now sold over ten million
records in the past two years, but David Geffen was known for
defiantly refusing such approaches.

'I'd heard from a very good friend of mine that Howard Kauf-
man, who managed Whitesnake, went into David and said,
"Listen, Coverdale has sold you five million albums. Let's renegotiate the contract and pay him better." And Geffen told him to
fuck off. Howard then made the huge mistake of going back to
Geffen, this time in the company of his artist, David. He thought
that if he walked into Geffen's office with the artist that that
would stand Geffen down. That he wouldn't say no to Coverdale
himself. Howard had to endure the humiliation of being told to
fuck off a second time, in front of his artist . . .

'When Aerosmith hit the five million mark and asked for a renegotiation too, [Tim Collins] got kicked to the kerb real fast. And
my friend at Geffen told me about this. So I knew that Howard
and Whitesnake and Tim and Aerosmith had been brushed aside.

So that told me that, in this instance, you don't *ask* David, you fucking *tell* him.'

Niven had devised a two-pronged strategy. For his then wife's birthday, he booked a private room at La Chardonnay, then one of LA's most chic restaurants. Chief amongst the guests were Geffen's president, Eddie Rosenblatt, and his wife. Having arranged to have Rosenblatt seated next to him, Niven waited while he counted the glasses of wine Eddie had. 'Waiting until he's had just the right amount. Then I lean against his shoulder and I say, "Please don't react badly to this, and react quietly. But I need you to take a message back to David Geffen." He looks at me, and I go, "Tell David that if he doesn't renegotiate the contract we're gonna go out on tour without finishing the album."'

The other arm of his strategy was his awareness that Geffen was then planning to sell the label to the Matsushita Electric Industrial Co. in Japan, in a deal that would make David Geffen a billionaire. Rosenblatt and Niven had already estimated 'we'd do a hundred million [dollars] in gross from the first week of sales of the *Use Your Illusions* worldwide'. So Niven 'knew I had [David Geffen] up against the wall a little bit because he wanted the *Use Your Illusion* [albums] sold and in his profitable pocket before he sold the label to the Japanese'. He adds: 'To my knowledge it's the only time that David Geffen has ever renegotiated an extant contract.'

There was, though, a coda to Niven's renegotiation, which occurred once he was out of the picture. According to Doug Goldstein, the deal that Niven had negotiated was for a massive upfront payment of $10 million, with the royalty points left as they were, which, he says, 'started at thirteen and went to fifteen. Which for a superstar act is absolutely fucking deplorable. Normal would have been somewhere around twenty to twenty-two. So I called David Geffen's office, and I said, "Look, I need to have a meeting with David."'

Geffen was then in New York but a meeting was arranged at the executive's home; an extraordinary face-off that Goldstein claims ended with him physically strong-arming Geffen. 'We're sitting at breakfast across from each other and [Geffen] says, "Why are you here?"' Goldstein replied that 'with all due respect' he was recommending to the band that they don't sign the deal Niven had worked out for them with Geffen. At which point, says Goldstein, an outraged Geffen 'starts poking his finger in my face . . . I took his arm and twisted it in such a way that his face was now on the table. I said, "Again, sir, with all due respect, I was told you do your research on people before you meet with them. If you did your research on me you'd find out that if you stick your finger in my face I'm gonna snap your fucking arm at the elbow."

'I said, "Here's what you and I are gonna do. I'm gonna pretend that this little fucking escapade never happened. I'm gonna let you up. I'm gonna walk outside, knock on your door, and we're gonna start again." I said, "Does that work for you?" and I applied pressure on his head. He's like, "Yes, yes." So I let him up and I walked outside, knocked on the door, "Hi, Mr Geffen, Doug Goldstein." And he's fucking livid, right? He kept screaming at me for, like, three hours. And finally, it occurs to me what his issue is. He's a guy who believes in being a man of his word. Unlike a lot of people that got to where he is but doing just the opposite. If David Geffen tells you that he's going to do something, *he fucking does it*. That's one of the things that I love about David Geffen. He is a man of his word. He's a very, very, very ethical person when it comes to shit like that. And if he tells you something he's gonna make sure it happens, and conversely he expects the same respect.'

The problem, Goldstein decided, was that Geffen had already agreed a deal with the Japanese based on the figures of the new deal Niven had negotiated. He was loath to go back and tell them things had changed. So Goldstein started telling Geffen that he had done *his* research. 'I appealed to the ex-manager in him. I said, I have a band waiting for me in St Louis, and they're totally expecting me to come back with good news. Do I have to fly back to St Louis and say, "David gave me the choice between bubblegum and dick and we were out of bubblegum"?

'He goes, "Doug, I don't ever want to talk about this again. I don't care if I never speak to you again. But I am not going to get involved in a renegotiation. You can start talking to David Berman, who is the head of business affairs, and Eddie Rosenblatt, and whatever you come with you come up with." I thanked him and I went on my way to St Louis. The net result is, it took me six months, but I got the royalty points up to the highest any act in the history of music had ever had at that point. Thirty-four points. More than doubling what they had received in the past.'

Flying from New York down to St Louis that afternoon, Doug Goldstein felt sure he now had things under better control. That from here on in the band's main worries were over; the *Use Your Illusion* albums, delayed while contract negotiations had dragged on with Geffen, would now get an official release date and the tour would start to make real money.

Then the band went onstage in St Louis and all hell broke loose again.

There had been onstage rumblings since the band's 17 June show at Nassau Coliseum in Uniondale, New York, when Axl arrived late onstage and told the crowd: "Yeah, I know it sucks . . . If you got any real complaints, you could do me a favour though. You could write a little letter on how much that sucked and send it to Geffen Records. Tell those people to get the fuck out of my ass.' He returned to his record company frustrations a few songs later: 'The new record will be delayed again,' he said, pacing along the edge of stage. 'Geffen Records decided they wanted to change the contract and I'm deciding, "Fuck you." And since I don't have time to do both, go back there and argue and bitch with them or be on tour, I guess we'll just be on tour and have a good time and fuck them. It's a shame but . . . So we'll play a lot of the new shit tonight and it really doesn't matter, does it?'

Axl had flared briefly a few days before, too, at the Spectrum in Philadelphia, where he saw a member of the crowd fighting with the band's photographer, Robert John, and stopped the show until the fan was ejected, but these were minor things always likely to happen when so many combustible elements are thrown together. What happened in Missouri three weeks later, however, was far more serious, and seemed to leave a greasy trail of bad karma that would follow Guns N' Roses for the next two years.

The band were 15 songs into their show at the Riverport Am-phitheatre in St Louis when Axl saw a member of the audience quite close to the stage filming the show with a video camera. In the middle of 'Rocket Queen' he started shouting to the security guards to 'take that . . . Get that guy and take that . . .' Adrena-lin pumping through him, when nothing happened right away, he shouted, 'I'll take it, goddamn it!' and hurled himself from the edge of the stage towards the fan. There was a brief melee while the band continued playing the 'Rocket Queen' riff, and then security wrestled Axl back to the stage. When he got there, he grabbed his mike and yelled, 'Thanks to the lame-ass secu-rity, I'm going home', and threw the microphone to the stage so violently it made a sound like the crack of a gunshot. The band kept playing for a few moments ('We had a full bag of tricks to keep things moving whenever Axl made a sudden exit,' said Slash archly), but when the singer didn't return, the guitarist shuffled towards the wings, where Doug Goldstein yelled in his ear that the show was over.

They had played for more than the 90 minutes that they were contracted for, but it was unfinished business and the crowd was far from happy. With the band in their dressing room in the bowels of the arena, a full-scale riot broke out above them. Axl had calmed down somewhat and suggested going back on, but as they neared the stage it was clear that was now impossible. The place was being trashed, unconscious fans were being carried out and the police were at full stretch trying to limit the damage. They retreated back to the dressing room, where they hunkered down until the police could transport them safely through the chaos back to their hotel.

Doug Goldstein describes it now as a night he will never forget. 'There was this young kid who was a big Guns N' Roses fan, and Axl's telling everybody, "Look, you need to get this guy out of the crowd." We found out later that the guy worked for the local security, he had taken the night off to see his favourite band. So they're not gonna do anything about it. More importantly, I've got eight guys doing security, and yet not one of them jumped into the crowd to take care of it. Axl is like, "Really? Nobody's gonna take care of this? Are you serious?" So he finally took it upon himself.'

After Axl stormed off stage, Goldstein followed him. 'I go into his dressing room. I go, "Hey, bud, it's going to get really ugly if you don't get back out there." He had a cut on his knee. He goes, "Doug, you know how I do this. Just leave me alone for two minutes. I'll be fine. I got to clear up this blood then I'll come back out. Go get the other band members and tell them we're going back on." I say, "Great. Thank you."

'So I assemble the band and we're ready to go onstage and the promoter and the chief of police are there and they go, "What are you doing?" I go, "I'm taking the band back out there." They go, "Fuck you, you are. You've done enough damage, get the fuck out of here!" I said, "Guys, you don't get it. If you put the police in front of these people they're gonna rip this place to shreds." And the promoter gets in my face. "You heard me. Get the fuck out of here!" I said, "All right. It's on your hands then."'

Goldstein told the band's new tour manger, Josh, to get the band on the tour bus and call ahead to their hotel in Chicago that they were going to be arriving early. Then walked back out and did his best to help police quell the riot. 'To see guys running with Marshall stacks, off the stage and out of the building. Video screens! What are you going to do with video screens?'

The next morning the sun rose on a scene from *Apocalypse Now*. The crowd had levelled the place. Everything the band had left onstage had been trashed. The damage to the venue ran to almost a quarter of a million dollars. The next show in Chicago had to be cancelled, and Guns N' Roses didn't play again for almost a week, when they appeared almost 1000 miles away in Dallas, Texas. Axl was charged with inciting a riot, but wasn't arrested for almost a year. So, again, Axl ends up having to deal with all of that crap and it's not only unfair and unnecessary but he will not defend himself. He's like, "I'm not about to explain who I am or what I'm about." I don't know where that comes from, quite honestly, but it's there.'

Slash would recall in his autobiography that when he returned to St Louis four years later with his solo band, Snakepit, he ran into the fan who had been holding the camera. He'd just been awarded a sum of money from the lawsuit won by the city against Guns N' Roses, but had also endured death threats, and for a while had been unable to leave his house.

The band snuck a reference to the riot on the inside of the *Use Your Illusion* sleeve notes ('Fuck you St Louis!') but their reputation was set. And, though it wouldn't become evident until later, Axl had, in his strange way, asserted his control over what happened onstage – he decided when they went on, and what was and wasn't acceptable from the people who came to watch them.

After a triumphant – and lengthy – homecoming with four nights at the Inglewood Forum, where on the third night they played for more than three and half hours to celebrate the completion earlier that day of the *Use Your Illusion* album mixes, Guns N' Roses headed for Europe. They called the run the Get in the Ring, Motherfucker tour. Skid Row accompanied them. The levels of debauchery remained epically high and the gang of three had a new accomplice in Skid Row's singer, Sebastian Bach, a young and green Canadian eager to learn from the masters . . . 'We'd done it all before but we did it all again with Sebastian,' remarked Slash. 'That leg of the tour through the States to Europe was debauched and sick and took hedonism to a new level.'

Offstage, Slash and Duff and Matt and whoever else cared to join them partied while Axl and, increasingly, Izzy, slipped away and did their own thing. While the gang of three quickly grew used to Axl's absence – that split had been happening all the way through the recording of the albums – Duff was pretty sure that he knew the exact moment when Izzy Stradlin checked out of Guns N' Roses: 'I remember when he got sober, I was watching him,' Duff said. 'Really early on, early-Nineties, while we were still on the road. And the moment that he became at peace with himself was the moment I also recognised, he's not going to be here very much longer . . .'

Axl's habit of going on late now became so regular the others found it stifling. Getting angry with him didn't work. Pointing out how much money the band was being charged in fines for breaking curfews held no meaning. Eventually, they simply re-signed themselves to hanging around waiting . . .

At first it didn't seem like a big deal: this was the most dangerous band in the world after all, and the crowd had come to get a taste of that danger, that unpredictability. They arrived in Helsinki on 12 August and went straight from the plane to a club to watch The Black Crowes play. The following evening the tour opened at the Jäähalli and a pattern that was becoming as predictable as Slash, Duff and Matt getting happily fucked up began again: Axl walked offstage an hour into the show, just as the band were launching into 'Welcome to the Jungle', and came back 25 minutes later. Four days later in Stockholm the band went on after 11 p.m. as Axl was reportedly playing blackjack and then watching a firework display. Two days after that, the show in Copenhagen was halted when a firecracker was thrown onstage and Axl led the band off until the culprit turned themselves in. The band flew on to Oslo and checked into their hotel, only to take a call from one of Axl's team telling them that he had travelled to Paris instead, and the Oslo show was cancelled.

The next scheduled date was in Mannheim, Germany, on 24 August, where they'd sold more than 38,000 tickets in two days. The band went on late again, and again Axl walked offstage. The venue's design meant that the band's dressing rooms were almost a mile from the stage, and so a fleet of vans had been organised to shuttle them back and forth. When Axl didn't return, the rest of the band went to look for him and found him sitting in his van. As Slash remembered it, he and Duff tried to persuade Axl to return, and when they failed, Matt Sorum went stomping down towards the van, the last threads of his temper finally snapping. Just as he did, Axl stepped out of the vehicle and began to walk towards the stage.

'What the fuck are you doing?' Sorum yelled. Axl turned around and got back in the van. By now, fearing another riot, the promoters had closed the gates around the backstage area to prevent the band from leaving, and police in riot gear had begun to enter the arena. Axl returned to the stage and the set was completed.

'Wow, that was close,' thought Slash, as they walked off after the encores. In fact, it was worse than close. The next morning Izzy sent word that he was quitting the band. The show may have been the last straw, but the reality was that this had been coming for a long while now. Izzy was in neither camp – the Slash–Duff–Matt party boys nor the Axl play-when-I-say-so faction – and the bullshit all around him had simply become too much. Rock'n'roll was supposed to be a simple life, lived to the full but enjoyed to the full, too, and that enjoyment, as far as Izzy could see, was not predicated on private jets and huge crowds, nor on living in a haze of drugs and booze. The man that Alan Niven called 'the heart of the soul' of Guns N' Roses, the guitarist whose effortlessly loose groove gave them their unique swing, was gone. Slash spent several days trying to change his mind, but he knew it was no good. The seeds had been sown when Izzy had quit drugs the year before, then departed Los Angeles for a quieter life back in Lafayette. 'I needed to get out of LA for my own sanity,' he remembered. 'I was tired of the whole scene. I didn't move there as a junkie. I became one in LA. It came with the turf. Once I quit drugs, I couldn't help looking around and asking myself, "Is this all there is?" I was just tired of it; I needed to get out.'

Izzy said he regarded the excesses of the *Use Your Illusion* album and tour with the same cool eye: 'I think you make more decisions when you're sober. And when you're fucked up, you're more likely to put up with things you wouldn't normally put up with. I didn't like the complications that became such a part of daily life in Guns N' Roses. Sometimes for the simplest things to happen would take days. You're sitting there in the dressing room at a hockey rink and for, like, two hours the walls are vibrating while the audience is going, "Bullshit! Bullshit!" That time goes *slow* when you're sober. And they have to send a helicopter to the hotel to get him [Axl]. He would just "get ready", and sometimes he would "get ready" for a long time. I don't know what goes on upstairs with him. To me it's simple. Get an alarm clock, ya know? There's a modern invention that seems to work for people. You set it, and then you wake up when you're supposed to.'

As Alan Niven says now, when Izzy Stradlin walked out on Guns N' Roses, 'I wasn't expecting it but it didn't surprise me. For the record, I had nothing to do with that.' Niven was in Switzerland with Great White when Izzy told him the news. 'I got a phone call. He said, "I'm quitting, I can't stand it any more." I said, "Let's meet up in London and talk about this." He had one gig left on that leg, which was Wembley, and he wasn't gonna go [to Wembley]. There had been a gig in Germany where Axl was late and the security was not good. There were Germans walking around with submachine guns and Izzy totally wigged. Like, what if this goes fucking south? I had to talk him into playing Wembley.'

Alan found out there was a hotel right near to the stadium, a Hilton. He took it upon himself to rent a suit there for Izzy. 'He still hasn't paid me for this, the fucker!' he laughs. 'I said, "You go and sit in the Hilton and have somebody on the crew tell you when Axl turns up. And when he turns up you can be there in five minutes."' So that's what Izzy did, playing his final show with the band before 72,000 fans that had no idea they were witnessing history. A few days later Guns N' Roses were back in LA, taking a break while they awaited the release finally of the *Use Your Illusion* albums – and looking for somebody to fill Izzy's shoes.

Izzy Stradlin's departure from Guns N' Roses was made official on 7 November 1991: the second of the original five-piece to find himself gone: one for being too much of an addict, the other for being far too sober. Izzy now rehired Alan Niven as his manager and set about making a solo album. Slash was distraught. Duff was in a daze. Axl just had one more reason to feel angry and betrayed. In an interview with *Rolling Stone* some months later, Axl put the blame for Izzy's abrupt departure squarely at the feet of his childhood friend.

'My personal belief is that Izzy never really wanted something this big,' Axl told Kim Neely. 'There were responsibilities that Izzy didn't want to deal with. He didn't want to work at the standards that Slash and I set for ourselves.'

Asked for examples, Axl claimed Izzy didn't want to make videos; that even getting Izzy to work on his own songs on the

Use Your Illusion albums 'was like pulling teeth . . . Izzy's songs were on the record because I wanted them on the record, not because Izzy gave a shit either way. If people think I don't respect Izzy or acknowledge his talent, they're sadly mistaken. He was my friend. I haven't always been right. Sometimes I've been massively wrong, and Izzy's been the one to help steer me back to the things that were right. But I know that I wanted to get as big as we possibly could from day one, and that wasn't Izzy's intention at all.'

He also called Izzy 'an asshole' for 'the way he went about' leaving the band. 'We got this letter saying, "This changes, this changes, and maybe I'll tour in January." And they were ridiculous demands that weren't going to be met. I talked to Izzy for four and a half hours on the phone. At some points, I was crying, and I was begging. I was doing everything I could to keep him in the band.'

When I had the opportunity to speak with Izzy personally about why he left, however, a few years later he said he simply couldn't take it any more. 'The shows were completely erratic. I never knew whether we'd be able to finish the show from day to day, cos [Axl] would walk off. I said to Duff and Slash, we gotta learn a cover song or something, for when [Axl] leaves the stage. They were like, "Ah, let's have another beer . . ." They didn't care.' The final straw, he said, came after he reversed his initial decision to leave, and Axl – in a repeat of the Steven Adler situation 18 months before – issued Izzy with a contract to sign. 'This is right before I left – demoting me to some lower position. They were gonna cut my percentage of royalties down. I was like, "Fuck you! I've been there from day one, why should I do that? Fuck you! I'll go play the Whiskey." That's what happened. It was insane.'

By then, said Izzy, the control issues seemed to have completely taken his old friend over. 'And I never saw it coming. I mean, this is my side of it, he'd probably say I'm completely fucking crazy, but I think he went power mad. Suddenly he was trying to control *everything*. The control issues just became worse and worse and eventually it filtered down to the band. He was trying to draw up contracts for everybody! And this guy – he's not a Harvard graduate, Axl. He's just a guy, just a little guy, who sings, is talented. But, man, he turned into this fucking maniac! And I did, too, but it was a different kind of maniac. I was paranoid about the business aspect – freaking out going, 'Where's all the money?' For [Axl] the money wasn't as big a deal. But he had this power thing where he wanted complete control. And you can say, well, it goes back to your fucked-up childhood where his dad used to smack him around, you know, and he had no control, so now he's getting it back. But it's like, it's still kooky, you know? You don't have to have everybody signing stuff.'

Whatever the truth, with the next leg of the tour starting in less than a month, there was simply no time to reflect on the impact that Izzy's loss would have. 'Even when we lost Izzy because we had all those shows booked, I was just like, let's keep going,' Slash said. 'But when the tour was finally over and it was time to get back to work, it was impossible, because Izzy wasn't there, Steven wasn't there, and it really dawned on me, the harsh reality that Axl and I had grown so far apart and we weren't really all that close to begin with. We'd grown so far apart there was no putting that back together.'

The band shot a video for 'Don't Cry' without Izzy and then took a short hiatus that was mostly taken up with trying to find a new guitarist and then get rehearsed in time for the resumption of the tour. Axl's first thought was to try and recruit Dave Navarro, whose vast, trippy soundscapes had pushed Jane's Addiction to the forefront of the alt-rock movement that sat halfway between Guns N' Roses and the grunge scene that was rapidly emerging from Duff's hometown of Seattle. The pair met in LA to discuss the idea, and after they'd spoken at length, Axl thought he'd found the right man. Slash was less convinced. He was a fan of Navarro's musicianship but Dave was a lead player like him rather than a rhythm player like Izzy, and what Guns N' Roses needed at this point in time was a rhythm player. Nonetheless Axl was insistent and so Slash had the band set up at Mates rehearsal rooms in North Hollywood and asked Dave Navarro down. But Dave Navarro didn't show – three times.

After the third occasion Slash spoke to Axl, who spoke to Navarro, who assured them he'd be along, and so Slash went back to Mates and Navarro stood up them up once more. His name was not mentioned again. 'There were a number of reasons it didn't work out,' Navarro said candidly some years later. 'If I could pick one, it would be my own heroin addiction.'

Slash had a guitarist in mind too, the memory of a show way-back-when at Madam Wong's, when Candy had opened for Hol-lywood Rose. Candy had a guy whose style was not unlike Izzy's, loose-limbed, hip-rolling . . . His name was Gilby Clarke. Slash tracked him down to his most recent project, Kill for Thrills, and when they hooked up there was an instant chemistry, plus, im-portantly, a willingness from Clarke to throw himself into the job.

With the resumption of the tour looming, Gilby learned 60 songs in two weeks and flew through his audition – a couple of weeks after that he was in full rehearsals, and before anyone could really process the change, Guns N' Roses were back on the road, the *Use Your Illusion* records high in the charts and, to the big bad world out there, little damage done. 'Izzy's departure had happened so quietly, with no fanfare and no media awareness,' said Slash. 'It was such a major change within the band, but to the outside world it was a non-event.'

It was the classic push-pull that they were all becoming used to. Success, in the form of record sales and sold-out shows, seemed unending, and yet every day seemed to bring more 'crazy assed shit' to deal with.

11

BOUGHT ME AN ILLUSION

With the *Use Your Illusion* albums on their way to selling a combined total of over 30 million copies worldwide and a seemingly limitless demand for tickets to see them play, by 1992 Guns N' Roses should have been the richest band in the world. Yet from the moment the *Use Your Illusion* tour proper had begun in East Troy, Wisconsin, on 25 May 1991, the band were deep in a hole financially. On a tour of this scale, everything cost money. Firstly there was the band, of course, expanded to include the keyboard player Dizzy Reed – with plans for later in the tour for additional stage musicians led by the piano player and 'pit boss' Teddy 'Zig Zag' Andreadis, including a horn section featuring the baritone saxophonist Cece Worrall-Rubin, trumpeter Ann King and tenor sax player Lisa Maxwell; plus three back-up singers, Roberta Freeman, Traci Amos and Diane Jones. There were also a crew of 232 and two huge identical stages that leapfrogged one another from city to city. There was the private jet, plus hotel costs and other incidental expenses, plus costs borne by the promoter as a part of their fee: everything from venue hire to printing and distributing tickets. To cover them, the band earned an average gross from ticket sales of $601,000 per show. As Duff McKagan, who would later graduate from business school, put it: 'Oh, we generated a lot of dough, but it took us *two years* to break even – just to break even – on that tour . . .'

And these were just the standard costs that any tour accountant would have factored in long before the whole thing lumbered
off around the world. What kept Guns N' Roses in the red for
so long was actually the real, underlying story of the tour: fees,
penalties and fines paid to venues, promoters and local author-
ities for going onstage late and breaking curfews, the riots that
took place, plus all of the other waste that comes with the madness and boredom of being on the road: the yachts they rented;
the boat out to the Barrier Reef; the go-kart tracks and the restaurants that they paid to close down; the endless no-expense-
that-anyone-could-think-of-spared theme parties – Roman baths,
Mexican fiestas, a travelling casino – organised every night by
Axl's half-brother, Stuart, and his sister, Amy. In those details
lay the story of a band careening inexorably off the rails. Doug
Goldstein, now manager rather than tour manager, was nonetheless on the road almost full-time, there, as Slash and several others felt, to pacify Axl and keep the peace by any means
necessary.

As Goldstein says now: 'Ninety-nine per cent of managers
wouldn't have even been at the show. Just sitting in their big
homes in Palos Verdes or Bel Air or wherever, collecting their
fucking huge cheques and not doing any of the work that's really
imperative with a band like GN'R. The amount of *stress* that you
go through *every day* that there's a show. Fuck, even when there's
not a show. What's gonna happen today that I'm gonna need to
put my thinking cap on and be able to react to *in seconds?* Cos I
tell you what, if you say the wrong thing, Axl's gone. He's gone!
You're not getting him back onstage. No way.'

It had always been that way with Axl and Guns N' Roses, he
says. But this was now something different. 'Clearly from the beginning it was just as frenetic and as risky but you're playing in
front of eighty people in a club, and it's a lot easier to finagle
your way around an eighty-person instead of an 80,000-person

crowd. The amount of lives in jeopardy grows exponentially, at that point.'

The support bands on every leg of the tour were big acts in their own right – Skid Row; Nine Inch Nails; Smashing Pumpkins; Blind Melon; Faith No More, Motörhead . . . all there for the same reason: to have a good time. At least as far as Slash and Duff and Matt – the unruly gang of three – were concerned. Not quite everyone felt the same way though. Faith No More's keyboardist, Roddy Bottum, described the scene backstage as 'excess, excess, excess. There were more strippers than road crew.' Reprimanded for 'laughing about the absurdity of the touring environment in the press', his band were 'told that we'd have to apologise to Axl or leave the tour. We made an attempt to explain where we were coming from, but I think it went over his head because as a sort of peace offering he brought us to a trailer backstage where two naked women strippers were having sex.'

Touring for a while with Soundgarden in tow was another uneasy fit. The third prong in a Seattle trident that also included Nirvana and Pearl Jam, Soundgarden – despite their Zeppelin-worshipping roots – were perceived as dour grunge icons apparently set on doing away with the self-indulgent excesses of the hair metal scene that had originally birthed GN'R. The disconnect between the two bands was best illustrated by the disastrous prank pulled during their final show, in Arizona, in February 1992. As Soundgarden played their last song, Slash, Duff and Matt walked onstage holding three blow-up dolls. Slash, who was naked behind his, fell over and gave the crowd more of an insight into his life than he'd intended. Yet for Soundgarden's singer, Chris Cornell, these were harmless high jinks, behind which the band hid, while their leader glowered in the shadows.

'Without saying anything negative about Axl,' commented Cornell in 2012, 'what I remember the most was Duff and Slash and everyone else being regular, sweet, warm guys in a rock band that just wanted to play rock music. And then, like, there was this Wizard of Oz character behind the curtain that seemed to complicate what was the most ideal situation they could ever have been in: they were the most successful and famous rock band on the planet. Every single show, hundreds of thousands of fans just wanted to hear songs. For some reason there seemed to be this obstacle in just going out and participating in that. That is what I remember the most. It's sad.'

Slash, in an interview from around the same time, put it more simply. Soundgarden, he said, 'came from a place where there was no fun to be had while rocking . . .' It was clear – to Slash and Duff and Matt, at least – that they needed some real rock'n'roll accompaniment on tour. It was soon to arrive.

Once the tour had lapped America and sped through Japan, Mexico and London for an appearance at the Freddie Mercury tribute show at Wembley Stadium – where Axl was able to make amends to Elton John for the 'One in a Million' fiasco and play 'Bohemian Rhapsody' with John and Queen – the band arrived back in LA for a press conference at which they announced a co-headline tour with Metallica.

It was a thrilling concept, an idea of commercial genius: here were the two flat-out biggest rock bands on planet Earth, both known for the brilliance and excesses of their live shows, together as co-headliners on the same bill. The tour was to begin in July, allowing Guns N' Roses to make another circuit of Europe in the meantime. They were road-ready and playing well, and they needed to be. Like them, Metallica were reaching a creative and commercial peak, the officially untitled record known universally as *The Black Album* that they'd released the preceding August was blowing up, its mix of no-limits thrash metal tempered by grandiose arena rock ballads like 'Nothing Else Matters', and even a hit single with the sneakily catchy riff of 'Enter Sandman' powering their breakthrough into the mainstream. They were an utterly formidable live act, too, battle-hardened and blue collar, known for the intensity of their performance and the no-bullshit attitude they brought along with it.

This was in stark contrast to the reputation Guns N' Roses had now built up as the band that was always late onstage – with a singer likely to walk off at a moment's notice. Doug Goldstein would always be the one expected to coax Axl back. He depicts one memorable occasion in Lisbon, Portugal, in July 1992, a couple of weeks before the tour with Metallica was to begin, when the band was headlining a massive outdoor show at the Estádio José Alvalade.

'The stage is the furthest from the dressing room of any building I've ever been into in my life. Like a fire walk, right? So somebody throws a pipe bomb on stage and it goes off next to Axl and Axl's like, 'Fuck this! I'm fucking out of here!' Throws the mike down and I'm telling you it was the longest walk from stage to dressing room of any venue I've ever been into. It was, like, a two-mile walk! I tell the security guy Earl [Gabbidon], who's Axl's personal security guy, 'I don't care if they play wipe-out, keep the fucking band playing.' So I walk back to the dressing room with Axl. He's not saying a word. I'm not saying a word.

'Finally, we get to the dressing room and he goes on this diatribe, right, for I don't know maybe thirty minutes. 'Fuck this motherfucking shit! Fuck, fuck, fuck! I'm not here to blow up for people! That's not why I'm here! I'm here to fucking entertain!' So finally after thirty minutes I realise I've eaten two pizzas. I'm like, oh my god! This guy's gonna turn me into the Stay Puft Marshmallow Man! Then he goes, "What do you think?" I go, "Pardon me?" He goes, "What do you think?" I go, "Wait a second, this is where I get to interject my thought?"

'He goes, "Shut up, Doug. Yes, what do you think?" I said, "First off, happy anniversary." He goes, "What the fuck are you talking about?" I said, "Exactly one year ago today we were in St

Louis." He goes, "You're fucking kidding me." I go, "No. It is exactly one year ago today. So, what do I think? We have 230 people on the road with us. I personally hired every single person. So I stuck you guys into a car in St Louis and I stuck around to defend my friends. I saw half of them crying, because they were fearful for their lives.

'"So what do I think? I think that you owe it to the guys who have been setting up and tearing down your stages for the past two years to go back onstage. Because I don't want to see them petrified and crying again." He just said, "You know what, let's go." So we fucking went back and he finished the show.

'The rest of the band, I don't think they know to this day the shit I had to go through. First off, I have absolutely tried to empathise with what it's like to be up in front of 120,000 people without a singer. I mean, that's gotta just, like, eat your fucking gut to pieces. Not having any clue if he's coming back. But I don't think any of them ever put themselves in my position, empathetically, and tried to realise if I don't get this fucking guy back on stage, my band is in jeopardy, the fans are in jeopardy, and the 232 people working for me are in jeopardy.

'So every single fucking person in that venue is contingent upon me figuring out the right fucking thing to say to Axl Rose at that given moment, to get him to go back. And you know what, *not one fucking time* was I unable to get him to go back. Not one fucking time.'

So far anyway . . .

Guns N' Roses landed back at JFK airport in New York on 12 July 1992, a Monday, with the first show of the co-headline tour with Metallica scheduled for Friday at the RFK Stadium in Washington, DC. Axl was arrested at the airport on the outstanding warrant for the St Louis riot, bailed by a judge two days later and told he was free to go on tour. (GN'R were eventually banned from

St Louis for life, and Axl was charged with four counts of mis-demeanour assault and one count of property damage and fined $50,000.) Slash managed to fill those same few days by agreeing to marry his girlfriend, Renee. Nothing was ever quiet, it seemed.

Metallica had negotiated to go on first throughout the tour, which proved a smart move. Both bands were keen to impress one another and there was some natural competition, too. There was a mutual respect, one that showed itself from Guns' side with Axl's idea for the post-gig theme parties that were to become infamous for their lavishness and expense. His inspiration came from the Rolling Stones and the lounge they had at every show to entertain their guests. 'We'd spend $100,000 a night on parties,' said Matt Sorum. 'For two and a half years, there was something every night.' As well as an 'open bar', several pinball machines, pool tables, hot tubs and strippers dancing from tables, one night would be 'Greek night – four greased-up, muscle-bound guys [carrying] in a roast pig.' Another night would be 'Sixties night', with lava lamps on all the tables and slogans spray-painted on the walls: 'Acid is groovy'; 'Kill the pigs'. There were also limos on-call 24 hours a day. 'The first night we played Giants Stadium,' says Matt, 'there was one pinball machine and a few bottles of booze backstage. Axl came in and said, 'This isn't the Rolling Stones!' So the next night there's a full casino, tons of lobster and champagne flowing everywhere.'

While Metallica were onstage, Guns N' Roses would be at their hotel. None of the band would have got to bed much before 7 a.m. Lemmy, for so long one of the band's heroes, whose band, Motörhead, opened the show when they played the Rose Bowl in Pasadena on 3 October, recalled how 'they were already fragment-ing. Axl was on his own. It didn't feel like they were thinking as a band any more.' As Slash would write in his autobiography: 'Our inability to get onstage on time was like the big elephant in the room every night. Lars Ulrich [Metallica's drummer] never said anything to me, but he did to Matt and it was humiliating and embarrassing how lame those parties were and how disappointed Metallica were that we couldn't even get onstage on time.'

There was another aspect to the tour, however, that Axl also instigated which was much less publicised. Doug Goldstein explains: 'Well, you know, Axl did come up with a great idea on the Metallica tour . . . different educational organisations, homeless causes, Greenpeace, anybody that had kind of a nice message to be delivered, we allowed them to set up in the concourse and deliver their messages. And that was Axl's idea and it was a great idea, because those were very, very well-attended booths, and the organisations that were brought in loved the opportunity to do that. You know, when you're in a 100,000-person stadium and you get to pass out educational material to people, that was Axl's successful attempt at giving back.'

Behind the scenes, Axl was also doing everything he could to try to get to the root of whatever it was that continually scratched at his insides like an unfinished feeling. Interviewed in 1992 for Andy Warhol's *Interview* magazine, he spoke candidly of the intensive therapy sessions he had been undergoing, in terms of improving his mental attitude to his relationships with both men and women. 'I reached a point where I was basically dead and still breathing,' he said. 'I didn't have enough energy to leave my bedroom and crawl to the kitchen to get something to eat. I had to find out why I was dead, and why I felt like I was dead. I had a lot of issues that I didn't really know about in my life and didn't understand how they affected me. I didn't realise that I felt certain ways toward women, toward men, toward people in general, and toward myself. The only way to get through that was to go back through it and find it and re-experience it and attempt to heal it. I'm still working on that but I'm a lot further along than I was.' Meanwhile, he likened his relationship with the band as 'kinda like a marriage and a half, or a marriage and a household'.

Especially his relationship with Slash, which was 'definitely a marriage'.

He also spoke of his radically new perspective on the rock'n'roll lifestyle; specifically, the drug taking and heavy drinking Guns N' Roses appeared to endorse. 'I would also like it to be known that I'm not a person to be telling the youth of America, "Don't get wasted."' Too many bands that had publicly cleaned up 'talk about things they did and how they were wrong. I don't know if it was necessarily wrong. It helped them survive. At the time they weren't given the proper tools to do the proper healing. I personally don't do any hard drugs any more, because they get in the way of me getting to my base issues, and I'd rather get rid of the excess baggage than find a way to shove it deeper in the closet, at this time in my life.'

He confessed that the overwhelmingly negative critical reaction to 'One in a Million' had also helped him change. 'I went out and got all kinds of video tapes and read books on racism. Books by Martin Luther King and Malcolm X. Reading them and studying, then after that I put on the tape and I realised, "Wow, I'm still proud of this song. That's strange. What does that mean?" But I couldn't communicate as well as I do now about it, so my frustration was just turned to anger. Then my anger would be used against me and my frustration would be used against me: "Look, he's throwing a tantrum."'

Meanwhile, onstage, once they eventually got there, Guns N' Roses were as brilliant as ever, with Gilby slipping unobtrusively into the Izzy role, his cool good looks and easy style fitting well with Slash's shirt-off, king-of-cool persona. But the show was affected so often by Axl's lateness, his unpredictable moods, the atmosphere being punctured like a balloon, Slash likened it to an athlete preparing for a race: there was an optimum moment when they were ready to go, but when that moment passed, adrenalin began seeping away to the point that, once they were onstage, it took a few songs for the rush to return and the band to really hit their groove.

'The reality is that touring for Axl was a painstaking process,' says Goldstein. 'We had the $10,000 exercise machine put into his room every day that he'd get on. His routine was about a four- to five-hour routine daily, between chiropractic, massage, two hours of vocal warm-up and warm-down.'

The singer now had his own expensively assembled retinue of chiropractor, masseuse, vocal coach, bodyguard, driver, personal assistant, PR, manager and gaggle of friends like Del James and Dana Gregory, his psychotherapist, Suzzy London, and a new, even more influential figure in his life: a professional psychic he had recently become enthralled by named Sharon Maynard. The head of a non-profit organisation based in Sedona, Arizona, Arcos Cielos Corp (from the Spanish for 'sky arcs'), describing itself as an 'educational' enterprise, specialising in 'channelling' past lives, extra-terrestrial intelligence and the power of crystals, Maynard was a short, middle-aged Asian woman who had started to take a central role in Axl's life that would stretch throughout the rest of the decade. Operating out of her own countryside home, where she lived with her husband, Elliott, a kindly grey-haired man, 'Dr Elliott and Sharon Maynard' had both been thanked in the *Use Your Illusion* liner notes. Known to the rest of the band and touring crew as Yoda (after the goblin-like mystic in *Star Wars*), Maynard had a role on the road that was less specific than London's, but Axl's reliance on them both grew equally import- ant. According to a crew member, Yoda and her own assistant 'were like aliens'.

Every major decision Axl now made was in consultation with Maynard. 'Slash and Duff – *everybody* – would say, who is this gal and why is she involved in a lot of the business decisions? I said, "You know what? I told Axl my opinion." Which I did. I just ques- tioned certain things and said those to him. And she was able to turn that around. Didn't attack me. I think she knew better than that, cos Axl and I were very close and she didn't want to play whose dick was bigger. But she handled it incredibly well. I'm a firm believer in that we all have our own beliefs and that we're entitled to those. I had a responsibility as his manager to air my feelings. I told him that I respect any and all of the decisions that he made about his life cos it's his life . . . I told him, "All I am is a conduit to your dreams. I'm not a dream maker, you tell me what your dream is and I'll figure out how we're gonna get there. I'm a facilitator of dreams."'

According to Axl, 'It's like, I have a pit crew. And it's like, I'm a car.' The chiropractor also stood at the side of the stage each night so that Axl could get adjusted between songs. And for a while he was taking up to 60 vitamins a day. 'We do muscle testing and kinesiology,' he explained. 'We do chiropractic work and acupuncture. We do cranial adjusting. Oh, yeah. On a daily basis. I'm putting my life back together, and I'm using everything I can.'

Everybody – from the lowliest bag carrier to the loftiest record company executive – was also now forced to sign confidentiality agreements forbidding them from commenting publicly on any aspect of the tour without Axl's express permission first, and then only in writing. Whatever 'regression therapy' he was undergoing, paranoia was still the main order of the day and Axl was more determined than ever to exert complete control over any given situation he now found himself in.

For all their efforts behind the scenes, though, the one thing Maynard, London and co. could not protect Axl from was random acts by his own fans. Ten days into the tour with Metallica, at Giant Stadium in Rutherford, New Jersey, on 29 July, during the last song, 'Knockin' on Heaven's Door', swaying back and forth in his white spandex shorts, white buckskin jacket and white cowboy hat, Axl was hit in the genitals by a cigarette lighter thrown from the audience. Doubled up in pain, he turned his back on the crowd, threw his microphone into the air, tore off his hat, and staggered to the side of the stage where he complained to Doug Goldstein that his voice had gone. 'He literally came over to the side of the stage and goes [gruff voice], "I can't talk. What do you want me to do?"'

Duff took over briefly on vocals while the crowd began chanting, 'Axl, Axl, Axl!' But there was no way he was coming back and when the house lights came on the crowd just stood there for a while before filing out, dejected. The very next day an announcement was made claiming Axl had sustained 'severe damage to his vocal cords' and that the next three shows – in Boston, Columbia and Minneapolis – would all have to be rescheduled, although it was whispered amongst the crew that the latter had been cancelled on the orders of Yoda, who was 'concerned' about disruptive 'magnetic energy concentrations' around Minneapolis.

Slash began to wonder whether Axl actually felt that he was heightening the atmosphere and anticipation with his elaborate preparations. 'I think it was all building up what Guns meant to him in his mind,' he observed in his memoir. 'And in the face of that he simply could not comprehend how what he was doing did not make complete sense to us or the rest of the world.'

Maybe he was onto something. It's tempting to interpret Axl entirely through his actions, to see him as some kind of ego-riddled tyrant dictating his terms of business to the world, placing himself and his needs above those of the band, the crew, the paying punters and everyone else with a stake in seeing Guns N' Roses play live. Yet run the film backwards and watch it through Axl's eyes and another reality suggests itself. Guns N' Roses is his life's work, his greatest achievement. He has just poured into it his best songs about the rawest and most difficult moments in his life. He's immensely proud of what he has created and he wants to present it to the world in the best possible way. Ranged against him are people in record companies, promoters, managers and a million other hangers-on, plus a band with whom he used to be tight but who now spend most of their time blasted out of their brains and failing to understand why he's not having a good time, too. All of these people have agendas, be they business or personal, and they want something from him – time, money, something – and all of it in some way detracts from what he is trying to do. As a perfectionist, it drives him crazy, fuels the rage. He can see it, so why can't they? So he controls whatever he can still control.

He was a sensitive, shy, angry guy, clever and misunderstood and living in circumstances very few people could imagine. All of the past-life regression and the various therapies and thinking and searching he'd done came back to one thing: his childhood, and how it had been taken away from him; how his father's abuse had left him marooned emotionally in his early years. 'When they talk about Axl Rose being a screaming two-year-old, they're right,' he once said. Now he wasn't medicating that pain but trying to express it artistically.

When the film was run that way, a lot of what Axl Rose did and how he was made to do it made much more sense. There was no denying that, when it worked, the Guns N' Roses of 1992 was the most spectacular event in rock: 250,000 watts of power, a maniacal fireworks display featuring 20 bangs, 28 sparkles, 15 airbursts, 20 flashes, 25 waterfalls and 32 fountains. Axl, now relying for parts of the set on a teleprompter for his lyrics, took to changing his stage outfits on almost every other song, from spandex shorts to leather kilt to Jesus/Bukowski/Manson T-shirts, to another that read: *Nobody Knows I'm a Lesbian*. The highlight was always his beloved 'November Rain', which he sang his heart out to while seated at a grand piano that rose into the middle of the stage with the piano designed to look like a motorcycle seat. Slash would casually climb atop the motorcycle for his back-arching guitar solo.

'Knockin' on Heaven's Door' would end the set, a large red sign flashing the words: GUNS N' ROSES, GUNS N' ROSES, GUNS N' ROSES ... If Axl allowed an encore, which was never a given, they would stride back on for a blood-pounding version of 'Paradise City', the whole 12-piece band returning one last time for a bow, arm in arm, looking for all the world like the cast members surrounding the star of a major theatrical production, right down to the moment when Axl would toss roses into the crowd. Followed by more fireworks, the red lights now flashing: THANK YOU WE LOVE YOU, THANK YOU WE LOVE YOU ... The very last thing the crowd would see each night would be a cartoon of a butcher chopping off his thumb and yelling, 'Son of a bitch!' before chopping off his arm and then his head, which was left twitching in a large pool of blood. What the hidden meaning of that was no one knew, but it made Axl laugh.

Meanwhile, back in the so-called real world, Slash was planning his wedding to Renee Suran, although the relationship, which would be made official in October 1992, when the pair were finally hitched in Marina Del Rey, was by his own admission interrupted by various dalliances, including a fairly serious involvement with Perla Ferrar, who would later become his second wife. Duff married his second wife, Linda Johnson, a month before Slash married Renee.

The subject of Slash's prenuptial agreement led to trouble soon after the Metallica dates had resumed. In San Francisco the couple got into a row about it, and Slash sloped off to score some dope from a pornstar friend of his and her boyfriend. The trio got loaded on crack and smack in Slash's hotel suite, the guitarist taking it too far and briefly OD'ing. He was taken to hospital and when he got back to the hotel, a furious Doug Goldstein sent a bottle of Jack Daniel's flying through the TV set in Slash's room. 'You know the Narcan scene in *Pulp Fiction*?' Goldstein asks, referring to the scene where the unconscious Uma Thurman character is jolted back to life after a heroin overdose by the drug dealer stabbing her in the chest with a syringe full of naloxone, a prescription medicine used by paramedics in emergency situations to reverse an opioid overdose. 'We carried that,' he says matter-of-factly.

'I hit Slash with that on five different occasions. The fifth time that he went code blue, we were in San Francisco on the Metallica tour. I got a call at three o'clock in the morning: Slash is dead outside the elevator. I ran outside with the Narcan. Hit him in the chest. The EMT showed up, took him away, and myself and a couple of the other guys, we kicked the shit out of the drug dealers.'

When Slash returned from the hospital early the next morning Doug was waiting for him in his suite, along with Earl Gabbidon, Axl's personal security guy, John Reese, the tour manager, and Slash's bodyguard, Ronnie, 'who we used to call Slash on steroids. He looked just like Slash, *identical*, only very muscular,' recalls Doug. 'We're sitting there and I said, "Slash, you're done. You don't do this any more." And Ronnie his bodyguard's crying. I saw that and I'd known Ronnie since I was seventeen years old, and I'd never seen him emote at all. I said, "Slash, look at Ronnie, you're really gonna do this to your best friend?"

'He says, "You know what? Fuck you! Fuck Ronnie! Fuck all you guys. Get the fuck out of my room. I'm gonna continue to do whatever the fuck I wanna do!" And some trigger snapped in my head and I started throwing shit and by the time I left I'd done $75,000 damage to the room. And I quit. I said, "You know what, I'm fucking out of here! Go fuck yourself! I'm not gonna watch my family kill themselves." So I woke up my wife, put her in the car. We were off to the airport.

'Then John Reese went to Axl and told him what happened, and Axl said, "Well, if Doug's gone, I'm gone." Then he went to

Slash's room and said, "Just wanna let you know, now that Doug's quit, I'm quitting too. I suggest you try and make amends with Doug or I'm not gonna be at this Saturday's show with Metallica at the Rose Bowl."' Back in LA the next day, Slash drove down to Doug Goldstein's place in a limo. 'He said, "What's it gonna take?" I said, "Rehab. As soon as the Metallica tour's over, you're going straight in."'

He pauses, sighs. 'Whenever I talk about it I allude to the bunker mentality in wartime. You know, three guys in a bunker and shots are being fired over their heads and they're bunkered down for a week at a time. By the end of that week there's so much PTSD [Post Traumatic Stress Disorder] that takes place and you've gotten so much closer because of it.'

It was also left to Doug Goldstein to have a serious word with Duff, when his drinking became so bad he could barely play the bass any more. He had the sound engineer make him a record-ing on DAT purely of Duff's playing. 'Listening to it, it was like, doink! Doink! Then a gap. Then . . . doink! I'm like, what the fuck? I'm like, "Look, man, you need to stop drinking so much before the show. I don't care how much you want to drink after the show. That's between you and your god. But it's affecting the show therefore it's affecting the kids who paid a ton of money to come to the show." Duff's like, "You're crazy. I'm not playing like shit."'

Goldstein waited a few days, then called Duff into his hotel room one afternoon, where had a stereo was set up with a DAT player, and at a time when he knew he wouldn't be drunk yet, and played Duff the tape. 'It was a recording of the bass channel from the desk, so that was all you could hear. I played him 'Sweet Child'. Again, it's like, doink! Doink! Doiinnnkkkk!!! Not only is he not playing the parts, he's not even playing them on time. I'm trying desperately not to laugh. You can tell he's really embar-rassed. But after that Duff cut down on his drinking before the show. He would drink [before] but substantially yes. Cos he was pretty much pickled the entire tour.'

Goldstein, who still maintains that Axl Rose is 'the most talented, intelligent, giving guy I've ever worked with, who has a wonderful sense of humour, which people don't know about', now feels, however, that, as he says, 'I don't think there would have been Slash's and Duff's horrendous drug and alcohol use had they not been scared shitless that Axl was gonna leave them hanging on a stage again.'

Had they grown fearful of him by then, I wondered?

'I don't think they were fearful at all. I think they grew angry at having to stand up on stage and play alone. Matt Sorum used to come to me all the time and say, "I'm going in there and kick his fucking ass!" I used to say, "Come on, man. You do that we're all on the way home." Finally he comes to me at Axl's dressing room door, and he goes, "That's it, get the fuck out of my way!" And I'd had it with Matt's bravado so I said, "Go ahead." He walks in and I don't hear any trashing of furniture or anything.' Instead, when Doug went in to check on the situation a few minutes later, 'He's sipping champagne with Axl. Like, oh yeah, way to go, tough guy. You had your golden opportunity . . .'

In order to try to stay on top of everything, Goldstein would find himself staying awake round the clock for days at a time – 'I've never really been a sleeper' – but on the *Illusion* tour, he says, 'For three nights in a row I wouldn't sleep and the fourth night I'd sleep for four to six hours. The really cute thing is Slash and I were so close he knew my sleeping pattern, so on the fourth night he'd come to my room and he'd answer the phones so that my sleep wouldn't be disrupted. Oh my god, yeah. It was so cute. He'd show up, "Hey, go to sleep." "Okay, man."'

That was when things were going good. After nearly two years on the road, though, even Slash was flagging. 'Slash used to come to me about once every two weeks,' Goldstein says. 'And whenever there was something would happen he'd say, "This is fucking insane. I'm outta here." My response was always the same: "You know what, Slash? If you wanna leave this train and go do clubs in LA, let's go." Or whenever Slash would bring up: "Axl's costing us a ton of money." I'd say, "He *is* costing us money I'll give you that. If you wanna go play the Whiskey, we can do that. But, remember, we just played in front of 220,000 people at the Maracana Stadium, in Rio, for two nights, and we picked up $7 million. The [outgoing expenses] cost us $500,000 to do that. So we will end up with $6.5 million, where the Whiskey we're gonna pick up a $250 to $500 guarantee." But it was what it was. Basically, I was just trying to keep it going as long as I could.'

Nevertheless, with the benefit of a quarter of a century's hind-sight, Doug Goldstein now says he regrets not allowing Slash and Duff to confront Axl more directly with their grievances. 'I used to say the best thing that I did for the band was I never let Axl know how much the rest of the band hated his fucking guts. Because if he would have known that Slash and Duff and Matt and even Izzy . . . To Axl, he thinks Izzy quit the band because of the rampant drug use. That wasn't it at all.'

Now, though, he says, 'If I had one thing to do over again it would be, I wouldn't keep the band away from Axl. I thought at the time that I was doing the right thing. But in retrospect clearly I was not. Because they had no idea how much Axl loved them. In retrospect, I should have let them have their disputes heard, because Axl, I protected him from hearing that in fear that we'd all be going home.'

What about the relationship between Slash and Axl?

'There wasn't one.'

Did Axl and Slash still connect on any level?

'I think on the stage they did. But other than that, not really. I have to take some responsibility for that again, because if I were to . . . who knows? I mean, Axl was so sensitive that if Slash would have said, "You're being a big fucking cunt", I think maybe we would have all gone home. I don't know. Hindsight's 20/20. But . . . I really don't know the answer to that. Had I let them sit in a room and figure out each other's grievances maybe they would have been able to work things out. Maybe they wouldn't have. I don't know.'

Then there was Montreal. A week after the tour had been put on hold while Axl recovered his vocals, the Guns N' Roses–Metallica tour resumed with a huge show at the Olympic Stadium in Montreal. It was to prove another pivotal moment on the tour. After a strong support bill featuring Motörhead, Faith No More and Ice T's Body Count, Metallica were three songs into what was shaping up as a typically powerful set when James Hetfield was badly burned by a rogue pyro stage effect. By Hetfield's account, 'During "Fade to Black", I'm up there playing the part, you know, and these coloured flames are going off. I'm a little confused on where I'm supposed to be. I walk forward, I walk back, the pyro guy doesn't see me and "whoosh" a big coloured flame goes right up under me. I'm burnt – all my arm, my hand completely, down to the bone. The side of my face, hair's gone. Part of my back . . . I watched the skin just rising, things going wrong.'

A quick-thinking stagehand dumped a bucket of cold water over Hetfield's injured arm, which temporarily cooled the injury, but by the time he'd been led backstage, the pain from the second- and third-degree burns was intense. Metallica had no choice but to abandon their set. Guns N' Roses were at their hotel when a call came asking them to travel to the stadium and cover the rest of Metallica's show. They agreed immediately and en route Slash discussed with the other musicians what extra material they could play to extend their set. There was, however, no Axl. Guns N' Roses took the stage two hours later than their regularly scheduled time and the crowd was already tilting dangerously on the edge when Axl cut the planned two-hour set short at the ninety-minute mark, complaining the onstage monitors were not loud enough for him to hear himself sing. He'd already told the baffled crowd, before 'Double Talkin' Jive', that this would be 'our last show for a long time'. Then, at the end of 'Civil War', he growled, 'Thank you, your money will be refunded, we're outta here.' Cue another riot as more than 2000 fans fought with police, resulting in over a dozen injuries. As Metallica's Lars Ulrich later commented wryly: 'That was the wrong night to have monitor problems.'

When the tour finally got going again, at the International Raceway in Phoenix, Arizona, on 25 August, it was almost midnight before Axl led the band onstage, announcing to the exhausted crowd, 'Maybe I was just too fucking bummed-out to get my ass up here any quicker.' Or as he put it afterwards: 'Maybe I couldn't move any faster than I was because it was a bitch.'

Says Doug Goldstein now: 'Everybody blamed Axl for not getting to the show at an earlier time. But the reality is I called him and just said, "Where are you in the process?" And he said, "What's up?" I told him and he said, "Doug, I'll do the best I can but you know what I go through." I said, "Right, no, I understand." People say it was two and a half hours [before Axl got to the show], that's bullshit. It was more like fifty minutes when he showed up. Maybe an hour and fifteen, tops. And here's the reality on the Montreal riot. Nobody knows what *really* transpired.'

He claims that during the break while Axl waited for his voice to repair itself, Lars Ulrich had instructed Metallica's production manager to have his drum riser moved 'so that the first fifteen rows of fans can see him. Thereby causing the sites of the pyro cubes to be moved. But he [Lars] doesn't tell anyone that they've change the pyro cubes, and so James is standing in an area which normally is a safe spot for him. And the pyro blows up right on top of him . . . Axl gets solely blamed for it, and he had fucking nothing to do with it.'

Trapped in the dressing rooms beneath the stadium, the band heard the riot begin. It sounded like a stampede, the ominous thunder of thousands of people laying waste to everything around them. The sky boxes were trashed, the merchandise stalls looted, cars in the parking lot upturned and set alight. There were more than a dozen arrests, with ten rioters and three police officers taken to hospital and damages estimated next morning at half a million dollars. It was St Louis all over again, only this time with less of an excuse.

'It was a very tense time,' said Slash in his autobiography in 2007. 'It was actually a huge issue for me because I'd lost face with everyone in Metallica . . . when it mattered most it felt like we'd given even less. I couldn't look James or Lars or anyone from their band in the eye for the rest of the tour.'

It's a tribute to the toughness of James Hetfield that he was back onstage less than three weeks later, unable to play guitar but patched up and ready to sing. The band had even found time to rehearse a stand-in rhythm player, Metal Church's John Marshall. The experience wasn't an entirely comfortable one for Hetfield: his arm was heavily bandaged, moving about was difficult and he wasn't sure of what to do with himself during the lengthy instrumental passages in some of Metallica's more epic songs – 'Maybe I should go off and do some laundry' – but he was there. It emphasised the apparent gulf in the attitudes of the bands towards their work. What's more, James Hetfield was the kind of classic alpha-male biker-type dude that Axl sometimes seemed to aspire to be. Axl spent part of the ensuing break in New York, where one of his management team, Craig Duswalt, met his future wife. As he said: 'I'm married to Natasha because James Hetfield stood on a flash pot in Montreal . . .'

Even on the longest and most arduous tours, life went on. Axl, having had his marriage to Erin Everly annulled 18 months before, was in a new and consuming relationship with the model Stephanie Seymour which had begun in the summer of 1991. Seymour would appear in the infamous video for the 'November Rain' single that had come out in February 1992, a vast and overblown production that cost $2.1 million to make and that featured Axl 'marrying' his girlfriend in a wedding that soon turned into a mini-riot, Slash seen soloing on the edge of a mountain as cameras mounted on helicopters whirled around him in faux epiphany. Given Axl's attachment to the song the symbolism was heavy; the po-faced nature of the storyline – drawn from a Del James concept – adding to the merriment of the band's detractors. Indeed, with grunge the new flavour of the day, bands like Nirvana and Pearl Jam seemed to be bringing a ground zero approach to everything that had come before, their sights set firmly on what were now perceived to be ridiculous metal trolls like Mötley Crüe and Poison, Def Leppard and Bon Jovi. Ironically, Guns N' Roses had probably done more to help usher in this new age of rock than any other Eighties artist besides Metallica. But things like the wincingly over-the-top 'November Rain' video and Axl Rose's increasingly self-indulgent demands were eroding their image. Street rock was now epitomised by the frill-free riffs and thrift store chic of grunge. The *NME*, then still Britain's most influential music weekly, had gone as far as labelling Nirvana 'the Guns N' Roses it's okay to like'.

Nowhere was this made more clear, symbolically, than on 9 September 1992 when Guns N' Roses performed 'November Rain' live at MTV's annual Video Music Awards, held that year at UCLA's Pauley Pavilion. Elton John had agreed to join the band on piano and backing vocals and Axl was tremendously excited about it. Nothing must go wrong! The fat had already hit the fire, however, when Nirvana, who opened the show with 'Lithium', stole the show by busking a few bars of a completely different song, the as yet unreleased 'Rape Me', which the MTV organisers had expressly forbidden them from doing, only segueing into 'Lithium' as MTV's vice-president, Judy McGrath, was about to order the director to cut to a commercial break. It caused a major frisson backstage and set a precedent that made Slash and Duff swearing at the America Music Awards the previous year look asinine by comparison. It also set a defiantly anti-establishment tone Axl would find impossible to match with his much more studied and showbizzy duet with Elton. The comparison between the old, ornately garbed gods and the new, lean and hungry pretenders was there for all to see. Things turned really nasty though when, as Nirvana left the stage, Kurt Cobain spat on the keys of the piano he believed belonged to Axl, but which actually belonged to Elton.

Then, to add insult to injury, Cobain's wife, Courtney Love, whose taste for confrontation was the equal of Axl's, called out as he wandered past with Stephanie, 'Axl! Axl!' Holding aloft her and Kurt's baby daughter, Frances Bean. 'Will you be the godfather of our child?' Furious, Axl marched over to where she and Cobain were seated and pointed his finger in Kurt's face. 'You shut your bitch up,' he ordered, 'or I'm taking you down to the pavement!' The Nirvana entourage burst into laughter. All except for Kurt, who pretended to be affronted, glaring at Courtney and telling her, 'Shut up, bitch!' At which his band and friends all burst into laughter again.

In an effort to take the sting out of the situation, Stephanie sweetly asked Courtney, 'Are you a model?' But Courtney merely regarded her coldly. 'No,' she replied. 'Are you a brain surgeon?'

It didn't end there, though, and when Nirvana returned to their trailer after the show, waiting for them was a posse from the GN'R camp, including Axl's bodyguards. Kurt ran into the trailer to check that Frances was untouched, but Nirvana's bassist, Krist

Novoselic, was immediately surrounded. A lot of pushing and cursing ensued, in which Duff made it pretty clear he intended to personally see to Novoselic. But an even larger crowd of industry onlookers began to gather and the situation was eventually re-solved without anyone getting hurt. Pissed off but still supremely paranoid, Axl told friends that Love was actually trying to pos-sess him. 'He believes people are always trying to find a window through to control his energy,' said a friend. Axl's way of dealing with it was by 'controlling the people who have access to him'.

With a sense of irony not even Kurt could have dreamed up, the final show of the Guns N' Roses–Metallica tour, on 6 October, was at the King Dome in Seattle, the home of grunge's biggest stars. After it was over, *RIP* published one of Axl's most revealing interviews yet. In it, he owned up for the first time to feelings of inadequacy. 'I'm a difficult person to deal with,' he admitted, 'I'm a pain in the ass to understand, and I've had my share of problems.'

He didn't take drugs any more though, he said, even the pot smoking had been almost eradicated. Instead, he was 'on very specific, high-tuned vitamins'. He was also involved in 'extensive emotional work to reach certain heights with myself that doing hard drugs would interfere with', undertaking several detox pro-grammes at once, he said, in order to 'release trapped toxins that are there because of trauma'. This was one of the reasons why he was so often late onstage, he said. He didn't mean to 'inconven-ience the crowd' but he was 'fighting for my own mental health, survival and peace'.

The work he was doing was 'so I can do my job'. He had learned that 'when certain traumas happen to you, your brain releases chemicals that get trapped in the muscles where the trauma oc-curred. They stay there for your whole life. Then, when you're fifty years old, you've got bad legs or a bent back.' That wasn't going to happen to him. 'But as soon as we release one thing and that damage is gone, some new muscle hurts. That's not a new injury; it's a very old injury that, in order to survive, I've buried.' Every day he was on the road he received some form of either 'muscle therapy' or 'kinesiology, acupuncture . . .' He wasn't about 'escaping through drugs and sex any more,' he insisted. 'I've reached a point where I can't escape. There *is* no escape . . .'

He also admitted that he was basically the leader of the band now. Matt Sorum, Gilby Clarke, Dizzy Reed, even Duff were 'all members of this gang' but 'the business is basically run by Slash and myself. Then we run whatever it is we're discussing by Duff and see if he's cool with it. Guns N' Roses is basically Slash, Duff, Doug Goldstein and myself.'

Asked what came next for the band, he answered prophetically, 'We've pretty much stayed within the parameters of rock'n'roll music as we know it. I'd like to see if we could add anything to GN'R, possibly bring in a new element that hasn't been there before . . . There was a certain focus we all wanted to keep for *Illusion I* and *II*, but when I did 'My World' everyone dug it and wanted it on the record. By the next record I think we can branch out a lot further . . . I don't feel now like I did when I wrote "Estranged". I'm not as bummed out as I was then. I've grown past that.'

While Metallica had made millions of dollars from the co-headline tour with Guns N' Roses, even though the bands were on an equal split Goldstein found himself in the unenviable position of having to explain to Axl and Slash why GN'R had lost around 80 per cent of their fees in costs associated with going on late plus the untrammelled spending on entertaining themselves. The only remedy was to keep touring and claw it all back. In the event, they would play on for another ten months, heading down through South America and the Pacific Rim, followed by another trek through North America and then Europe – almost

50 shows in all, and ending up in South America once more, for two climactic gigs at the River Plate stadium in Buenos Aires.

There were some magical moments: in Colombia, at the magnificent El Campín stadium in Bogotá, they played 'November Rain' in the middle of a tropical storm, steam rising up from the 36,000 crowd, as if the very heavens were answering Axl's call. And then there were some moments everyone wanted to forget. Being 'smart enough to know that going to Bogotá in '92 was an arduous task and you're playing with some guys that are just not above board', Doug Goldstein had demanded – and got – all the band's fees upfront. 'I also hired US Embassy security to complement the eight or so security guys that I already employed.'

The signs were not good, though, when the band's equipment was delayed leaving Simón Bolívar International Airport in Venezuela, where they had just headlined a sold-out show at the 20,000-capacity Caracas Polyhedron. Booked to perform two shows – a Friday and a Saturday night show in Bogotá – the group arrived at their hotel late on Thursday night, early Friday morning, where an already worried Goldstein was concerned to find the three promoters of the shows sitting in the hotel bar 'absolutely blasted out of their minds. Between the booze and the coke I couldn't tell if they were gonna fall down or jump over the fucking bar.'

A noisy stand-off ensued with the Colombian promoters demanding half their money back as the band would only now be able to perform one of their two scheduled shows. Goldstein, however, insisted the band was happy to stay on and play a second show on the Sunday, to make up for the lost date on Friday. He picks up the story.

'They were like, "No, fuck you! You have to give us the money back!" I said, "No, fuck you. I'm going to bed. Goodnight." So I go to my room and about four o'clock in the morning they call me.' They informed Doug that they had taken one of the band's PR people hostage. 'Oh, and by the way, the three guys that are promoting the event, one guy owns the television station, one guy owns the radio station and the other guy owns the newspaper. The chances of getting *my* story out are fucking nil. So I go, "You know what, she's not that good." Click. Hung up the phone.'

Having called their bluff (the so-called hostage was allowed to go back to her hotel room), Goldstein then had to find a way to keep the band calm. 'Back in '92 in Bogotá, it was *crazy*. The entire day and night, all you hear is machine-gun fire in the hills. We're all going, why in the fuck are we here, right?'

He was on the phone the morning of the show when suddenly there was a huge boom. 'A huge bomb outside the hotel rocks back and forth. So Duff, who looks like a fucking ghost he's been doing so much blow, he comes into my room and he goes, "What the fuck was that?" I go, "What was what?" He goes, "Don't say what! The fucking bomb!" 'I say, "What the fuck?" he says, "Fuck you, Doug! The bomb!"

'I hang up the phone. I go, "Dude, what are you talking about?" He goes, "Doug, fuck you. I'm on my way to the airport. I'm fucking going home, this is crazy!" I go, "Duff, if you go catch a plane before the show, they're gonna kidnap me until we return all the money. You can't fucking do that to me." He goes, "Are you out of your fucking mind, man? I am not fucking staying here!" I go, "Duff, I'm gonna take you back to the Old Compadre ..." He's shaking his head as I'm talking. I go, "One of the first questions I asked you guys [when we met], what do you guys wanna be? You guys collectively said you wanna be the biggest band in the world. You know what? To be the biggest band in the world you have to play the world."' He laughs. 'Duff's rebuttal was one of the greatest comeback lines ever: "No, no, Doug. I remember that dinner. Axl, Slash: biggest band in the world. Duff: biggest band in North America. *Okay for me ...*"'

Axl is escorted to a police car after being arrested as he stepped off an Air France Concorde jet from Paris, 12 July 1992, at New York's Kennedy Airport. He was arrested on charges stemming from the St. Louis riot a year before. (Press Association)

Duff McKagan, Slash, Axl and Gilby Clarke onstage at The Freddie Mercury Tribute Concert at Wembley Stadium on 20 April 1992. (Getty Images)

Axl and Erin Everly. The girl he married and divorced in less than a year – and wrote 'Sweet Child O' Mine' for. (Getty Images)

The infamous MTV Video Music Awards show in New York, in 2002. According to Nick Kent, 'Rose looked deeply frightened... his one new song, a terrible self-pitying dirge'. (Getty Images)

Velvet Revolver: Duff and Slash onstage with the late Scott Weiland, LA, 2004. (Getty Images)

Above left Buckethead, whom Axl had built a chicken coop for him to record in. (Getty Images)

Left No Axl. No Izzy. The rest pose in the press room during the 27th Annual Rock And Roll Hall Of Fame Induction Ceremony on 14 April 2012. (Getty Images)

Axl on his 'throne'. Coachella festival, 16 April 2016. (Getty Images)

Above left Slash and Meegan Hodges – the love of his life who he was reconciled with after 25 years and a big part behind his decision to reform with Guns N' Roses – at The Greater Los Angeles Zoo Association's 46th Annual Beastly Ball on 11 June 2016. (Getty Images)

Left Axl and Angus Young of AC/DC perform at the Olympic Stadium in London, 4 June 2016. (Press Association)

The man with the plan. Alan Niven, at his mountain home in Prescott, Arizona, 2016. (Fraser Harding)

Goldstein wasn't laughing when they arrived at the venue that afternoon. The promoters, still convinced there would only be one show, oversold the event by some 30,000 tickets. 'So there are kids everywhere outside of the building that have tickets but there's no seats for them so the fire marshal and the cops aren't letting them in. The cops are on horseback and they're wielding these huge wooden sticks, just pounding kids. The band, of course, they have no fucking clue what's going on.

'So they're continuing to play. It was a stadium with no roof. So, like clockwork, Axl hits the beginning notes to "November Rain" and a *huge* fucking downpour! It was actually really cool. But they looted the streets of Bogotá, the kids. All of the storefronts are being busted down and they're stealing all this shit and stuff from the shops. Turning over cars. I mean it was a fucking scene . . . I used to say we were the signature CNN band. Every night there was something on CNN about GN'R . . .'

They weren't clear yet, though. At seven o'clock the following morning, there was a fierce pounding on Goldstein's hotel door. 'I open the door and it's some guy with a machine gun. He sticks a machine gun in my chest and hands me a letter. I'm like, uh oh.' The letter was to inform Goldstein that he had 'a mandatory meeting with the mayor that day at three o'clock. So in Spanish I tell the guy as soon as Mr Goldstein gets back I'll let him know.'

He then went to the phone and called his US Embassy security contact and asks him to come to his room, where Goldstein showed him the letter. 'He goes, "There's no meeting." I go, "Right, I'm being kidnapped, right?" He goes, "Absolutely." Then he goes, "Time to get out of Dodge."'

Goldstein moved fast to get the band out of the hotel by 7.30 a.m. and straight to the airport. 'We had to sneak out of town. We were never so happy to leave a place . . .'

Nobody had time to think about what *might* have happened, though. Too much real stuff was still going on. Forty-eight hours later they did a show in Santiago, Chile, then two in Buenos Aires, Argentina, then three in Brazil, two in São Paulo, one in Rio. There was a three-week break after that for Christmas and New Year, and by 12 January they were back on the road, starting with three nights at the 42,000-seater Tokyo Dome in Japan.

They said farewell to the horn section and the backing singers to save money and instead played an intimate little middle section of acoustic songs that sometimes sent shivers down the spines of all in attendance – musicians and fans alike. Then there was more bad luck: Duff was knocked unconscious onstage in Sacramento by a bottle full of piss thrown from the audience. Then Gilby broke his arm falling off his motorcycle, while practising for a celebrity race in honour of the TJ Martell Foundation for leukaemia, cancer and AIDS research. It nearly scuppered their planned return for more European dates, but then Izzy agreed to return for that leg of the tour,

'Izzy and I grew up together and we're like a family in lots of ways – including having our differences,' Axl explained. When I later reminded him of that quote, Izzy simply smiled and shook his head. 'Well, what else could he say? They were kind of in a spot and if I hadn't agreed to help out they might have missed out on that whole leg of the tour.' The temporarily reunited band rehearsed together in Tel Aviv then played some sloppy but terrific rock'n'roll right through the rest of the tour. The crowd in Tel Aviv got a nice glimpse of Axl's sense of humour when he came onstage in a T-shirt that read 'Guns N' Moses'. After a show at the Olympic Stadium in Athens, the supermodel Claudia Schiffer joined them afterwards for a party at the Mercedes Club. Then on 26 May they performed in Istanbul, where Axl stopped the show after just three songs to berate the audience for throwing lit fireworks at each other. 'Someone will get hurt and the band will be forced to leave the stadium,' he told them. Remarkably, the crowd stopped and the show continued.

Still, though, the dogs of doom kept snapping at their heels. Doug looks back at one huge concert in Germany: 'It was one of the ones where Gilby had broke his arm and we needed to bring Izzy back. So he was playing and Axl left the stage and Izzy just, he left. He said, "You know what, I'm not fucking doing it. This is crazy." So I tried to get the wives out on a bus back to the hotel and the local cops literally shut down our access to the exit. So I couldn't even get the wives out, let alone the band. We got shut in.'

At the end of May Guns N' Roses headlined the first of two shows to over 50,000 people at the National Bowl in Milton Keynes. After the encore of 'Paradise City', Axl threw two dozen red roses into the crowd. For Izzy, 'it was weird. We toured Israel, Greece, Istanbul, London – I liked that side of it, seeing some places I'd never seen.' But that was the only thing he liked about it. 'Money was a big sore point. I did the dates just for salary. I mean, I helped start this band . . .'

The second show the following day saw the return of Gilby and his wife, who had flown in especially for the occasion. With Gilby's wrist injury now healed, this was also Izzy's last show with the band. For the encores they were joined by the Rolling Stones guitarist Ronnie Wood and former Hanoi Rocks vocalist and Axl acolyte Mike Monroe. Afterwards, Izzy told me he left without even saying goodbye. 'I didn't actually say, "See you" cos they were all fucked up. Duff and these guys, they didn't even recognise me. It was really bizarre. It was like playing with zombies. Ah, man, it was just horrible. Nobody was laughing any more . . .'

12

BEAUTIFUL AND FUCKED UP

After one last show in Paris, on 13 July, Guns N' Roses flew straight to Argentina, where the final show of their world tour was scheduled to take place four days later at the 70,000-capacity River Plate stadium, in Buenos Aires. As if to give them the send-off they had grown accustomed to on tour, the night before the show more than 50 cops from the city's narcotics division forced their way into Axl's top-floor penthouse suite, where he was having dinner. They turned the place upside-down looking for drugs. Then, when they couldn't find any, they left again, without apology. 'They'd have had better luck trying one of the others' rooms,' quipped a crew member. 'By then, Axl was about the only one not doing drugs on a permanent basis.'

Broadcast live on TV in Argentina and Uruguay, for once the show the next night kicked off promptly at 9.30 p.m. Starting the 21-song set with 'Nightrain' and ending it with 'Paradise City', by midnight the band were already back at the hotel, where Axl, Slash and others remained in the bar until six o'clock the following morning, Axl at the piano for some of it, treating the assembled throng to one last tune. They had been on the road for two and a half years, played 192 shows in 27 countries and sold more than seven million tickets while doing so. It would go down in history as one of the last great rock'n'roll tours, a monument to industry and excess, perhaps never to be repeated.

Back in LA the sense of dislocation they'd experienced after returning from the *Appetite* tour three years before now returned with some force. Even a road rat like Slash confessed he was happy to hang his top hat in the same spot for a while, although he'd sold the Walnut House up in the hills and bought a much bigger new place on Mulholland Drive where he and Renee could begin their married life. 'We tried to stop the wheels for a second,' he said, 'but it was very hard to do . . .' It was perhaps a portentous moment when the house was destroyed six months later in the Northridge earthquake.

Axl was back in court a month after the tour ended, this time to testify in the lawsuit brought by Steven Adler against the band after his dismissal. The case centred on the legalities of Adler's termination agreement and his entitlement to future royalties. Axl's evidence focused on Adler's contribution to the *Use Your Illusion* sessions, and he told the court that the drum track for 'Civil War' had to be assembled from more than sixty takes laid down by Steven (he was referring to the session at which Adler admitted he'd been given an opiate blocker and was too out of it to play properly). During the court hearings, Axl described the agreement he and Slash had come up with for splitting royalties in the lead-up to recording *Appetite*. 'There was lyrics, melody, music – meaning guitars, bass and drums – and accompaniment and arrangement. And we split each one of those into twenty-five per cent . . . When we had finished, I had forty-one per cent [of overall takings], and other people had different amounts.'

With the judge calculating that the 'different amount' Steven would have received came to roughly 15 per cent, the case came to an abrupt end when, on 24 September, the band agreed to an out-of-court settlement: a one-off payment of roughly $2.5 million to Steven, plus a further agreement giving him 15 per cent of all future Guns N' Roses royalty payments related to the period he was in the band – i.e. their first two albums. 'It wasn't [a] pay-off,'

Steven pointed out. 'It was what they owed me. And I got all my royalties back.' Furious, Axl was unable to concede that Steven had played a critical part in the band's rise to stardom. 'He didn't write one goddamn note [of *Appetite*] but he calls me a selfish dick!' he fumed. They did not speak again for nearly 15 years.

'We weren't lawyers, we were rock'n'rollers,' said Steven somewhat ruefully in 2001. The money was little consolation – he missed the band and missed his friends and his sad decline began: being young, rich and addicted to drugs was not a good combination. It would take a prison sentence, numerous over-doses (31 trips to the emergency room, he once estimated), two strokes and a heart attack to eventually bring Steven back to some sort of normality.

Duff was back in the city for barely a month when he hit the road again. Still drinking heavily and snorting cocaine round the clock Duff felt unable to do anything other than keep moving. He'd recorded a solo album in a matter of weeks called *Believe in Me*, a typical rich rock star effort full of guest appearances – Slash, Matt, Dizzy, Gilby, West Arkeen and Teddy Zig Zag, plus Sebastian Bach, Lenny Kravitz and Jeff Beck. It was recorded quickly, with Duff handling much of the instrumentation, and reflected his influences: mostly punk, but also Prince and a little hip hop. Almost nobody bought it. But the album sessions had drawn Guns N' Roses together long enough for them to lay down the backing track for a cover of Johnny Thunders' 'You Can't Put Your Arms around a Memory', again with Duff on lead vocals but which was held back, at Axl's insistence, for Guns N' Roses.

They still had several punk covers stretching back to the *Illusion* sessions, which they'd originally planned to issue as an EP or mini-album. Now Gilby went over Izzy's guitar parts and they threw a few more songs into the mix, mostly old punk rockers that had inspired them at some point along the way: the New York Dolls ('Human Being'); The Stooges ('Raw Power'); The Damned and the UK Subs ('New Rose' and 'Down on the Farm') . . . In spirit it was like Metallica's *Garage Days* EPs, an acknowledgement of their roots that also meant a nice payday for some ageing punks (imagine getting the call from your publisher – 'Hey, the biggest band in the world want to cover that song you wrote years ago and put it out. Is that okay with you?').

Most controversial – and perhaps unsurprisingly at the insistence of Axl – was a version of 'Look at Your Game, Girl', an almost forgotten acoustic dirge written by America's most infamous thrill-killer and wannabe muso Charles Manson as part of an album designed to fund his trial defence back in 1970. 'The song talks about how the girl is insane and playing a mind game. I felt it was ironic that such a song was recorded by someone who should know the inner intricacies of madness,' explained Axl. But even the band baulked at this, and the recording features only Axl, Dizzy Reed on bongos and guest guitarist Carlos Booy. In all, there was enough for an album rather than an EP, and it emerged in November under the title *The Spaghetti Incident?*, a band in-joke that referred to evidence given at the Adler lawsuit about a food fight between Axl and Steven, with the Manson song as a 'hidden' extra not included on the track listing. The band had been persuaded to keep it after they were reassured that all of Manson's royalties would be paid over to the family of one of his victims, Wojciech Frykowski.

Although it was a stop-gap and was never claimed to be much more than that by the band, *The Spaghetti Incident?* debuted at Number 4 on the US album chart and Number 2 in the UK, and sold over 200,000 copies in its first week. Rough and ready but lacking the leering, cheap ferocity of some of the originals, the album nonetheless kept Guns N' Roses connected to their roots in some small way, however distant they may now have become. As *Rolling Stone* pointed out in its review: 'Punk rock is sometimes best read as a vigorous howl of complaint against one's own powerlessness, but Axl doesn't quite connect to the punk rock material on *Spaghetti* as anything but a conduit for pure aggression.'

It was as if they had just enough energy left to get the record out before things really fractured. The intense, often negative energy of the *Use Your Illusion* era demanded a sign-off, some kind of symbolic marking of what it was and what it had forced its participants to become. It got one, and it almost cost Duff McKagan his life. As soon as he heard that Duff had booked a solo tour to begin almost as soon as the *Use Your Illusion* shows were complete, Axl called the bassist. 'Are you fucking crazy?' he asked. 'You're insane to even think about it.'

The truth was, Duff felt that if he stayed in LA he was as good as surrendering to his cocaine addiction, so readily available was the drug and so empty were his days. He told himself that at least on the road he had a chance to keep ahead of it all. It was an addict's logic. There was a price to be paid for the years of drinking and drugging and partying and for Duff the bill was about to come in. He kept the coke under control while he spun through Europe yet again, but the booze was running riot, he was in end-stage alcoholism, the room next door to death. He deluded himself into thinking that switching from vodka to wine would keep the lid on it all, but soon he was drinking ten bottles a day. He wasn't eating and his body began to bloat. After the tour he flew back to LA, where 'I felt sicker than ever. I kept getting nose-bleeds, I had sores . . .'

He picked up the phone and cancelled a planned tour to Australia. Instead he flew home to Seattle, where he'd bought a house on Lake Washington. He'd barely even seen the place, but felt drawn to go. On the same flight from LAX was Kurt Cobain. They sat talking: 'He had just skipped out of a rehab facility. We were both fucked up. We ended up getting seats next to each other and talking the whole way, but we didn't delve into certain things.

I was in my hell, he was in his, and we both seemed to understand,' Duff ruminated in his autobiography. At the airport in Seattle he almost asked Kurt to come over to his place and stay for a while, but they lost each other in the queue somewhere and so Duff went home alone. A few days later, Doug Goldstein called to tell him that Cobain had committed suicide at his own place on the lake. Duff had been one of the last people to speak to him.

A month later, on the morning of 10 May, Duff woke up in pain – not the normal backwash from booze and coke, but something far worse, the kind of pain that made it impossible to move as far as the phone to call 911. He was dying. He felt it. But all he could do was lie there on the bed waiting. All that saved him was chance: a childhood friend stopped by to say hello and found him in the bedroom. Somehow he got him out of the house and a few doors down the street to where Duff's long-term doctor had his offices. He was given two shots of Demerol by the doctor, then a shot of morphine in the ambulance. But none of it touched the pain. Duff's pancreas had swollen so much that it had burst, spilling digestive enzymes into his abdomen. The powerful stomach acids burning holes through his tissue and organs caused the pain. His only chance was surgery to repair the tear, and a probable lifetime of dialysis. Once again, he got lucky. The surgery saved him. He stayed in hospital for a couple of weeks and when he got out, he started drinking again – this time water.

'For the first few months I still had the shakes and I didn't know anybody sober,' he later reported. 'So I rode my mountain bike and first of all it was like self-flagellation, I was beating myself for failing my mom and some of my friends. But it also started to make me feel whole, I was drinking water for the first time, I literally didn't drink water for ten years. I started eating healthy food, and reading books . . .'

It was a transformative moment for Duff McKagan. Just like Izzy, his days of hedonistic excess were now over. Others in Guns N' Roses were still to reach that point in their journey.

'I knew there were times I could have pulled up and been a real voice of reason, because I think I was looked at as a voice of reason in that band,' Duff told Jon Hotten in 2011. 'I didn't know how to and I didn't do it, but at least in my lifetime I have come to terms with it. I think the path of Guns happened the only way it could have happened. It was fucked up from the beginning, it was beautiful and fucked up.'

In 1990, Slash had told *Rolling Stone*, 'We really would all feel sort of lost and lonely if it fell apart and we had to go out and do solo records, because it wouldn't be Guns. None of us could reproduce that. Axl's got so much charisma – he's one of the best singers around. It's his personality. He can go out and do something. What freaks me out is if the band falls apart, I'll never be able to shake the fact that I'm the ex-Guns N' Roses guitar player. And that's almost like selling your soul.'

Five years later the 'For Sale' signs were now up. For Slash, the big turning point in his personal relationship with Axl had been reached on the summer tour of 1992. 'At some point during the Metallica shows, I just lost Axl,' he told me. 'I just didn't know where he was at any more. I didn't know where *I* was at any more! Steven was already gone, and then losing Izzy . . . And it was all nothing we had control of. Everything was kind of . . . out of hand. Then all of a sudden, we got off the road after two and a half years of touring, and everything just kind of . . . stopped. Dead.'

Slash spent the early weeks and months of 1994 writing new material for the next Guns N' Roses album, drawing from a Geffen advance worth $10 million – crazy fuck-you money. No lyrics yet, that was Axl's department. But a plethora of dirty riffs and moody melodies, songs without titles that carried on from where he'd left off on six-string-razor tracks from the *Illusions* albums like 'Garden of Eden' and 'Locomotive'.

But when he sent Axl a demo tape of what he had so far, the singer rejected them wholesale. Hurt but defiant, Slash decided to use them as a launchpad for a solo album of his own under the aegis of a new 'band' to be called Slash's Snakepit. Not only that, but he hired Mike Clink to produce it for him, and invited Gilby, Matt and Dizzy to contribute to it. He also hired the frontman of Jellyfish, Eric Dover, to be his new singer – a 27-year-old powerhouse vocalist not a million miles in style away from Axl at his most ferocious.

When the album, titled *It's Five O'Clock Somewhere*, was eventually released on Geffen in February 1995, commercially it was a flop. Critics were mostly kind, acknowledging that Slash's playing was as scintillating as ever, but almost unanimously wondering where the songs were?

Doug Goldstein tells the story of Tom Zutaut calling him about the album. 'He said, "Look, have you heard the record?" I said no. He said, "You need to. It's abysmal. I can't put it out." I said, "Well, you're the A&R guy, you need to tell him." He goes, "Never gonna happen. Not a fucking chance. There's no way that I'm gonna tell him that his record sucks. That's your job." I go, "It's not my fucking job! You're the A&R guy. This is what you do." He goes, "I'm just telling you. I'm not fucking doing it, and I'm not putting it out."'

Goldstein phoned Eddie Rosenblatt, and told him what Zutaut had said, and how he was refusing to be the one to tell Slash. 'Eddie goes, "Well, I'm not!" I go, "Well, you're a fucking big help!" He goes, "Look, you're gonna have to tell the kid." Great. So I called Peter Mensch and asked him what he would do. He said, "Doug, I always tell the truth to my artists, regardless. I don't care if it's Metallica, Def Leppard, whoever. I tell them the truth. You have an ethical responsibility to do just that."'

Goldstein took Slash out to eat at Hamburger Hamlet. 'I said, "How many songs on the record?" He said, "Twelve." I go, "Well, we're only about twelve songs from being able to release the record." He goes, "*What?*" I go, "Yeah. You're gonna have to re-visit this because the label's saying they're not gonna put it out." And that was a *huge* issue with Slash and I. I believe that that was the falling out for him and I. I was trying to manage it at the time because I didn't want other people getting involved. But Slash thought that I thwarted the success of that record, which just isn't true. I worked as hard on that record as I would the Guns N' Roses record. But you're just not dealing with the same level of musicality, for lack of a better term. Certainly, lyrically, not even remotely close. The music wasn't that bad. But lyrically it was just . . .' He tails off. Then adds, 'It made Axl look like a hell of an A&R guy.'

Even Gilby now worked up enough material for a solo album. Only Axl, who would retreat into the Malibu hills and the strange half-life of the reclusive rock star, had no plans for music outside of Guns N' Roses. He didn't need to. Though the outside world hadn't become aware of it yet, W. Axl Rose and Guns N' Roses were now indivisible – legally.

In 2008, during a conversation on GN'R's online forum, Axl explained how the contract that Doug Goldstein had renegotiated with Geffen contained a clause that gave Axl legal control of the use of the name 'Guns N' Roses'. It was a clause that wouldn't fully detonate until 1994, when things had really begun to fall apart, but, according to the singer, it caused little upheaval at the time.

'When Guns renegotiated our contract with Geffen, I had the bit about the name added in as protection for myself, as I had come up with the name and then originally started the band with it,' he said. 'It had more to do with management than the band, as our then manager [Alan Niven] was always trying to convince someone they should fire me. As I had stopped speaking with him, he sensed his days were numbered and was bending any ear he could, along with attempting to sell our renegotiation out for a personal payday from Geffen.

'It was added to the contract and everyone signed off on it. It wasn't hidden in fine print, etc., as you had to initial the section verifying you had acknowledged it. Now, at that time, I didn't know or think about brand names or corporate value etc. All I knew is that I came in with the name and from day one everyone had agreed to it being mine should we break up, and now it was in writing. I still didn't grasp any other issues until long after I'd left and formed a new partnership which was only an effort to salvage Guns, not steal it.'

Beautiful logic. Fucked-up repercussions. There were now just three original band members left in Guns N' Roses, but only one of them owned the name. According to Doug Goldstein, though, things weren't quite that simple. 'The most important date in the band's history is July fifth of '93,' he says. 'What transpired on that day, the band was in Barcelona, Spain, and I'm given a directive to go to Axl's room. Axl says, "Look, either the band signs their rights to the name back to me or I'm not going onstage and there will be a riot and people will die and that will be on them." Well, I'm not a dumb guy. If you present a contract like that, that's signing under duress. You might as well wipe your ass with that contract.'

Maybe so, but on that night in Barcelona neither Slash nor Duff saw things like that. As Duff relates in his memoir, he and Slash were handed documents signing over the band's name to Axl a short time before going onstage that night, by their tour manager. 'What the fuck?' Duff asked. Only to be told it was simply about the fact that he and Slash were 'not in good shape' and that if one of them died 'nobody wants to have to spend years battling your families or whatever'. According to Duff, though, 'There was nothing about death in these documents.'

In the end, convinced, as Duff writes, that, Guns N' Roses could not 'possibly exist without us', he and Slash signed. Anything to get this shit out of the way and the band onstage without any more hassle. 'I was so *fucking* exhausted,' explained Duff. 'It felt as though I'd been dragging a house around behind for me for those two years.'

Now, a year later, the reality of the situation began to kick in. Slash and Duff still owned their equity in Guns N' Roses – but not the name, and as Mick Jagger, David Lee Roth, Liam and Noel Gallagher, even Paul McCartney would attest, in the music biz it's the *name* of your band that counts for everything. Suddenly, the hideous truth dawned: Slash and Duff no longer had a real say in whatever direction Guns N' Roses took next, because Guns N' Roses now in effect belonged to Axl. Slash and Duff didn't even have a manager to turn to for help. Doug Goldstein had long since recognised that there would never be an active, working Guns N' Roses without the consent of Axl Rose. All that had changed in that regard was that it was now official.

As Stephanie Fanning says, Axl 'put the screws to the band, took the name. The things that he's done, for whatever reason he does things, he had the power, he used it. And at that point Doug went with it and did stay loyal and went with Axl – and so did the band.'

After that, she says, 'it was just a downward spiral . . . I don't wanna take away from Doug but Doug is a yes man. He's a sweetheart. He's a great guy. But it was easier to just go along with it and just kind of keep your mouth shut. He's keeping his job, he's staying the manager, one of the biggest managers in the world, and that's what he chose to do. And for maybe a couple of years of the *Illusion* tour it worked.'

Now, though, things quickly began to unravel. When Slash showed at LA's Complex studios in August 1994 for the recording of a cover of the Rolling Stones' 'Sympathy for the Devil' intended for the soundtrack to the Tom Cruise and Brad Pitt movie *Interview with the Vampire*, he was mortified to be told that Axl had brought in his own replacement for Gilby – an old pal from Lafayette named Paul Huge. According to an insider, Huge was a 'nice enough guy', but 'they're Guns N' Roses, for God's sake'. Huge was simply 'not that good' and didn't have 'the chops'. Or as Slash later put it: 'Paul is in my mind completely useless. I hate that guy. I'm sorry, I'm sure he's very nice, but in a rock'n'roll context he's pathetic. As far as his relationship with [Axl], they're Indiana kids, I can understand he feels comfortable, but I refuse to ever play with [Paul] again.'

Axl, however, was not prepared to take no for an answer. To his mind, Huge was the perfect replacement for Izzy. As a guitarist, he wasn't in the same league as a Slash. He didn't need to be. He just needed to play the chords he was given. More importantly, from Axl's point of view, Paul was a genuine friend – something he was no longer sure either Slash or Duff were. And though he was loath to admit it, Axl needed somebody like that right then. Somebody he could trust not to talk trash about him behind his back. Somebody who looked up to him and would be forever grateful for the opportunity Axl had given him. Somebody who would never challenge him.

This, though, would be the final straw for Slash. Unwittingly, Slash now found himself asking Axl to choose between his original, and arguably most important, musical sidekick or his old school pal. Cornered, threatened, Axl did what he always did in that situation and simply dug in. He chose his old school pal.

It didn't have to be that way. Not according to Doug Goldstein, who insists that Axl had been open to Slash and Duff bringing in their own choice of replacement for Gilby, but that they simply gave up and allowed Axl to have his own way. 'I'd get these frustrated calls from Slash primarily, and Duff occasionally, saying, "Look, get this fucking guy out of there.' Slash would call and say,

"I fucking hate the guy. He's an asshole. He can't play . . ." And I would say, "*Then – find – someone – else.*" But they wouldn't even look for somebody else.'

In fact, there had been several attempts to bring someone else in before Paul Huge appeared on the scene. First, Slash had bent over backwards trying to keep Gilby in the band – leading to Gilby finding himself fired three times from the band in as many months. Then there was talk of Ozzy Osbourne's former guitarist, Zakk Wylde, coming in. Goldstein managed Wylde's solo project, Pride and Glory, and Zakk was already drinking buddies with Slash. But Zakk was a star lead player and Slash objected furiously to the suggestion that he should share solos. There was a revival of the idea of having Dave Navarro join, but again Slash rejected that out of hand for much the same reason.

'Slash just kept saying, "You know what? I'm not fucking sharing solos. Fuck this. I am not even remotely interested,"' says Goldstein. 'Had Slash been a little more pliable to that end Guns N' Roses never would have broken up.'

In a rare interview in 2002, Axl still insisted that Paul Huge 'was one of the best people we knew who was both available and capable of complementing Slash's style . . . Paul was only interested in complementing Slash, laying down a foundation of a riff or something. That would accent or encourage Slash's lead playing.'

Slash would have none of it, though, insisting that he'd actually made his mind up to leave Guns N' Roses the day after discovering Huge in the studio, saying he couldn't even sleep that night he was so distraught. 'I was suicidal. If I'd had a gun with me at that time, I probably would have done myself in. If I'd had a half-ounce of fucking heroin with me, I probably just would've gone. It was heavy. It was a headspace I'd never been in before. Somehow I managed to go back to sleep. Then, when I woke up later that morning, I made a decision.' At which point, 'I felt the whole weight of the world drop.'

*

Everyone now had more on their minds than just the band. They were all worried for their lives. Axl especially. As well as trying to solve the riddle of what to do about Slash, he now had the ignominy of facing his ex-wife, Erin Everly, and ex-fiancée, Stephanie Seymour, across a crowded courtroom. Axl had broken up with Seymour in 1993, in the aftermath of a terrible row between the two at Christmas.

When they had first got together, Axl gave a phone interview to Andy Warhol's *Interview* magazine in which he talked about his new affair with Stephanie. When the piece ran it was accompanied by pictures of Axl and Stephanie French-kissing. Axl was quoted as saying, 'Steph and I have a really good time talking with each other and we want to try to see if we can have that, in our lives, for our lives. We don't know, but we're definitely trying to communicate as much as we can.'

He went on: 'Sometimes your friends are your lovers, or have been at one time, or are at some time or are at different times. Maintaining the friendship and taking the responsibility of being a friend and also helping the other person be a friend to you, and expressing your feelings about your friendship . . . Stephanie and I do that with each other. It's a good thing.'

But that was then. Now, in 1994, according to Seymour's sworn declaration in connection with the legal action she was taking against him, the trouble began after 'a verbal argument' Stephanie had had with Axl, after which he 'announced that there would be no Christmas party'. She went on: 'Guests began to arrive in the late afternoon [and] at some point in the middle of the party, [Axl] entered the house, slammed the door, was obviously very angry, went upstairs and then came downstairs and left the house again.' When Seymour's mother tried speaking to him, Axl 'began yelling and screaming at her and ultimately told her in no uncertain terms that she was not welcome in his house. Thereafter, most of the people at the party left.'

Seymour went on to claim that once they were alone Axl had pushed over a kitchen table, sending bottles and glasses smashing to the floor. According to Seymour's testimony, Axl then grabbed her by the throat and dragged her barefoot through the broken glass. Axl would respond by claiming Seymour had grabbed his testicles and that he was merely defending himself. Inevitably, it was left to Doug Goldstein to try and fix things. 'I had to drive up there to kind of clean up that mess. Not literally, but emotionally. Because he was distraught and down and . . . I loved the guy to death so I wanted to be there for him.' Trying to put Axl back together again after a major meltdown had become a regular practice, says Goldstein. 'It wasn't something that only transpired through that two-year period.' In the end, he says, 'I was making those trips for seventeen years. He could go a week long, where I'd talk to him and he'd be in tears. I could never really figure out the derivation. I would just try to be here for him . . . Clearly the relationship stuff with Stephanie *really* got to him. I mean, *really* got to him. He loved her to death . . .'

Axl and Stephanie had had bad fallings out before, but they had always made up again. Goldstein recalls after one bad break Axl phoning him and asking: '"Do you know anybody with a white horse?" They had split and he was trying to win her back. I said, "Let me see what I can do."' Goldstein, who prided himself on always being able to come up with whatever bizarre requests his boss made, made the arrangements and the next day a trailer containing a white Arabian charger showed up outside Stephanie's Hollywood home.

'Axl gets on the horse and pulls up to the front door, and I knock on the door and go hide in the bushes.' Next thing, 'He's on the horse apologising to her and, you know what, honest to god, it was one of the cutest things I'd ever seen. I'm hiding in the bushes watching this guy. I mean, he's pouring his heart and soul out. He's never been on a horse in his fucking life! And the horse is moving back and forth and he has no idea how to control it. It was just adorable. What we do for love . . .'

By 1994, however, the relationship had broken down so badly that Seymour was ready to take Axl to court, claiming compensation for certain 'domestic' issues she alleged she had been a victim of. Axl was devastated. He knew Stephanie had begun seeing a millionaire businessman, Peter Brant. (According to a former Geffen employee, Axl had managed to obtain a photograph of Brant's wife, Sandra, which he sent to Yoda, in order to 'cast a spell around Sandra to protect her from Peter, because he felt that she, too, had been cuckolded [sic] as he had been, and he had a great deal of sympathy for her'.) Nevertheless, Axl had always hoped for some form of reconciliation with Stephanie. This lawsuit crushed that hope.

Things got messy quickly. Axl's lawyers petitioned for a restraining order after alleging Seymour had taken cocaine in his house in the presence of her two-year-old son, Dylan. According to another friend, Axl also believed he and Stephanie had been together in more than 15 past lives. Then, when Erin Everly found herself subpoenaed to give evidence in Seymour's lawsuit, she decided to file one of her own, accusing her former husband of assault and sexual battery.

Axl now had to endure the grimmest details of his personal life being discussed openly in court. Erin's former flatmate Meegan Hodges-Knight testified under oath about such things as the night she woke up to overhear Erin begging Axl, 'Please stop. Don't hurt me, don't hurt me', as Axl screamed at her. 'And then all of a sudden he'd come out and he'd, like, break all of her really precious antiques, and she would be, "Please don't break them, please", and trying to get them back from him. And he'd push her and he'd break everything that he could get his hands on. I remember sleeping and waking up to crystal flying over my head, shattering on the floor.'

Meegan had been the love of Slash's life when she was in her teens. She stated that she had told Slash she was going to 'do something' about Axl but that the guitarist had stopped her, saying, 'No, you're going to make it worse.' Meegan also asserted in her sworn deposition that she'd witnessed Axl kicking Everly and dragging her around by the hair one night. He then threw a television set at her, she said, which had luckily missed, and then spat on her. 'That pig,' said Meegan scowling.

In her own sworn deposition, Erin described in shocking detail the occasion when Axl tied her hands to her ankles from behind, put masking tape over her mouth and a bandanna over her eyes, then led her, naked, into a closet, where he left her bound and gagged for hours. When Axl finally allowed Erin to leave the closet, she said, he picked her up and placed her face down on a convertible bed. He then 'forced himself on me anally really hard. Really hard.'

Erin also testified that Axl believed she and Seymour had been sisters in a past life and were now 'trying to kill him'. Axl had also told her 'that in a past life we were Indians and that I killed our children, and that's why he was so mean to me in this life'. Erin also claimed that Axl had removed all the doors in her apartment in order to keep an eye on her wherever she went.

For Axl this was all too much. He wasted no time instructing his lawyers to settle the case out of court. Erin reportedly walked from court with an undisclosed sum reckoned to be over a million dollars. Axl also ordered his minions to hurriedly gather up the few existing copies of a tape containing the unreleased version of the 'It's So Easy' video from five years before, which featured Erin tied up in bondage gear, with a red ball pushed into her mouth, while Axl screams at her, 'See me hit you! You fall down!'

Neither Erin nor Stephanie ever pressed for criminal charges. The damage was done, however, and the story of their joint actions against Axl hit the front page of *People* magazine in 1995. Coming only a month after the magazine had led with the story of OJ Simpson's being arrested for and charged with the murder of his estranged wife, Nicole Simpson, most people took a decidedly dim view of this new domestic-abuse story. Ironically, Erin herself still seemed to retain some sympathy for her beleaguered former spouse, admitting, 'I felt sorry for him' and 'I thought I could make it all better.'

The Seymour case was also hurriedly settled before the case could come to court, with Axl paying out a reported $400,000. Stephanie's lawyer, Michael Plonsker, would neither confirm nor deny the sum involved, except to say that the suit was eventually resolved 'amicably'.

Stephanie Seymour married Peter Brant in Paris just a few months later. She gave birth to the first of two sons by Brant shortly after, and they remain happily married to this day. Says Doug Goldstein: 'Oh my god, Axl was just fucking crushed! The guy deserves to have love in his life because he is so loving himself. He would be an *amazing* father, if given the opportunity. He really wanted to adopt Stephanie's son, Dylan. But obviously was never given that opportunity.'

According to Stephanie's nanny, Beta Lebeis, who went to work for Axl as his housekeeper after the couple split, 'When the band was over, he thought he could have a family, he would be married and would have children. This would be the second part of his life. He would have enough money and would dedicate his time to his family. He dreamed of a family, children, everything he never had.'

Losing Stephanie had put paid to that dream. 'Axl is a person who wants to do everything right,' says Beta. He was 'that kind of passionate man a lot of women would like to have in their lives. He was like a charmed prince. He did, for Stephanie, all kind of things you could find in a romantic book. What he did doesn't exist in real life any more! I think a lot of women would have loved to be in her place. I would never leave a man like that. But Stephanie is very pretty and sexy; she can have any man she wants. She uses men as toys.'

Beta added, 'Have you ever seen a child with a new toy? They play with it and later they don't want to play any more. I always told her she could hurt Axl more than she thought. Other men who fell in love with her would never suffer like Axl did. He wanted to do everything right, and he really thought everything was going right. He took this relationship very seriously. She almost killed him.'

Indeed, says Doug Goldstein, the loss from his life of Stephanie Seymour and her son, plus the crumbling of Guns N' Roses, sent Axl to the brink. He got used to getting phone calls in the dead of night, from a near-hysterical Beta, begging him to come over and talk to Axl, who was lying in bed in tears clutching a loaded gun.

The rest of the time, Axl Rose now became a near recluse. 'I'd be on the phone talking to the people at Geffen telling them Axl was in the studio working every day on the next Guns N' Roses record,' says Goldstein, 'and I was still getting maybe five, ten calls a day from him. Primarily he was just continuing to try different things while still involved in the writing process. But really nothing else was going on. For a while . . .'

On 20 January 1994, Axl Rose had been one of the guests at Elton John's induction into the Rock and Roll Hall of Fame in New York, giving a short but heartfelt speech about what both Elton John and his lyricist, Bernie Taupin, had meant to him through the years, ending with the words: 'When I first heard "Bennie and the Jets", I knew at that time that I had to be a performer. So now a man who, in ways, is responsible for more things than he ever planned on – Elton John.' Cue thunderous applause.

Later that night, Axl sang 'Come Together' with Bruce Springsteen. Dressed down in his own version of post-grunge stage attire
– jeans, boots, white tee and plain open shirt, he looked nervous
next to Springsteen's ultra-cool presence, his vocals squeezed out
like drops of blood: a far cry from the strutting, peacocking hot-
shot who had blown Tom Petty off the stage at the MTV awards
what now seemed like a lifetime before.

It was the last time he would perform in public for six years.

'Axl called me one day when we were off the road for a couple
years,' Doug Goldstein recalls. 'He said, "What do you think, in
retrospect, was the biggest mistake I've made in my professional
career?" I said, "Probably the 'November Rain' video, showing
the big mansion that the general public has paid for." He went,
"Wow. Yeah. You know what, you're probably right." So we let it
go and then he called me about two days later and he said, "Hey,
Doug, I want to go back to your point about showing my house.
I understand because now it's all about being one of the crowd,
with Nirvana and Pearl Jam, flannel shirts, and it's no longer su-
perstars, they want you to be one of them. But nobody ever told
us that the world changed." I said, "You know what, you're right."
It was a very valid point that he turned up . . . We would get on
our bus or plane and we had *no fucking clue* what was happening
worldwide. We were just doing what we enjoyed doing and that's
it, no more or less.'

Not any more. Suddenly everything had changed, and not just
for Axl Rose. Duff McKagen had put another side project together,
called Neurotic Outsiders, along with Matt Sorum, the former
Sex Pistols guitarist, Steve Jones, and Duran Duran's bassist,
John Taylor. Duff would later admit to feeling left behind by the
Seattle grunge bands that so dominated the rock scene in the first
half of the Nineties. Although Neurotic Outsiders were based in
LA, with half their line-up coming from England, a newly sober

Duff, still crawling from the emotional wreckage of the past ten years, was determined to make up for lost time. He cut his hair short – as did Matt Sorum – and appeared onstage with the band at the Viper Room in LA shirtless, pogoing up and down to what for all the world sounded like a cross between the Sex Pistols and Nirvana – though lacking the key elements of both, in a frontman to rival Johnny Rotten or Kurt Cobain. Instead, a paunchy Jones took lead vocals and the result, epitomised by the bish-bash-bosh single, 'Jerk', sounded like what it was: a grunge wannabe; an after-the-fact-vanity release. There was one self-titled album, released on Madonna's Maverick label in 1996, followed by short tours of Europe and the US. Before everything fell away again.

Meanwhile, over at The Complex, the west LA studios, where a massive soundstage was now on 24/7 hire to Guns N' Roses, it was as if time had stood still. By 1996, convinced that the next album had to be more forward thinking than the *Use Your Illusion* sets, Axl had ordered in a huge barrage of new equipment – and staff. Along with the pinball machines, pool tables and catering facilities, he now had a full-time computer expert tutoring him in the ways of new technology. Newly smitten by the outré electronica of Nine Inch Nails, The Prodigy and Moby – and still struggling with the fall from grace he had suffered in the wake of what he saw as the disrespectful grunge generation – Axl was desperate to reposition Guns N' Roses as far into the future as he could. He had cringed when he'd listened to Slash's ideas for the next album: the kind of substandard bad-boy boogie that even Duff had privately dismissed as 'Southern rock'. He had winced just as much when he heard Duff's late-to-the-party faux-grunge with the Neurotic Outsiders.

Most excruciating of all for Axl, though, was the fact that they and Matt seemed to wilfully disregard his latest attempts to keep Guns N' Roses on the bleeding edge of rock, shrugging off his imprecations to find something 'new' to say with their music as just the latest expression of an ego now completely out of control. This last was not helped by the fact that both Slash and Duff were now bitterly regretting the papers they had signed in 1993 handing over the rights to the Guns N' Roses name: the deal that effectively left Axl as their leader.

This, though, was a typically squint-eyed way of looking at things. Both Slash and Izzy had been complaining about Axl's 'interference' in their music since the *Illusion* sessions. Slash claimed he had a tape of an early, rough mix of the *Illusion* material that was much more 'strong and powerful' than the recordings overseen by Axl that eventually emerged – 'before the keyboards and horns and backing vocals got added'. Izzy, too, had bemoaned the fact that Axl always wanted to take the demos he brought in and turn them into big production numbers. As Axl had told *Rolling Stone* in 1992: 'When Izzy had 'em on a four-track, they were done. I mean, I like tapes like that, but we'd just get destroyed if we came out with a garage tape. People want a high-quality album. And it was really hard to get Izzy to do that, even on his own material.' In the end, said Axl, 'Izzy's songs were on the record because I wanted them on the record, not because Izzy gave a shit either way.'

As Doug Goldstein says now: 'The rest of the band, they were happy being AC/DC or the Rolling Stones, where every album is primarily the same. And Axl wanted to be the Beatles. He wanted every album to evolve. He didn't want to put out *Appetite for Destruction* again. But the band, they were totally fine putting together songs that were simplistic, to the point, concise, easy to do. They just wanted to go fucking tour again. The Beatles came off the road and spent the rest of their career in the studio. Axl wanted to do something similar. But the Beatles only had four, then eight tracks to play with and it was the dawn of time recording-wise. Six weeks in the studio then was like six years now.'

But while Axl was dreaming of building the same-sized musical cathedrals as previous studio perfectionists like Phil Spector and Brian Wilson, Slash and Duff and the rest of the world were still hung up on the fact that Guns N' Roses had come crawling out of the same Hollywood sewers as Poison and Mötley Crüe. Nobody was even asking for anything more than that from him. And that riled the boy who had grown up studying Queen and Elton John, Led Zeppelin and Billy Joel, to the point where he was damned if he was going to let what he saw as the short-sighted stupidity of the others get in his way.

'Nobody talks about the brilliance of Axl Rose as the song creator,' says Goldstein. 'They talk about Guns N' Roses as being this incredible band. Yet who fucking put that together? Granted, I was with Slash and Duff when they were writing the music for *Use Your Illusion*. And "Locomotive" and "Coma", they were doing that shit without Axl's participation. But I'd get these phone calls from the studio, and Axl would say, "I fucking hate Slash. Have you heard this song 'Locomotive' yet? How the fuck am I supposed to write lyrics to this shit?" I'd go, "Hey, man, I don't know. That's your gig, right? I do the management. You do the songwriting."'

For Slash, who'd grown up loving David Bowie and Stevie Wonder, as well as Aerosmith and the Stones, attempting to take Guns N' Roses to a new level musically was definitely not out of his field of vision. That wasn't the problem, as he saw it, though. It wasn't even the creatively stifling presence of Paul Huge. The main problem, said Slash, was that Axl was now openly acting as self-anointed leader. 'It seemed like a dictatorship. We didn't spend a lot of time collaborating. He'd sit back in the chair, watching. There'd be a riff here, a riff there. But I didn't know where it was going.'

Finally, in September 1996, Slash told Axl he'd had enough. 'There's a certain personal side to it, too,' he told me. 'I can't *relate* to Axl. Maybe I never could. I mean, Axl came with Izzy, I came with Steven, and then we all hooked up with Duff.' Now though, 'I realised I was out alone, and that meant me and Axl had to come to terms with . . . not our animosity, but having a different opinion about everything. And, I mean, you know, Axl works as hard as anybody else but only on what *he* wants to work on, and I . . . I just lost interest.'

Ultimately, he said, 'It all comes down to this: if I hadn't quit, I would have died, hanging round with nothing to do, no mutual artistic relationship, nothing. I mean, I tried to hang on in there, but it was like a big, revolving door, from really hi-tech equipment, guitar players, all kinds of shit going on . . . I was just waiting for the dust to clear. Eventually, I thought, we'll *never* be able to put this on the right path.'

When Slash told Axl he was leaving, the singer braved it out in public. No announcement was made. No private arrangements made to bring in an immediate replacement. As with his painful breakup with Stephanie Seymour, there was a part of Axl that secretly hoped Slash would come running back. Axl knew that without Slash there could be no Guns N' Roses. Not one that would be instantly recognisable to the world at large. He decided to keep the news quiet until he could figure out what to do.

When, though, in October 1996, Slash did an online interview where he admitted that 'right now, Axl and I are deliberating over the future of our relationship', Axl felt angry, hurt and utterly betrayed. He rushed to get his side of the story out, sending a fax to MTV on 30 October in which he suggested it was his decision that Slash should leave, one he had actually made as far back as 1995. He could no longer work with him, he said, because the guitarist had lost his 'dive in and find the monkey' attitude. Privately, however, Axl felt more alone than he ever had before. First Steven, then Izzy . . . now Slash? What was happening to him? In the most fragile moment of the night, he blamed himself. That's when Doug would get the calls from Beta, begging him to come over and talk Axl down. Up to face the day, though, Axl would know again that it wasn't him it was them. Fuck 'em all!

'Axl had a vision that GN'R should change and Slash had an attitude that Guns N' Roses was Guns N' Fucking Roses and that's who they were,' explains Tom Zutaut. 'I don't think they could get over their breakdown in communication. It wasn't announced publicly [initially] because nobody wanted to say the band had broken up.'

Speaking about the split to the official GN'R website in 2002, Axl remained defiant. 'Originally I intended to do more of an *Appetite*-style recording,' he recalled. 'So I opted for what I thought would or should've made the band and especially Slash very happy. [But] it seemed to me that anytime we got close to something that would work, it wasn't out of opinion [sic] that Slash would go, "Hey, it doesn't work", but it was nixed simply because it did work. In other words, "Whoa, wait a minute. That actually might be successful, we can't do that."'

Slash scared of success? It would have been a laughable statement to make if it hadn't been so obviously desperate. Axl had made similar claims about Izzy after he'd walked out, too, insisting he would have been happier if the band had not been so successful. 'I wanted to get as big as we possibly could from day one,' Axl had told *Rolling Stone*, 'and that wasn't Izzy's intention at all.'

The fallout from Slash's departure, though, would be devastating. As Duff said later, 'Slash turned his back and said, "This is shit." He and Axl didn't talk to each other any more. It had become quite irrational.' By the end, he said, he had become 'the one both came to see, and I got the impression I arbitrated little kids' quarrels'. Duff loved Slash but he wasn't ready to throw the towel in himself. When, though, some months later, Axl decided to fire Matt Sorum, Duff couldn't bear it any more and told Axl he was quitting too.

According to Matt, the spark that caused him to be fired had been an argument he'd had with Axl about Slash. They had been in the studio when Paul Huge remarked he had seen Slash play with his band, the Snakepit, on the David Letterman show the previous night and that it had 'sounded like shit and looked like shit'. According to a still angry Sorum, 'I said, "Listen, mother-fucker, when I'm sitting in the room, I'd appreciate it if you don't fucking say shit about Slash. He's still my friend. You can't even hold a fucking candle to that fucking guy. He's got more talent in his little toe than you, motherfucker, shut up!" And then Axl got in my face. I said, "You know what, Axl, man? You're fucking smoking crack if you think this band's GN'R without Slash. You're gonna go play 'Sweet Child o' Mine' with fucking Paul Huge? Sorry, dude, it ain't gonna sound right. Fucking 'Welcome to the Jungle' without Slash?" [Axl] says, "I'm Guns N' Roses – I don't need Slash." I said, "You know what? No, you aren't." We got into a big pissy match; it went onto a bunch of other bullshit for about another twenty minutes. And then he finally said, "Well, are you gonna fucking quit?" I said, "No, I don't fucking quit." And then he said, "Well, then you're fucking fired."

'Paul Huge chased me out to the parking lot and said, "What the fuck, man? Just come back in and apologise!" I said, "Fuck you, Yoko! I'm gone!" And that was it. I went home to my fucking six-level palatial rock star estate with two elevators and my Por-sche. I was producing a band called Candlebox at the time, they were living in my house. And I said, "I just got fired." They said, "Ah, fuck, he'll call you back", and I said, "No, not this time." Cos he'd fired me before but he always called me back. I said, "No, I don't think so." And about a month later I got the letter from the lawyers.'

Duff: 'Matt was never a full member of the band, he was on an ejector seat and Axl said, "I'm gonna fire him." I answered that this decision required more than one person to be taken since we were a band, that he alone didn't own the majority. All of this because Matt told him he was wrong. The truth is Matt was right and Axl was wrong indeed.'

But Axl didn't care what Duff or anyone else thought any more. 'I thought, I never played for money and I'm not gonna start now,' said Duff. 'I've got a house, I'm secure financially.' This, though, 'was the worst moment of my career in Guns. I went out for dinner with Axl and I told him, "Enough is enough. This band is a dictatorship and I don't see myself playing in those conditions. Find someone else."'

13

2000 INTENTIONS

The second half of the 1990s would be a bleak time for Guns N' Roses. Slash and Duff and Izzy continued to work sporadically as solo artists, usually draped under the banner of a band, as if trying to conceal themselves from a now unforgiving spotlight. Steven Adler was still fighting his drugs demons, living off the fumes of his thinning celebrity. (When he approached me to help him write a memoir I couldn't find anyone interested in publishing it.) By the end of the decade Matt Sorum had agreed to go back to The Cult, who had reformed after six years in a wilderness of their own. Meanwhile, the music scene quickly moved on, as it always does, past grunge, into nu-metal (a conflation of street rap and hard rock) and finally the yawning gape of the Napster generation. Marilyn Manson had taken over as the new shock rockers in America, while in Britain a parochial battle for supremacy between Oasis and Blur had stolen everybody's cheese.

It was the same for W. Axl Rose, as the last man standing in a band that had become a joke to the outside world – and a very unfunny nightmare for those having to live inside it. The impression was that Axl had exiled himself deliberately. There were no interviews granted, no new pictures released, no personal appearances, nothing to dispel the growing conviction that he had become the Howard Hughes of rock, a clearly brilliant, yet remote, figure for whom everything had now simply become too goddamn much.

Even when he did venture out into the world, very few people even recognised him any more. Just like every other Eighties rock star still hoping to transition successfully into a more grunge-friendly apparition, Axl had now cut his hair short and abandoned the full-on LA Strip duds in favour of faded blue jeans and nondescript shirts. He had also put on weight. 'He had personal hurt,' says Doug Goldstein of those days. 'If it wasn't Stephanie, he was *devastated* about Slash leaving. Because he clearly loved Slash to death.'

According to the LA performance artist Vaginal Creme Davis, Axl would also occasionally wear 'those Michael Jackson-type disguises – fake moustaches and Members Only jackets'. Even when he occasionally went to concerts – always in the company of his faithful bodyguard, Earl Gabbidon – he often went unrecognised. According to Moby, 'If you were walking down the street and Axl passed you, you'd never notice. He look[ed] like a regular, decent guy.'

Working in the studio with a new set of hired-hand musos, Axl suffered from a similar malaise: unsure quite what it was he was after, hesitant where he had once been supremely confident that his path was the right one. He even began to shrink from the job of recording his own vocals, a sure sign of the crisis of confidence and lack of self-esteem he seemed to be labouring under. It was one thing to be the leader of a gang of rebels who all had strong ideas about what they wanted to do, marshalling them into a cohesive musical force; quite another to be the only guy in the room who was supposed to know what the hell was going on, trying to forge a new, more adventurous musical identity while everyone else simply waited to be told what to do.

Dizzy Reed was the only other survivor of the *Use Your Illusion* sextet, and Dizzy had been little more than a glorified session player. Paul Huge was no help either. Brought in to act as buffer between Axl and Slash and the rest of the gang, now they were gone Huge's role was indistinct. Axl liked to include Paul in the writing, but only as a strand in a complex sonic weave of ideas – the track that would eventually become the title of the album, 'Chinese Democracy', would feature a co-credit for Huge amongst seven others. But this was not like working with Slash and Duff and, in particular, Izzy, who would bring in whole tracks ready to go.

The new 'band' now included Nine Inch Nails' former guitarist Robin Finck – originally recommended by Matt, advising Axl that he would make a great foil for Slash, who could then be coaxed back, to which Axl retorted: 'No, he would be a great *replacement* for Slash' – bassist Tommy Stinson (formerly of alt-rock pioneers The Replacements) and former Vandals drummer Josh Freese (aka 'the Bruce Lee of drums').

At first, Axl had invited Mike Clink to come in and see if he could add a little weight to the sessions. But Clink didn't get it, as far as Axl was concerned. The singer didn't want to merely make another Guns N' Roses album. He wanted to create something that lifted the whole enterprise into the future. Next through the studio doors was the rising techno star Moby, then Killing Joke's former bassist Youth, and then, in April 1998, the former Marilyn Manson and Nine Inch Nails producer Sean Beavan.

Youth (real name Martin Glover) left feeling that Axl's problem was 'partly perfectionism. The psychology is that if you have something out you get judged – so you want to stay in a place where you don't get judged.' While Moby recalled 'an emotionally reserved' man who became 'a little bit defensive when I asked him about the vocals. He just said that he was going to get to them eventually. I wouldn't be surprised if the record never came out, they've been working on it for such a long time.'

Adrift in a darkening ocean of sudden thoughts, abandoned ideas, flashes of inspiration and second-guessing, even when almost-complete song ideas began to shape themselves Axl would order his studio engineers to keep recording anything and everything that the musicians spent longer than a few seconds on. By the end of each week he'd have as many as five CDs with various versions of different songs on them, until he had amassed a stack of more than 1000 CDs and DAT tapes, all painstakingly filed and labelled. 'It was like the Library of Congress in there,' observed one engineer.

That 'cold black cloud coming down' that Axl had sung of in 'Knockin' on Heaven's Door' now seemed to follow him everywhere. Every year when Stephanie Seymour's birthday came around he would 'shut down for weeks' at a time. A great many of the songs he was now writing were, he later confessed in *Rolling Stone*, directly about her, adding he hoped that one day her son, Dylan, would listen and 'hear the truth' about the relationship. The split with Slash – which he viewed as 'a divorce' – was similarly mourned. When Shannon Hoon died of an OD in a New Orleans hotel room, Axl was devastated all over again, seeing himself as something of a mentor to the Blind Melon singer.

Not long after that, Axl heard that his mother, Sharon, was ill with cancer. She was 51, far too young to die, and though Axl still hadn't forgiven her for not 'protecting' him as a child against the physical and mental abuses he suffered from both his fathers, Axl, Amy and Stuart flew to Indiana to be with their mother not long before she died in May 1996. When, a year later, West Arkeen died of an overdose of prescription painkillers, at the even more terrifyingly young age of 36, Axl began to think in terms of a curse. When not in the studio, he lived behind the electric iron gates of his secluded Latigo Canyon estate, rising late, working out, sitting on the computer. He had to 'educate myself' he said about the new technology that was redefining the making of music. At the same time, he also began taking guitar lessons. Everyone who worked for him was still expected to sign confidentiality agreements, which, along with photographs of themselves would be sent to Sharon Maynard for 'psychic inspection': motives; strengths, weaknesses; what kind of energy they emitted. Even photographs of an employee's children were sometimes required.

As if to emphasise the seesawing contrasts in his personality, Axl also began hosting special Halloween costume parties for friends – mainly employees, lawyers and other members of his inner circle – and their children, decorating the house with pumpkin-lanterns and fake spiders' webs. There would be special mazes erected. Dave Quakenbush, vocalist with LA punk band The Vandals and a guest at the 1999 Halloween party, remembers Axl 'wearing a dinosaur outfit. When some kids approached him and asked if he was Barney the Dinosaur, he said, "Nah! Barney's a fag!" Then he stopped himself and said, "Oh, uh, I mean Barney's a pussy."'

'It would be every Halloween and every Easter,' explains Goldstein. 'At the Easter party he used to dress as the bunny! All the little kids are coming up and sitting on his lap. He was a doll! The Easter parties were in the morning time, around noon. Then the Halloween parties would be starting at, like, three or four p.m. so the young kids could come. Then it would go on till very late in the evening with all the adults. They were *hugely* attended and incredibly . . . you know, everybody felt well looked after cos Axl invited everybody. All the attorneys and the attorneys' assistants, and the accountants' families. 400 to 500 people. And he brought in all these entertaining rides and fun things for the kids to do and a haunted house every year.

'Then some asshole from the LA *Times*, who had been there for, like, seven years at these Halloween parties, wrote in the paper about how they were not as popular any more. It was just bullshit! And it totally . . . because Axl loved doing that and it broke his heart. So he just stopped doing the parties. It really broke his heart doing this once a year for everybody who worked hard on his behalf.'

Occasionally, a real friend would try to break through the barriers Axl had set up for himself. 'I'd moved back out to LA [and] was riding around one day and I thought, fuck it, I'll go by his house,' Izzy told me. 'Bastard, he lives up in the hills, he's got a big house, I'll go and see what he's doing, you know? And I go up and he's got security gates, cameras, walls, all this shit, you know. So I'm ringing the buzzer and eventually somebody comes and takes me up and there he is. He's like, "Hey, man! Glad to see you!" Gives me a big hug and shows me round his house. It was great.

'Then, I don't know, probably a month later, one night he calls me [and] we got into the issue of me leaving Guns N' Roses. I told him how it was on my side. Told him exactly how I felt about it and why I left.' Suddenly, the conversation became very one-sided. 'I mean, he had a fucking *notepad*. I could hear him [turning the pages] going, "Well, ah, you said in 1982 . . . blah blah blah . . ." And I'm like, what the fuck – 1982? He was bringing up a lot of really weird old shit. I'm like, whatever, man.'

The two old high-school friends would not speak again for nearly a decade. 'Every two or three years I'd put a call into the office and say, "Hey, tell Axl gimme a call if he wants to." But I mean . . . the weirdness of his life. To me, I live pretty normal. I can go anywhere. I don't think people really give a shit. But for Axl, I know for the longest time, because his face was all over the television and stuff, I don't think he could really go anywhere or do anything. And I think because of that he kind of put himself in a little hole up there in the hills. He kind of dug in deeper and deeper and now I think he's gone so fucking deep he's just . . . I mean, I could be completely wrong. But I know he doesn't drive and he doesn't . . . he doesn't do anything. I've never, never seen him in town. Isolation can be a bad thing, but Axl's been at it for a long time now. You know, he always stays up at night . . .' Izzy drifted off, shaking his head, no longer quite knowing what to say.

On 6 February 1998, a Friday, Doug Goldstein organised a 'surprise' party for Axl, to celebrate his thirty-sixth birthday, inviting around 40 people – much the same crowd, minus the kids, that came together for his Halloween parties. Everyone brought presents, and a gigantic birthday cake was rested on a dais in the corner of the restaurant. But when it got to midnight and Axl still hadn't turned up, people started to leave. Goldstein called Axl on his cell: the news was predictable. 'Axl's not going to be coming,' Doug informed the remaining guests. 'But order whatever you want and have a good time.'

Four days later, Axl, travelling incognito to Phoenix, was arrested at Sky Harbor International Airport after tussling with security personnel. 'I'll punch your lights out right here and right now!' he had screamed as they attempted a routine search of his baggage. 'I don't give a fuck who you are. You are all little people on a power trip!' Threatened with arrest, Axl roared back: 'I don't give a fuck. Just put me in fucking jail!'

He duly spent the next few hours in a locked cell at the local police station. A year later, after pleading 'no contest' to a misdemeanour charge of disturbing the peace, he was fined $500 and a day in jail – which he was already deemed to have served. According to friends, Axl had been carrying some of the birthday presents he'd received for 'review' by Sharon Maynard, whose home in Sedona, the self-styled New Age capital of America, lay 115 miles north of Phoenix. According to a Geffen press statement issued at the time: 'Axl had some birthday presents in his bag, including a glass object that a friend had given him for his birthday. The way they were going through the bag he was afraid it would get smashed.'

A couple of months after that, in a bid to change the conversation, Doug Goldstein let it be known that there were now around 30 finished tracks for the new Guns N' Roses album, including such titles as: 'Prostitute', 'Cock-a-Roach Soup', 'This I Love', 'Suckerpunched', 'No Love Remains', 'Friend or Foe', 'Zip It', 'Something Always', 'Hearts Get Killed' and 'Closing In on You' – only two of which would actually end up on the album. A title for the album was also revealed: 2000 *Intentions*, which most took to be a strong hint that the album would be out in time to mark the new millennium. But, again, that proved to be a premature announcement, the title being amended to the deliberately anomalous *Chinese Democracy*.

Nearly ten years since GN'R had unveiled the *Use Your Illusion* sets, people were now vague on where the group's narrative had got to. The band had gone, barring Axl, and there was a new album but it still hadn't been released? Say that again.

When, in March that year, they had been named among the inaugural artists to be presented with the new Diamond Award from the Recording Industry Association of America (RIAA), marking sales of over ten million copies of *Appetite for Destruction*, Axl pointedly refused to attend the ceremony in New York – as did Slash, Duff and Izzy. In fact, only Steven Adler showed up to receive the award and say a few words of thanks.

For Doug Goldstein, the only connection Axl still had with his musical past, this was a time of 'focusing on the minutiae instead of the overall. That's the thing about Axl [and] he never changed. Everybody thought he did but he was consistent with me right up until the end. There was nothing that caught me by surprise. I knew the same guy all the way throughout. And I have to say he's probably the most loyal individual I've ever met. Certainly the most loyal band member I've ever worked with. If you're on his team, you're on his team to the end.'

Nevertheless, admits Goldstein, 'It was pretty frustrating in that I'm a marketing guy. International marketing was kind of my deal in college. So all of a sudden I'm thrust into the position of having nothing to market. All I'm doing is spending and spending and spending, for the ten years it took to make *Chinese Democracy*.'

Even during those periods when Axl wasn't working in the studio, his huge staff of musicians and engineers remained on a monthly retainer totalling some $250,000 (including more than $50,000 in studio fees, a combined payroll for seven band members of approximately $65,000, plus guitar technicians on about $6000 per month, a recording engineer earning $14,000 per month and a 'software engineer' being paid $25,000 a month).

Goldstein says he was in the office of the new label chief, Jimmy Iovine, 'every month lying, saying the album's coming along great. Sometimes it was supposed to be a half-hour meeting and it would end up to be two and a half' – a situation made more galling when some of the musicians became so fed up waiting around that they began bailing out – in the case of the studio engineer, Billy Howerdel, and drummer, Josh Freese, forming their own band, A Perfect Circle, and recording the million-selling album *Mer de Noms*, an uncomfortably close yet apparently far more easily achieved approximation of the kind of rock-industrial sound Axl was striving for on *Chinese Democracy*. When the guitarist Ron Finck then left to rejoin Nine Inch Nails, all Axl's feelings of betrayal and abandonment resurfaced.

Says Goldstein: 'Axl was making great choices like Josh Freese, one of the best fucking drummers out there and one of the nicest people on the planet. Unfortunately we lost a lot of the great guys because the process was just seemingly taking too long, and they were all given opportunities to jump into something that there was a real tour to get on. All of these guys. That's the one thing that I have found out is Axl really enjoys the recording process. And he's very, very, very, *very* calculated about how that goes, and most of the musicians that I come into contact with, they just wanna go play. So the recording process is not even remotely thought of in the same light as the way that Axl takes it. You know, Axl wants to put something out that is going to be remembered for ever and ever, and again most of the musicians I know are like, 'Let's just put it down and get the fuck out there.'"

A chink of light finally appeared in the darkness in September 1999 when the track 'Oh My God' appeared on a trailer for the new Arnold Schwarzenegger movie *End of Days* – only after Finck's contributions to the track had been wiped and Dave Navarro and Circus of Power's former guitarist Gary Sunshine had been brought in to rerecord them. Axl also took the opportunity to issue his first public statement for five years, in which he described 'Oh My God' as a song that dealt 'with the societal repression of deep and often agonizing emotions – some of which may be willingly accepted for one reason or another – the appropriate expression of which (one that promotes a healing, release and a positive resolve) is often discouraged and many times denied'. Whatever it meant, it was clear we were now a million miles away from visiting Rocket Queens in Paradise City.

Two months later came the release of the double CD live album, *Live Era '87–'93*, an orphan born after the fact which Axl refused to take responsibility for. Indeed, most of the work on the album had been overseen by Slash, who told me, 'I figured if it was gonna come out anyway, it might as well be as good as we could get it.' Slash and Axl had not even spoken about the album directly, he said, communicating only through intermediaries. 'Suddenly there's lots of faxes and phone calls, everybody avoiding each other.' And what did Axl make of the final mix? 'I don't know. I didn't ask and nobody said anything.'

Neither the critics nor, more importantly, the fans seemed to care much about the album either. Peaking at an embarrassingly lowly Number 45 in the US charts, barely selling enough copies – over 500,000 – to even go gold. A similar fate befell the *End of Days* soundtrack that included 'Oh My God', while the track itself was largely ignored by radio. Instead, Axl's attention was now focused on two new musicians: the guitarist Buckethead – a virtuoso who wore a mannequin-like face mask and an empty KFC bucket upside down on his head, and only conversed via a small handheld puppet – and the drummer Bryan 'Brain' Mantia: a 35-year-old Californian, born in the South Bay city of Cupertino, previously known for his work with Tom Waits, Praxis, Godflesh and, most recently, Primus, who had been brought into the line-up at the suggestion of Buckethead, whose solo albums he had also played on.

Buckethead (real name Brian Carroll) was a strangely charismatic 31-year-old who had grown up in an LA suburb close to Disneyland. He was a shy, nerdy kid obsessed with comics, video games, Kung Fu movies and slasher flicks who also studied music theory at college, and his musical signature was a fondness for incorporating splashy classical influences into his raucous, 'shredding' guitar style. Uncomfortable onstage, he developed the Buckethead persona, he said, after eating a bucket of KFC one night. 'I put the mask on and then the bucket on my head. I went to the mirror. I just said, "Buckethead. That's Buckethead right there."' From which he developed his absurdly detailed chicken fetish – insisting that he had actually been raised by chickens and that his long-term ambition was to alert the world to the on-going chicken holocaust in fast-food outlets the world over. Before signing on as Axl's latest replacement for Slash, Buckethead had been recording as a solo artist for almost a decade, going from the 'post-metal psycho-shred' of his 1999 album *Monsters and Robots* to the eerie ambience of his next release, *Electric Tears*. He also recorded under the anagram Death Cube K. The only reason he had joined Guns N' Roses, he said, was that when Axl invited him to his house he gave him a rare collector's edition of the Leatherface doll, which he took as a good omen, deciding that Axl 'must understand me somehow'.

According to Goldstein, who thought he'd seen it all until now, 'To get Buckethead's signature, Axl took him to Disneyland and they rode rollercoasters together. I was like, you know, this is a little fucking out there. I was told that his television was covered in Saran Wrap cos he masturbates so much. Too much fucking information! I could have gone the rest of my life without hearing that. It started getting really funky, though, when I got a call that we had to build a chicken coop for Buckethead. He did his leads in the studio with the chicken wire and the fencing all around. Until one day Axl's pet wolf cub got in there and that was the end of that. I thought, you know what, maybe this *is* a little fucking crazy now.'

Increasingly, Axl's only solace came from his home life with Beta Lebeis and her own extended family. Born in São Paulo, Brazil, in 1956, she was a divorced mother of three grown-up children now in their twenties. In a rare interview given to the Brazilian daily paper *O Globo*, in 2001, Beta described her role in Axl's life as 'his personal assistant, I organise his house, I coordinate his personal life'. She also spoke candidly of her role as what she called the 'mother' of the band. 'I always light candles for them.' Axl, she explained, had never known the love of a good mother, 'like the good-night kiss' and because of that didn't know 'how to demonstrate this kind of love, and it is very difficult for a grown-up to deal with this'. No wonder he found it so hard to trust others, she said. Axl needed 'someone who listens to what he has to say and I am here for that'.

She explained how she and her eldest son, Fernando, had lived with Axl at his Malibu mansion for the past seven years, although she now owned her own house 'very close to Axl's house'. Even when she wasn't at the Malibu mansion, she never went out without her cellphone and pager, or anywhere where Axl couldn't contact her 24/7. Quizzed about Axl's interest in past lives, she replied, 'Yes, Axl and I believe.' It was 'impossible', she thought, 'for two people who never met before, to get along this well. When I opened the door and he was there, I felt as if I knew him from ages ago.'

Surrounded by his new 'family', Axl now worked out 'for four hours a day', Beta said, including running 'almost eight kilometres every two days'. There was also 'a doctor who tells us what we must eat'. The reason he was rarely seen in public, she said, was because 'he doesn't like bars or clubs'. Instead, Axl and Beta would 'go a lot to the movies'. 'According to his grandmother,' said Beta, Axl 'had never liked the day ... He writes a lot in the night, because there's no phone or other thing that could interrupt him. He is more creative late at night.' Both Amy and Stuart Bailey had lived at the Malibu house at different times, but only Beta had remained a constant companion, there to 'give him advice when he asks me for it. I know he values my opinion a lot.'

Slowly, things were coming full circle. A new generation of Guns N' Roses fans were now discovering the *Appetite* and *Illusion* albums for themselves. MTV still rolled out the 'Sweet Child' video once in a while and always got a great reaction to it. Ozzfest had now replaced Lollapalooza as the most popular annual festival in the world, and a new 'classic rock' market was emerging that would breathe life into a scene considered moribund just a couple of years before. When, in November 1999, Axl accepted an invitation from *Rolling Stone* to speak by phone briefly to Kurt Loder, it was treated like the second coming. Axl claimed there were now more than 70 new songs in various states of readiness for the next Guns N' Roses album – 'at least two albums" worth of material, some of which he felt was 'too advanced' for most people to handle. 'It's like, "Hmm, I have to push the envelope a little too far. We'll wait on that."' He compared what the new Guns N' Roses were doing to 'listening to Queen. [They] had all kinds of different-style songs on their records, and that's something that I like. Cos I do listen to a lot of things, and I really don't like being pigeonholed to that degree . . .'

Asked to explain the title of the album, *Chinese Democracy*, he replied, 'Well, there's a lot of Chinese democracy movements, and it's something that there's a lot of talk about, and it's something that will be nice to see. It could also just be, like, an ironic statement. I don't know, I just like the sound of it.'

Reassured by the way the magazine had carefully handled the piece, Axl allowed them back, this time into the studio, for a face-to-face interview. The resulting feature spoke of a man that 'looks a bit older and more solidly built than the lean rock god of his "Sweet Child o' Mine" days'; who was dressed in Abercrombie & Fitch 'with his reddish hair intact and cut to a Prince Valiant-ish mid-length'. In the interview Axl confessed that during the early years after putting together the new line-up, 'this wasn't Guns N' Roses', adding, 'But I feel it is Guns N' Roses now.'

Pressed on why he hadn't done as the other original members had and simply continued as a solo artist, he stonewalled: 'I contemplated letting go of that, but it doesn't feel right in any way. I am not the person who chose to try to kill it and walk away.' No mention of the fact that he owned the name – and was damned if he was going to let go of it. Why should he? Hadn't he been the chief instigator behind the band and everything that became so great about it? For Axl, when Slash left it wasn't because the singer had become a dictator, it was because a still drug-addled Slash didn't have what it took to try to take the band to the next level.

He also shrugged off stories of him becoming a recluse. He simply didn't 'find it's in my best interest to be out there'. He was 'building something slowly', he said. 'If you are working with issues that depressed the crap out of you, how do you know you can express it? At the time you are just like, "Life sucks." Then you come down and you express "Life Sucks" but in this really beautiful way.'

It was time for Axl Rose to come out from wherever he'd been hiding. It was still a surprise, though, when he chose to do it in such a low-key way – making an unscheduled appearance onstage at the Cat Club, on Sunset, in June 2000, swaying through a few numbers with the part-time Thursday night band, the Starfuckers, led by the Cat's proprietor, the former Stray Cats drummer 'Slim' Jim Phantom, and featuring, of all people, Gilby Clarke. Over six years since he'd last set foot on a stage, Axl admitted he didn't know what to expect. 'He was psyched,' recalled one onlooker. 'It seemed like it boosted him [that] people still want to hear him.'

When he'd arrived with just Earl for company, Axl had done so in as no-big-deal a way as he could. With a baseball cap pulled down low over his eyes, nobody recognised him at first. When Slim Jim and Gilby first caught sight of him, this stocky, hunched-up figure nursing a beer at the bar, neither man was convinced it was actually Axl. So they went over and 'tapped the guy on the shoulder', said the drummer. 'He turns round and Gilby says, "That's not him." But Axl grins and says, "Hey, Gilby, how are you doing?"'

Inviting him up to join them onstage for covers of Rolling Stones classics – 'Wild Horses' and 'Dead Flowers' – Axl stuck around afterwards, hanging out and talking to his one-time bandmate until dawn. 'I guess he ran into some friends of mine at the Roger Waters show at Universal Amphitheatre, and they told him that we were playing down there and he came by,' said Gilby.

'Maybe he just wanted to have some fun.' Axl was 'very, very excited about his new record and the new band'.

Not yet excited enough, though, to call time on his endless deliberations and release it. Axl was now confidently predicting the album would contain up to 18 tracks, accompanied probably by an extra CD containing a further ten tracks. Back at his record company, though, things were getting desperate as the massive costs continued to escalate. Interscope – who through various corporate deals were now the inheritors of the Geffen catalogue – thought it might please Axl and speed things up if they brought Queen's former producer, Roy Thomas Baker, out of retirement to oversee the project. But within a few months he was gone, too.

Partly to appease the label executives who were now pulling their hair out and partly to dip his toes in the water again as a live performer, on 6 December 2000 the first official Guns N' Roses concert for seven years was announced: a special New Year's Eve show at the 2000-seater House of Blues, in Las Vegas. This would also serve as a relatively low-key live debut for the 'new' Guns N' Roses, which now comprised guitarists Paul Huge, Buckethead, and – to Axl's delight – a returning Robin Finck, plus the bassist Tommy Stinson and drummer Bryan Mantia, Dizzy Reed on keyboards, and an additional keyboardist and the most recent recruit, former Replicants member Chris Pitman.

Kevin Morrow, Senior VP of Entertainment at the House of Blues, couldn't believe his luck. 'I thought it was a joke. I said to myself, "There is no way this can be real."' But with tickets priced at between $150 and $250 each, this was no joke. With the new band also now booked to appear at the Rock in Rio festival in Brazil in January, Axl saw this as a small but hugely significant step in rehabilitating the reputation of the band he had, to his mind, singlehandedly rebuilt.

Nobody, not even Doug Goldstein, could be really sure how things might go, though. When the start time for the Vegas New

Year's Eve show – 1 a.m. – came and went without Axl going anywhere near the stage, he feared the worst. Then, at 3.35 a.m. precisely, Axl and his new Guns N' Roses strode out onto the stage
to huge applause.

'Good morning,' said Axl as the opening, footsteps-down-a-
dark-alley notes to 'Welcome to the Jungle' echoed around the
room. 'I've just woke up. I've been taking a nap for about eight
years.'

The set lasted for nearly two hours, built mainly around guaranteed crowd-pleasers like 'Sweet Child', 'Patience', 'Rocket
Queen' and a new, semi-acoustic version, more akin to the Dylan
original, of 'Knockin' on Heaven's Door'. Then, towards the end
of the set, came six new numbers, beginning with a scorching
version of 'Oh My God'. This was followed by 'The Blues', a piano
ballad very much in the 'November Rain' mould, Axl crooning
like a sheep-killing dog about his lost love, Stephanie: *'You know I
tried so hard to make you change your mind . . . I don't know what to
do, everywhere I go, I see you . . .'*.

Next up was 'Oklahoma', said to have been written by Axl in
response to the 'lies' told about him by Erin in court, but later
to surface in revised form on the finished *Chinese Democracy*
album as 'Rhiad and the Bedouins'. Then 'Chinese Democracy'
itself, the most immediately exciting of the new songs, almost
like something the original line-up might have spat out. Then,
another obvious highlight, 'Madagascar', another portentous
ballad, with looped samples of movie dialogue, triggered by Chris
Pitman, including a snatch from Martin Luther King's famous 'I
have a dream' speech, Axl standing defiantly atop the mountain:
'I won't be told any more, that I can't find my way any more . . .' And
then, just in case anyone was getting too comfortable, the last
and strangest of all the new numbers, 'Silk Worms', a keyboard
and synthesiser special-effects blowout 'put together by Mr Dizzy
Reed and Mr Chris Pitman', announced Axl, proudly. When the

cacophony ended suddenly, to polite but baffled applause, the band sent the crowd home happy by bringing the hammer down on 'Paradise City'.

'I have traversed a treacherous sea of horrors to be with you here tonight,' Axl announced at one point. No one doubted it, least of all the exhausted and relieved band of musicians who now stood about him dressed as Guns N' Roses.

Two weeks later they were back in Rio, playing much the same set and to almost identical effect. Perhaps it was the fact that he had his adoptive Brazilian 'mom' Beta with him, or perhaps he simply felt the Brazilian fans required a more direct statement from him about where Guns N' Roses were at in the twenty-first century, but Axl took the opportunity onstage to talk to the 150,000-strong crowd about 'the old band'. Bringing Beta on-stage to interpret for him, he said, 'I know that many of you are disappointed that some of the people that you came to know and love could not be with us here today', this, to loud cheers and screams from the audience. Axl continued: 'Regardless of what you have heard or read people worked very hard, meaning my former friends, to do everything they could, so that I could not be here today. I say, fuck that!' The crowd cheered even more loudly, though what they thought they were cheering for was impossible to say.

The next day, Axl was also interviewed for *O Globo*, chilling out by the Intercontinental Hotel swimming pool, sipping a caipirinha – a traditional Brazilian drink prepared with cachaça – and tequila. For nearly two hours Axl held forth about the ugly demise of the original band. 'Everybody hated each other in the band, with the exception of me,' he was quoted as saying. 'Slash was fighting for power with Izzy because he wanted to take con-trol of the band and destroy it', adding that Duff had suffered panic attacks during the performances. 'Do you remember that movie *Pulp Fiction*?' he asked. Then spilled the beans about Slash getting similar Narcan injections to the one Uma Thurman's character famously received in the movie.

Emboldened by the success of the Vegas and Rio shows, 'new' Guns N' Roses dates were announced in March for London, Glasgow, Manchester and Birmingham: part of a 14-date summer tour of Europe, scheduled to begin in Nuremberg on 1 June. But then things got weird again and the tour was cancelled in late May because, according to official sources, Buckethead had been ordered to rest after suffering 'internal haemorrhaging' of the stomach – despite the fact that he had played a solo show just prior to the announcement. The release of *Chinese Democracy* was also postponed from the 'June release' previously suggested by Doug Goldstein's office, until autumn at the earliest, pending some unspecified 'adjustments'. Hopes were still high for an end-of-year release when it was announced that all the cancelled summer shows would not be rescheduled for December.

Vicious rumours circulated amongst the cognoscenti that the real reason the tour had been pulled was because Axl's recent hair transplants had reportedly left him with 'big, scarred patches on the back of his head', while yet another unconfirmed report suggested he was also undergoing liposuction. Certainly, newly taken pictures of the singer suggested he had succumbed to the lure of botox, as had several top-line entertainers of his generation and older. And that those suspiciously lustrous braids he was now sporting were the result, most likely, of a skilfully designed weave.

When the rescheduled dates were also then cancelled – again, just weeks before the tour was due to start in Holland on 2 December – the rumour mill went into overdrive, with several promoters up in arms. Axl, though, put the blame this time firmly at the feet of Doug Goldstein, who was forced to issue a laughable official statement to the effect that he had 'forgotten' to tell Axl about the planned tour. The statement read: 'Following the euphoria of [the band's appearance at] Rock in Rio, I jumped the gun and arranged a European tour as our plan was to have the new album out this year. Unfortunately, Buckethead's illness not only stopped the tour, but it slowed down our progress on *Chinese Democracy*. I am very sorry to disappoint our fans, but I can assure them that this is not what Axl wanted, nor is it "Another page from the Howard Hughes of rock," as some media will no doubt portray it. I made a plan, and unfortunately it did not work out.'

Speaking now, however, Goldstein explains what really happened. The day after the Rio show in January, he and the band's London agent, John Jackson, were walking in from the pool just as Axl was walking out. 'Axl goes, "Guys, I'm having a fucking blast. Can we book a European tour for this summer?" I looked at John. He said, "We can make that happen. When are you looking at, Axl?" He goes, "I don't know. June to middle of August?" John says, "Certainly. We can do that." I said, "Axl, do you want to see the routing?" He said, "No, just book it and sell the tickets." I said, "Okay, you got it."

'So I see the routing from John Jackson and I say, "Yeah, looks good. Let's go." I called Axl and said, "Hey, we sold all the tickets in, like, ten minutes. The entire European tour is sold out." So fast forward about four or five months and we're about three weeks from leaving, and Axl calls me up. I'm on my way home. He goes, "I'm on my computer. What the fuck am I looking at, these European dates?" I said, "Dude, what are you talking about?" He goes, "I never fucking agreed to these." I go, "Axl, look, I'm walking back in from the Hotel Intercontinental pool in Rio with John Jackson . . ." Give him the whole rundown. And he goes, "No. Never fucking happened. I'm not going on the tour. It's all on you. Fuck you." Click.'

The last-minute cancellation of the European tour in December didn't prevent Guns N' Roses making a return appearance in

Las Vegas for another New Year's Eve show, this time at a modest-sized venue called The Joint housed at the Hard Rock Café. Again, it was a sell-out, with jubilant holiday fans packing in to see Axl Rose and the new line-up. One longstanding fan from the band's very earliest days was refused entry though. His name: Slash. He was in Vegas anyway for New Year's Eve, so decided to check out the new band – only to be told he was not welcome and would actually be blocked from entering even if he showed up at the door with a ticket. According to Doug Goldstein, forced yet again into explaining the inexplicable, 'We didn't know what his intentions were. If nothing else, it would have been a distraction. Axl was really nervous about these shows. We decided on our own not to take any risk.' According to Slash, 'I was trying to be discreet but apparently [Doug Goldstein] found out and it was major pandemonium. It was like they sent out an all-points bulletin.'

This was also the last show for the guy who had helped force Slash out of the band in the first place: Paul Huge. Surrounded by lavishly well-paid session stars, all from other well-known bands, Huge was even more out of his depth than he had been when ostensibly replacing Izzy. The guitarist they now brought in to replace him said it all: the 35-year-old Richard Fortus, most recently of Psychedelic Furs offshoot Love Spit Love, who was given the nod for the job by Axl's new 'musical director', Tommy Stinson, an old amigo from way back. Axl issued a brief statement via the official GN'R website in which he emphasised how much Huge had 'helped us a lot in the writing and the recording of this record and to me was a vital part of not only the band but also my life'. The problem was Paul disliked touring, claimed Axl. 'We're fortunate to have found Richard. [He] has this vibe kind of like Izzy but with amazing feel . . .' Something, it seemed, Paul Huge had been lacking.

A tour of the Far East followed before the band finally arrived back in London in readiness for the first Guns N' Roses show in

Britain for nine years, headlining the Saturday night bill at the Carling festival in Leeds, on 23 August. As if to remind British fans of exactly what they'd been missing all these years, Axl did not take to the stage with the band until nearly 11 p.m., over an hour past the advertised stage time. When he did so, though, he did it in style, exiting his private dressing room backstage straight into a chauffeur-driven stretch limo in which he was driven to the stage, less than 50 yards away, past the bemused assemblage of other acts that had already appeared that day, including members of The Prodigy, Offspring and Slipknot, as if to say: make way for the king, the PA blasting out 'Gimme Danger' by Iggy Pop and The Stooges.

The 60,000-strong Leeds crowd, already teased to its limit, went crazy as the familiar echoing riff to 'Welcome to the Jungle' began bouncing around their heads and the video screens began flashing up psychedelic visions of some skull-infested hell. Axl Rose was back, baby. Fuck you very much. For many people in the crowd, though, there was still something missing.

'Where's Slash?' cried one daring soul during 'Patience'. 'He's up my ass, that's where he is. Go home!' snapped Axl.

Later into the set, as Axl took his seat at his grand piano for 'November Rain', he turned to the crowd and said, 'Well, it appears that we're gonna have an interesting evening. You see, the city council and the promoters say we have to, like, end the show.' He gazed out at the sea of faces, waited for the catcalls to die down, then added, ' . . . they could say maybe I'm inciting a riot. Now I'm not, cos I don't want anyone to get arrested or anyone to get in trouble or anything like that. But I think we got a good seven or eight fucking songs left at least. And I didn't fucking come all the way over to fucking England to be told to go back fucking home, by some fucking asshole!'

Axl got what he wanted as most of the 60,000 roared their approval. He wasn't done yet though. 'All I've got for the last eight years is shit after shit after shit in the fucking press and Axl's this, Axl's that. I'm here to play a fucking show and we wanna play! So, if you wanna stay, I wanna stay and we'll see what happens. Everybody ... Nobody try to get in trouble or anything. Try to have a good time.'

It was now past midnight. Earlier in the afternoon, festival officials had witnessed around 500 drunken fans gang together to fight police, knocking down and setting fire to 71 toilet blocks and a Portacabin. Nobody wanted to even guess at the kind of trouble the crowd might cause now if Axl walked off. As the next song ended, Axl was given the news. 'We've got more time,' he told the crowd triumphantly. 'And to whoever is responsible for that I'd like to say thank you.' The show eventually ended without further incident just before 1 a.m.

Forty-eight hours later, onstage at what was still then known as the London Arena (now the O2), Axl informed the audience that most of the new songs they had played so far on the tour were no longer actually going to appear on *Chinese Democracy*. He went on to explain that he and the band had, in fact, already completed the recording on a follow-up to *Chinese Democracy*. 'By the time the record company release the second group of songs, and we do this all over again, who knows? Maybe I'll have finished the third album.' The crowd cheered and cheered, but as was becoming more and more the norm these days, afterwards nobody was quite sure exactly what it was they were supposed to be cheering for. Just the sheer daring of the guy, perhaps? The sheer bad-ass craziness? Or just the fact that he had even turned up at all?

Three days later Guns N' Roses had been ready to launch their first US tour for a decade with a 'surprise' appearance live onstage at the MTV Video Music Awards show. This was an old stomping ground for Axl. The first time he'd done the show with Guns N' Roses in 1988, they had torn the place apart with a blissfully out-of-control version of 'Welcome to the Jungle'. Four years later they had given the watching millions a taste of the deliciously over-indulgent theatricality of 'November Rain'. What more perfect setting could there be to relaunch the new twenty-first-century version of Guns N' Roses live on national American television?

This time, though, the performance was a disaster. Once again, they had decided to begin with 'Welcome to the Jungle', but all it did was serve to underline the contrast between the new band and the old, Axl out of breath as he ran around the stage overcompensating for the fact that he was no longer the svelte snake-hipped gunslinger of the Eighties but an overweight, over-costumed guy who looked like his much angrier father. When the band then launched without introduction into 'Madagascar', it became clear that Axl was hurting. That the real surprise to the appearance of the new band was that they believed they could get away with it. As the British rock-writing legend Nick Kent later observed: 'Rose looked deeply frightened that night and his one new song was another terrible self-pitying dirge.'

Ending with 'Paradise City', the last image the dumbfounded crowd had was of a wild-eyed Axl staring out from the stage in typically messianic stance, arms aloft, eyes closed, mouthing the words: 'Round one.'

The ensuing US tour was doomed from that moment on, with the dates soon collapsing beneath the weight of riots, no-shows, delayed appearances, cancellations, tantrums, 'health problems', even the hiring of a new latter-day Suzzy London-type 'tour psychiatrist' in order to try to coax Axl onto the stage each night. By the time the tour had reached its first major stop, in New York, on 5 December, for a show at Madison Square Garden, where all 20,000 tickets had sold out the day they went on sale, it found Axl on a high. As he told the crowd that night, 'I managed to get enough of myself together to do this.' Afterwards he told everyone he met at the after-show party that this had been 'as good as the band could get' and that it was 'time to cut our losses' and get on with things again – specifically, the release of a new album.

The following night, however, the demons returned and armed police were called in to quell what threatened to be another riot amongst the 14,000-capacity crowd at First Union Center arena in Philadelphia. Just minutes before the band were scheduled to take to the stage, an announcement was made that the show would have to be cancelled due to the non-appearance of not just Axl this time but the entire band. Ripped-up seats and broken beer bottles rained down on the stage. The next day a spokesman explained the decision by saying they had received a phone call 'shortly after 11 p.m.' informing them that an unspecified band member had been 'taken ill' and that the group would therefore not be able to perform that night.

Within days shows in Washington, DC, Albuquerque, Phoenix, Sacramento and San Jose were also unceremoniously cancelled. While Axl refused to offer any further excuses or vapid explanations, the promoters, Clear Channel, publicly warned ticket-holders to expect more cancellations. It seemed only a matter of time before the announcement was made that the rest of the tour was pulled – which it eventually was on 11 December.

Privately, some members of the band's entourage wondered if Axl had 'lost his nerve' following the critical lambasting his appearance at the MTV awards show had received. Stinson and Finck were rumoured to have already tendered their resignations, while Buckethead was also said to be seriously out of sorts.

According to the *New York Post*, the band 'had been previously frustrated by the delays and Axl's pathological perfectionism, tardiness and general insanity. Now they're back in the same boat, and they'll probably split.' According to another 'friend', 'Axl has never been so totally alone before – this time he had nobody to blame but himself.'

With the new line-up apparently blowing up in his face, speculation now mounted that Axl was ready to discuss some sort of reunion with the original Guns N' Roses line-up. This last, though, was pure invention, idle rumours sparked by the fact that Slash, Duff and Matt were now very publicly back together again in LA, while talking privately of working together in some capacity again. There was even speculation that Izzy was involved somewhere in the background. All they needed, it was said, was a singer. Could it be true?

Meanwhile, a story in the *Chicago Sun-Times* published in January 2003 claimed: 'Sources say that Rose is very close to checking himself into a psychiatric clinic to deal with "exhaustion" and a number of other emotional problems.' Quoting another unnamed source, the paper went on: 'Famous for his outrageousness, the aging rocker lately has been "even more whacked than usual." The singer himself has openly admitted he's battling inner demons.'

Axl wasn't the only one now asking himself serious questions about the future. Doug Goldstein, who'd agreed to sell his Big FD management company – and, with it, his overriding control over Axl and Guns N' Roses – to the giant Sanctuary Music Group, decided he could take it no longer and announced his decision to 'retire' to Hawaii, where he had a wife and son. 'For two years I'd been flying from LA to Hawaii every Friday night, then back to LA again on the red-eye Monday morning. I just couldn't do it any more,' he says now.

In a further twist, he now says that he had to return half the money he'd received from Sanctuary for his company – reportedly in the region of $8 million. 'That was the condition for getting out of my deal with Sanctuary.' By then, he says, half of his salary was already going to Sharon Maynard, 'Axl's guru in Sedona, at [Sanctuary's] directive . . . It got really weird once [Sanctuary] got involved. I mean, *really* fucking weird. [They] had no clue how to talk to Axl. He was way out of [their] league.'

Be that as it may, the real cause of the problem, Doug confesses, was that he and Axl had never resolved the fallout from the cancelled European tour in 2001, which Axl still maintained was all Doug's fault. Things between them had never been the same. Once Doug Goldstein 'retired' to Hawaii, they never would be again.

Speaking now, more than a decade since the split, Goldstein admits he is still heartbroken. 'I lived for him every day of my life. And it kind of blows me away that he . . . I believe that Axl feels like once you've abandoned him he turns his back on you. Even if he wanted to let me back into his life, he would stop himself. It's sad, because him and I, I mean, we loved each other. I was his – for lack of a better definition – I was his big brother. I was there through thick and thin. When he needed me at four o'clock in the morning, I was in the car and up. It probably cost me my first marriage . . . She honestly thought when I was leaving at four o'clock in the morning that I was going to my girlfriend's home. She didn't believe that I would actually muster up the coffee and energy to get out of bed to go to his fucking call. But I did. And it had zero to do with the money and everything to do with the fact that I loved him to death.

'I was very fearful that he was going to become part of the 27 Club. Even when he was older than that. I knew that I could separate him from thoughts of suicide. And so for me to not do that, what kind of a friend would I be? For me to drive for two hours from south Orange County to Malibu, it was nothing for me. It certainly beat the alternative. Which was him making some desperate move. If I could thwart that by stepping in, I'd do it seven days a week. Beta would call me crying, 'He's gonna kill himself!' So I'd have to go up to his home and find him lying in bed with a gun in his mouth crying. I'd have to sit there and talk him off the fence. So I wasn't just a manager, right? I had a brother who was manic-depressive, and suicidal at times – which kind of honed me for my craft or my profession with Axl. Which is, just be there for him. I have other people in my life who have the depressive side of bipolarity. Basically, they don't really want to harm themselves, they just want to be loved, and know that they're cared about. So that's all I've ever done with Axl is just love him, and try and be there as a friend and be supportive. I don't know who serves that role now.'

On 19 June came an even more savage blow to Axl's plans – when Slash, Duff and Matt played their first official show together in LA, at the El Rey Theatre, with their new singer – the former Stone Temple Pilots frontman Scott Weiland. The new band even had a name: Velvet Revolver. Following favourable reviews in *Rolling Stone* and *Spin*, the new band also had a whopping new multi-million-dollar record deal, with RCA, to go with it. Axl was enraged that his former bandmates were 'cashing in' on the Guns N' Roses name. They would fail, he was sure. That's what he told Beta and anyone else crazy enough to bring up the subject with him. When he lay in bed at night alone though, he wasn't so sure.

Axl Rose was no longer sure about anything.

14

THE PROJECT

After he was fired as the manager of Guns N' Roses, in 1991, Alan did not hear from any of the band – barring his fellow ex-pat Izzy Stradlin – for nearly nine years. Then one night, sitting in his local bar, he got a phone call. 'It was Curly,' he says now – 'Curly' being his nickname for Slash. 'It was just a delight to hear him after eight years.' Slowly, over the months and years, they pieced back together the trust they had once shared in Guns N' Roses. When Slash called again one night and invited Niven down to LA for a meeting with him and Duff, 'I went down and we all had dinner. That's when they told me they wanted me to work with them on "The Project".'

The Project was the original name for what eventually became Velvet Revolver: Slash, Duff, Izzy and Matt Sorum reunited, with the addition of an as yet unknown singer. Or put another way: Guns N' Roses without Axl Rose. Niven was at once delighted by the idea, then horrified, then flattered, then dismayed. Had the offer been made five years before, or even five years later, he might have been on the next plane to LA. Right now, though, from his vantage point in the new mountainside home he'd made for himself in Prescott, Arizona, Alan Niven felt he had no choice but to decline.

'There were two reasons. I had started to write songs again and they were the best things I'd ever written and I wanted to follow that, see where that went. As regards The Project, I thought if we reconvened everybody apart from Axl and Doug, that we'd be setting a bar that would be unfair for them. An expectation that I thought would be an albatross. And there was perhaps a third reason that I wasn't articulating to myself. In that I wasn't in the best of spirits.'

In fact, Alan Niven hadn't been 'in the best of spirits' since being fired. The brutal nature of his firing from Guns N' Roses had caused him to descend into an emotional black hole.

As he puts it now: 'It took me ten years of accumulating experience and contacts to form a skillset that I could apply to, amongst others, Guns N' Roses. It took five years to get them to selling out Wembley Stadium, and that was done under my watch. I put Wembley up for sale. Which was kind of sweet, in a way, because it's English. One of my heartbreaks was, that was going to be the moment when I was going to have my mother driven down from Wales, I was gonna put her in a box at Wembley and let her see it and let her understand what I do. And that was denied of me and that's sad but . . . anyway, it took ten years to acquire the skillset, five years to do the work. It took [Goldstein] *three months* to break it. Because of Izzy leaving three months after me means that it's broken. It took [Goldstein] only two and a half years to completely destroy it after that. Two and a half years after Izzy leaving, it was just Axl and totally, totally destroyed.'

It would take years for Alan Niven to recover. Meanwhile, things got worse before they could get better. The first Great White album that followed his split with GN'R, *Psycho City*, in 1992, had been a total flop, not even cracking the US Top 100. Co-produced and co-written by Niven, it had a cover featuring a gaudy neon sign with a big advertisement for the Rose Motel. The title track also featured a snippet of an answering phone message Erin once left for Niven, allegedly while Axl was being violent towards her. 'Yes, I did use Erin,' he admitted in an interview with the *LA Times* in 2016, 'but I was hurt and angry and in the process of writing my anti-LA, anti-betrayal, anti-Goldstein content for the *Psycho City* album. So now you know.'

A man on the verge of a breakdown, Niven was convinced by then that he was, as he puts is, 'under psychic attack' from Axl. Convinced that Axl was utilising the forces offered to him by Sharon Maynard and her circle of crystal-gazing, future-reading, aura-controlling followers, Niven had gone in search of his own form of magical defence. Stephanie Fanning, who had initially left to work with Niven, had firsthand knowledge of some of Niven's occult intentions at this time. 'I think he dabbled in some things when the band was gone,' she says. 'He was kind of talking to a couple of interesting people that I think were dabbling in that as well. But Axl was doing the same thing. I felt like they were duelling each other with a little bit of their whatever you want to call that – black magic, whatever. I think they were duelling each other. One would hear like, "I hear Axl's doing this to me, I'm gonna do . . ." I feel like it was kind of going on between the two of them. I don't know how much credence I place in that but, yeah, he was. He was. He definitely was. A little bit, for sure. I don't know exactly if Alan was wishing Axl ill or hoping maybe to bring clarity between the two of them, cos to be honest as soon as I heard about it I kind of shut my ears off. I was like, I don't want to get mixed up in any of that. I don't know what that is. Maybe it scared me, I don't know. I don't know whether it was black or white, evil or good. Bring us back together; tear him apart . . . But I know he was talking to people who dealt in that world.'

Eventually, Fanning left Niven – to go and work with Doug Goldstein again. 'Alan, he went kind of underground. He stayed in LA for a couple of years while he was building the house [in Arizona]. But I was really hoping he'd get back in the game. Like, get back in the game. I'd bring him music into the office like, hey, check this out. And he just couldn't . . . He just wasn't . . . I don't know if something left him. Look, it was even hard for me to wake up the next morning when GN'R was over. There was a huge emptiness in my stomach. A huge emptiness in my soul not to be with that band any more. So I can imagine what it was like for him.'

'I already knew that [Niven] was into the Crowley, Jimmy Page, that whole kind of thing,' says Doug Goldstein. 'Him and Izzy used to go into New Orleans quite a bit.' When Steph went back to work with Doug, she felt obliged to tell Doug of some of Alan's strange behaviour. 'She said, "He hired a black-magic specialist from New Orleans and every single day after work before he would go home he would go over there and they would put on black robes, and the candles and the incense, and they would cast evil spells on you and Axl.' I was like, what a rat bastard, man! I mean, a) what a waste of fucking money. But b) what an evil bastard.'

As far as Alan Niven is concerned now, though, 'the psychic attack was definitely manifest in the deliberate undermining of [Izzy's solo outfit] the JuJu Hounds by Goldstein and [Axl].' He feels this 'psychic attack' was also manifest in the sharp decline of Great White's fortunes: specifically by the arrival at their label, Capitol, of the former Zoo Entertainment promotions chief Ray Gmeiner, as replacement for Michael Prince, who had long been a supporter of Great White. 'Gmeiner was Goldstein's former roommate,' he adds ominously.

This was the last straw, he says. He had been 'on the dark side of the moon to everyone in West Hollywood' since losing the GN'R gig. A couple of tentative feelers from big-name acts had come his way in the immediate aftermath of the split, but Niven wasn't interested. The big one was when David Geffen invited him to work with Bon Jovi. But it nearly made him puke, he says, when Jon Bon Jovi turned up at their first meeting with his lawyer and accountant in tow. 'How could I possibly get excited, it was diametrically opposed to the nature and essence of my passion? This is not a job to me. It's something that I value beyond a job.' He sighs. 'It was a very dark period for me and it got darker and darker.'

Next he discovered that his wife had been having a long-term affair with Great White's vocalist, Jack Russell. 'He was terrified I was going to find out.' It was a discovery that led to the overwhelming realisation that she had in fact 'compromised pretty much every relationship that was of value to me. And who the hell would want a toxic individual like that in a business structure?'

With his marriage in tatters and his career being held back by what he was convinced were 'psychic' forces, he recalled a place in New Orleans he'd once visited with Izzy called Barrington's: 'A retail mausoleum of ritualistic cornucopia. That covered all kinds of spiritual expression, from elephants' feet with weird things buried in them packed with mud, to drinking skulls . . . I still have a couple of items from there', including a large wooden rosary, a cross made from the staff of a bishop . . . 'I'm a fucking atheist. I'm managing a rock'n'roll band. I have very little knowledge but I'm curious . . . I have two Coptic Ethiopian healing scrolls. One of them is intact, about seven feet long. It's very rare to find a whole one because they're concertinaed. They're stunningly beautiful. I bought two Coptic bibles there that were about 400 years old. The pages are like bark. All hand-constructed and handwritten . . .'

He stresses, though: 'I'm curious but I'm always going towards the light. So when things were going bat shit and I couldn't figure anything out . . . I got to this point of: "This is ridiculous. There's something to all this. Maybe I've been hexed. Maybe someone's put a fucking curse on me." So I called the guy at Barrington's . . .'

Niven was put in touch with someone who offered help – at a price. 'I'd walked through the door. Whatever scepticism I had, I'd knocked on the door and it had been opened so I walked through it.' For several months, he studied under 'a mad monk – he was huge and looked like he'd been picked out of a medieval monastery. To this day I still don't know how much of a bullshitter he was. I do know how much of a manipulator he was because I had to fly him here. I had to fly him there. I had to take care of him at this point. But he introduced me to a whole area of reading that I'd been oblivious to. Which was basically occult reading . . . the secret knowledge. I learned that the simple truth is that truth is simple. That you simply find the truth by simply being truthful.

'At this point in my life I have a real clarity of darkness and light. But at that point I was just in pain. Isolated and confused. And this guy said, "I can ceremonially get rid of the negatives that are attacking you." And I was being psychologically attacked and I was in a psychological and spiritual warfare. There was a lot of negativity being put my way. Goldstein is just one of the people who was putting out that energy in my direction. Axl was another who was putting out that energy in my direction. Yoda was probably another one that was putting out that energy because she wanted to exploit him.

'I was his guard. Once I was out of the way they could feed off him like fucking maggots. So I had to go and have these special knives made, crudely, out of a particular copper. And there was going to be some ceremony of putting the knives in a certain way. And the fact that a water pipe broke was supposed to be symbolic. And I started to go, I think I'm being fucking had here. And I eventually cut myself off from this guy. But, yeah, my open mind, at that moment, to such as hexing and hoodoo was an act of defensive desperation . . . nothing was working and all felt unpleasant . . . I couldn't figure what the hell was going on . . . and not going on . . .'

At the time Slash and Duff had come to him with their idea for him to manage The Project, Alan Niven had reached rock bottom.

Checking himself into a hotel, he washed down 172 pills with a bottle of 'good Graham's port' – then sat there waiting to die. 'I remember it so well because I put out the piles of ten and I had two left over and I thought, if I don't start with these suckers I'll never get to them.' Painkillers, sleeping pills, 'Ambiens, just anything I could get my hands on. The management of the hotel dragged me out of there after a few days ... I got to a situation where I could see somebody down below going, "I'm not sure he's on our list." And upstairs they're going, "Well, he's not on our list either. If he's no good to either of us let's just throw him back." I mean, how the fuck do you survive 172 pills?'

When he came to after 72 hours, he found he had vomited all over the room. The hotel management got him up and dressed and packed, then virtually dragged him to his car. 'They put me in my rental truck and I immediately hit a very expensive car sitting in front of the hotel. So they called a limo and got me down to the airport and I got on a flight down to LA, where a friend picked me up and took me to his home and I was out of it for a week. It was weeks before I could even walk straight. I got up one morning and went to the window and looked out at the ocean and went, "Where the fuck am I?" That's not the desert. And my friend said, "That's exactly what you said yesterday."'

The gilded hallways of major labels are littered with the ghosts of bloated rock star vanity projects that should never have seen the light of day. Central to these over-publicised debacles is a starry-eyed failure to recognise that just because you're a rock star, that doesn't mean you can carry a band. In the wake of his departure from Guns N' Roses, Slash put together a new version of Slash's Snakepit – led by the more generic-sounding rock vocalist Rod Jackson. Where *It's Five O'Clock Somewhere* had offered Slash a low-pressure opportunity to unburden himself of the gathering tensions within GN'R, it had been a time-killer, badly lacking the sense of urgency that pervaded his work in Guns N' Roses. Re-booting the Snakepit in 1999 felt more like knee-jerk reaction than a statement of intent, and the Snakepit's 2000 release, *Ain't Life Grand*, withered from a gaping lack of originality, not to mention an embarrassingly ham-fisted rap sequence to kick off the first single, 'Mean Bone', that sounded like it had been grafted on by some well-meaning but clueless record label drone.

Slash desperately needed to channel his creative energies into something vital and dynamic, but without an equal and opposing force operating within his process, creating a sense of tension within his ideas, he was a man adrift. Even Matt, who kept time in the original iteration of Slash's Snakepit and who played on *It's Five O'Clock Somewhere*, understood that Slash's Snakepit was never a long-term deal, referring to it as 'a way for me and Slash to go and play music in the beginning when we were waiting around for Axl . . . I think it turned into more of a thing for Slash, cos just . . . you know, Slash just loves to play his guitar, and he is the consummate musician, you know?'

Sorum had largely avoided the spotlight until 2001, when he rejoined The Cult to record and to tour behind their first album for seven years, *Beyond Good and Evil*. Duff had moved back to Seattle and reignited his old punk band, Ten Minute Warning, who were among the early progenitors of the city's pre-Nirvana grunge scene. Pearl Jam's Stone Gossard has credited Ten Minute Warning as his inspiration for learning guitar and it was at his urging that Duff re-formed the band when he returned to Seattle in 1998. In true punk fashion, they recorded an album on Sub Pop and broke up shortly thereafter when their lead guitarist, Paul Solger, left the band. Bolstered, however, by his newfound sobriety and a disciplined diet and martial arts regimen, Duff dived headlong into other pursuits, mainly family life and academia, ravenously devouring the principles of business and finance in one-off community college courses and self-study. In 1998, Duff recorded a solo album, *Beautiful Disease*, where he sang and played most of the instruments alongside guest appearances from Slash, Izzy and Faith No More's drummer, Mike Bordin. But when Duff's parent label, Polygram, was bought during the album's promotional campaign, *Beautiful Disease* fell among the earliest casualties. According to Duff, one of the new executives told him, 'I'm going on a ski vacation and I'm going to listen to all the upcoming releases with my kids. We'll decide whether they have a future with the label or not. When I come back I'll let everyone know. I'll have each artist into my office to tell them personally where they stand.' Instead, 'I never heard what his fucking kids thought of my record. In fact, I never heard from the guy again. On my birthday – the day of the album's supposed release – an intern from the label called and left a message on my answering machine to say it wouldn't be released that day or any other day.' The album has never been released.

Rather than sit around and mope, though, Duff enrolled in a string of business courses at a community college – notching up an impeccable 4.0 grade point average, no less – with one eye towards attending a proper university. Now 35, Duff had come a long way from the coke-fuelled alcoholic who'd glibly signed away his rights to the name Guns N' Roses. Having seen rock stardom from both before and after, Duff was now happy to divert his energies into creating a vibrant personal life wholly unconnected to his music. He was now independently wealthy, thanks to some sound investments he stumbled onto when he first got sober. 'God bless him he has more money than god,' chuckles Doug Goldstein, money made, he suggests, 'by decisions that myself and the accountant helped him with. Once he had some money, we took him to the accountant's office, and said, "Duff's interested in investing and I obviously support that." And the guy – his name was Michael Oppenheim, he was a great guy – said, "Do you have any idea what you want to invest in?" And Duff had no clue at that point. So he asked a great question. He said, "What are you passionate about?" Duff said, "Well, my hometown – Seattle." So we immediately put his money into Starbucks and Google. Next thing I know he's got his own radio show and daily newspaper column about what a financial guru he is. I'm sure he is today. But back when those first investments were made I don't think he could spell "investment".'

Nothing, though, could diminish Duff's passion simply for making music, and by 2001 he had his own new band, Loaded, recording and playing dates around the world. By 2002, Loaded had added a new lead guitarist into the mix – some cat that had been at high school with Slash named Dave Kushner.

Slash was also going through some big life changes. He'd been diagnosed with cardiomyopathy and had a defibrillator inserted. 'Years of drinking had swollen my heart to the point of bursting,' he said in retrospect. 'It reached the point where the doctors gave me between six days and six weeks to live. They installed a defibrillator to keep my heart from stopping and keep it beating at a steady rate. After the operation I began therapy and miraculously my heart started to heal. I was out of circulation for four months before I picked up a guitar. It was the darkest period of my life.'

He thought he'd pulled through when, four months after the op, he was invited to play at Michael Jackson's birthday celebration. 'This was my first gig since the operation so I was looking forward to it. It certainly turned out to be memorable.' He had worked through two days of rehearsal for the show, which boasted a bill including the reunited Jacksons, Marlon Brando, Liza Minnelli, Gloria Estefan and several other of Jackson's celebrity 'friends'. 'On the day it was a great show,' said Slash. 'Everyone in the Michael Jackson entourage was rocking out, and I was doing the best I could to stay away from alcohol. After all, I now had a pacemaker. When the doctors put the defibrillator in me, it was for maintaining a normal heart rate. For most people this isn't a problem, but it was for me. Once I get up onstage my heart rate sky-rockets. When I took the stage with Michael and got into it, I was suddenly hit in the chest by a shock and my vision flooded with electric-blue light.

'This happened about four times during each song, and I had no idea what was going on. I thought I had a short-circuit in a guitar cable or a photographer's flash had popped in my eyes. Each time it happened I had to stand there and make it look as if everything was normal. I saw it later on TV and you couldn't tell, so I guess I pulled it off.'

He had been halfway through a Snakepit tour when he first became ill. Had to cancel dates. He didn't believe the doctors, but he followed their instructions, to sober up, and do some minor exercises. 'And I recovered. Which is an amazing thing. A couple of people I know have died from the same thing.' He also gave up drugs, at least for a while. But he still drank – and he still smoked. It would be quite some time before he was finally able to do something about that. In the meanwhile, he disbanded Slash's Snakepit in 2001 and began collaborating with Steve Gorman, the drummer with The Black Crowes, who had recently quit the Atlanta-based band and moved to LA. The two put together an early version of what would eventually become a huge hit for Velvet Revolver called 'Fall to Pieces'. But without other key players or any long-range vision for their project, the one-off collaboration would prove to be just that and nothing more.

Then, in April 2002, a gathering of Hollywood's rock illuminati descended upon the Key Club on Sunset Strip to pay tribute to Ozzy Osbourne's former drummer Randy Castillo, who had passed away from cancer a few weeks before. A noisy, sold-out crowd of 800 enjoyed a parade of classic rock covers played by a rotating cast of musicians that included Ronnie Montrose, Ritchie Kotzen, Steve Lukather and a raft of other big names. Slash, Duff and Matt had all turned up to donate their talents to raising money for Randy's family, and along with the guitarist Keith Nelson and Buckcherry vocalist Josh Todd they stormed through a blistering set that included 'It's So Easy', 'God Save the Queen', 'Nice Boys' and Buckcherry's bouncy, shout-out-loud coke anthem, 'Lit Up'. They closed with 'Paradise City' (aided by Cypress Hill's Sen Dog on backup vocals) and a roof-lifting cover of 'Mama Kin', on which they were joined by Steven Tyler himself.

In the sweaty, electrified aftermath of the show, the three former GN'R members were on fire. 'It was like a 747 jet taking off in that room,' recalled Duff. 'Powerful yet familiar, comfortable and friendly. There were no assumptions or ulterior motives. We were doing this for a friend's family in need. End of story.' Though their intentions were charitable, they recognised that their chemistry remained as strong as in their *Use Your Illusion* days. 'Slash, Matt and I faced a bona fide dilemma,' Duff went on. 'It felt too good together not to continue after that gig. We didn't have any new material yet, and had only the foggiest of ideas about what we might do, but the sheer power of us playing together was unmistakable, and we knew that if we worked hard, the rest would somehow come.'

The next piece fell into place after a Loaded gig at Johnny Depp's Viper Room, when Duff introduced Dave Kushner to Slash. The two guitarists had attended junior high school together, but through the years had only enjoyed a casual friendship. As Slash's star began to rise, Dave joined Waysted Youth and later The Electric Love Hogs, who recorded an album produced by Mötley Crüe's drummer, Tommy Lee. Kushner had also appeared in Sugartooth, Infectious and Danzig before securing a regular gig playing with Dave Navarro and serving as his music director. Guys like Dave Kushner were always in high demand around Los Angeles; through playing in so many different bands and drawing from influences as diverse as Black Sabbath and the

Ohio Players, Dave boasted a prismatic versatility that producers and musicians valued highly.

Duff, Slash and Matt invited Dave to take part in their new 'project' as the band's rhythm guitarist, but the opportunity came with an extra complication in the shape of Izzy Stradlin, who had also been jamming with the band for a few weeks. Complicating the dynamic, Izzy remained silent about his intentions with regard to The Project, keeping Slash in the dark as to whether he planned on sticking around or whether he viewed this as an opportunity to jam. 'Izzy did one of his disappearing acts,' comments Alan Niven. 'He was involved and then he didn't turn up for rehearsal any more. Didn't want to be involved. He doesn't like the palaver. He's skittish. As absurd as it sounds, that's actually a valid point of view. All of us in some way or other suffered from our GN'R experiences. There's no class at UCLA for dealing with what happens when you become successful. And it can be a tremendous trauma. It starts with the onset of fame because people around you start to change in the manner that they deal with you faster than you realise what's going on. You're not quite sure of anybody's motives any more.'

According to Slash, however, Dave Kushner was now their first choice anyway. 'Dave brought a cool vibe to what we were doing. There was no deliberation; that was it, it was a perfect fit.' Kushner could now set about the Herculean task before him: learning how to play with Slash. 'I play nothing like Izzy,' he explained, 'and Slash even said that he'd never really been able to play with anyone except Izzy, so for the second guitar player to be really comfortable with him, it's just a matter of playing open chords when he's playing barre chords, or if he's playing a riff, trying to come up with something good underneath it instead of doubling the riff. It's about trying to find the right balance of not doubling him, but yet adding something to it or trying to play off of him rhythmically.'

In September 2002, The Project placed ads for a singer in various newspapers and magazines that read: 'Unnamed artist looking for singer-songwriter somewhere in the realm of early Alice Cooper/Steve Tyler, the harder-edged side of McCartney–Lennon.' They had a specific vocalist in mind; however, that singer was already committed. In fact, he had only just got out of rehab. Still, they saw no harm in floating the idea and so Duff reached out to Stone Temple Pilots' frontman, Scott Weiland.

Scott Richard Weiland was a hugely talented but deeply fucked-up singer-songwriter who, by 2003, had become known more for his drug busts, abandoned spells in rehab, relationship breakdowns and arrests by police than he was for the handful of very good albums he'd made in the 1990s with his band, Stone Temple Pilots. Routinely portrayed in the rock press, in their earliest, most successful days, as the great grunge pretenders, in reality their crime consisted solely of not coming from Seattle but from Los Angeles. That and the fact that on their breakthrough hit, 'Plush', in 1993, Scott Weiland sounded a little like Pearl Jam's singer, Eddie Vedder (who sounded a little like Tim Buckley, but no one ever pulled him on it, because most *NME* and *Spin* writers then had never heard of Tim Buckley).

I had first met – and championed – Weiland when the Stone Temple Pilots toured Britain in 1994. Every day of the tour I was told to get ready for my interview with him, but come the appointed hour, come the bullshit excuse from the band's manager, Steve Stewart. Scott had a cold; Scott was busy; Scott's head was 'not in the right place'. What really made it weird, though, was that I was staying in the adjoining room to Weiland at one hotel and I could hear him through the walls, yelling and cursing, followed by what sounded like loud weeping. Jeez, I thought, what's up with this guy?

Then, when we got back to London, I got a call at home asking me to meet up with Scott at his hotel. He was finally ready to talk, they said. Having been there so many times before, though, I turned up later that day with zero expectation that he would actually keep his word this time and sit down with me. Except he did. Turning up in an ankle-length black leather trench coat he told me he'd just bought that afternoon from Kensington Market, he added that he'd have to be 'kinda quick' as he was meeting his wife, who'd just flown in from LA, to take her to a movie. 'Which movie?' I asked nosily. 'The new Quentin Tarantino,' he said, '*Pulp Fiction*.' Oh, I said, that's cool. I heard it was quite good. 'Yeah,' he said.

So we sat together in the coffee shop of his hotel, where other nearby guests bothered us not at all. STP may have sold three million copies of their latest album, *Purple*, but that don't mean shit, daddy, in the UK. This, though, was something he seemed to enjoy. Weiland did not fetishise fame the way most rock stars did. Money was also not his deal. 'Money isn't really an issue; that's all relative,' he told me. 'There's security in the fact that we can own a home, but that's it. I spend more money eating out than I used to, but I still buy pants and shirts for $1.25. There's other elements of success that are far more confusing, like the idea of celebrity. That's such a misconception. Unfortunately, people think that a public person is always a public person, and that you have these responsibilities to other people because you influence them. But the only thing we feel ultimately responsible to is music.'

A few days after our interview, Weiland shaved his head completely bald. Interesting, I thought. R.E.M.'s Michael Stipe had just unveiled his own newly shaved pate in the then current 'What's the Frequency Kenneth?' video. Three months later, I had also shaved my head completely bald. Like Stipe's, my hair was already thinning, shaving it off was the only way I could see to keep some dignity. Unlike Michael and me, Scott shaved his off because he wanted to make some sort of statement. About what I could only guess – pressures of fame, insistence on private personal concerns over public perception and popularity? Just feeling, you know, fucked up? 'I just, uh, felt like it,' he told me when I asked. 'So I did it.'

As a young man he'd been through the tragedy of seeing his younger brother die. 'We thought [it] was an overdose,' he said, 'but it was cardiomyopathy, due to just years of substance abuse. But he died in his sleep and at such a young age. There's a part of me that still grieves for him every day. He and I were so close, losing a person that's your brother and your best friend – we were creative partners as well . . . it was just beyond anything . . . you never quite get over it.'

In 2011, he would write in his autobiography, *Not Dead & Not for Sale*, of being raped by 'a big muscular guy, a high school senior', an incident so traumatic he had suppressed it 'until only a few years ago when, in rehab, it came flooding back'.

In a phone interview we did at the time, I asked him about that. 'I've always been a very driven person and I kind of look at it like, every time you falter and fall you have to pick yourself back up again, and every time you do it just gives you a further sort of a belief that you don't have to quit. Just take an experience that is bad and turn it into something positive. Take a good experience and turn it into something even better. That's sort of overall my philosophy.'

I asked if he had been able to bring that philosophy to bear when he'd been sentenced to jail for six months in 2009 after admitting to using heroin while on probation. 'Yeah, definitely. I was in this part where everyone was a drug addict so we had groups every day and did a lot of work. It wasn't pleasant at all being in jail. I don't think the jailing of people that are just users is necessarily the right way to go. But at that time there was a programme within the system that allowed me to deal with the issues.'

He'd first heard about The Project when 'I ran into Duff at the gym,' Weiland later recalled in the *Washington Post*, 'and he told me they were forming a new band and that I should check it out and see if it's something I'd be into. They gave me two different CDs with about forty to fifty songs. The first CD was basically atrocious. It was stuff they'd also written with Izzy, and it sounded like Bad Company gone wrong. I told them I was busy and wasn't really interested in the idea.'

In his autobiography, Duff relates how he'd been introduced by his wife, Susan, to Scott Weiland and his first wife, Mary, who was a friend of Susan's. 'Scott and Mary had kids, too, and our families had gotten together for dinner on a few occasions. Scott was having problems with his band, Stone Temple Pilots, and he had been through trouble with addiction – on those occasions when our families met up, we had a lot to talk about. But I didn't consider him for the new band because he had a band.'

By 2003, The Project had leaked into the hive mind of social media and Guns N' Roses fans were frothing at the mouth for a taste of that iconic *Appetite*-era sound, as Axl stood mired in the sludgy morass of writing *Chinese Democracy*. Slash announced that the band would release an album that year, yet while he boasted to *Rolling Stone*, 'We got the baddest fucking be-all, end-all rock'n'roll band', he confessed that the sort of vocalist they vaguely had in mind continued to elude them. 'There are no rock'n'roll singers out there right now . . . except Billy Idol.'

In October, Slash sat in with LA's rotating all-star cover band, Camp Freddy, featuring Matt Sorum and Dave Navarro. Skid Row's Sebastian Bach joined in for 'Time Warp', from *The Rocky Horror Picture Show*, and 'Paradise City', also featuring Ronnie Wood. The club erupted and Slash began to wonder if the former Skid Row frontman might just be the guy The Project were looking for. Duff was less convinced. So Slash gave Bach five instrumental tracks, asking him to throw some vocals on top of them, but the collaboration ended there. Early in 2003, seeking to capitalise on the cheap appeal of reality television, VH1 sent over a film crew to capture the process of the band trying to find a singer, which they would later release as a documentary. Once again, for a group of musicians who had literally put their lives on the line to taste success to invite the distractions of a television crew, not to mention opening such a public window into band business, underscored how badly they lacked the internal force to push them ahead. If the guys grew frustrated with having nothing to show after a ten-month search, they missed the point; it wasn't that the world lacked great vocalists, more that their selection process was bereft of real urgency. Accustomed to letting others pilot their ships, not one of them possessed the Jagger-like ambition to take control, to push others and to act decisively. Thrust into the roles of co-pilots, The Project were in danger of failing badly when Slash put in his call to Alan Niven. But Alan had other mountains to climb. He couldn't afford to look back any more.

Meanwhile, audition tapes and CDs arrived by the hundreds; try-out invitations were extended to a broad spectrum of vocalists, seemingly without regard to genre, range or style. They auditioned Neurotica's Kelly Schaefer and Josh Todd, though neither slipped smoothly into the chemistry generated by the other four. They would also audition Steve Ludwin, of Carrie and Little Hell, and Travis Meeks, the frontman from Days of the New, whose business partner, Jonathan Hay, was only too happy to publicly comment on the audition. In one of the most comically absurd displays of putting the cart before the horse, Hay declared, 'Slash, Izzy, Duff and Matt have all been working on new material that I have been blessed with the opportunity to hear and witness ... This is the best rock music I have heard since *Appetite for Destruction*. Guns N' Roses fans and Days of the New fans will not be disappointed. They will be ecstatic! The new material has that vintage GN'R feel that millions craved and loved in the late-Eighties and early-Nineties. I can honestly say that as a witness, this band is back and better then ever [sic]. Travis Meeks and the remaining members sound completely natural, comfortable, and astoundingly incredible. Travis, like Axl [Rose], is from Indiana. Both diverged from their original bands. This is a match made among the stars with a sound that is out of this world.'

After such an appalling breach of band etiquette, nothing ever came of Meeks's audition and his next brush with fame would be a tragic appearance on an addiction-centred American television show called *Intervention*, chronicling his grim spiral into meth addiction. He reportedly has since gotten clean.

A Canadian bassist, Todd Kerns, would also audition for the role, offering a substantially more grounded take on the process. The tall, good-natured musician, whose collaboration with Slash would eventually come about a few years later, remarked, 'I was sent three songs to work on. Every singer on the planet has been sent three songs to work on. I am to write lyrics and record vocals to three instrumental tracks that the guys recorded . . . *Appetite for Destruction* is still in my Top 3 greatest rock records of all time, so I do find the entire thing amusingly surreal.' The band took a pass. Ian Astbury of The Cult, Mike Patton of Faith No More and Myles Kennedy of Alter Bridge would also receive invitations to audition, but each would decline. Kennedy, like Kerns, would eventually secure a spot in a future Slash project, but it too would be a few years down the road. By April, just as the audition process appeared hopelessly stalled, word arrived that Scott Weiland had just split from Stone Temple Pilots.

2003 was another difficult year for Weiland. In the wake of commercial indifference to STP's 2001 release, *Shangri-La Dee Da*, the troubled singer's drug problems approached dire proportions. His latest split from STP came on the heels of a drug-fuelled backstage blowout with the guitarist Dean DeLeo that had seen the two of them squaring up for a fight. The band members left that show in different cars and, for the first time since 1985, Scott Weiland was a man without a band. And that was just fine with him. 'I never fucking tried out for Velvet Revolver,' he maintained. 'I've never tried out for any band. I wouldn't even try out for the fucking Rolling Stones. Stone Temple Pilots broke up and I was working on my solo album. The last thing I wanted to do was join another fucking rock band after all the fucking drama I went through with Stone Temple Pilots.' When news spread of STP's dissolution, Duff received a call from one of his managers, urging him to reach out to Scott. 'I was reluctant at first because Scott and I were friends in a completely different context and I wasn't sure I wanted to cross that bridge. Besides, he still went through periods of pretty serious drug use and I hadn't spent big chunks of time with anyone in full-habit mode for about eight years. Still, I did have a lot of sober time under my belt and no harm could come from just asking Scott if he would be interested.'

The Project needed a vocalist who could do more than just sing, one who would invest the band with a real sense of risk, both in the material and in live performances. Having assiduously cultivated their roguish outlaw personae, to turn around and play it safe with some skinny, straw-haired kid who worshipped at the altar of GN'R would be tantamount to shooting themselves in the collective foot. Sebastian Bach would have created a drama-fuelled sideshow and at the other end of the spectrum, some no-name up-and-comer would have vanished into the background of the others' towering celebrity. They needed somebody with his own weight, fame and swagger. Someone who would speak up and assert himself as a major contributor. They needed a true peer – somebody as brilliant, committed, fucked-up and ballsy as they were. Scott Weiland was all of those things. But would he want to join them? Was The Project up to his low-life standards?

Three months after Weiland rejected the first clutch of material, they sent him over another CD, full of new stuff. This time, something clicked. 'There were two that I thought were pretty good,' Scott said. 'One was called "Slither". I thought it sounded a lot like Stone Temple Pilots around *Core* – like "Piece of Pie" or "Wicked Garden". In my head, I was thinking, "What would I do with this?" If you listen to the vocal on it, it's, like, very much *Core*-era Scott Weiland. What ended up happening was, my wife and I separated. She was with the kids in LA and I was living in our apartment in Hollywood, doing a lot of drugs. And those guys were clean at that time. I said that if I did get into this band, it might be an opportunity to hook up with some guys who aren't using and had gone down the same sort of path that I had. Right around that time, their manager called me and said there were two soundtrack opportunities on the table for a lot of money. Do the songs, get a big pay-cheque and if you find out you work well together, just take it from there. I didn't show up the first day because I was loaded and couldn't make it. But I came the next day and we got together and started working out Pink Floyd's "Money" and writing a new song, "Set Me Free". And I joined. But never, ever, ever, never did I try out.'

One can only speculate as to Weiland's mind-set at the time this was all going down. A man plummeting into full-on addiction lives out his day as a series of impulsive, shortsighted decisions with little regard to the future or consequences. At this point in his well-worn cycle of using, crashing and heading into rehab, Weiland was physically dependent on drugs to simply avoid the agonizing grip of dope sickness, and finding a predictable source of income and a place to cool his heels surely made sense, even though he wasn't yet wholly invested in the concept. Scott would test the waters, although he later admitted that joining the band was purely a financial decision, telling *Spin*, 'I can't call it the music of my soul.'

Or as he told *Classic Rock,* 'So there was this period of time before Velvet Revolver that I really didn't want to play in a rock band again. I was knee-deep in recording my solo record. I was in the process of putting together my record company and I was producing other bands. I co-produced two of the Limp Bizkit records. Not my favourite band by any stretch of the imagination, but it definitely put me on the map as a producer. I also had kids and didn't want to spend the rest of my life on the road.' Joining Slash and the guys 'was almost like coming together off a rebound. At first it was very exciting and we did jive. We had the same common interests. Duff and I shared a lot of the same musical interests with punk rock. Matt and I shared an interest in experimental music. Dave and I had known each other from back in the days of playing clubs in Hollywood. And then you had Slash and I who were – and I don't want to come over as self-serving – two iconic figures, which the media tried to turn into a Mick–Keef kind of thing. We did have that gang-type camaraderie at first. At the same time, I was in the worst period of my drug addiction I'd ever gone through.'

During their first week together, the musical director Kathy Nelson connected them with F. Gary Gray, the director of the 2003 update of *The Italian Job.* He wanted to use Pink Floyd's 'Money' in the film but the original version was too fast, and he wanted to see if they'd be interested in knocking out a slower cover. It proved an excellent opportunity for easing everybody into the new dynamic; they learned and recorded it in a day. '[Scott] was just the guy, you know,' said Dave. 'It was so undeniable. It was *him* . . . just the complete package. The look, the attitude, you know . . . the stage presence, the performance and especially the vocals. It's like he came in and we gave him a demo of one song, and he came back a day and a half later and it was "Set Me Free"', another track that also ended up being used on the soundtrack to a Hollywood blockbuster: *The Hulk.*

Speaking with me years later, Weiland confessed that his insouciance about hitching his wagon to the ex-GN'R crew was mainly for show. In truth, he said, joining Velvet Revolver 'was a magical thing too. That was right when I was getting off dope and those guys were all sober and clean, and I had, like, a very special kinship because we'd all experienced the same things. So it felt like, kind of us-against-the-world and we're gonna play just pure rock'n'roll.' To underscore his excitement, on 12 May, at a Marilyn Manson concert in Hollywood, Scott announced that he was the singer for the new band, which he now referred to as Reloaded, jumping the gun on the band name, leaving their publicist rushing to clarify the next day that Reloaded was only a working title.

Six days later, LAPD officers approached Weiland, sitting in a parked car with its lights off, and arrested him for possession of heroin and cocaine. He pleaded not guilty at his arraignment two weeks later and voluntarily entered another rehab in advance of his next court appearance. That the band moved forward in the face of this bleak augury only emphasises how confident they were that Scott was indeed their guy. And how desperate they were to keep him.

Also, in June, they finally settled on a name. 'Coming up with a name was an eventuality we were dreading,' McKagan told Gavin Edwards. 'We were like, we have to come up with a fucking name.' They had seen a movie financed by Revolution Studios, inspiring Slash to suggest Revolver. 'But I did a Google search on a Revolver,' Duff said, 'and there was, like, a thousand bands, so that was impossible.' Weiland countered with Black Velvet Revolver, but the band rejected that because it had the same rhythmic cadence as Stone Temple Pilots. They eventually settled on Velvet Revolver, entirely missing, until it was too late, that it sounded eerily, some might say mockingly, like Guns N' Roses, with the hard-soft resonance merely flipped to soft-hard. Guns, Revolver, Roses, Velvet . . . anyone?

On 19 June, 2003, Velvet Revolver made their first public appearance with a brief, six-song set at the El Rey Theatre, in LA, where they played 'Bodies' by the Sex Pistols, 'Set Me Free', 'Sex Type Thing' (Stone Temple Pilots), 'It's So Easy', 'Slither' and 'Negative Creep' (Nirvana). The brevity of the set and the inclusion of only two originals suggest that it was more of a statement of purpose than a platform for showcasing the band's creative heft. It was now that they were approached about using 'Set Me Free' as the end-title song for *The Hulk*. Not only was the new band hitting a collaborative stride but, at long last, it had begun to generate some cash. 'The deal gave us some breathing room,' said Duff. 'Everyone had some scratch, and we recouped some of the costs of our rehearsal space.' Without a deal, a label or any formal PR machinery, 'Set Me Free' entered the US charts, peaking at Number 17 on *Billboard's* Mainstream Rock chart.

By now, the new band had accumulated a trove of demos, jams and other ideas, which Weiland brought to his own studio to add vocals. On some, he sang over the existing music, but on 'Big Machine' he torqued the original arrangement, twisting the guts of the song into something that suited not just his voice but his style. The significance of this play did not go unnoticed by the band. Duff wrote: 'It instilled confidence in us about Scott's ability, despite his being strung out on opiates and various other supporting drugs.' Although they knew Scott was still using, songs began quickly flowing. At his son's birthday party, Weiland played a demo of 'Got No Right' for Dave and Duff, saying, 'I think this is the best thing I've ever done.' Having worked with Axl Rose, the silo approach of four guys creating music in one time and space and a singer adding lyrics and vocals in another was not new territory for Slash and Duff and Matt. Weiland, though, was forced to develop a new approach to his craft. 'A lot of times, on certain songs, the riff and the beat inspired me to write music that's pretty fucking sleazy and dirty and, for lack of a better term, music that girls and guys should fuck to,' he said. 'It's good stripper-fucking music, and there's nothing wrong with that. You know why? People should spend more time fucking.'

In a room full of strong-willed, creatively driven egos, their ability to tap into a verdant songwriting chemistry was less impressive than the notable lack of personality clashes. But their path to a debut album proved anything but linear. Either unaware or uninterested that he was running out of chances, early one morning in October – his thirty-sixth birthday – Weiland was popped for driving under the influence when his BMW smashed into a parked van. He fled the scene. Duff tore over to Weiland's apartment, where he found Dave Kushner already there, trying to talk Scott down. Exploding in a vitriolic rage, Duff began giving Scott all manner of holy hell for letting everybody down. Scott's response was not what Duff anticipated – the singer asked for help and, when he did, Duff softened. 'This guy's a dad, I thought. In fact, I had originally become friends with Scott because we had that in common: we were fathers.'

When the LAPD officers caught up with him they charged him with DUI and hit-and-run. It was his fourth arrest in eight years. Once again, the judge committed the singer to an inpatient detox programme, followed by six months in a residential outpatient programme, during which he was allowed one ten-day stretch to finish the album. Only in LA could the court system broker such a generous arrangement: police would escort Weiland to and from the studio and he would be drug-tested immediately upon his return to his halfway home.

Duff said they knew when they formed the band that 'We'd get the "Guns N' Roses without Axl" crap, but it was too good to let go. And then we just needed to find a singer. And everyone was saying, "Oh, these guys will never find a singer." And then when we got Scott it was like, "Oh great, they got a junkie for a singer."'

15

SMELL THE POPPIES

For years now, Duff had been working with a martial arts instructor – a Sefu – in a gruelling regimen that had turned Duff from a bloated, out-of-shape, coke-addled alcoholic into a lithe, muscular athlete. Dejected by one failed rehab after another, Scott Weiland asked Duff if that regimen might help him clean up. Dave Kushner, who was the most sober of them all, took Duff and Scott to a doctor in LA who supplied them with the drugs they'd need to detox Weiland and, just like that, they were off to Seattle, heading for the mountaintop retreat of Duff's Sefu, where together they put Scott through a 360-degree wellness programme that included punishing intervals of exercise, followed by meditation, more exercise, writing and a strict healthy diet. After three weeks, the light in Scott Weiland switched itself back on and Duff could add 'Miracle Worker' to his list of accomplishments.

Meanwhile, Slash and Matt Sorum were both anxious and sceptical, wondering if, instead of booking studio time for an album, a search for a new singer should be next on the band's 'To Do' list. But when they saw the hale and laser-focused singer back in LA, their concerns evaporated and they finally got down to the business of recording the first Velvet Revolver album, although as part of his court-ordered outpatient rehab, Weiland was only allowed to work a few hours each day so he could return to his halfway house by curfew.

During the writing, Slash resurrected the melodic little ballad that he'd conjured up with Steve Gorman and handed it over to Scott, who, inspired by his most recent crash and all the terror and damage it inflicted on his wife and children, added the lyrics that became 'Fall to Pieces'. 'If it hadn't been such a powerful song, on a musical level, I wouldn't have been moved to write those lyrics, that melody,' he said. 'That song was the exact moment where I realised that Slash and I could really be one of those classic songwriting teams.' Accompanied by a grim, emotionally charged video that drew from the real-life events of the singer's addiction, the song showcased the very best of Velvet Revolver – Weiland at his most broken and vulnerable, Slash back in his element as the architect of chiming, anthemic riffs, and the band together again, playing grimy, four-on-the-floor rock'n'roll.

With a hit song already enjoying broad exposure and an album on the way, a bidding war erupted among the major labels and the band ultimately signed with Clive Davis at RCA. It was during these meetings that Duff first appreciated just how deeply his financial classes were paying off: he actually understood the complex financial considerations underpinning the deal, matters that he had never before bothered to learn. 'People took me more seriously in business meetings. Cool shit. Sometimes I looked into the eyes of industry types and saw a flash of panic: Shit, I wonder if Duff knows more than I do.'

Weiland finished his vocals during the first week of December and the finished masters were sent to New York for mastering, with RCA announcing a release date of 27 April 2004. During this time, Weiland took to the band's official site to call out the media for what he saw as their cynical portrayal of his high-profile struggles, writing: 'First of all let me say that *Rolling Stone* magazine's gossip columns exist only so rich college boys can wipe their fucking asses with the rag. As for the lad that interviewed me and then printed that I was drunk driving . . . get your facts straight you moron paparazzi fuck.'

They hadn't planned it that way, but nevertheless the timing of the release of *Contraband*, as the band had decided to call the album, could not have been more perfect, in terms of snagging disaffected Guns N' Roses fans. By 2004, Axl Rose's 'new' Guns N' Roses had lost whatever momentum they had built up with their unveiling three years before: *Chinese Democracy* was now the most well-known unreleased album in the world, its title a jokey euphemism for any black hole endeavour with little purpose or ending in sight. As the spring eased into summer, some observers wondered if a similar fate had befallen Velvet Revolver's debut when the album's release date was pushed from April to May, then to June. 'We finished it sometime around Christmas,' Matt recalled, 'and I think that was just a record company thing, you know, as far as, like, the setup, and doing a lot of press . . . Duff and Slash went to Europe on a couple-week run over there, we had to do a video – there were a lot of factors. And we just really believed in Clive and . . . everyone at RCA. We weren't worried.'

In fact, the delay was caused by concerns over whether Weiland would be legally able to tour with the band. Finally, in April, a California judge cleared the singer to tour with the band and they played a brief acoustic set on LA's KROQ morning show later that month, running through 'Slither' from the upcoming album, and versions of STP's 'Interstate Love Song' and GN'R's 'Used to Love Her'. In an effort to combat illegal file sharing on P2P platforms, RCA flooded fan-related websites with recordings of Scott, his brother and Doug Green reading poetry, naming the files after actual songs from the album.

Contraband was released six weeks later with the supporting tour starting in May. A thoroughly polished modern rock record, *Contraband* struck the halfway point between the *Use Your Illusion* sessions and *Purple*-era Stone Temple Pilots. It was a crowd-pleaser, a muscular blood-storm of bare-knuckled, fucked-up hard rock, erupting with vitality, tooth-rattling hooks and infectious, earworm choruses that begged for big, swaying crowd singalongs. The element of risk was not in the style of music, but in the band chemistry, and with Weiland's vocals dovetailing seamlessly into Slash's prismatic melodies, it was eminently clear from the radio play, the media coverage and the industry buzz that the risk had paid off handsomely. Reviews were mixed. 'Anyone expecting *Use your Illusion III* will be in for a slight buzz-kill,' declared *Entertainment Weekly*. 'The songs suggest the pop grunge of Weiland's old band more than the careening overdrive of GN'R.' David Fricke in *Rolling Stone* was considerably more bullish, hailing the album as 'a rare, fine thing', saying that '[Weiland's] grainy yowl – which, at the height of Seattle rock, earned Weiland a lot of lazy, cruel comparisons to Eddie Vedder – is actually a precision instrument that cuts through Slash and Kushner's dense crossfire with a steely melodic purpose that, when Weiland piles up the harmonies in the choruses, sounds like sour, seething Queen.' In the main, critics reluctant to reach for the word 'safe' described the album instead as 'mature', with one going so far as to call *Contraband* an '*Appetite for Destruction* for grown-ups'.

Behind the strength of chart-smashing hits like 'Set Me Free' and 'Slither', and power ballads like 'Fall to Pieces' and 'Loving the Alien', *Contraband* would sell over a quarter of a million copies in its first week, making it the fastest-selling debut album by a rock act in US chart history. Their debut would generate two supporting tours, stretched out over nearly two years, and land them a Grammy award for 'Slither' (Best Hard Rock Performance) and two additional nominations – 'Fall to Pieces' (Best Rock Song) and *Contraband* (Best Album). To date, Velvet Revolver's debut has sold over four million copies worldwide. Interviewed retrospectively in the *Mail on Sunday*, Slash pointed out how 'At first everyone thought we were just doing it for a quick cheque. But, trust me, getting this band off the ground required ultimate sacrifice and commitment. We toured *Contraband* for nineteen months, playing five shows a week in every country we could get into. It was never for the money. I can't even say it was for the girls. Really, it was a music thing.' In the same interview, Duff added, 'Money's never dictated me. I came up at the time of punk. People like Iggy and The Stooges were my heroes. They were never about the money. They never sat down and said, "Hey, let's be rock stars", they were just like, "Fuck you", and that's always stayed with me. When the three of us, me, Slash and Matt, played the benefit gig for Randy Castillo, it was the first time we'd played together for maybe eight years. And it just felt right.'

In the press junkets, the band fielded the same tired questions about working with a singer prone to such exceedingly public and outrageous behaviour. 'I'm just not that judgemental,' said Slash. 'Look, I'm one of the biggest fuck-ups I ever met. So all things considered, how am I going to pass judgement on this guy? I don't know one brilliantly talented individual in this business that doesn't have a burial ground worth of skeletons in their closet. It was a given that Scott had this baggage that he'd been dealing with for years. He said he wanted to get clean and we could all relate. So we rallied for him. We had to jump a lot of hurdles, but it was worth it. Scott's got a great rock'n'roll voice and charisma. Had we not taken those chances, we wouldn't have the band we do.' As Velvet Revolver lined up their touring commitments for the summer of 2004 amid a wildly successful radio launch, they received an intriguing offer. 'We were offered a gig in Lisbon, Portugal, opening for Guns N' Roses,' Slash revealed. 'The new Guns N' Roses, whatever that consists of, but we actually said okay. We'd love to be there. It'd be very exciting. I think it would be quite a spectacle.' However, the gig never materialised. Guns N' Roses wouldn't return to Portugal until the Rock in Rio

Lisbon festival in 2006, when they were supported by The Darkness. Meanwhile, after finishing the 'Fall to Pieces' video in July, the band recorded cover versions of Cheap Trick's 'Surrender', Aerosmith's 'No More, No More' and Queen's 'Tie Your Mother Down' to use as B-sides in subsequent releases.

The Velvet Revolver world tour began with 24 dates in America, playing the sorts of venues Guns N' Roses had made their bones in nearly 20 years before, theatres and ballrooms, clubs and big halls. *Contraband* may have been Number 1 but the band were determined to start at the bottom and work their way up, building a solid fan base that reached beyond diehard Guns and Pilot fans, into a people-stratosphere all their own. They followed that with 22 shows around 15 countries in Europe. Headlining at the Hammersmith Apollo in London, the scene of GN'R's early triumph 17 years before, they put on the most genuinely thrilling rock show seen there in many years. Led Zeppelin's Jimmy Page was there, turning to his friend, the photographer Ross Halfin, as they left the building and exclaiming, 'Now *that's* what I call rock'n'roll!'

They carried on in this fashion for the next 12 months, selling out rammed theatres and auditoriums, and becoming the big draw on the 2005 Ozzfest summer tour. With two big hit singles to their name in 'Slither' and 'Fall to Pieces', the band had been eager to make the fourth and final single from *Contraband*. RCA had other ideas, though, and instead released 'Dirty Little Thing', which presented an issue with the next video, as they had already fleshed out a concept for 'Sucker Train Blues' – a part-animation performance piece that takes place on a speeding train, crowded with dancing, under-clad women. The band was bummed at the thought of ditching the idea. Then Scott said, 'Hey, why don't we use the same treatment, just use a different song?' The result made it hard to tell the difference, but the single was not a hit.

*

On tour in June 2005, Scott Weiland caused a minor stir in Germany, where the media accused him of wearing Nazi regalia on stage, an illegal act in Germany. Vigorously denying any Nazi sympathies, Weiland responded to the allegations by saying, 'The Nazi SS hat that I wear in fact symbolises the loss of democracy and the shift to totalitarianism. One could make an argument that indeed the Government of the US is evolving into, or is already, a fascist police state, hiding under the guise of a republic.' While nobody who knew him would ever mistake Weiland for a Nazi sympathiser, his explanation hung heavy from the weight of the sort of lazily contrived anti-authoritarianism one would expect to hear at a teenage punk show.

The RIAA certified *Contraband* as double-platinum in July, with the band latching on to the Ozzfest tour for August and September. Celebrations were soon quietened when Matt broke his hand in a water-skiing accident in August. He posted the following statement to fans: 'Just wanted to say to all the fans that came to see Velvet Revolver on the last leg of the tour, including Ozzfest, how sorry I am that I couldn't make it. It was very hard for me to sit on the sidelines while my band went out on the road without me. But it's what they had to do and with my blessing. It was just a week before the tour when I went to my Mom's house on Lake Havasu near the Colorado River. I was water skiing when I had a freak fall on the water skies by getting tangled in the ski rope and being dragged.' The band brought in a former Ozzy Osbourne drummer, Brian Tichy, to handle Matt's commitments until he himself had to leave for a tour with Billy Idol. The band then hired Mark Schulman, formerly the drummer with Simple Minds, for the remainder of their Ozzfest tour.

August would also prove contentious for other reasons. Later that month, Slash and Duff filed a suit against Axl in the federal court, alleging that Axl had changed the publisher of GN'R's copyrighted songs and kept the royalties for himself. Earlier in the year, Axl had negotiated a multi-million-dollar deal with the Sanctuary Group – Axl's new management, following the departure of Doug Goldstein – for the rights to GN'R's back catalogue. Although this deal was reported by the press, Slash and Duff claimed that they had not been clued in to the details and argued that Axl had 'omitted and concealed' the scope of his dealings. It was their position that they weren't aware of the scope of the deal until their royalty cheques stopped arriving. The lawsuit read: 'Suffering an apparent attack of arrogance and ego . . . Rose recently decided that he is no longer willing to acknowledge the contributions of his former partners and band-mates in having created some of rock's greatest hits.' Duff's lawyer, Glen Miskel, explained, 'When the ASCAP cheque didn't come, we called and they looked into it. We didn't know all the facts at first.'

Yet while aggressively confronting Axl in the courts, in public, Slash still wore his chill, confrontation-avoiding persona. In February 2006, Slash said that he'd 'always been supportive' of his old singer and that he was as excited as anybody for the release of *Chinese Democracy*. If Slash offered such comments as something of an olive branch, Axl wasn't having it. A month later, Axl filed a countersuit against Slash and Duff to clarify the property rights surrounding the copyrighted material in the GN'R back catalogue. Sanctuary issued an utterly scathing statement that branded Slash as 'a consummate press, photo and media opportunist and manipulator' who 'has attacked Axl Rose on a number of levels'. The statement additionally alleged that 'Slash has continually made negative and malicious statements about Axl [in the press] in order to garner publicity for himself', further accusing Duff and Slash of making 'numerous false allegations about Axl . . . [and that] Mr Rose believes that once apprised of the true facts, the judge or jury deciding these lawsuits will rule in Axl's favour on every issue before them'. The statement went on to allege that Slash and Duff's lawsuit 'attacks [Axl's] integrity as Slash and Duff, in a vindictive attempt to aggrandise their own stature, rewrite history through false statements, which have been repeated by the media. Their attacks on Axl stand in sharp contrast to Rose's conduct. Axl has at all times worked diligently to maintain the artistic integrity of the band by choosing with great care which properties to license Guns N' Roses songs to.'

In true scorched-earth fashion, the statement went on to claim that Slash had turned up at Axl's house in October to offer a truce. According to Sanctuary's statement, 'Slash came to inform Axl that "Duff was spineless", "Scott [Weiland] was a fraud", that he "hates Matt Sorum" and that in this on-going war, contest or whatever anyone wants to call it that Slash has waged against Axl for the better part of 20 years, that Axl has proven himself "the stronger". Axl regrets having to spend time and energy on these distractions, but he has a responsibility to protect the Guns N' Roses legacy and expose the truth,' the statement continued. 'Axl believes he has been left with no alternative but to respond to these lawsuits. It would have been Axl's preference to resolve disputes with Slash and Duff in private. The courthouse is not his choice of forum. However, Axl could no longer sit quietly and allow the continuing dissemination of falsehoods and half-truths by his former band-mates.'

Never one to knowingly walk away from a fight, Weiland weighed in with an open letter to Axl that read: 'Get in the ring. Go to the gym, motherfucker, or if you prefer, get a new wig, motherfucker. I think I'll resist the urge to "stoop" to your level. Oh shit, here it comes, you fat, Botox-faced, wig-wearing fuck! Okay, I feel better now.' Then he continued: 'Don't think for a second we don't know where those words came from. Your un-original, uncreative little mind – the same mind that had to rely on its band-mates to write melodies and lyrics. Who's the fraud now, bitch? Damn, I couldn't imagine people writing for me.

How many albums have you put out, man, and how long did it take the current configuration of this so-called "band" to make this album? How long? And without the only guys that validated the name.

'How dare you! Shame on you! How dare you call our bass player "spineless"? We toured our album over a year and a half. How many shows have you played over the last ten years? Oh, that's right – you bailed out on your long-awaited comeback tour, leaving your remaining fans feeling, shall we say, a trifle miffed?! I won't even list what I've accomplished because I don't need to. What we're talking about here is a frightened little man who once thought he was king, but unfortunately this king without his court is nothing but a memory of the asshole he once was.'

Many months later, Beta Lebeis told the official GN'R website the following: 'I was the one whom Slash spoke with when he came to Axl's house in [October] 2005 and expressed his negative comments regarding the others in his new band.' She went on: 'Behind the scenes it is a very different story than what the public is told.' Forced to respond, Slash now admitted in an interview with New Jersey's *Home News Tribune* that, yes, he had visited Axl's home in an effort to call a truce. 'I actually did go to Axl's house at one point, but I never saw him. I never talked to him. I left a note with his person over there having to do with the lawsuit that we were in. I don't know how it got turned into what it got turned into.'

April 2006 found the members of Velvet Revolver returning to Earth long enough to consider producers for their second album, bringing in both pop and hip hop maestros Pharrell Williams and Lenny Kravitz. Duff said, 'I've always been a huge fan of early Motown and soul and Prince, so to explore something like that with Pharrell would be amazing. There's nothing like that out there. It's uncharted territory. Dude, it's going to be way cool. It's going to be stinky. Pharrell's a genius.' There was also talk, however, of working with Rick Rubin, even of making the second album a concept album. In November, however, Velvet Revolver turned to the Midas touch of the Stone Temple Pilots' former producer Brendan O'Brien. 'We were really excited about six months ago, when we first began writing,' Weiland explained. 'Then we really kind of flat-lined for a while, We didn't know which way we were going. Once Brendan came on board, it was kind of like a shot in the arm. It was a new energy.'

Serious work on the album, now titled *Libertad* – Spanish for 'freedom' – began in December. According to Weiland, he hadn't been 'this excited about a rock record since 1993, when I went into the studio to record [STP's] *Purple*', hailing *Libertad* as 'a really inspired rock and roll album, but it's got many textures. It's multi-dimensional, which I think is one thing Brendan brings out in artists. I mean, [Slash, Dave, Duff and Matt] are amazing players, and they're capable of anything. They've reached completely new heights, and pulled something out of themselves. Instead of doing what's completely comfortable, what they've done before, they have gone to new places, emotionally, musically and spiritually.'

If publicly the musicians appeared inspired and energised, privately they had begun to fall apart, one man at a time. 'I was clean and sober for two years and then I started drinking,' Weiland later confessed, 'and that all seemed cool for about a year, but then it started escalating. During that time is when the guys started falling off the wagon. Matt relapsed and went into treatment, then Duff relapsed and went into treatment, and then Slash had his situation. So everybody in the band ended up falling off, except for Dave, of course. At that time I was maintaining my problem in a sane way and I really didn't fall off intensely until my brother died.' Indeed, while it had seemed like they had found new designs for living that insulated them from the cravings and emotional obsession over drinking and using, the success of *Contraband* had pushed them back over the edge. 'I definitely went way down the fucking drain for a minute there after the *Contraband* record came out and we went on tour for two years,' said Slash. 'I started drinking heavily and revisited my opiate passion.'

Though Dave Kushner had been sober the longest of anyone in the group, Duff had always appeared to have transcended his alcoholism in the most inspirational sense, replacing drinking and self-destruction with a robust exercise and academic rigour. As the realities of success and touring began piling up, however, even the stolid bassist caved in. While touring, Duff said, he let the stress of trying to be the band's decision-maker get to him. 'I've had panic attacks since I was seventeen,' he told his home-town newspaper, the *Seattle Times*, 'so I keep a pack of Xanax on me, for stress. But I'm a drug addict and an alcoholic. A guy like me can't take anything for stress. I got myself caught up in a nice habit for two weeks. Luckily, I had my kids and my wife; I didn't let myself go too far. But I didn't see that stuff coming. I've learned relapsing is part of recovery. I did twenty of those [Xanax] pills a day, and I'm thinking, "Hey, I'm not doing blow, I'm not drinking, I'm not doing heroin or Vicodin . . ."'

As 2007 unfolded, Weiland's situation grew progressively darker. He split with his second wife, Mary Fosberg, his mother was diagnosed with cancer and his younger brother, Michael, died of an overdose. Michael's death would cripple the singer, who was called to identify the body of the man he considered 'the best friend I ever had'. Publicly he admitted to a brief slip-up, stating, 'I had a setback after Michael, I had a coke binge, but then I put myself back in rehab.' But comments from Slash and later interviews with Weiland suggested that the wounds ran far deeper. 'I was suicidal,' he told the *Mail* in 2008. 'I wanted to kill myself. My wife kicked me out. I'd barely seen my two kids. I'd missed birthdays, Christmas, Easter. I wanted to stop, I just couldn't. I'd go into detox, clean up and go fix again as soon as I got out. It was just horrible.'

A few days after Michael Weiland's fatal overdose, Daniel Sorum, Matt's 11-year-old brother, passed away from brain-stem cancer. A day after the funeral in Minnesota, Matt had to fly back to meet the rest of the band to play a pair of Van Halen songs at their Rock and Roll Hall of Fame induction ceremony in New York City. They played a song by each of the two Van Halen singers – 'Ain't Talkin' 'bout Love' from the David Lee Roth era and 'Runaround' from the Sammy Hagar era. The event was not without drama. According to Weiland, Roth had wanted to sing 'Jump', one of Van Halen's biggest hits. But the band demurred. 'We felt from an artistic standpoint, and I'm being totally honest with you, that it wasn't a song we felt comfortable with. We don't have keyboards. To bring a keyboard on stage wouldn't work for us. We said we'd do "Jamie's Cryin'" or "You Really Got Me", and he was adamant that wasn't okay.'

The tension backstage was not helped by the personal crisis everyone in Velvet Revolver except Dave Kushner was now embroiled in. While Duff, Matt and Slash would all straighten out sooner rather than later, Weiland continued his terrifying slide backward. Slash reflected: 'We all eventually came out of it and made the *Libertad* record, which I thought, musically, was a good record, but we lost Scott and we never regained that. I thought the overall spirit of everything was declining at that point . . .'

On Thursday, 3 May 2007, Velvet Revolver played a show at the Avalon, a small club at the top end of Sunset Strip, in the promotional run-up to the release of *Libertad*. It was a tribute show, for the benefit of Michael Weiland's family, and Scott spoke of the passing of both his brother and Matt's brother, saying, 'It literally crushed us. It made this record happen for both of us.' He turned his back to the crowd, and the band launched into Pink Floyd's 'Wish You Were Here', with Matt singing harmony and a video screen above showing montages of Michael, his wife and his two daughters. The band debuted a number of tracks from *Libertad*, including 'She Builds Quick Machines', 'The Last Fight' and 'Get Out the Door', all of which would later be released as singles, plus another new song, 'Just Sixteen'. Everybody said how great the gig was. How special the band was. But everyone in Velvet Revolver already sensed the band had turned a corner – and suddenly found themselves lost.

For two years, Velvet Revolver had managed to balance their herculean egos, they had survived lawsuits, bitchy media speculation and the onset of relapse, but in August 2007 Scott Weiland admitted that bad cracks had begun rippling through the band's foundations. 'When things really go south,' he told the *Washington Post*, 'and we start getting in that big drill car and driving to hell, we usually get together and talk. How successful that is depends on everybody's state of mind at the time. Usually it works out fairly well. But lately there's been some things that have happened that definitely shouldn't have happened – where band members have irresponsibly used the media as a tool and said things that they shouldn't have said. And that's fucking blasphemy, because a band should be a safe haven regardless of what goes on. It doesn't matter what kind of problems a family is having; it should always stay in the family. The fucking media is bad enough as it is. It seems like everyone's got an agenda, and the agenda seems to be selling magazines or air time with sensational stories. Look at the shit with Britney Spears and Lindsay Lohan, these tragic figures. It's not like any of that stuff is new; that kind of shit has been happening for years. It's just that the media didn't hound them. When people fell, they either fell again or they picked themselves up and figured it out. But it wasn't on *E!* or the celebrity news shows 100 per cent of the time. It's become an addiction for the

American public. People are more interested in that shit than the upcoming election.'

Weiland was referring to a recent *Rolling Stone* article in which Matt Sorum had seemed to suggest that Velvet Revolver were on the verge of breaking up after just two albums, prompting a band meeting to circle the wagons. Matt subsequently sought to emolliate his comments, stating, 'A lot of that stuff I said was taken out of context. We're getting along pretty good right at this moment. We have days here and there where we have a beef just like anyone else who might be in a working relationship or like a relationship with a husband and wife. It's about ten million times better than when it used to be when Guns N' Roses was running back in the day where everything was so dramatic all the time.' Pressed to comment on possible Guns N' Roses or Stone Temple Pilot reunions – rumours of which had both been gathering momentum throughout recent months – Matt stonewalled: 'We don't know anything about it. I'm sure our managers and agents and everybody else probably have got something up their sleeves. We're so in Velvet Revolver right now; we're booked on this tour for another year. [The reunions] are not going to happen anytime soon. There's never been any mention of it between us.'

In fact, there had been tentative discussions behind the scenes to do with reuniting Slash and Duff with Axl but there were still several stumbling blocks. Top of the list: Axl's raw need to save face and get *Chinese Democracy* out of the way first. But with Axl still insisting the album was about to be released anytime now and Velvet Revolver gearing up for a second and final album together, the feeling was that it could happen within the next couple of years. The money was certainly there, millions of dollars just to do some weekend festivals; a great deal more if they could actually keep it together long enough to make a new album. Easygoing Slash was certainly up for it, even though it was fairly obvious that Axl would not countenance working with Matt Sorum again, nor with Steven Adler. As for Izzy Stradlin, that question would remain moot. After he had bailed out early on from Velvet Revolver, nobody was ready to engage with that question unless it became a necessity. In the meantime, born-again businessman Duff presented the biggest stumbling block when he insisted he and Slash would only consider a reunion tour if Axl was made accountable for any financial penalties or losses incurred from the singer either not showing up on time, not showing up at all, and/or, God forbid, walking off mid-set, thus triggering another riot on the scale of St Louis. According to one insider, it was this last point that killed the deal.

Meanwhile, Velvet Revolver had finished *Libertad* in February, and the mixing was completed in March. They released its first single, 'She Builds Quick Machines', in May, with the full album release on 3 July. By most standards, its entry into the charts would have been impressive, debuting at Number 5 and selling over 90,000 copies in the first week. Compared to *Contraband*, however, it was a disappointing performance that did little to engender the sort of us-against-the-world camaraderie of its predecessor. Which was a pity as, musically, *Libertad* was much more of an instant hit than its sometimes murky predecessor. As soon as the pumping riff to 'Let It Roll' came tumbling out of the speakers like a machine gun spraying bullets, it became clear that all those months on the road had helped rub off the rough edges, helping the bloody stumps left peeking out of their fancy new clothes heal into a brand new multi-limbed creature no longer reliant on their mangled former musical bodies to make sense. It's the same story with tracks like 'She's Mine' and 'Get Out the Door': top-drawer, shades-on rock delivered with such private-plane panache the album goes straight to the mainline.

The only perplexing moment was the inclusion of a cover of the 1974 ELO hit 'Can't Get It Out of My Head'. The original was a classic orchestral pop moment. This sounded like unnecessary filler. Conspiracy theorists had a field day, however, pointing out that while none of Velvet Revolver's principal members had ever professed a liking for ELO, they had famously always been one of Axl Rose's favourites. The album's coup-de-grâce came in the final track, 'Gravedancer', a toxic ballad built around a sinuous Slash guitar figure in the 'Fall to Pieces' mould, Weiland once again apparently speaking to himself as he stares in the mirror: *'Every time it goes down / Every time she comes down / Every time we fall down / She dances all over me . . .'*

Libertad was also pervaded by a strong sense of the dominant artist on each track: 'For a Brother' (Weiland's ode to his brother) and the audaciously infectious 'Mary, Mary' (the name of the singer's ex-wife), while tracks like 'Let It Roll' and 'Spay' tapped into the serpentine pulse of *Use Your Illusion*-era Guns N' Roses. Reception was again mixed, with *Rolling Stone*'s David Fricke hailing *Libertad* as boasting 'plenty of thrill in the fuzz-lined hard-rubber bends of Slash's guitar breaks and the way bassist Duff McKagan keeps time, like a cop swinging a billy club. There is honest depth here too.' *Entertainment Weekly* gave the album an A–, calling the album 'so chock-full of the tight'n'crunchy pedigreed hard rock that's in short supply these days, it feels both comfortingly familiar and vaguely exotic . . . Our advice? Stop pining for a new Guns N' Roses release, break out your air guitars, and bask in the glory of *Libertad*.' The *New York Times* offered a more critical assessment, stating, '*Libertad* sounds old, heavy, wrapped in a tough skin. At the same time, by virtue of sheer out-dated flamboyance, it seems almost wilfully naive.' Time has revealed the truth to be somewhere in between. Aided by O'Brien's talents and vision, *Libertad* felt sonically much more cohesive than *Contraband*, with considerably greater depth and scale. Lyrically, *Libertad* revealed Weiland to be at the very top of his game, summoning a confessional intimacy that at times felt disconnected from the chugging riffs and sleaze-rock posturing. Ironically, while some dogged on *Contraband* for suffering a lack of connection between singer and material, that criticism rang true on *Libertad*, with Weiland's clean, velvety croon often at odds with the jagged thrust of Slash and Kushner's dual-fretted onslaught. Fair or not, had another band released *Libertad* in 2007, they would have been hailed as the new standard-bearers of classic rock. Measured against the impossibly high commercial watermark set by its predecessor, though, and overshadowed by the towering legacies of Velvet Revolver's feeder bands, it never stood a chance.

They filmed videos for 'She Builds Quick Machines' and later 'The Last Fight' and headed out on tour in September 2007 with Alice in Chains opening for them. 'This has been one of the best tours I've ever been involved in,' Slash said at the time. 'It's cool because this band is really good friends with the Alice in Chains guys. We're from similar backgrounds, a similar period. We've all been through a lot, and it's all been really cool.' However, the guitarist would later reveal that the weather in the Velvet Revolver camp wasn't quite so sunny, confessing that he felt like the band were losing their connection with Scott, whom he described as appearing 'out to lunch'. Certainly the shadows now appeared to be swallowing them. Although they had planned to tour Japan and Australia for a second time and added shows in Nagoya, Osaka, Yokohama, Tokyo, Brisbane, Sydney, Melbourne and Adelaide, the Japanese dates were cancelled when the band's request for visas was refused.

Internally relations between Weiland, Slash and Duff were now in tatters. In January 2008 they kicked off the Rock' N' Roll As It Should Be tour, cutting the campaign short after just ten dates so Scott could check into another detox and rehab. They first cancelled their 7 February show in San Diego, then released a statement that read: 'Velvet Revolver regret to announce they're unable to perform their five upcoming concert dates in Australia that were scheduled for February 15–20. The cancellation of these shows will allow lead singer Scott Weiland to continue treatment at a rehab facility, which he voluntarily entered after the band's February 6 performance in Los Angeles. Velvet Revolver deeply apologize to their fans in Australia and thank them for sticking by the group when various members have relapsed during the last year and a half.'

According to Slash, the Australian cancellations were the last straw, so that even before leaving for their final tour in the UK, they had agreed to fire their singer, stating, 'When [Scott] came back [from the January tour], he was supposed to go to rehab, so we postponed our Australian tour but he didn't really go to rehab. That was the final blow. We had a lot of commitments, like the tour in the UK, which we didn't want to go back on, so we wanted to finish those before telling him.' As if the situation could bear any additional complexity, the Stone Temple Pilots announced that they were reuniting with Weiland for a 65-date North American tour, beginning in May with Ohio's Rock on the Range festival. Apparently unfazed, Slash announced that the band would return to the studio at the completion of the STP tour to begin work on Velvet Revolver's next record. But few inside the VR camp actually believed that. Or that, if there were to be another album, Weiland would be on it.

Velvet Revolver's disastrous final tour took place in Europe, beginning in March. With the smiling subterfuge of a mafia hit, unbeknownst to Weiland, the band embarked on the campaign having already decided to fire the singer when the tour concluded, though the singer soon sussed the plans because of how they all now treated him. 'We basically didn't speak a word [to Scott] that whole time,' said Slash. 'We gave him the cold shoulder in the UK like nobody's business. There were a couple of arguments around the stage, but, other than that, nobody spoke to him. I imagine he was quite uncomfortable. No wonder he didn't have a good time. Then he told everyone in Glasgow that the whole band was over. We were like, "Oh well, I guess we've got a surprise coming for you, Scott." For the most part, I don't really remember seeing much of him. We flew to Dubai together . . . Well, I think I remember him being on the plane, anyway. We sort of got used to him not being around. He's never really been part of the mechanics of the group, he's always been separate and doing his own little thing.'

On 20 March, at a sold-out show at Glasgow's SECC, Weiland announced from the stage that the audience were seeing something special – 'the last tour by Velvet Revolver'. Weiland had only articulated what everyone had been thinking for months, and with that simple statement the singer brought to a close the most commercially successful and transfixing supergroup of the 'oos. In the wake of the show, a vitriolic war of words raged, beginning with a statement from Matt Sorum the morning after the Glasgow show: 'So last night was interesting. Had a little band turmoil on stage, as you probably all could tell. Being in a band is a lot like being in a relationship. Sometimes you just don't get along. I guess there has been more turmoil lately, with the cancellations and all. It has been frustrating, I am not going to lie. My career and life in rock'n'roll has come with its ups and downs. Unfortunately, some people in this business don't realise how great of a life they have. Touring the world, meeting great people and fans all over the world. And just playing music for a living. I feel truly blessed. But sometimes the road can be draining for some. Being away from home and family does grind on you sometimes, with all the travelling and different beds. Personally, I love this shit and sometimes can't believe I am so lucky to still be doing what I do for a living. Everybody could see who was unhappy last night, but all I can say is let's keep the rock alive, people! In this life, you just pick up and keep moving. And don't ever let anybody stand in your way.'

Weiland wasn't going to let him get away with that, responding swiftly: 'Well, first of all, the state of my family affairs is really none of his business, since he is too immature to have a real relationship, let alone children. So don't attempt to stand in a man's shoes when you haven't walked his path. Secondly, "keeping rock'n'roll alive"? I've made many attempts to remain cordial with the members of VR, but mainly, the likes of you. Funny though – this is your first band, as opposed to being a hired gun. I've been making records (now on my ninth), which have sold over 35 million copies worldwide and have maintained a level of professionalism regardless of how many drugs I've ingested into my system. I have only cancelled one tour during the entire course of my 16-year run and that was the "make-up" Australia tour. Now, shall I open that can of worms, Matthew? Release the Kraken? Serve . . . Volley! You cancelled the Aussie tour in the fall because you went to rehab, but I won't say why . . . As for our fans – I will sweat, bruise, and bleed for you. And will continue to do so until the end of this tour. However, you deserve to hear Velvet Revolver playing . . . not certain individuals singing along to get a muddied-up sound. God forbid – could one imagine if I grabbed a guitar and started soloing along with Slash? That would never happen because I know my place. It's a shame . . . we were a gang. But ego and jealousy can get the better of anyone. I wish the best and plan to annihilate the stage in the last few shows.' Then the coup de grâce: 'On a separate note, we did an STP photo shoot before this tour and it was fun, inspiring and it gave me that thrill – that feeling that got my rocks off from the get-go.'

On 1 April 2008, the band made it official, announcing that Velvet Revolver had parted ways with Scott Weiland. According to a press release from Slash, 'This band is all about its fans and its music and Scott Weiland isn't 100% committed to either. Among other things, his increasingly erratic onstage behaviour and personal problems have forced us to move on.' Though both Slash and Duff would insist that Velvet Revolver would find another singer and carry on, four years would pass before the band would play another gig, and then only as a one-off, as a kind of belated farewell.

Unsurprisingly, Weiland's response the next day was both swift and withering. 'I find it humorous that the so-called four "founding members" of Velvet Revolver would decide to move on without me after I had already claimed the group dead in the water on 20 March in Glasgow.' Referring to his reunion with STP, the singer said, 'I choose to look forward to the future and performing with a group of friends I have known my entire life. This also speaks to my commitment to the fans who I feel would much rather watch a group of musicians who enjoy being together as opposed to a handful of discontents who at one time used to call themselves a gang.' Unable to resist a parting shot, he concluded with a snarky valedictory call to his former bandmates, saying, 'Good hunting, lads, I think Sebastian Bach would be a fantastic choice.'

They would audition a fresh raft of singers, including Slipknot's Corey Taylor, who seemed enthusiastic about a role in the band, although Slash felt that stylistically the pairing lacked the vibe he sought, saying, 'Corey came in, just like a lot of other guys came in. Of course, Corey's Corey, and he's probably one of the best guys out there. I love Corey. I just thought it was a different style than what Velvet Revolver was trying to capture. But, still, the songs are cool. But if we were gonna do anything with that, they would have to be rerecorded and . . . Cos, I mean, it was very raw and very, sort of, "making it up on the spot" kind of deal. And so we'd have to revisit everything and then we'd put it together, I think. But that's not really a plan. I'm just saying if it was . . . I don't wanna get any ideas in anybody's head. That would be the only way that it could be released, [and] I'm not saying that it's going to.'

As the next few years rolled by, Slash would embark on a solo career, bringing in Alter Bridge's Myles Kennedy as frontman. Duff toured again with Loaded and Dave Kushner and Matt Sorum engaged in various side projects. By any reasonable estimation, Velvet Revolver appeared to be on ice – permanently. That is, until the band announced that they would be reforming for a special one-off appearance in January 2012. The singer? Scott Weiland. '"Love You Madly:" A Concert for John O'Brien' took place at West Hollywood's House of Blues, boasting an eclectic roster that included Maroon 5, Tom Morello, Stephen Stills, Sheryl Crow and Fishbone. While Maroon 5 were the only performers currently charting (their Mutt Lange-produced *Hands All Over* album had just spawned a huge international hit with 'Moves Like Jagger'), it was clear that the evening belonged to Velvet Revolver. The group had announced that they would perform three songs and, beyond that, no one was prepared to predict their future. The mere sight of Velvet Revolver walking onto the stage, though, detonated a rousing hail of applause as the band took their positions, with Weiland bouncing at centre stage, cigarette and bullhorn in one hand, microphone in the other. Duff fired off the intro to 'Sucker Train Blues' and, just like that, four years disappeared. Weiland, looking like a young Howard Hughes with his retro leather jacket and slicked-back hair, gyrated and spun as Slash prowled the side of the stage, stepping forth to issue blistering leads before retreating into the corners during the verses. Each time the spotlight hit him, the audience roared with approval.

The rejuvenated band followed with 'She Builds Quick Machines' and 'Slither', which showcased a roof-destroying solo from Slash that suggested he was in the best form of his life. Whatever water might have passed under the bridge was not apparent. In fact, the band could have been in the middle of the *Libertad* tour, so polished was their execution. Though three songs were promised, the band could not resist a fourth, closing the evening with Pink Floyd's 'Wish You Were Here'. Afterwards it was hoped this had been a curtain-raising event in lieu of a full VR reunion. But it was not to be. Slash would go back to his progressively successful solo career, Duff would record with Loaded and later form Walking Papers, Dave found a lucrative second life writing and scoring television soundtracks, co-writing the theme song for the mega-popular biker drama *Sons of Anarchy*. Matt would bounce around a number of side projects and Scott Weiland would eventually split from Stone Temple Pilots again in 2011, attempting to reignite his flagging solo career. He was found dead on his tour bus on 3 December 2015, the victim of an accidental drug overdose.

Before he died, I had one last phone conversation with Scott Weiland. As usual he was a hard man to pin down. I'd been trying to speak to him for weeks, but each night as it got to the time when I was supposed to call, one of his 'people' would call and give me the same old excuses I'd got when I first met him nearly 20 years before. He was unwell. He was unexpectedly called away. He just wasn't answering the phone. Finally, I gave up. Told them not to bother him any more. And then he rang me.

He sounded sad on the phone, but then he always sounded at something of a loss whenever I had spoken to him. Not at all like the way he came across in his angry press statements, when he'd be flogging at Slash and Duff and even Axl. It was the first time we'd spoken since he'd published his autobiography, *Not Dead & Not for Sale* – a chillingly frank self-portrait in which he talked for the first time about being raped as a 12-year-old – and where he claimed Velvet Revolver 'came out of necessity, not artistic purpose'. He had also recently designed his own 'English Laundry' clothing range and completed a set of paintings which he planned to exhibit. But I didn't really want to talk about that. I wanted to know what he meant by the 'came out of necessity' remark about VR?

'Well, I think we did a really good job of it,' he said wistfully. 'It was a great band to see live and I think we made two exciting albums.'

So . . . no hard feelings? I mean, were they the kind of people he would invite to dinner?

'Oh, yeah,' he said. 'We patched things up and we get along. I see them every now and again, we text each other. And, you know, I mean, you can never say never. But, you know, it's like, uh, um, who knows, maybe we'll do some shows sometime . . .'

The conversation drifted. I found myself asking him what, when he looked back, was he most proud of? I was thinking in terms of his career. He was thinking of something else.

'I am definitely most proud of my children,' he said with a whisper. 'They are what keep me up when I feel low, seeing the light in their eyes and that kind of unconditional love is even more important than my music, they keep me going definitely.'

Was there such a thing as a 'secret to success', I wondered?

'I don't believe so. People often think that it's luck, because there are so many talented people who don't ever get to have success or even a record deal. But I have this mantra that is: you really create your own luck. But it's part of serendipity too. If you work hard, you have talent and you put yourself in situations enough of the right times, you'll meet people along the way that eventually notice you . . . Serendipity, timing, God and hard work, they all sort of have to merge together – having a vision of where you want to be and what it's gonna take to get there.'

God? Did he accept there was a higher power?

'Oh, yeah, I believe in God, definitely. When I was a kid I went to church every Sunday. My brothers and I would be watching cartoons and my dad would be, "All right, Mark, Scott, Michael, get dressed." I'd be like, argh! [But] I look back on it fondly and when I go to church, I don't go regularly, but it brings like a sense of [getting] back in touch with what you believe in. I was very lucky with the church that I went to, a Catholic church, it was very sort of progressive and wasn't all that dogma-based. And my mother and father also were brought up with believing in God and Jesus. But that's a personal thing [not] something you try to push on others, that spiritual connection that you have.'

How did you look back on grunge?

'That was a magical time for music and art and social change. It was a different climate and there really hasn't been such a massive movement in rock'n'roll since – though [STP] never really considered ourselves a grunge band. But it was a real time of enlightenment and a lot of hope.'

It was getting late. We'd run out of things to talk about. And there would always be a next time. Lastly then, I asked him, out of the blue, what he would like written on his tombstone? Here lies Scott Weiland . . .

'. . . he loved his family. He loved his children. He loved his friends. And never ceased to pick himself up off the ground.'

We left it like that.

16

BLAME IT ON THE FALUN GONG

Having informed his label, Interscope, at the start of 2003 that there were only some 'last-minute' tweaks, to do with his vocals, Axl confidently predicted that *Chinese Democracy* would be ready for release later that year. By August, however, Axl had abandoned the studio and become a virtual recluse again behind the gated walls of his Malibu mansion. At which point, in a desperate attempt to claw back some of the millions they had thrown at an album that after nearly ten years in the making was still not finished, Interscope announced the forthcoming release of a *Greatest Hits* collection. Axl, understandably, was outraged. Didn't they get it? Why didn't anybody ever see what he saw, that he had spent years rebuilding a new Guns N' Roses? That the last thing his fans needed was a sharp reminder of why the old Guns N' Roses had been so damn great.

Merck Mercuriadis of Sanctuary, now Axl's de facto manager, called in some favours and persuaded Interscope to hold back on the hits album in return for a cast-iron guarantee that *Chinese Democracy* would be ready to go in time for the big Christmas market. When that didn't happen, the label pressed the button on *Greatest Hits*. The resulting 14-track CD was released in March and went on to sell more than 13 million copies worldwide, making it the band's biggest hit since the double *Use Your Illusion* sets 13 years before. None of which appeared to pacify Axl. But by now the label had had enough. In a letter dated 2 February 2004, Axl was informed that, 'having exceeded all budgeted and approved recording costs by millions of dollars', it was now 'Mr Rose's obligation to fund and complete the album', and no longer the record company's.

It meant that, just as *Greatest Hits* was riding at Number 1 in the UK and Number 3 in the US, work on *Chinese Democracy* was closed down and the band's gear packed away. A planned appearance – scheduled for May – at the fourth Rock in Rio festival, relocated this time to the Portuguese city of Lisbon, was also cancelled: according to the official press release, because Buckethead had left the band. There was a further release headed: 'A Message from W. Axl Rose', as follows: 'The band has been put in an untenable position by guitarist Buckethead and his untimely departure. During his tenure with the band Buckethead has been inconsistent and erratic in both his behaviour and commitment – despite being under contract – creating uncertainty and confusion and making it virtually impossible to move forward with recording, rehearsals and live plans with confidence.' Erratic behaviour? Uncertainty and confusion? Surely these had been hallmarks for Guns N' Roses decades before Buckethead was signed on? Axl's press release went on: 'There is not a member of this camp that is not hurt, upset and ultimately disappointed by this event. Regardless of anyone's opinions of me and what I may or may not deserve, clearly the fans, individuals in this band, management, crew and our support group do not deserve this type of treatment. On behalf of Guns N' Roses and myself, I apologise to the fans who planned to see us at Rock in Rio.' Then one last dig at Buckethead: 'It appears his plans were to secure a recording contract, quit GN'R and use his involvement in the upcoming Guns release to immediately promote his individual efforts.' However, there was a light at the end of the tunnel: 'This unfortunate set of circumstances may have given us the opportunity to take our recording that one extra step further. Regardless we hope to announce a release date within the next few months. Sincerely, W. Axl Rose.'

Was anybody keeping up with this stuff? Of more interest to the press in Europe and America was the lawsuit against Axl that followed just a few weeks later, which Slash and Duff filed at the LA Superior Court. Claiming they had been deprived of at least a million dollars after Axl had unilaterally, and without telling them, turned down lucrative offers from the makers of movies such as *We Were Soldiers*, *Death to Smoochy*, *Old School* and *Just Married*, and, potentially most lucrative of all, had refused offers from producers of the 2001 blockbuster *Black Hawk Down*, to let them use 'Welcome to the Jungle' on the soundtrack. Axl denied the charges and lawyers for both sides rubbed their hands in glee.

When, in July, VH1 broadcast the latest episode in their popular *Behind the Music* series, this time on the story of Guns N' Roses, Axl again refused to take part, leaving the juice to Slash and Steven, even Gilby and Matt. There was only one mention of Axl's new Guns N' Roses right at the end of the programme, when it explained that that their first album together, *Chinese Democracy*, would be released in November. Even Axl must have had a laugh about that.

Indeed, no more was heard until over a year later when Axl, accompanied by his still faithful bodyguard, Earl, stood at the gates of his mansion and told a bunch of fans that *Chinese Democracy* would finally be released just a few months later, at the start of 2006. Not only that, but a track from it would be featured on the soundtrack of the forthcoming movie version of the best-selling book *The Da Vinci Code*. Although the rumour was never verified, Merck Mercuriadis declined to comment either way. In the event, neither of these two things occurred. But rumours persisted throughout 2006 that the album was now imminent. Certainly, Axl was back in the spotlight again. Attending the launch party in January for the American band Korn's latest tour, he told a writer from *Rolling Stone*, 'We're working on thirty-two songs, and twenty-six are nearly done.' Of the completed tracks, he added, 13 would be included on *Chinese Democracy*, and the rest on two subsequent 'sequels'. His favourite tracks, he said, were 'Better', 'There was a Time' and 'The Blues'. Dressed in a Toronto Maple Leafs jersey, a large ornate cross hanging from his neck, he puffed on a cigar and declared, 'People will hear music this year. It's a very complex record. I'm trying to do something different. Some of the arrangements are kind of like Queen. Some people are going to say, "It doesn't sound like Axl Rose, it doesn't sound like Guns N' Roses." But you'll like at least a few songs on there.'

Taking over an entire floor of the mega-expensive Trump Tower hotel, in New York, Axl could now been seen hanging out at 'late-late' clubs like Stereo, in the Chelsea district, which didn't get going until 4 a.m. When, a few days before his forty-fourth birthday, he showed up with his entourage at around 5.30 a.m., he blew everyone away by allowing the club DJ to play tracks from two ten-track CD copies of *Chinese Democracy*. 'He was talking with everybody freely about how he's been off for ten years, and how even though Slash and the rest of the guys [had started] Velvet Revolver, he's been holding back,' described the club's owner, Barry Mullineaux. 'He was freely answering questions about his work, the band, what happened with the split [with the original line-up], the direction he's headed in – and the music sounded great.'

When, in May, it was announced that Guns N' Roses would play four 'warm-up' shows at the 2000-capacity Hammerstein Ballroom on West 34th Street, everyone was convinced the album was definitely on the way. When this was followed by confirmation of a European tour in the summer, including a headline appearance in Britain at the annual Download festival in June, fans really did begin to believe again. So did the band and management. Even the record company began making nice again. The icing on the cake was Axl turning up unannounced on Eddie Trunk's syndicated Saturday night radio show to publicise the gigs – along with a promise that *Chinese Democracy* would be released 'sometime this fall or late fall. It will be out this year.'

As one record company exec put it to me at the time, 'If you say something enough times it's got to be real, right?' But trouble was brewing again before the band had even arrived for the sound check at the Hammerstein. Axl had a meltdown when both his band and management tried to talk him out of adding a third guitarist to the line-up. With Buckethead having flown the coop, so to speak, and having resisted all attempts to lure him back, Axl had been happy to go with just Robin Fink and Richard Fortus, but the closer they came to the opening night of the Hammerstein shows, the more convinced he became that he simply had to get another guitarist in. Tommy Stinson and Brain the drummer are said to have threatened to quit. To which Axl allegedly replied, 'Who cares? We'll just get Duff and Matt.' With Izzy now also secretly rehearsing a few numbers with the band, someone else half jokingly suggested Axl get Slash in the line-up too. Then immediately regretted it when they saw the thunder on Axl's face. In the end, Axl got his way, and halfway through the first Hammerstein show on 12 May he introduced the fans to Ron 'Bumblefoot' Thal – a New Yorker and a technically gifted shredder once described as a heavy metal Frank Zappa.

With the exception of Bumblefoot, the band was identical to the line-up which had ground to a gear-wrenching halt three and a half years before: Axl on vocals and occasional keyboards; guitarists Finck, Bumblefoot and Fortus; bassist Tommy Stinson; keyboardists Dizzy Reed and Chris Pittman; and drummer Brain Mantia. With Sebastian Bach, Limp Bizkit's frontman, Fred Durst, Lenny Kravitz and the actor Ethan Hawke watching from the roped-off VIP area, naturally, they were an hour and a half late onstage, and it was long past midnight by the time Axl seated himself at the piano for 'November Rain'.

Most of the set, as before, was classic-era GN'R fare, with Sebastian Bach joining them onstage for 'My Michelle'. The most precious moment, though, was when Axl stopped to address the baying crowd between the new numbers 'Chinese Democracy' and 'There was a Time' and quipped, 'I see you people singing the new songs. You downloaded them, fuckers!' Pause for comic timing. Then: 'You can hold your breath a lot longer than David Blaine. I want to thank you for that . . .'

The most attention-grabbing moment of the four-night stint occurred at the last gig, when Izzy Stradlin strolled onstage. He and Axl stood and embraced, before the band ripped into 'Think About You'. Axl had tried to say something to announce his old school pal's arrival but he was drowned out by screams the minute the crowd caught sight of Izzy shuffling around in the shadows. During a wonderfully heartfelt performance of 'Patience', Izzy could be seen wiping tears from his eyes. It seemed that both Axl and Izzy had come full circle since the last time I'd spoken to the guitarist. 'Well, it's obviously *not* Guns N' Roses,' he'd said of Axl's new band. 'I think all the fans [know that]. It's not even right that he uses the name, because he's the only guy [left]. I think ultimately it's gonna work against him, because people are gonna say fuck you – that's not Guns N' Roses!' Izzy was paid $25,000 a show for just showing up, plus all his hotel and travel expenses. Making him the best-paid player on the stage – after Axl, of course.

Three weeks later they opened the European leg of the tour with a show at London's Hammersmith Apollo. Late again, not coming onstage this time until nearly 11 p.m. – 'We know he's in the building,' said a venue security guy. 'He's just insisting he needs two masseuses for a "Deep Heat massage" before he goes on stage. He fired both his personal masseuses this morning. He's also complaining because his personal hairdresser [from Africa] couldn't enter the country because of visa issues. But there's not much we can do about that.' The review of the show that followed the next day in *The Times* was not good. 'Rose appears very much at home as the grand rock showman,' it began, 'The 44-year-old's reputed face-lifts are indicated, too, by his pinched features and unblinking eyes, and he's sweating profusely as early as the second song as he pirouettes and canters restlessly around the tiered stage . . .'

None of which augured well for their headline show at the Download festival, on 11 June. When sections of the 59,000-strong crowd grew restless with the performance they began hurling plastic bottles of urine at the stage. Axl seemed unexpectedly unnerved. Mumbling about 'technical difficulties', he left the stage twice – the second time after slipping over on a pool of piss during 'Sweet Child o' Mine'. Tommy Stinson tried to put himself in the way of the abuse, threatening to take the whole band off if the crowd didn't stop throwing bottles. To which some shouted, 'Fuck off then!' And 'Pussy!' When Axl, too, told them he would walk off after 'Better' had been spoiled by more bottle throwing, it merely prompted more booing and jeering. Even the arrival of Izzy – for 'Patience', 'Nightrain' and 'Used to Love Her' – and Sebastian Bach once again for 'My Michelle' couldn't save the day.

Backstage after the show, Axl went ballistic at Merck Mercuriadis – who bravely offered to resign. Axl stormed off to his limo, which carried him at speed to the private plane that was waiting to fly him back to London. Returning to his Knightsbridge hotel, the Mandarin Oriental, he went straight to the bar, where he met Lars Ulrich, whose band, Metallica, had headlined Download the previous night, though to a spectacularly different crowd.

The summer 2006 tour never recovered. At the Paris show on 20 June they came on almost two and a half hours late. Seven days later Axl was arrested in Stockholm after an early-morning fracas at the band's hotel, during which he fought with a security guard, biting his leg like a rabid dog, before the police arrived and arrested him. Charged with damaging property, assaulting a security guard and threatening police in the squad car on the way to the station, as one of the arresting officers, Fredrik Nylén, told local journalists, 'He was aggressive and acting out', adding pointedly that in Sweden 'threatening a police officer is punishable by jail time'. After admitting the charges, Axl was fined 40,000 kronor (approximately £3000) and released 12 hours later. He was also ordered to pay 10,000 kronor (approximately £750) in damages to the security guard, who had been taken to hospital with his injuries. Issuing a press statement, Axl said, 'We had a great gig in Stockholm and I am not going to let this incident spoil that. My assistant Beta and I were talking in the lobby of the hotel when the security started to give us a hard time. My only concern was to make sure she was okay.'

The final show of the tour, the second of two at London's Wembley Arena, at the end of July, ended early after Axl collapsed at the side of the stage before the encores. Sebastian Bach stepped in for him. According to the official press release, Axl had become 'ill after performing two concerts' the night before: the first at Wembley and the second an unannounced semi-acoustic at London's Cuckoo Club, which had begun at 4 a.m. The fact that Axl had been 'partying' with Lars Ulrich for several hours after the Cuckoo Club probably hadn't helped either.

From there the tour continued on to America, where it took an even steeper nosedive. Still coming on way behind schedule, Axl came up with a new saying: 'This isn't McDonald's or Burger King. It isn't "Have it your way."' Sebastian Bach was still putting in his nightly appearances on 'My Michelle' and Izzy was said to be lined up for a handful of dates, too, but Guns N' Roses were now viewed as more of a freak show than one of the last giants of rock. Internet speculation amongst even diehard fans was now centred on bets about what time they would, or wouldn't, arrive on stage; how many numbers they would get to play before Axl stormed off; when the tour would eventually be cancelled.

Looking for someone to blame for this latest embarrassment, Axl fired Merck Mercuriadis, a few weeks before Christmas, releasing a statement via the internet. Under the heading, 'An open letter to our fans from Axl', dated Thursday, 14 December, 2006, he began by announcing the cancellation of the band's January 2007 touring schedule, to save 'valuable time needed by the band and record company for the proper setup and release of . . . *Chinese Democracy*'. Uh huh. He went on: 'To say the making of this album has been an unbearably long and incomprehensible journey would be an understatement. Overcoming the endless and seemingly insane amount of obstacles faced by all involved, notwithstanding the emotional challenges endured by everyone – the fans, the band, our road crew and business team – has at many times seemed like a bad dream in which one wakes up only to find that they are still in the nightmare. Unfortunately, this time it has been played out for over a decade in real life.' Pinpointing 'on-going, behind-the-scenes triumphs and casualties' and 'various legal issues', Axl said it was 'easy for people to point out how others [would] have handled similar situations' but that 'without full knowledge of the various dynamics and circumstances involved, these types of comments or commentary are just uninformed, disassociated, generally useless – and often hindering – speculation'. Problems that had been 'compounded by an overall sense of a lack of respect by management' had also now resulted 'in the end of both Guns' and my managerial involvement with Merck Mercuriadis'.

At which point he actually gave a release date for the album: 6 March 2007. Pending 'certain minor – and I do mean minor – additions, as well as contract negotiations'. He concluded: 'We thank you for your patience . . . We do hope you can hold on just a bit longer, and if not, please take a break and we'll be more than glad – if you so choose – to see you again later. All the best to each and every one of you over this holiday season, thank you and God bless. Sincerely, Axl Rose.'

Watching all this from afar was Doug Goldstein, now on the outs but still to his mind a concerned party. 'Everybody thinks Axl's this big, bad guy, who doesn't care about his fans,' he says now. 'I couldn't disagree more strongly. I believe, after my experiences of travelling with multitudes of bands, he has the most heightened fear of failure of anybody I've ever met in my life. He would much rather just cancel a show than give a mediocre performance. He cares so much about putting on the best show that his pre-show routine is about four hours. It's the masseuse on the road, and the chiropractor-slash-acupuncturist, it's the vocal warm-ups, it's the vocal warm-downs. You know, he has to have a steak. I mean, all of these things that the little guy Hans von Leden taught him, to be the best possible singer out there, he goes through all of those kind of pre-conditioned exercises to get him in the best possible shape. But during that process if he doesn't hit the mark, as far as he's concerned, he starts it again.'

There followed an extended period when various big-name managers were sounded out for the job. Initially, the post was given to Doc McGhee, famously the manager who had steered both Mötley Crüe and Bon Jovi to success in the Eighties, and now managed Kiss, Hootie & The Blowfish and several others. Few inside the biz doubted that Doc was merely positioning himself for the inevitable reunion that would finally come, if not now then someday – for sure. When Axl began to get the same feeling, on a flight to Japan, where Doc attempted to question him at length about what his problems with Slash and the guys might be exactly, suddenly he was looking for a new manager again. Years later, Doc would look back and laughingly tell friends how he 'got sick and tired of the fact I could only speak to Beta. That whenever a meeting was taking place she was always there. That whenever I had managed to get Axl's direct phone number she had changed it.'

Next came Irving Azoff, one of the most powerful men in the music business. Irving had managed The Eagles, been the chairman of MCA Records and then started his own label, Giant, under the aegis of Warner Bros. Now he was back in management, overseeing the careers of Christine Aguilera, Maroon 5, Jon Bon Jovi and several others. After The Eagles had been apart for nearly 15 years, famously telling the press that hell would freeze over before they reformed, it was wily, brilliant Irving Azoff who talked them into doing just that in 1994 with the squillion-dollar *Hell Freezes Over* tour and accompanying live double album. Irving was rock biz royalty. If anybody could handle Axl Rose, get him to do the right thing, it was Irving Azoff, surely?

And yet, to no one's great surprise, except perhaps Irving's, *Chinese Democracy* wasn't released on 6 March 2007, nor on any other date that year. This time, however, there were no 'open letters' explaining why. Apparently, even Axl Rose had finally run out of excuses. A tour of Japan, scheduled for April, was 'postponed' two weeks before it was due to start after Tommy Stinson reportedly fell down a flight of stairs. In the official press release, Stinson was quoted as saying, 'I feel so bad right now. I accidentally fell down a flight of stairs. I put my hand down to break my fall and heard a loud pop. The next morning my hand looked like a balloon. I went to see my doctor and while the good news is that it's not broken, the bad news is it's severely sprained and I may have done some ligament damage.' He added, with feeling, 'We had our last rehearsal a few days ago and shipped the gear to Japan and then this happened. I feel horrible. We'd like to sincerely thank our fans worldwide for their patience and support.'

A month later a tour to South Africa was cancelled for the same reason. The tours of Australia and New Zealand that had been scheduled were also then cancelled. Some sprain. Next came talk of Velvet Revolver and the 'new' Guns N' Roses actually doing a co-headline tour, with a temporarily reformed Stone Temple Pilots opening the show. Weiland would perform a brief set with the Pilots each night, before resuming with Velvet Revolver. A neat idea that also left the door open for a short set in which Slash, Duff and Matt hooked up with Axl and the guitarists and keyboardists from his band. Slash was even quoted on MTV in Brazil as saying, 'It would be a good idea to get, just for a couple of shows, the original STP and the original Guns N' Roses just for the fun of it.' Still, insiders said it was never gonna happen. But then, when Slash said Velvet Revolver had recently agreed not to perform any GN'R songs in their set, even the most hardened cynics began to take the idea seriously. The fact that both bands had new albums ready to pop later that year – *Libertad* and *Chinese Democracy* – had promoters wading in with sky-high offers for such a tour. It would be like the GN'R–Metallica mega-tour of the early Nineties, only even more profitable.

Word round the campfire was that Axl was on the point of agreeing. Then he pulled back and did a 180-degree turn at the last minute. Shrewdly, Axl had foreseen the outcome of such a high-profile pairing – and that Slash and the other guys would most likely be the ones who came out on top in the comparison stakes. And, worse, how the clamour for the original line-up to get back together permanently would be hugely enhanced. Axl was damned if he was about to throw away a decade's worth of work on *Chinese Democracy*, or the ultimate control he now had over Guns N' Roses, just to make Slash and Duff happy. Instead, by the time *Libertad* was released in July, Guns N' Roses had already taken off for shows in Mexico, followed by the rescheduled tours of Australia and the Far East.

*

One show Axl Rose had pointedly declined to put it an appearance at was the one Steven Adler had decided to stage at Hollywood's Key Club on 28 July, to mark the twentieth anniversary of the release of *Appetite for Destruction*. But then Steven had already announced that he expected both Slash and Duff and Izzy to make an appearance, and again Axl wasn't going to be ambushed into getting up on a stage with them. Tracii Guns, though not actually having been part of the *Appetite* album, was also scheduled to appear, and Steven boasted on the Key Club's website: 'I'll be down there with my band and Slash, Izzy and Duff will be there too. It's gonna be great.' Although he knew there was almost no chance of Axl being there, he cheerfully added that he had recently been discussing a reunion with the singer: 'Axl and I spoke to each other in Las Vegas recently, and I know there's a chance. It's just too big. Whatever the Stones make when they play, we'd triple it. It'd be ridiculous not to do it. He can't be that goofy.'

Come the big night, Izzy and Duff were there as promised to join Steven on stage for a blast through a few numbers. Slash was there, too, but not to play. He just wanted to watch, he said. 'I believe I made it this far for some reason,' Steven declared triumphantly after the show. 'I want to finish what we started, and with the love and support I got from those guys, I think we can [reunite]. I'm gonna leave it up to Axl. That's gonna be Axl's call, and I love Axl and I know he'll make the right call.' Slash, though, had a more pragmatic take on the situation. 'I went down there for a minute to say hi to Steven. What happened was Steven has finally come out of that sort of haze that he's been in for the last seventeen years. I was sort of instrumental in getting him out of the place he was in, into a little bit more sober kind of environment. So I've been hanging out with him and supporting him and stuff. He had that gig that was about to happen, and I'm really jazzed that he's gotten back on the drums and he's gotten ambitious again and he's gonna go out and play.' But that didn't mean the old gang was about to burst back in town, though. 'Steven's just an excitable guy and he meant well when he said it. But he said that there was gonna be this reunion, that I was gonna be there and Duff and Izzy and Axl possibly, and that just fuelled that already rapid-fire kind of Guns N' Roses rumours that go on. Once I started getting phone calls and emails from all over the world about this gig, I said, "You know what? I can't support it as such cos that's not what it is." So I went down there but I didn't wanna get up and play because I didn't wanna fuel that any further . . . Duff got up and played, and Izzy got up and played, and it was what it was, but I don't see any reunion happening for real.'

With a release date for *Chinese Democracy* now no longer even being speculated on, by the start of 2008 most serious people had stopped even asking about it, demoting it to the same category in their minds as those other great 'lost' albums in the past, like The Who's *Lifehouse*, or *Smile* by The Beach Boys. But not even those had inspired more bare-knuckled hammering. The album's incessant delays, middling dramatic sub-plots and bloated, eight-figure budget had reduced the project to an industry punchline.

And then, on 23 November that year – miracle of miracles, and to almost no fanfare whatsoever, not even a video or a tour – *Chinese Democracy* was finally released. Distributed exclusively through the US electronics retail giant Best Buy – a deal struck by Irving Azoff similar to the one AC/DC struck with Wal-Mart the same year for their album *Black Ice*, and intended as a shrewd means of recouping at least some of the eye-watering $13 million that had been the estimated cost of the album. It was reported that Best Buy ordered 1.3 million copies up front in anticipation of a frenzied assault by GN'R fans.

The album debuted at Number 3 in the US and Number 2 in the UK, and made the Top 5 in eight other countries, selling over a million copies worldwide in the first week alone – impressive numbers in an era when physical CD and vinyl sales had declined drastically. Critically, opinions were generally favourable, too, with outlets like *Spin* and *Allmusic* awarding decidedly positive reviews. Few, though, were as effusive as long-time GN'R watcher David Fricke, who gushed in *Rolling Stone*, 'The first Guns N' Roses album of new, original songs since the first Bush administration is a great, audacious, unhinged and uncompromising hard rock record. In other words, it sounds a lot like the Guns N' Roses you know.' While Robert Christgau, the godfather of American music critics wrote, 'This effort isn't just pleasurable artistically. It's touching on a human level. Noble, even. I didn't think he had it in him.'

Note that 'he', as opposed to the 'they' a real band would have deserved. At the same time, the detractors were many, with the *Village Voice* calling the album 'a hilariously painstaking attempt to synthesise that lightning, a lost cause taken to delirious extremes, a fascinating catastrophe inspiring equal parts awe and pity'. Others lambasted the album for a perceived excess of pretence and absence of heart. The acclaimed American biographer Stephen Davis described *Chinese Democracy* as simply 'the worst album ever'. You had to wonder at such extreme views, though. The truth was, had Axl released *Chinese Democracy* within three or four years of the *Use Your Illusion* releases, it would have been hailed as a mature and sharply focused follow-up to the meandering over-indulgence of its evil-twin predecessors. Drawing deeply from its industrial, pop and classic rock influences and spangled with flourishes of keyboards, electronica and even flamenco, *Chinese Democracy* fitted awkwardly into the GN'R canon, no doubt, but only in that it is really an Axl Rose solo album in all but name. And, as such, was a masterwork of its type, towering over the Velvet Revolver albums, barely able to register such specs of dust as whatever Loaded or the Juju Hounds may have been up to these long gone years, it soared so much higher than they.

Thematically, Axl had tapped back into the jagged vulnerability, sneering resentment and embattled paranoia that dominated *Use Your Illusion*. Mighty salvos like 'Riad n' the Bedouins' and 'Scraped' deliberately harked back to the pugnacity and wild abandon of the band's early works, though what Axl meant exactly with lines like 'Blame it on the Falun Gong', from the aggressively romping title track, was anybody's guess. Described as 'a Chinese spiritual practice that combines meditation and qigong exercises with a moral philosophy centered on the tenets of truthfulness, compassion and forbearance', it seems an odd addition to verses otherwise powered by words like 'hate', 'iron fist', 'hell' and 'masturbation'. Perhaps Axl was merely applying a bit of yin to his yang?

It hardly mattered. Not when placed in the context of meatier fare such as 'There was a Time', with a breathtaking build-up that eclipses the song's hopelessly puerile acronym, and the poppy tunefulness of 'Catcher in the Rye' revealed a provocative cinematic vision tailor-made for the new generation of ear-bud listeners.

Nevertheless *Chinese Democracy* was confounding for those who had been chomping at the bit to pass judgement on it; for many, it became a creeper album that divulged new secrets with each progressive listen. For others it was a mystery wrapped within a mania. Compared to historically similar overworked classics it yielded no obvious hits. When, in 1976, Fleetwood Mac had entered the studio with unlimited time and money at their disposal they emerged a year later with *Rumours*, one of the best-selling records in history.

This, though, was different. Notoriously averse to speaking with the media, Axl granted an interview to Jonathan Cohen of *Billboard* magazine in February 2009 in which the singer explained the album's withering delay with a now familiar list of excuses. 'There aren't too many issues of the hundreds [we ran into] that happened as quickly as anyone would have preferred, from building my studio; finding the right players; never did find a producer; still don't have real record company involvement or support; to getting it out and mixed and mastered.'

In short, everybody's fault but Axl's. Didn't he already have the right 'players' in Slash, Duff, Izzy and Matt? But that was a stupid question. Axl also expressed satisfaction with the final product while seeming to address criticisms that perhaps the original GN'R line-up might have put the album out more quickly, by pointing out, 'It's the right record and I couldn't ask for more in that regard. Could have been a more enjoyable journey, but it's there now. The art comes first. It dictates if not the course [then] the destination artistically. For me, once the real accompanying artwork is there with a few videos and some touring, the package was achieved and delivered. And to do so at this level in terms of quality, both artistic and performance-wise, both on record and live, is something that's a miracle at minimum and something that wouldn't have happened, no matter how anyone tries to convince others, with old Guns, regardless of anyone's intentions. It was just as ugly in old Guns, regardless of our success.'

This last was undoubtedly true, in its way. It also meant that those hoping for a reunion of the original line-up would see their hopes dashed against the rocks of Axl's virulent refusal to set aside past grievances. In that same *Billboard* interview, he categorically stated that while he was open to collaborating with or touring with Izzy or Duff, he would never again make music with Slash, icily vowing, 'What's clear is that one of the two of us will die before a reunion and however sad, ugly or unfortunate anyone views it, it is how it is. Those decisions were made a long time ago and reiterated year after year by one man. There are acts that, once committed between individuals, they are what they are. To add insult to injury almost day after day, lapsing into year after year, for more than a decade, is a nightmare. Anyone putting his own personal entertainment above everything else is sickening.'

In 2009, Axl brought in Sixx:A.M.'s guitarist, DJ Ashba, for the *Chinese Democracy* World Tour – a tour that had actually begun in 2001 but that, like the album, seemed impervious to the constraints of time and space. They would play 117 shows worldwide on that leg, although stretching back to 2001 the total number of shows played was 239, with 48 cancellations from 2001 to 2007 and five cancellations between 2009 and 2011.

Business as usual then, GN'R style. But while Axl had publicly praised Azoff's handling of *Chinese Democracy*'s release and its associated deal with Best Buy, that relationship, like so many others in Axl's life, had now turned sour. In 2010, Azoff sued Axl, alleging that the singer had breached an oral agreement to pay him 15 per cent of the earnings from the tour, which Azoff estimated to be approximately $2 million. Axl swiftly countersued for $5 million, alleging that Azoff had deliberately botched the album promotion and had mishandled tour dates for the band. Axl insisted that Azoff had tried to force him 'into a position where he would have no choice but to reunite with the original members of Guns N' Roses for a reunion tour'. Axl also alleged emotional distress stemming from Azoff's use of Axl's real name, complaining that the use of the name 'William Bailey' was done 'out of spite and vindictiveness to cause Rose emotional distress and harm', because 'Azoff knew that the name William Bailey carries significant emotional damage.' Azoff, known for his practical jokes, responded by stating, 'On advice of counsel I cannot respond at this time, but will discuss in my upcoming book, *My Life with William Bill Bailey*.' Not to be left out, Azoff's attorney, Howard King, when apprised of the substance of Axl's allegations by *Billboard*, deadpanned, 'He didn't accuse Irving of being on the grassy knoll in Dallas on November 22, 1963?'

Even Slash weighed in on the drama as it played out in the media, saying, 'I don't even know what that's about. I don't know where Axl is coming from. I mean, I know where Irving is coming from, he's looking for commissions for a tour that he booked. [It's a] pretty reasonable kind of thing. Axl's countersuing, so I'm not sure exactly what the merit is that he's countersuing, exactly. Anyways, I don't keep up with that, I don't follow it.' Eventually Azoff and Axl settled out of court, with the terms kept largely confidential, although it was reported to involve 'a comprehensive touring agreement' for the band to perform at a number of venues favourable to Azoff's position.

It was now that another old face from Axl's past tried to step in and save the day: Doug Goldstein. Having spent five years in Hawaii, as he puts it, 'drinking umbrella drinks and helping raise my family', Goldstein now felt ready to get back in the game and thought he saw a way of both solving Axl's troubles and making him a ton of money. Unable, though, to get to speak to Axl personally, he wrote him a letter. 'I wrote a letter to Axl, gave it to Beta, and said, "Don't let anybody else see it", and next thing I know it's on the fucking internet. I've had some people since go, "Why on God's green Earth would you put together a letter like that?" And I've gone through that letter a number of times and I thought I had some great ideas.

'I told him, "Let's go start by opening for the Van Halen stadium tour. Let's kill 'em on their stage. Then the band would be solidified in the public eye and then we'll go on and do our own thing." And I mentioned having something called the Rose Fest, which basically was just ripping off the business model of Sharon Osbourne and Ozzy of Ozzfest. My point behind it was, you know, Axl, you're getting to the point where you don't like to tour, so Ozzy only does like one in every three Ozzfests. Yet every year it's still called Ozzfest and he reaps the rewards. They make more money than any of the artists playing on the bill. Just by cruising the event. So that was all covered in the letter as well. And unfortunately I was never communicated with back in return to the letter that I sent him. All I know is he was really angry that Beta and I had met in private.'

Goldstein also touched on the thorny subject of a reunion, but coming out on the side of *not* doing it. 'What I said was, the Azoffs, the Doc McGhees of the world, they're not gonna back your artistic play. They're really only interested in the reunion. My point was, whatever you want to do professionally, I'll be there for you. If you don't wanna do the fucking reunion, fuck the reunion. That's fine. The reunion will always be there, but if you wanna do Axl Rose's Guns N' Roses for the next twenty fucking years before the reunion, then let's go. I'll be your guy. I can do a great fucking job. You already know that.'

But when the letter was published on the internet, Goldstein became a figure of ridicule. It seemed an unnecessarily harsh way to repay the 17 years he'd spent watching Axl's back.

Throughout the next leg of the *Chinese Democracy* world tour, the band criss-crossed the globe. Internet trolls had a field day with Axl's physical appearance; no longer the lithe, sinewy frontman, writhing in skinny jeans and snug T-shirts, the singer had packed on weight over the years. He also continued his long tradition of starting shows egregiously late, often without explanation. As audiences grew less tolerant of this routine, the band's appearance on the first night of the 2010 Reading Festival kicked their fury into high gear. The show had opened with riotous sets from NOFX, Biffy Clyro and Queens of the Stone Age. Guns N' Roses were the hotly anticipated headliners, but as their set time approached then passed, there was no sign of the band. Waves of boos gathered force and crashed against the empty stage until finally, an hour beyond the scheduled start, Axl and co. turned up and launched into the title track from *Chinese Democracy*. But the damage had been done. The outraged fans continued the boos and catcalls through the opener and it was reported that some fans began leaving during the early part of the set. With a firm curfew from Reading Council controlling the performances the band were forced to cut short their set, stopping at midnight. The delay had cost the fans an entire hour of performance time.

Nick Hasted, writing for the *Independent*, excoriated the band's antipathy for the audience, writing: 'Even "Welcome to the Jungle" is dribbled out with no meaning. Fireworks flare to fool the rubes, Axl sputters, and lets his career die. Only the bellboy still owed money at whatever Royal Berkshire hotel he's staying after this nightmarish one-night stand might wish him well, for one night only. For "Sweet Child o' Mine", he changes into a red check shirt that would go down well in a country bar on a slow Monday. He tinkles away at a keyboard – as if he's an artist – but never says sorry when he falls far short. The contempt of this tinny, redundant show by a blissfully ignorant ex-star is mutual long before the end.'

Two days later, the band closed the Leeds festival, taking the stage 30 minutes late. If the Leeds fans were more forgiving than the noisy Reading crowd, the people waiting in Dublin two nights later would prove considerably more antagonistic when the band came on nearly 45 minutes late. In a video of the show that's widely available on YouTube, the fans are heard to be already hurling abuse at the stage when DJ Ashba kicks off the set with the intro to 'Welcome to the Jungle'. Irate at being forced to wait without any explanation or apology, some ticketholders began throwing plastic cups and bottles onto the stage. In the video, Axl runs out and begins singing but seconds later, another object falls dangerously close to him, prompting him to stop the show and say, 'All right, here's the deal – one more bottle, we go home. It's up to you. We would like to stay. You want us to stay?'

Speaking in a calm and measured tone, Axl tries to control the situation as the catcalls continue. 'We want to stay. We want to have fun. If you don't want to have fun, all you've gotta do is let us know and we got no problem. We'll go on our way.' The band starts the song again, another bottle hits the stage, and Axl says, 'Have a good evening' and leads the band offstage.

Promoters rushed into damage control mode, laughably announcing that they were addressing technical difficulties, but later admitting that they were trying to coax the band, i.e. Axl, back out. Eventually the lights came up and announcements were made that the evening was over and that refunds would be given. Then, after many of the fans had already left, the band retook the stage at 11.30 and performed a full set. Huh?

The promoters issued a statement the next day, confirming the band's late start and blaming the support act for running late (though not explaining the 45-minute window between the support act finishing and Guns N' Roses taking the stage). The statement confirmed that the band were being pelted with plastic glasses containing 'unknown substances', adding that 'While the artist has a long history for being late on stage, NO artist should be subjected to missiles and unknown substances being thrown at them. However, despite this the band went back on stage after people stopped throwing items performing their full set of songs in full [sic]. MCD and The O2 wish to apologise for any inconvenience caused due to late running of the show.'

Just before noon on 27 September 2011, Steven Adler stepped into the Rainbow on Sunset, where he was scheduled to do an interview for *Metal Hammer* magazine, and shouted, 'We just got nominated for the Rock and Roll Hall of Fame!' Discussion quickly turned to the induction – who would walk up on stage? Had Steven spoken with any of the other members? Could this be the first step in the long anticipated reunion of the original line-up? Only hours into the news, Adler had as much information as anybody, although he pointed out that in recent months, with a brand new stretch of sobriety, he had mended fences with most of his old bandmates, saying that he was even on speaking terms with Matt Sorum, his eventual replacement. One thing was clear – Steven Adler was not remotely entertaining an induction ceremony that did not include him standing at the podium, along with Slash, Duff, Izzy – and Axl.

Nevertheless, it was implicitly understood that any Hall of Fame induction format would largely hinge on Axl's willingness to share the stage with the original line-up – the four other men who had forged the band's legacy through its game-changing debut album as well as the band's fearsome reputation for drinking, drugging, brawling and dominating every room they entered. But if the worst thing you could give a control freak was complete control, the next worst thing was zero control, and this was what became the crux of Axl's predicament.

For their part, the other members of the original line-up were open to any of the obvious scripts – either going up as just the original line-up (indeed, they were the ones being inducted, not the new line-up), or sharing the stage with the current line-up. Speaking shortly after the nomination was made official in December, Duff described his reaction to the news with equal parts disbelief and apprehension: 'It's weird, you know? I've never striven to get into the Rock and Roll Hall of Fame. Never in my life have I thought, "Man, I gotta get a Grammy." In sports you try to win it all, but music's a different deal. So the Rock and Roll Hall of Fame was never on my radar.'

With the official announcement came the decree that the members being inducted would be as follows: Axl, Slash, Izzy, Duff, Steven, Matt and Dizzy Reed. Nobody else. It appeared fairly certain that Duff, Slash, Steven and Matt would attend. Izzy and Dizzy Reed declined to attend, though. Reed was still playing with the current line-up and presumably under heavy manners from Axl. 'Obviously there's a lot of great, great people that I respect and grew up admiring and idolizing who are in and part of that institution,' he was quoted as saying. 'So just to be mentioned in the same breath as them, I take it as an honour.' He also made sure to add that as far as he was concerned the then current GN'R line-up was 'The best version of Guns N' Roses that I've ever been in. I think everyone is just super-talented, and it's just great chemistry. Everyone is a lot of fun to be around and a lot of fun to play with, so to me it's definitely the best line-up we've had.'

Meanwhile, the internet bristled with frothy emotional appeals to Axl to take the podium with his original partners, but almost inevitably such entreaties were ignored. On 8 January 2012, Axl tweeted, 'I'd like to thank the Rock and Roll Hall of Fame and our fans. This is your victory', and remained pointedly silent thereafter, until the proverbial eleventh hour, when in vintage Axl fashion he announced his verdict via an open letter on 11 April – the day before the induction ceremony – stating, 'I won't be attending The Rock and Roll Hall of Fame Induction 2012 Ceremony and I respectfully decline my induction as a member of Guns N' Roses to the Rock and Roll Hall of Fame. Neither I or anyone in my camp has made any requests or demands of the Hall of Fame. It's their show not mine.'

As in the past, his letter appeared to presuppose the arguments for a reunion of the original line-up and anticipates the inevitable backlash, adding with a straight face, 'There's a seemingly endless amount of revisionism and fantasies out there for the sake of self-promotion and business opportunities masking the actual realities. Until every single one of those generating from or originating with the earlier line-ups has been brought out in the light, there isn't room to consider a conversation let alone a reunion.' To those insisting that he overlook his differences just for one night, his response was unambiguous: 'So let sleeping dogs lie or lying dogs sleep or whatever. Time to move on. People get divorced. Life doesn't owe you your own personal happy ending especially at another's, or in this case, several others' expense.' Finally, with regard to the possibility of a reunion, Axl flatly wrote: 'In regard to a reunion of any kind of either the *Appetite* or *Illusion* line-ups, I've publicly made myself more than clear. Nothing's changed.' Axl would finish the letter with a tribute to Armand 'Butts' Crump, the Slayer guitar tech who died just weeks before: 'P.S. RIP Armand, Long Live ABC III.'

Anybody surprised by Axl's decision – or the way he delivered it – had not been paying attention over the past decade. And yet, with the uncertainty removed, it was as if the band, the fans and the rest of the watching world could finally breathe and move forward to honour the men who co-authored the immortal Guns N' Roses sound, who co-wrote the band's biggest and best-known hits and who, for a number of wild and untamed years, richly earned the reputation of the Most Dangerous Band in the World. The show would go on without Axl – a predicament with which the others were entirely too familiar. And so, on 12 April 2012, Slash, Duff, Steven and Sorum took the podium to accept their induction into the Rock and Roll Hall of Fame, also bringing up one-time guitarist Gilby Clarke for the honour. Green Day's frontman, Billie Joe Armstrong – at first blush, a curious choice to induct the band – delivered a gem of an induction speech, hailing *Appetite* as 'the greatest debut album in rock'n'roll history'. The cacophonous applause that followed showed that he was not alone in his opinion. 'The opening riff of "Welcome to the Jungle" is a descending trip into the underworld of Los Angeles,' Billie Joe continued. 'It was all about the seedy underworld of misfits, drug addicts, paranoia, sex, violence, love and anger in the cracks of Hollywood. It was a breath of fresh air,' he cracked.

As he rattled off the names of the original line-up, Axl's name drew a chorus of boos, but Billie Joe deftly derailed the catcalls by yelling over them, saying, 'Shut up! Shut up. He was the greatest frontman to ever step in front of a microphone. But he is . . . crazy. And I can vouch for that.' With broad, triumphant smiles, big waves and peace signs, the five men drank deeply of the applause – the first that they had received together as Guns N' Roses in nearly 20 years. Diplomatically, in his induction speech, Duff said, 'I don't know that it matters who's here tonight, because it's about the music that these bands played', also seizing the opportunity to criticise the Hall of Fame grandees for passing over bands like Kiss, Deep Purple, Rush and Iron Maiden.

If anybody stirred up any controversy that night, it was Matt Sorum, who used the spotlight to lob some decidedly uncharitable barbs at Adler's recurring addiction issues. Not only did such jabs come across as mean-spirited and cheap, but Adler had always been the fans' hands-down, sentimental favourite of the two, and Sorum was forced to later issue a *mea culpa*, writing: 'In my speech, I made references to drugs and Steven being dismissed from the band, in which I referred to, "How could someone be fired from Guns N' Roses for doing too many drugs?" It was meant to be light-hearted. But knowing the struggles Steven has endured all these years I felt I needed to clarify that Steven was onstage, healthy, and ready to rock . . . Steven's passion for GN'R is something that no one can explain but him: it's a true love gone, but never forgotten. How many people have felt that in their lifetime?'

The comedian Chris Rock, who inducted the Red Hot Chili Peppers later that evening, could not pass up the opportunity to lob a dig at Axl, too, saying, 'A lot of people are disappointed that Axl Rose isn't here. But let's face it, even if he was going to be here, he still wouldn't be here yet.' The reunited line-up stormed through 'Mr Brownstone', 'Sweet Child o' Mine' and 'Paradise City' for their celebratory jam, with Myles Kennedy, from Slash's band, Slash and the Conspirators, handling the vocals. But it was only a matter of time before Axl – the Hall of Fame's newest and most reluctant member – weighed in, which he did via another open letter five days later. 'I still don't know exactly or understand what the Hall is or how or why it makes money, where the money goes, who chooses the voters and why anyone on this board decides who, out of all the artists in the world that have contributed to this genre, officially "rock" enough to be in the Hall?' The letter then lapsed into more punch-drunk defensiveness, as he groused, 'Now that the smoke's cleared a little, any desperate, misguided attacks have been just that, a pathetic stab at gossip, some lame vindictiveness, the usual entitlement crap, he's obsessed, crazy, volatile, a hater. I once bought a homeless woman a slice of pizza who yelled at me she wanted soup. We got her the soup. You can get your own.'

As if to emphasise how much better they really were than the originals, over the next couple of years members of the 'new' Guns N' Roses would go out of their way to suggest they all still had a big future together. DJ Ashba had said as far back as 2009 that they were already working on new songs for their next album and Dizzy Reed now confirmed that there was a wealth of unreleased material from the *Chinese Democracy* sessions, estimating that at some point the band would release new material. In June 2012, while touring with his side project, The Compulsions, Richard Fortus dropped something of a bombshell, when he reportedly told a French website that the band had been working on new material in the hope of finishing the *Chinese Democracy* follow-up by the end of the year. Indeed, he stated that the band would not play further dates on that year's *Up Close and Personal* tour so that they could funnel their energies into the studio.

Only Earth's newest residents would have placed any stock in such promises, which Fortus nevertheless continued to reiterate in the ensuing years. Later that summer, the band announced a

November residency at The Joint – a 4000-seat room in the Hard Rock Hotel and Casino, in Las Vegas, which they would film for an upcoming concert DVD. The 12-show, three-week residency was officially titled the *Appetite for Democracy* tour, in celebration of 25 years of GNR's debut and four years of *Chinese Democracy*, and would serve as a warm-up to the band's 2013 campaign through Japan, Australia and back through North America. The only other remarkable development in 2013 was the leak of a new song, called 'Going Down', which featured Tommy Stinson on lead vocals with Axl singing backup. Though Axl's camp would not officially confirm that it was a new Guns N' Roses track, *Spin* magazine seized on the story, citing not just cease-and-desist actions as adding credence to the rumour, but a tweet from the guitarist Bumblefoot that August which read: 'If you're in Corfu, you Better be Going Down to 'One for the Road' bar in Sidari for the big jam tonight . . .! @gnr.' The general response to the track fell somewhere between a shrug and a sigh when the 'jam' never happened.

There was another successful residency at The Joint, in Las Vegas, plus a high-profile headlining performance at *Revolver* magazine's 2014 awards ceremony in LA. But the circus coming to town no longer seemed to be the big event it once was, the sheer novelty of seeing Axl Rose alive onstage, surrounded by who cared what other band members, having long since worn off.

Slash released a star-studded solo album and later two more extremely well-received outings with his new band, Slash with Myles Kennedy and the Conspirators. In addition to constant collaborations with other artists, he launched his own horror movie production company, Slasher Films, in 2011. Duff also stayed active releasing material with Loaded and, more recently, Walking Papers. He also released a bestselling autobiography – as have Slash and Steven Adler – and became a popular blogger and columnist for *Seattle Weekly* and *ESPN*. He even, like Izzy before him, would show up occasionally on stage with Axl and his Guns N' Roses.

Izzy continued to release solo albums – 11 since leaving GN'R, many of these featuring members of the *Appetite* line-up, with his latest due later in 2016. He also appeared on Slash's first solo album. Steven Adler continued to struggle with addiction in his post-GN'R career, though still managing to play regularly, first with his own outfit, Adler's Appetite, and later releasing an album and touring with his band, Adler. He appeared on the television show *Celebrity Rehab* for two seasons and in 2013 he put Adler on hiatus to continue focusing on his sobriety. While it would have been naive to say that these men had all transcended the thrill or sentimentality of playing with Guns N' Roses and would never consider a reunion, they remained for the time being largely and happily focused on their respective projects, squarely looking to the future – right up until word first began to spread across the internet again, in 2015, about that possible, longed-for reunion.

In the spring of 2014, with Stinson committed to a reunion tour with his original band, The Replacements, official GN'R sources announced the return of an old friend – Duff McKagen. Duff would temporarily fill in for Tommy on five dates of their South American tour. A gracious Stinson explained to *Billboard*, 'I didn't want to fuck anyone up in Guns by saying, "Hey, I can't do this tour" or anything like that. Luckily someone was able to reach out to Duff and he was amenable to the idea and was into doing it. It's Duff being the kind of good sport he is, trying to help Axl out. So I'm like, "Thanks dude, for covering my ass on this one." I think people are gonna be really stoked about it. It's gonna be fun for everyone.' Not that Stinson actually had much say in the matter.

Later that spring, with the current line-up restored, Axl took the band back to The Joint for a second residency, stretching into June, this time called 'No Trickery! An Evening of Destruction'.

With this move, Axl had almost certainly – unwittingly – revealed his hand regarding the band's near future. While the other musicians had all discussed the writing of new material and the existence of several unused *Chinese Democracy* tracks, the choice to spend two weeks on another Vegas residency, rather than put the finishing touches to a new record, spoke volumes. Guns N' Roses were not about new music any more; they were a touring band stacked with hired guns, making their living off the fumes of its classic older albums, and a few of the strongest tracks from their latest album – not unlike a Thin Lizzy or Lynyrd Skynyrd.

Meanwhile, the latter half of 2014 saw the release of the band's first video in 22 years – *Appetite for Democracy: Live at the Hard Rock Casino, Las Vegas*, which captured the band's first residency, two years previously. Filmed in both 3D and 2D, and mixed in 5.1 Surround Sound, *Appetite for Democracy 3D* is a technological tour-de-force, showcasing crystalline graphics, brawny production and quick-cut edits that create a sense of speed and action, pacing the film far more effectively than the underlying material. Coming in at just under three hours, the 25-song set list includes seven tracks from *Appetite for Destruction*, five from *Chinese Democracy* and the rest a smattering of *UYI* and *Lies* tracks and even a pair of originals from Stinson and Bumblefoot. Giving it the feel of an old-school Vegas cabaret, there are scantily clad dancing girls and a bewildering Liberace-esque interlude where Axl plays piano from a platform floating above the audience. The musicians empty the drawer of live concert tropes – strutting, mugging and pouting for the cameras, and while their respective performances are polished to a man, entirely absent is any sense of chemistry, let alone the danger or unpredictability that once shrouded the very *idea* of a Guns N' Roses concert.

Critically, while the consensus was overwhelmingly favourable regarding the film's special effects and all-around razzle-dazzle, far more muted was the reception for Axl's vocals. Even with the inevitable post-production overdubs that would accompany any modern DVD release, tracks like 'It's So Easy', 'Welcome to the Jungle' and the whinnying of 'You Could be Mine' spoke of the singer's increasingly limited range. While heritage acts like the Rolling Stones rework certain songs to accommodate the inexorable deterioration of their frontman's vocal cords, new GN'R play the material as it was originally recorded, exposing the singer's struggles in reaching those edges that he once so confidently owned.

Compared to videos of Eighties-era performances by the original line-up storming through the belly of *Appetite*, or unleashing the gritty acoustic punch of the semi-acoustic 'You're Crazy', it became apparent that precisely what the new line-up delivered in showmanship, they lacked in soul. And how could they ever truly own these songs that were written years before they joined the band? Setting aside the potent production, *Appetite for Democracy 3D* plays more like a Broadway show – regardless of how flawlessly or passionately the cast onstage deliver their lines, every single person in the audience sees them as actors telling somebody else's story. Fun without the funk. Entertainment without the edge. Rock without the roll.

Earlier that year, the band headlined *Revolver* magazine's annual Golden Gods awards, at which Richard Fortus renewed his perennial proclamation regarding new material, telling the *Associated Press*, 'We are working on stuff and hopefully very soon we're going to have new stuff out. Well, in the next year.' Later that June, Axl would provide a bit more clarity on his plans, telling *Revolver*, 'We recorded a lot of things before *Chinese* was out. We've worked more on some of those things and we've written a few new things. But basically, we have what I call kind of the second half of *Chinese*. That's already recorded. And then we have a remix album made of the songs from *Chinese*. That's been done for a while, too. But after Vegas, we're going to start looking very seriously at what we're doing in that regard.' The release date for either of these albums was not provided.

Ultimately, the 2012 Rock and Roll Hall of Fame show (or no-show) would encapsulate the Guns N' Roses story better than any other event in the preceding 20 years, bristling with drama, ego and wild unpredictability. In the wake of their induction, one got the overwhelming sense that the band's first two acts had finally closed. On the neutral ground of the Hall's glassy edifice on the shores of Lake Erie, four modern rock legends gathered for one final time beneath the Guns N' Roses banner to take one last bow together. There was nothing left to say.

And yet, if anybody could shock the world, it would be W. Axl Rose. Reunion chatter would continue to fester on barstools and bulletin boards. Axl remained insistent that a reunion would never occur and with the eyes of the world on the 2012 Hall of Fame ceremony, he might have missed his best opportunity for not simply giving the fans what they so desperately craved, but the opportunity to recast his own embattled image through one single action. That one gesture – standing alongside his former bandmates for a few more hours in history – would have eclipsed all of the open letters, accusations and innuendo and might have been his own crowning moment.

But then anyone who still thought they could second-guess Axl Rose . . . well, they were fucking crazy.

17

IN THIS LIFETIME

The signs were there for all to see but after so many detours down the dark alleys of the Guns N' Roses story, no one was foolish enough to actually come out and say it. There was also the fear that the merest mention of – shhh – a reunion would send Axl Rose running off again into denial. The presence of Duff McKagan onstage with Axl in South America had re-stoked the fires. But even when Duff was also present as the band played an hour-long set at the US rock magazine *Revolver*'s high-profile Golden Gods awards ceremony, in April 2014, the rumours were still only smouldering, not blazing. Axl was there to pick up the Ronnie James Dio lifetime achievement award, named after the late Dio/Rainbow/Black Sabbath singer. For once, Axl was on his best behaviour – no tantrums, minimal tardiness and an uncharacteristic humility on the part of the frontman.

'It was actually kind of a surprise to me,' he told the magazine in a brief interview on the night. 'And I appreciate it and stuff, but, personally, I don't feel like I've done enough of anything to have a lifetime achievement award. But that's just me. I know other people were really happy for me about it so that was a good thing. I just feel like, you know, it's been a long, slow process beyond comprehension with *Chinese Democracy*, but it's still moving forward and there's a lot more that we hope to do.' Asked about the presence of GN'R's original bassist, Axl was effusive in his praise and seemingly happy at the resurrection of an old friendship. 'It went really well,' he said. 'He worked really hard on the parts and he liked playing the newer songs from *Chinese Democracy*. And, you know, it's pretty funny because we'd go to talk about certain things from *Illusions*, and there's things he doesn't remember, there's things I don't remember. We kind of finish some of each other's memories sometimes. And the Duff that played these shows with us isn't really the Duff that I knew from what I'd call "Old Guns", or the *Appetite* or *Illusion* line-up.'

More surprisingly, Axl also obliquely referenced 'Old Guns' in the short acceptance speech he gave when picking up the award, thanking 'our line-up right now . . . all of our line-ups'. It was hardly earthshattering – he studiously avoided mentioning any of his colleagues by name. But given the vitriol that he had heaped upon Slash in recent years – infamously describing him as a 'cancer' in an interview with the AOL website *Spinner* in 2009, a remark that was reported around the world, adding that there was 'zero possibility' of a reunion with him – it hinted at something approaching a détente on the singer's part. Few paid much attention to the reference, and why would they, but hardened Guns N' Roses watchers couldn't help but wonder if something was unfolding behind the scenes.

If there was, no one was letting on – not least the members of Guns N' Roses themselves. Despite sitting out recent dates, their bassist, Tommy Stinson, was still following the party line, suggesting that wheels might be grinding back into motion on the long-gestating follow-up to *Chinese Democracy*, even if it was said more in hope than with authority. 'There's rumblings of other things to come,' Stinson insisted, 'but I'm not sure what those would be at this point. I hope we would fucking throw ourselves in the studio and make another record. A bunch of us have been writing stuff, so hopefully we'll get something going.'

Those 'rumblings' turned out to be something less explosive than a new Guns N' Roses album. Instead, their second Las Vegas residency at The Joint, the 'No Trickery! An Evening Of Destruction', had promised to strip away the hi-tech, metaphorical crash-bang-wallop of recent GN'R shows and focus instead on the things on which the band had originally built their name way back when: music and attitude. While a cynic might suggest this streamlined approach was mainly to save money, the shows themselves were a success, even if the 4000-capacity venue was a step down from the arenas they'd played on their last few runs. With Stinson back on duty, they stretched their set out to three hours and 30-plus songs to make up for the lack of onstage explosions, throwing in covers of The Who's 'The Seeker' and an instrumental version of Pink Floyd's 'Another Brick in the Wall (Part 2)' for good measure.

During the last show, Izzy Stradlin' made a semi-traditional cameo, dropping by halfway through for a loose-limbed version of the classic *Use Your Illusion* number '14 Years'. But the Vegas shows were also surrounded by a strange uncertainty. As the residency kicked off, the website RadarOnline.com reported that Guns N' Roses were 'set to split'. According to what the website described as 'a source close to the band', 'Band members have been told their calendars are free following Vegas. Axl is considering retiring and it's done. Band members and support staff were surprised when told the news and are actively looking for work.' While according to another source, 'Axl has made enough money and wants to stop touring . . . He is considering retiring.'

The rumours were quickly shot down by Axl himself. 'I'm not going anywhere,' he wrote on Facebook. 'GN'R fans sure have a Radar for BS! Love you all!' But not everyone was on the same page. A source close to the band described the rumours of retirement as 'bullshit' but admitted that the members of the current line-up had been told that the calendar was empty for the foreseeable future, and that they were free to pursue other things. If that was true, then it looked like Axl could have been winding down the *Chinese Democracy* line-up. But if he was, nobody had told Slash. The guitarist's solo career was stronger than it had ever been. When the inevitable question of a Guns N' Roses reunion came up in interviews, Slash treated them with a polite weariness. His standard answer was that, no, he didn't know what Axl's problem with him was, but there was too much water under the bridge for it to happen anyway. Though that didn't stop him taking the odd sly dig at the current line-up. Asked what he thought about Duff standing in for Tommy Stinson earlier in 2014, he replied, 'It really isn't that big a deal. Duff told me he was going to fill in for what's his name.' Whatsisname being a man who had been part of the GN'R line-up for 16 years – five years longer than the guitarist himself.

Slash's third solo album, *World on Fire*, was released in September 2014. A double album, it gave him another Top 10 hit in several countries, including America, Britain and Germany. Since his stint as an unlikely stand-in as Guns N' Roses' bassist had come to an end, Duff had kept himself similarly busy, playing with his low-key side project the Walking Papers and the altogether higher-profile Kings of Chaos, an all-star collective featuring a rotating cast of musicians that included Def Leppard's Joe Elliott, Aerosmith's Steven Tyler, ZZ Top's frontman, Billy Gibbons, and his own ex-bandmates Matt Sorum, Gilby Clarke and Slash. With the latter in the line-up, the Kings of Chaos were the closest the world were going to get now to a classic Guns N' Roses reunion.

Over in the GN'R camp, things were altogether quieter after Vegas – suspiciously so, in fact. Concerned that their gravy train was about to grind to a halt, the current line-up kept their own counsel. The exception was the guitarist Ron 'Bumblefoot' Thal. Always the square peg in the round hole that was GN'R, in

December 2014 Bumblefoot hinted that all might not have been well within that world, and that his future and the band's future weren't exactly travelling in the same direction. 'I'm focusing on my stuff,' he said at a press conference to announce a new solo album. 'I'm sure it's going to be an exciting, interesting year for everybody – for Guns, for me, for everybody. A lot of stokes in the fire . . . for them, for me. We'll see what happens in 2015.' The unspoken message was clear – Bumblefoot was no longer a member of Guns N' Roses. He just wasn't going to talk about it. When I contacted him for an interview for this book in January 2016, he was open and friendly, wondering in an email 'what I can add that isn't shrouded in unpleasantness, if anything'. But then he became paranoid when I asked if he'd signed a confidentiality agreement as part of his contract with Axl? He emailed me again, writing in block caps: 'I DON'T WANT TO HURT ANYBODY.' Adding, 'I already don't like the feeling in my gut from all this. I'M OUT.'

But there was a much more seismic event for the future of Guns N' Roses on the horizon after Thal left, though as with many things related to the on-going Guns N' Roses soap opera, it was only obvious at the time if you were paying close attention. On 30 December 2014, Slash filed for divorce from his wife of 13 years, Perla Hudson. The pair had split once before, in 2010, but had soon reconciled. This time it was to be permanent. According to legal documents, the pair had separated six months earlier. Soon afterwards, Slash had hooked up with a new girlfriend, Meegan Hodges – the same Meegan Hodges whom Slash had first fallen in love with as a teenager, but who had walked away for the sake of her own sanity when things began to take off in earnest with Guns N' Roses, and the same Meegan Hodges who had been such a good friend to Erin Everly, and who was about to play a pivotal part in the future of both the guitarist and his old enemy, Axl Rose.

'Meegan was his nineteen-year-old girlfriend in 1988,' says Alan Niven. 'But Meegan bailed on him because it was so fucking crazy. And well done, Meegan, for having a sense of self-preservation and getting her ass out of there. Meegan coming back into his life now was sufficient for him to finally get out of a relationship that he was very unhappy with. But falling in love again with Meegan and having her support he could get out of the relationship.'

Coming back together with Meegan unlocked another door for Slash, says Niven. 'So Meegan has a best friend who lives in Atlanta. And that best friend is called Erin Everly.' Suddenly, 'Erin and Axl are talking again. That was the seed for getting Axl and Slash back together. It was Erin and Meegan.'

The idea of Axl considering a reunion was backed up by Ricky Warwick, the former Almighty singer who now fronted the resurrected Irish rockers Thin Lizzy. When Lizzy supported Guns N' Roses in 2012, Ricky and Axl had become friends, Warwick told *Classic Rock* magazine, 'Axl was quite realistic about the possibility of a reunion, saying: "Who knows?" He had fond memories of it. It was always a case of: "we'll see where the road takes us." It was never: "Over my dead body."'

Unbeknown to the public, by the summer of 2015 Axl, Slash and Duff were already in communication – albeit via their lawyers and business managers. Though according to Alan Niven, who remains close to Slash, 'Duff did most of the spadework at that stage', a statement backed up by the band's old friend Marc Canter, who said the bassist had acted as the main peacemaker. Just as it had been Duff who helped broker the deal with the DVDs a year earlier. 'Duff was a big part in getting them back together,' Canter told the *Mail*. 'He was working with Axl again and is a good middle man. There was no one else who communicated with Slash and Axl. When Axl was venting about Slash, Duff was able to help him see things through Slash's eyes.'

Both the Axl-led GN'R and Slash's solo band were set to release their own live DVDs. Both featured classic Guns N' Roses songs that required the other party to sign off on. Whereas in the past Axl would most likely never have allowed his old nemesis the privilege, this time he agreed to it seemingly without objection. The thaw had started. All that was going on in private. To the outside world, it was business as usual – that is, no business at all. At least it was until a single tweet set the alley cat amongst the pigeons. On 6 February 2015, Axl Rose celebrated his fifty-third birthday. Anyone watching his Twitter feed closely would have seen a string of birthday greetings from fans around the world, people the singer would have never met. But there was one tweet that stood out:

Happy Birthday @AxlRose iiii];)'

The message was from the very man that Axl had spent the best part of 20 years disparaging and publicly maligning: Slash. The crudely rendered top-hat-and-winking-face 'emoji' suggested the message was light-hearted but entirely serious. After two decades of acrimony, could the most damaged friendship in rock'n'roll have finally been repaired? And if it had, what did that mean for the greatest rock'n'roll band of its era? Slash himself wasn't letting on, at least not in public. Interviewed on the US TV show *CBS This Morning* in early May, he played his cards close to his chest. Asked about the rumours that he and Axl had finally made up, he chose his words carefully. 'Well, we haven't really talked in a long time, but a lot of the tension has dissipated,' he said. 'We don't have all those issues any more. It's not a lot of controversy. It's something that is more perpetuated by the media, more than anything.'

When he was asked directly if he wanted the classic Guns N' Roses line-up to get back together, he was no less cagey. Though what he didn't say said as much as what he did. 'I got to be careful what I say there. I mean, if everybody wanted to do it and do it for the right reasons, I think the fans would love it. I think it might be fun at some point to try and do that.' His erstwhile bandmates were no less forthcoming. In June, Duff was asked for his thoughts on a potential reunion. 'It could happen and it could not,' the ever-diplomatic bassist told the US radio station WIND-FM. 'And I think it would be wonderful, one day, if we reconciled, first and foremost. That alone would be cool.'

Amusingly, some members of the most recent Guns N' Roses line-up were still holding out that there was a new record in the pipeline. 'We're going to be doing stuff next year,' insisted Richard Fortus, the guitarist on *Chinese Democracy*, in June 2015. 'We're not going to have anything out this year. Next year it should be out and we'll be touring.' Whether Fortus was being disingenuous or just misguided wasn't clear. But at least one of his colleagues had had enough. In July, DJ Ashba confirmed that he was no longer a member of Guns N' Roses, citing family commitments as well as his renewed work with Mötley Crüe's bassist, Nikki Sixx, in the latter's Sixx:A.M. side project as reasons for his departure. 'It is with a very heavy heart and yet great pride that I announce that I've decided to close this chapter of my life and encapsulate the wonderful times that I've shared with Guns N' Roses into fond memories,' said Ashba in a suitably buttock-clenching press release, before losing control of himself completely. 'I was blessed with the opportunity to not only work with one of the most talented bands but also to share the stage with a living legend and a truly gifted human being, Axl Rose. The amount of confidence and trust that Axl placed in me was genuinely heart-warming and truly career-defining.' The same month, Bumblefoot also made it official. 'That is the thing I am not prepared to elaborate on,' he told journalist Gary Graff, when asked why he now wanted out. 'I think there's enough clues out there for you to figure out what I'm up to now . . .'

Everything pointed to the fact that 'new' Guns N' Roses was falling apart, and that it left the door open for a reunion of the original incarnation – or at least a version of it. Slash then fuelled the rumours even further during an interview with a Swedish newspaper, *Afronbladet*, in August 2015. Asked if he'd made up with Axl, the guitarist finally confirmed the pair were on speaking terms. 'It was probably way overdue, you know,' he said. 'But it's, you know, very cool at this point . . . dispel some of that negative energy that was going on for so long.' He still refused to go the whole nine yards and talk about the likelihood of a reunion, but by now only a blind man couldn't see a pattern merging. 'Oh, I couldn't answer that one,' he said. 'Let's get off the subject because that's an old one.'

Frank Ferrer, who drummed for the *Chinese Democracy* line-up, also dropped an oblique hint. 'I am a member of Guns, and Guns still exists,' he told the US radio DJ Mitch Lafon. 'Guns definitely has a lot of moving parts, and there's a lot of things in the works. And once we're ready to announce something, the whole world will know. But everything is moving forward.' Tommy Stinson, who hadn't played with Guns N' Roses since their second Vegas residency, also fuelled the speculation. Confirming that he was no longer part of the band, he expressed a desire to see the classic line-up get back together. 'I hope they do because when you go back to where you started from and just check that out, and feel that for a moment after you've gone on and done all these other things, you know, there's a reward that comes with that, and I had that with The Replacements,' he told the website *The Current*. 'It's a good thing. And I hope it works out for them, if it actually happens.'

In November, a film crew captured a US reality TV personality, Brandi Glanville, yelling, 'Guns N' Roses is coming back, mother-fuckers!' The fact that Glanville was a close friend of Duff's wife, Susan Holmes-McKagan, prompted a series of cryptic tweets from the Guns N' Roses camp: 'Whatever happened to no news is good news? Of course today, everyone is a journalist. If only they could read lips. Surely they'll read between the lines.' A few days after that, Nikki Sixx chipped in with his own opinion. Responding to a question on Twitter as to whether Guns N' Roses were reuniting, he responded, 'THEY ARE. EVERYBODY KNOWS.' Given that his other band, Sixx:A.M., featured DJ Ashba on guitar, it was a safe bet that Nikki had inside information. There was the odd red herring. When Duff was spotted in the studio with his old bandmate, Izzy Stradlin, observers suggested they were working up material for a new Guns N' Roses record. Not true – the pair had connected earlier that summer, but the songs were for Izzy's latest solo album. 'We were talking on the phone and Izzy said, "Let's go record a song,"' Duff explained. 'We'll probably do it some more. We just enjoy making music together and enjoy each other's company. We're allowed to do that.'

According to Alan Niven, though, looking on from his mountain in Arizona, where he is now happily ensconced with his beautiful mystic wife, Heather, there was more to it than that. 'Um . . . I could not possibly confirm that but if I were to speculate I would say that they realised that they needed an Izzy song or two – if it's going to be Guns N' Roses. And if I know Izzy at all, I think Izzy would have gone, "Yeah, OK, I don't mind writing something and recording with you guys."'

Would Axl really go for that, though? Just singing over music they've already made?

'Oh, absolutely. It's not like they haven't gone through that process before.'

But the biggest sign of a reunion of all was yet to come. In December, the much-anticipated new *Star Wars* movie, *The Force Awakens*, was released in cinemas. To the surprise of US cinemagoers, the film was preceded by an unannounced and unexplained trailer featuring snippets of 'Welcome to the Jungle' playing over black-and-white footage of a crowd at a Guns N' Roses gig. At the same time, the band's website was redesigned to feature the classic GN'R logo of two pistols wrapped in a rose. All the 'new' GN'R merchandising was also replaced by 'classic' GN'R merch from the *Appetite* and *Illusion* eras. Clearly, something was about to happen.

And then, finally, it did. On 4 January, the worst-kept secret in music was confirmed: Guns N' Roses were reuniting to headline the Coachella festival in April 2016. 'Upholding a three-decade tradition of breaking ground, creating trends and forever changing the face of rock'n'roll, Guns N' Roses announce the most significant and anxiously awaited musical event of this century,' announced a breathless press release that read like it was put together by committee. And then the rub: 'Founder Axl Rose and former members Slash and Duff McKagan will regroup to headline the Coachella Music & Arts Festival (April 15–17 & April 22–24) . . .'

The world immediately began to parse the statement for clues. 'Founder' Axl Rose and 'former members Slash and Duff McKagan'? Did that mean Axl was still in charge and the other two were barely more than hired hands? Would they revisit *Appetite* in its entirety, or would Slash and Duff be forced to pick up numbers from *Chinese Democracy*? Most important of all, where were the two men who, to many, were the heart of the band: Izzy Stradlin and Steven Adler. Nobody was saying. With such huge amounts of money at stake – on their last go-round, Guns N' Roses were being paid around $350,000 per show, according to a report in *Billboard*. For the reunion shows, though, estimates put their fees at ten times that number, at least – and with even bigger egos at play, the GN'R camp were understandably unwilling to risk any stray comment demolishing this house of cards. Everyone from the band members down to their publicists were in lockdown. Nothing was allowed in, nothing allowed out. As well as the two

Coachella shows, the promoters, AEG, had also done a deal for the reunited band to play two arena shows in Las Vegas. According to insiders, they would be paid $26 million for all four shows.

Lots of unexpected people now came forward to snatch some the credit for this astonishing development. Chief among them was Steven Tyler. 'I did meet Axl in a couple of clubs, a year ago, two years ago, three years ago, and I'd bump into him and I'd have that talk,' the Aerosmith frontman told the US DJ Howard Stern. 'I said, "You need to get the fuck back together again soon, because we all miss you." Same thing someone said to me when [Aerosmith guitarist] Joe [Perry] and I were fighting.' Amusingly, Tyler's claims were swiftly shot down by the GN'R camp in a Facebook post: '[We] would like to respectfully thank the many people taking credit for our upcoming shows and everything in between. Especially those whom we haven't spoken to in numerous years . . .'

Others merely wanted to carp. When Chris Pitman was told he wasn't going to be involved in the reunion, he tweeted, calling the tour 'a money grab'. Less than forty-eight hours later, though, he had taken the message down, sparking rumours that maybe he was involved after all. In the event, Pitman had blown any chance he might have had. He was now further out than ever before.

Their appearance at Coachella was unsurprising. The biggest music festival in the US and one of the biggest in the world, Coachella had built a reputation as being the place where bands reunited – and for big money. Guns N' Roses were no exception. *Billboard* claimed that the band would earn $7 million for each of their two Coachella appearances, and that it would be followed by a full US tour that would earn them another £3 million a show. 'You'd have to look at [the promoters] Golden Voice and AEG, sitting there with a festival that last year generated eighty million dollars in profits,' Tom Zutaut told *Classic Rock*. 'Axl Rose has never done anything for money in his life. Nor has Slash or Duff. But when the entire music world is clamouring to see you, the rush of that experience is hard to resist, especially when AEG is waving all those large wads of money at you. Coachella is considered one of the biggest and most influential festivals in the world . . . Suddenly it might have felt right for all of them to test the waters.'

In the absence of hard facts, speculation continued to spread like a virus. With that kind of money floating around, it was no wonder the members of GN'R were keeping quiet. Ironically, the first person to break ranks was one who, as far as anyone knew, wasn't actually involved in the reunion. In late February, Izzy Stradlin finally launched a Twitter account, apparently in response to rumours that he would/wouldn't (delete as applicable) appear at Coachella. His first tweet clarified his position: 'At this point in time, I've no involvement in the upcoming April 2016 GNR show.' That didn't stop the rumour mill from turning, though. Quite the opposite: multiple sources now claimed that the guitarist was offered $40,000–50,000 to appear for a few songs at each of the shows, but that Izzy wanted either a full-time spot in the band or nothing at all. But the splits had already been agreed with experts suggesting Axl would receive as much as 50 per cent of all the revenue generated by the reunion, while Slash and Duff would agree a share of the other 50 per cent. Bringing Izzy in meant diluting everybody's payday. Maybe next time then . . .

A few weeks later, however, Steven Adler, happy to accept any deal that saw him back onstage with the band again, seemed to confirm that he would be involved in the upcoming circus when he cancelled a show by his band, Adler's Appetite, due to take place on 1 April at the legendary Sunset Strip venue the Whisky, promising a 'big announcement' was imminent instead. All the signs pointed to a secret Guns N' Roses reunion warm-up show, with Adler on drums. Things were now approaching fever pitch.

By the time Friday, 1 April, rolled around, it was no longer a secret that Guns N' Roses would make their first appearance onstage since the reunion was announced, an official announcement being made that morning that a reconstituted GN'R would be playing that night – not at the Whisky, but at the Troubadour, the same club where they had made their live debut back in 1985. It was instantly the hottest ticket in town. And it wasn't the only big news. As predicted by *Billboard*, the band would be kicking off a 21-date US tour, dubbed – with knowing irony – the *Not in This Lifetime* tour, referencing one of Axl Rose's old quotes from the days when a reunion looked like it would never happen.

Hours before the announcement went out, clued-in fans were queuing outside the old Tower Records shop – now a Gibson Guitar show room soon to be fitted up with all manner of Guns memorabilia. By 4 a.m., there were already more than a hundred people waiting in line for one of the 250 $10 tickets. On the night, it seemed like all of Los Angeles had descended on the 400-capacity club. The 250 ticket holders were matched by music industry insiders and a sizable celebrity faction, including the actors Nicolas Cage, Jim Carrey, Bradley Cooper and Kate Hudson, Eighties' comedian Andrew Dice Clay and musicians Lenny Kravitz and Lana Del Rey, plus countless liggers and hangers on. Even before the band came on, the atmosphere could have charged the whole of the West Coast. Then, just after midnight – an hour later than advertised but a lifetime earlier than anyone could have anticipated – Guns N' Roses finally hit the Troubadour stage. Slash and Duff, both in shades, were first out, flanked by Frank Ferrer on drums, Richard Fortus in Izzy's place, Dizzy Reed there as always, and a mysterious new member, Melissa Reese, also on keyboards – a model and musician who had previously worked with ex-GN'R stickman Brian 'Brain' Mantia. Followed by – yep, it's him! – Axl Rose, looking the closest to his 'old' self that he had done for 20 years.

Any doubts about the legitimacy of the 2016 model of Guns N' Roses were answered within seconds. Axl was unrecognizable compared to the wheezing, ungainly figure he'd been for the last few years: lean, in-your-face and sporting a full head of shoulder-length hair, he was as close to the whirling dervish of old as you could expect a man in his mid-fifties to be (those sources who said he'd been hitting the gym were clearly on the money). Slash and Duff, by comparison, looked exactly like they always did: the former a human cartoon in lived-in T-shirt and top hat peeling out all those instantly recognisable riffs, the latter a human sinew anchoring the chaos around him.

The ferocious opening one-two of 'It's So Easy' and 'Mr Brownstone' instantly transported the crowd back in time 30 years, followed by Axl bellowing, 'Do you know where the fuck you are?' as Slash stood on a stage monitor and sliced away at the riff to 'Welcome to the Jungle' like an assassin doing his dirty work. Any notion, though, of this being a pure retro trip were dispelled three songs in, when Slash and Fortus cranked into a razor-wire version of 'Chinese Democracy' – yet more proof that maybe the mutual respect was back. Inevitably, they leaned heavily on the hits: 'You Could be Mine', Dylan's 'Knockin' on Heaven's Door' and McCartney's 'Live and Let Die', and the undying 'Sweet Child o' Mine', which found several members of the audience sobbing, plus a few deep cuts: 'Double Talkin' Jive' from *Use Your Illusion I*, covers of The Damned's 'New Rose' (from *The Spaghetti Incident?*) and The Who's 'The Seeker'. There was even a second *Chinese Democracy* track, 'Better', in which Slash silenced the doubters. No, there wasn't a lot of interaction between Slash and Axl up on the stage, but then there never truly was.

In the main, the performance answered some key questions. There was no Izzy, not even for a fleeting appearance, nor was

Steven Adler behind the drums (it turned out Adler was lined up to play, but had injured his back). But to the 400 crazed people in the crowd, the 'who' and 'what' of it hardly mattered. Guns N' Fuckin' Roses were back with a bang that echoed around the world.

There was just one cloud to this silver lining. A week after the event, the day before they were supposed to play their first official comeback show in Vegas, Axl announced via Twitter that he had broken a bone in his foot after slipping from the stage at the Troubadour gig. 'This is what can happen when you do something you haven't done in nearly over 23 years,' he tweeted, posting a link to a short video of his doctor explaining the damage and, more crucially, assuring fans that the show would go on. 'He's having a set designed for the stage so he can perform for everyone still,' the doc said.

What happened next was proof that Axl Rose in 2016 was a world away from the Axl Rose of yesteryear. Where once the show would have been blown out without a second's thought, he knew the eyes of the world were upon him like never before. Rather than scupper things before they'd even properly started, Axl came up with a plan that bordered on genius.

In the summer of 2015, the Foo Fighters' frontman, Dave Grohl, had fallen from the stage at a show in Scandinavia, breaking his leg and leaving him unable to perform standing up. Inspired by the TV show *Game of Thrones*, Grohl commissioned his own 'Iron Throne' of guitars, allowing him to perform sitting down. It was that very same throne that he now offered to loan Axl.

Despite the bizarre spectacle of Axl seated for the entire performance – not that it prevented him from changing hats at different intervals, the items brought on by various under-clad young ladies – the Las Vegas shows that followed were a full-blown triumph. With Axl seated regally on his throne, it was left to the rest of the band to bring the party, which is precisely what they did. If the Troubadour was warts-and-all, this was GN'R on the scale everyone was used to seeing them. It all boded well for Coachella.

But there was one more twist to come. A few weeks earlier, Aussie rock legends AC/DC had announced that their singer, Brian Johnson, had been forced to step down mid-tour due to career-threatening hearing problems. Rather than cancel their shows, the band announced that they would reschedule their US tour later in the year with a guest singer.

Almost immediately, rumours began to swirl that it would be Axl stepping into the breach. On paper, it looked ridiculous. Why would a man who had dedicated his life to Guns N' Roses moonlight with one of the few bands who were as big, if not bigger? Not least at the very moment he was engaged in putting his own situation back together? *While sitting down!*

Nothing about it made sense – with so much riding on the Guns N' Roses reunion, surely this was not the time to be gone fishing? But the rumours began to gain weight. The US DJ Jason Bailey claimed 'a very good source' had told him that Axl would indeed be joining AC/DC. A few days later, photos emerged of Axl leaving a venue in Atlanta – the same city where AC/DC's tour had ground to a halt. He was reportedly there to rehearse with the Australian band. Then, on the very morning of the band's first Coachella show, AC/DC released a statement confirming Johnson's exit and announcing they would indeed finish off the tour they started – with Axl taking Johnno's place. 'We are fortunate that Axl Rose has kindly offered his support to fulfil this commitment,' they said simply.

So it was true. Axl would be pulling double duty with Guns N' Roses and AC/DC. The most reclusive rock star on the planet was suddenly its highest-profile one. Depending on how you looked at it, the timing of the announcement was either lousy or a PR masterstroke. With Guns N' Roses set to play one of the world's biggest festivals a few hours later, it instantly undercut the impact of the reunion. If Axl could be lured away to AC/DC this easily, just how dedicated was he to GN'R? On the other hand, it cranked up the interest surrounding what was already the most hyped reunion of the decade even further. Whatever Slash and Duff were thinking, they weren't letting on. Word was, they'd already reconciled themselves to staying out of whatever craziness Axl got himself into on this tour. As long as he still turned up on time – or near as damn it – for their shows, everything would be cool, baby. That's what they told themselves anyway.

When the band took to the stage at Coachella that evening – just seven minutes late – it was with all the requisite blood and thunder they could muster. Once again, Axl ruled the roost from his chair, as a crowd of close to 80,000 people – many of them too young to have seen Guns N' Roses first time around – finally got to see what all the fuss was about. They had one more surprise up their sleeve. 'Since I can't run around for you,' announced Axl from his throne, 'we're gonna bring out a friend, put a little life into things for us.' Suddenly, Slash was joined by AC/DC's guitarist Angus Young, clad in his trademark schoolboy uniform. Young launched into an electrifying version of AC/DC's 'Whole Lotta Rosie', a tune that Guns N' Roses themselves had covered in their early days. If anyone had any doubts about either the politics of the situation or Axl's ability to step up to the plate as AC/DC's frontman, this dispelled them.

The second Coachella appearance a week later lacked the surprise factor of the first, but it was important in one key way: the band arrived on stage precisely on time. Something that boded well for the upcoming tour. But, then, the Axl of old was gone. This was the new, improved W. Axl Rose: punctual, forgiving, humble. At least, that's the way it seemed for now. 'It's going to be a much different tour than it used to be,' Arlett Vereecke predicted in *Classic Rock*. 'It's going to be a totally different situation this time because everybody is sober. Axl is still having a drink here and there, but Axl was never a big drinker before. Duff and Slash are totally sober. It's going to be interesting to see how long they can actually get along, all being sober.'

More pertinently, sources close to the band suggested that the band – or at least some of them – had already entered the studio to work on future material even before the reunion was publicly confirmed. 'I know they're doing some recording,' confided Vereecke. 'They're definitely doing something there in the studio. Axl hasn't been there, but Slash is definitely in there and it's not for anyone else.'

How Guns N' Roses' future pans out is anyone's guess. A band that once thrived on unpredictability still has the capacity to fly off the rails. This tour may be rooted in the past, but the people involved aren't likely to get hung up on nostalgia for too long. 'There has to be an element of creativity,' says Alan Niven. 'Guns N' Roses is about a spirit, about individuality. It can't just be purely fiscal. It must be about legacy. After all, you don't see many hearses with luggage racks.'

In the wake of Coachella, Axl found himself in the peculiar position of being the most in-demand and high-profile rock star on the planet. After years of intermittent public appearances on-stage and off, here he was pulling double duty with two of the biggest bands out there. The once famous recluse was now everywhere. The fear was that the Guns N' Roses reunion would be reduced to a sideshow by the announcement that he would be replacing Brian Johnson in AC/DC. To compound matters, the first batch of ten European dates would take place less than a month after GN'R's triumphant comeback. Suddenly, the reunion of the century had been superseded by something nobody could have predicted.

Not everybody was blown away by the idea of this Franken-stein's Supergroup. Roger Daltrey, the bullish singer with The Who and a friend of Brian Johnson's, couldn't have been more sniffy. He griped that AC/DC had treated his friend badly, not least in the way it was announced. When he was asked if he'd go and see the Axl-fronted AC/DC, he snorted dismissively. 'Go and see karaoke with Axl Rose? Give me a break.' It was a view shared by many longstanding AC/DC fans. At least, until they got a chance to check out exactly what Axl and Angus would be like together onstage. The press swiftly – and sneeringly – dubbed this ungainly hybrid 'Axl/DC', and bemoaned the way Johnson had been unsentimentally dumped on the scrapheap. They won-dered how one of the most livewire bands would cope with a man who was confined to a chair onstage and off. It would, predicted the Cassandras of the music press, be an unmitigated disaster. Meanwhile, ageing rockers fulminated on Facebook about how Angus Young was ruining the legacy of a once-great band, about how they would be boycotting these gigs, about how Bon Scott would be turning in his grave (ironically, oblivious to the fact that Axl Rose was the biggest Bon Scott fan around). People began clamouring for refunds – they wanted AC/DC, not Axl/DC.

For possibly the first time in their career, AC/DC picked up on what was going on outside their walled bunker. In early May, the tour's promoters announced that they would be offering money back to anyone who wanted it. 'The band made a decision to offer this,' said a spokesman. 'As they care about their fans and wanted to do right by them, they instructed local promoters to offer refunds.' While it was hardly a ringing endorsement of Axl/DC, it was also a masterstroke in damage limitation – though the band must have gulped nervously when it was announced that 7000 people had asked for their money back for a show in Bel-gium. In the UK, it was reportedly even worse. Rumours began to circulate that half of the people who had bought tickets for the show at London's Olympic Stadium had asked for a refund.

But the opprobrium directed towards AC/DC, and Axl in particular, was more than balanced out by the sheer novelty of it all. It's not often that the biggest rock'n'roll band in the world outside the Rolling Stones rope in the most talked-about rock singer ever. This was genuinely once-in-a-lifetime stuff. At least, it was unless things weren't as they seemed in the Guns N' Roses camp. Rumours circulated that the fences hadn't truly been mended between Axl and Slash, and the pair were barely interacting, let alone speaking. After all the hullabaloo of a month earlier, the Guns N' Fuckin' Roses comeback was in serious danger of fizzling out. Certainly the singer seemed more dedicated to making the Axl/DC project work than keeping momentum going with the band he'd just put back together. For a man who spent the best part of two decades keeping as much distance between himself and the press as possible, he was suddenly inescapable. Fan-filmed footage appeared of him hobbling through airports or leaving hotels, even talking to members of the general public. All of this without getting into a single fight with anyone.

This unlikely charm offensive even extended to a short promo video released a few days before the Axl/DC tour was due to kick off in Lisbon, Portugal. Perched uncomfortably on high chairs in an anonymous backstage room somewhere, Axl and his new AC/DC bandmates Angus Young and the bassist Cliff Williams attempted to sell the upcoming tour to the world. All three looked like they'd rather be somewhere else as they tried manfully but ultimately unsuccessfully to big up the dates. 'Lisbon, here we come,' croaked Angus Young, like a man who had only just been told they were playing in the Portuguese capital in a few days' time. 'We're really excited to be here in Portugal. We're here to give you a great rock show, so we hope to see you there.' Axl's contribution was even less edifying. 'Absolutely,' he added, forcing a smile for the camera. 'We're very excited to be there.'

If anything, the 30-second clip showed that AC/DC should never be allowed near a film camera. But, in a peculiar way, it was revolutionary – it was unlikely that they would have ever done anything like that with Brian Johnson. Or that Axl would have countenanced anything similar with Slash and Duff. But then there were still tickets to sell. A great many of them, for both bands.

Much more revealing was Axl's interview with the BBC. Talking about how the AC/DC gig came about, he explained: 'I called the day I read about it in the news, that there was a situation going on with Brian's hearing. I called a guy who's their production manager right now . . . because I knew there was going to be a problem with having dates on sale and dates sold and stuff like that. So if I could help and if I was able to do it and they were interested, I'd love to help. And that's how it started. I wasn't looking at it like, "I'm singing for AC/DC." I was looking at it like, if I can, and they think I'm able to do it.' The new, improved Axl even found time to crack a joke. 'It started out pretty good and it's gradually gotten better,' he said. 'I'm hoping to make it through the first show before I get fired.'

Axl/DC had decamped to Lisbon for two weeks of rehearsal before the first show, on 7 May. Fans outside the venue recorded Axl and his new bandmates running through AC/DC classics such as 'Back in Black' and 'Highway to Hell'. People were grudgingly forced to admit that it sounded great, even through thick concrete walls. Come the day of the show, though, the omens didn't look so good. The Passeio Marítimo de Algés on the banks of the Tagus River had been pelted with torrential rain all day – even the Big Guy Upstairs was apparently not keen on the idea of Axl/DC. But less than an hour before show time the rain cleared up, the clouds dispersed and the sun began to beat down. 'It's turned into a nice sunny day,' were Axl's first words to the 50,000-strong crowd. 'Nice to meet you.'

What followed was a revelation. Not only did Axl banish any doubts, but he did so with such conviction that Brian Johnson was swiftly forgotten. This wasn't so much karaoke as the ultimate fan-boy dream made flesh, with Axl the happy camper at the centre of it. Even seated on his 'throne', his charisma and energy seemed to galvanise Angus Young. As Axl yelped and hollered his way through a set that mixed AC/DC staples with the odd surprise – namely 'Riff Raff', a song they hadn't played live in decades – Angus seemed to slough off the years. This wasn't just the Angus show. This was the Angus'n'Axl show.

The reviews were unanimously glowing. 'Rose, who is familiar with both malevolence and misanthropy, delivers those songs perfectly, giving them fresh menace,' said the *Guardian*. 'Performance hinted at the new union's potential to be one of the touring hits of the summer,' added *Rolling Stone*. The tour rolled on, and those fans who asked for refunds were suddenly regretting their decision. Within ten days, Axl was out of his chair, back on his feet and adding more songs AC/DC hadn't played in years – or, in the case of the Bon Scott-era classic 'Touch Too Much', had never played before. Whatever the initial reaction had been, the fact was that Axl had unexpectedly given AC/DC a new lease of life – while at the same time lifting his profile higher than it had arguably ever been. Nasty, foul-tempered Axl now seemed just a memory, to be replaced by good-time, high-five Axl. 'For the first time in my life I'm looking at the guy and he looks incredibly happy,' says Doug Goldstein, 'and therefore I'm incredibly happy for him.'

The one thing nobody was talking about was the effect that Axl/DC's success was having on Guns N' Roses. In fact, nobody was talking about Guns N' Roses much at all. When Angus Young enthused of his new singer, 'I know he's very excited, he keeps saying can he do more?', it suggested Axl was more turned on by the prospect of fronting AC/DC than he was of leading his old band around the sheds of America.

Ironically, the roles had been flipped. Where once Axl was the silent recluse keeping the world at arm's length, now it was Slash and Duff's turn to keep shtum. Aside from a tweet from the latter wishing Axl luck with his first gig, both maintained a discreet but noticeable radio silence. Perhaps there was some truth to those rumours of lingering bad blood.

On 8 June, AC/DC pulled into London for a show at the 80,000-capacity Olympic Stadium. The same day Slash took to social media to announce that he was also in town. Word spread that Duff was with him, and that both had been flown in by AC/DC's promoter to surprise Axl. Would they both reciprocate the favour Angus Young did GN'R at Coachella and make an appearance onstage that night? As it turned out, no, they wouldn't, though a picture posted on Guns N' Roses' own Twitter feed showed Axl, Slash and Duff deep in conversation backstage. Not only did it counter suggestions that Slash had huffily refused to attend the show, but the trio's body language indicated that perhaps there wasn't any tension between them after all.

Just three middle-aged millionaires hanging out and having a laugh, not friends exactly, but businessmen just out to make an honest dollar . . . Was that what the Guns N' Roses saga had finally been whittled down to?

Don't be so easily fooled. Though nothing has been officially confirmed yet, there are well-advanced plans for Guns N' Roses to continue to tour the world throughout 2017, even into 2018, assuming everyone is still speaking civilly to each other. It's the thirtieth anniversary of *Appetite* in the summer of 2017, and there are plans afoot for deluxe editions of the album to be released, along with the usual plethora of alternative takes and extra tracks from the vaults. As I write this, Steven Adler has finally arrived for the party, playing two songs on stage in Cincinnati: 'Out ta Get Me' and 'My Michelle'. Axl introduced the drummer to the Brown Stadium crowd by simply saying, 'On the drums, you

might know this guy. Ladies and gentlemen, Mr Steven Adler.'
Cue berserksville! After hammering out a frenzied 'Out ta Get
Me', Axl said, 'I guess we should do another.' Since then, Steven
has reappeared at a handful more shows, again as 'surprise invited guest'.

The smart money is also on Izzy being involved at least in
some capacity, probably in 2017. 'Everyone knows Stevie would
have given his soul to be allowed near that stage again. But Izzy?
I think his attitude may we well be, "By the way, *if* I decide it's safe
and I want to come out and play at one or two shows, here's what
you'll pay me if I do it,"' says Alan Niven. 'Because we all know
that that sceptic doesn't want all the palaver and he'll sit on the
sidelines until he feels safe.'

Looking for an objective voice to end this with, I phoned
Stephanie Fanning and asked her for her thoughts on the new-
old-reunited Guns N' Roses.

'Well, they're all thin!' she laughed. 'I think it's great for them
to get out and play those songs again. Especially for Slash, because I think he's the one who probably missed it the most. That
band and its legacy, for him to have that, I'm just really happy.'

They simply belong together, she says. 'It's magic. It's magic!
It just is. I don't know how it happened but it happened. Those
five guys getting together – it was magic. That *Appetite* record? I
mean, come on. The first time you put that on, I mean, come on!
There's nothing like it. I remember hearing it for the first time
and thinking: *what the hell is this?*'

'It's too bad' that Steven and Izzy aren't a part of it, she says.
But then Izzy, who she is still in touch with, 'beats to his own
drum, for sure. But I guess you could say the same for Axl and
Slash, too. Which is what made them so special all along, right?'

Right.

After 30 years, many millions of words have been written
about Guns N' Roses, old line-up, new line-up, whichever one

you might be thinking of most. But the fact is none of them ever really got to the truth. Which is this: Guns N' Roses has always been a band out of time, the Last of the Giants. That solid gold, easy-action thing that every rock band since the Rolling Stones has purported to and nearly always failed to be: *dangerous*. Looking-for-trouble creatures from another realm, here to steal our souls, suck our blood. Fuck us.

They've never denied it. Not even in the 1980s, when they were just starting out, these watch-yourself, flash-ass, tattooed love boys from the LA strip that said 'fuck' in their very first single. These neon-addicted freaks who refused to play by the rules. You had to look twice because you couldn't quite believe your eyes. That at a time when smiling, MTV-friendly, safe-sex, just-say-no Bon Jovi was the biggest band in the world, here was a band that seemed to have leapt straight out of the blood-spiked, coke-smothered pages of the original, golden-age, late-sixties rock scene; a time when magical-mystical-musical acts like Led Zeppelin, The Doors and the Stones were writing their own rules, drawing maps to a world of weird dreams and forbidden fantasies. It didn't seem possible but nothing about Axl Rose, Slash, Duff and Izzy (where did they even *get* those names?) seemed possible. Which is why, in the end, we fell for them so hard then. And why we so want them to bring that feeling back again now – when we need it even more.

A mission statement more direct than crystal meth: Guns N' Roses weren't looking for a *career*. They weren't begging for your *love*. They didn't need to become rock stars first to have heroin habits, didn't require the consent of the rock press to piss up your leg. Weren't asking for *permission*, fuck you very much.

And then the most wonderfully startling thing of all: the music. Axl and Slash and Duff and the gang may have *looked* like Mötley Crüe, but they always *sounded* like something else. Like Elton John meets the New York Dolls. Like Queen sharing a ride with Iggy and The Stooges. You heard 'Welcome to the Jungle' and you knew you'd just turned a wrong corner into the very worst part of the neighbourhood. 'We got everything you want,' wheezed Axl as Slash flicked open his guitar like a switchblade, 'Honey we know the names . . .' And you shuddered to think of it, knowing it was true. Then you heard 'Sweet Child o' Mine', with that Disney-esque, carnival riff, Axl sweet-talking you suddenly, chillingly, felling you with pure poetry: 'Her hair reminds me of a warm safe place where as a child I'd hide', and you'd think: holy shit, Axl was once a child? Which means that all this is somehow . . . real?

Yes. Hard to believe but . . . yes. It was all true.

And that's what this book has been about. Nothing to do with me, nothing to do with that song, though it is still one of the greatest putdown songs of all time, right next to 'Positively Fourth Street' by Bob Dylan and 'How Do You Sleep?' by John Lennon. But you know that. That is old news.

What this book has been about is what happened when a gang of no-plan-B kids who would do anything not to be part of the so-called real world got together and, at no surprise at all to them, overnight became the biggest, greatest rock band of them all. A one-way ticket back to those times before heavy metal, before punk, before any of the pure stuff had been divvied up and stepped on and sold back to us as so-called good-time rock. The kind that made us sick to our boots in the Eighties, and has left us trembling feebly with withdrawal symptoms ever since.

Most of all, Guns N' Roses mattered because at a time when it looked like it was over for this kind of devil-don't-care, sure-thing deal, along came this utterly impossible band that stood for the kind of no-prisoners revolution in the head we hadn't known since 1969. Guns N' Roses brought the bad times back again and for that they won the black hearts of the entire bad-boy, cool-chick world. Even the straights loved Guns N' Roses, knew there was something real going on, even as it felt the bruises.

So this book is something new. Written with the clear head that 25 years later brings you, if you can just live long enough; the same deep mindfulness that now sees Axl and Slash and Duff – and Steven and, who knows, later maybe even Izzy – back together. One last time, before the glory-daze effects finally wear off. Before it's just too fucking late, dude. And while it can still be told with mad love and deep affection, with peace, love and understanding, no invisible strings attached.

Because when Guns N' Roses do finally go, so will the golden age of rock, gone for ever, no encores. When they go so will we, those generations of us that rejoiced in allowing our lives to become identified with this music, this message, this meaning. Those of us that recognise, finally, when all is said and done, that Axl Rose really is that thing we so desperately want him to be: the last of the truly extraordinary, all-time great, no-apologies, no-explanations, no-quarter-given rock stars. The last of his kind.

I hope he turns up late for every show on the rest of the reunion tour. I hope he gives everyone hell with every big-deal step he takes. Because that's who he is, the Great I Am. And that's why people love him more than ever. The authenticity, the risk taking, the sheer guts. Few ever really had it even in the 1960s. No one else has it now.

This ain't Mick Jagger, there's no growing old gracefully for Axl Rose. And Guns N' Roses is not Metallica, the corporate franchise skilfully plotting their next move. And this certainly isn't Black Sabbath, a tinker toy idea wound up by a big key in the back. A piggy bank.

This is Guns N' Fuckin' Roses, baby. And, like the song says, they will never, ever come down.

NOTES AND SOURCES

The foundations of this book, in terms of quotes and the facts of the story – of both W. Axl Rose and Guns N' Roses – are based on my own original investigations and archives, beginning with interviews and conversations with Slash, Duff McKagen, Izzy Stradlin, Steven Adler, and, of course, W. Axl Rose. Up to the present day and dozens of hours of interviews with Alan Niven, Doug Goldstein, Vicky Hamilton, and several others who have never spoken on (sometimes off) the record before and some of whom do not wish to be named here.

Other voices that have provided me with invaluable information and insights over the years, often from personal anecdotes or even chance remarks, include Scott Weiland, Lars Ulrich, Ozzy Osbourne, Vince Neil, Ross Halfin, Merc Mercuriadis, Stuart Bailey, Del James, Ola Hudson, Ross Halfin, Peter Makowski, Lonn M. Friend, Patrik Hellström and others who also might prefer to remain anonymous at this time.

I have also spent a great deal of time over the years compiling as much background material as possible from as much published – and, in a few cases, unpublished – material as there is available, including books, magazine and newspaper articles, websites, TV and radio shows, DVDs, demo-tapes, bootleg CDs and any other form of media that contained useful information, the most important of which I have listed here.

However, extra special mention should also go to a handful of articles that proved especially helpful, in terms of adding to my own insights and investigations. First and foremost to the series of excellently written articles back in the early 1990s by Kim Neely in *Rolling Stone*. Her interviews with Axl were particularly insightful, and full credit should be paid to her here for the impact these breakthrough pieces have had.

Also, to Del James, whose superb series of Axl interviews in *RIP* magazine between 1989 and 1992 are to be loudly applauded. A close personal friend of the singer's, James was in a position to ask the sorts of questions none of his music journalist peers of the time, including myself, would have been able to. They were enthralling reading when they were first published, and I found them no less so when writing this book.

There were also occasional one-off pieces which were so exceptional they forced me to rethink several parts of the overall story, such as the Duff McKagan interview published in *Hard Force* magazine in June 1999 and the stupendous oral history published in *Spin* in July 1999 under the heading: Just A Little Patience. And, of course, the consistently amazing work of *Rolling Stone*, *Mojo*, *Classic Rock*, *Uncut*, *Q*, and newspapers like the *London Times*, *The LA Times* and the *New York Times*, to name just the obvious ones. All hail to quality print journalism now more than ever before.

I would also like to draw attention to the sterling efforts of the most dedicated Guns N' Roses fan websites – such as heretoday-gonetohell.com and the official gnronline.com – whose Herculean efforts in keeping a detailed record of the ups and downs of Axl's incident-filled career go way beyond the realms of dedication, venturing worryingly deep sometimes into obsessional delusion. Only true love is likely to do that to you – God bless them for it.

Books

Loser: The Real Seattle Music Story by Clark Humphrey

David Geffen: A Biography Of New Hollywood by Tom King

Come As You Are: The Story Of Nirvana by Michael Azerrad

The Language Of Fear by Del James

The Dirt: Confessions Of The World's Most Notorious Rock Band by Motley Crue with Neil Strauss

Red Hot Chili Peppers: True Men Don't Kill Coyotes by Dave Thompson

Walk This Way: The Autobiography Of Aerosmith by Aerosmith with Stephen Davis

Tiny Dancer Really Elton's Little John?: Music's Most Enduring Mysteries, Myths, and Rumors Revealed by Gavin Edwards

Reckless Road by Marc Canter

The Days Of Guns And Roses by Danny Sugarman

The Autobiography by Slash

Watch You Bleed by Stephen Davis

My Appetite For Destruction by Steven Adler

It's So Easy (And Other Lies) by Duff McKagan

Appetite For Dysfunction by Vicky Hamilton

Magazines & Newspapers

'To Live And Die in LA' – *Spin*, 1986

'Colt Heroes' – *Kerrang!*, 11–24 June, 1987

'Guns N' Roses Marquee, London' (review of first night) – *Kerrang!*, 11–24 June, 1987

'Thorn To Be Wild' (Appetite For Destruction review) – *Kerrang!*, 23 July–5 August, 1987

'Guns N' Roses Marquee, London' (review of second and third nights) – *Kerrang!*, 23 July–5 August, 1987

'The world according to W. Axl Rose' by Del James – *RIP*, April 1989

'The Rolling Stone Interview With Axl Rose' – *Rolling Stone*, August 1989

'Guns N' Roses Working Up A Sweat' – *Metal Muscle*, May 1991

'Guns N' Roses The Illusion Of Greatness' by Lonn M. Friend – *RIP*, June 1991

'Tears Before Bedtime?' – *Q*, July 1991

'Danger Lurks Beyond The Doors' – *The Observer*, 25 August 1991

'Guns N' Roses' – *Sky*, August 1991

'Fans Riot at Guns Show' – *Rolling Stone*, 22 August, 1991

'Guns N' Roses Here Today Gone To Hell (And Lovin' It)' by Del James – *RIP*, September 1991

'Guns N' Neuroses' by Dean Kuipers – *Spin*, September 1991

'There's A Riot Going On!' – *Musician*, September 1991

'Guns N' Roses – Outta Control' – *Rolling Stone*, 5 September, 1991

'Guns N' Roses: Wimps 'R' Us' – *Village Voice*, 1 October, 1991

'Slash Speaks' – *Music Life*, 17 November, 1991

'Axl gets in the ring' – *Metallix*, 1992

'Guns N' Roses From The Inside an Exclusive Report' by Lonn M. Friend – *RIP*, March 1992

'Axl Interview' – *Interview Magazine*, March 1992

'Axl Rose: The Rolling Stone Interview' – *Rolling Stone*, 2 April, 1992

'No Axl to Grind: Rock Star Pleads Innocent' – *New York Post*, July 1992

'Axl Rose: The Mussolini Of Mass Culture' – *The Modern Review*, Summer 1992

'I, Axl Part I' – *RIP*, September 1992

'I, Axl Part II' – *RIP*, October 1992

'I, Axl Part III' – *RIP*, November 1992

'Trial by Fire' – *Guitar World*, November 1992

'On the Road with Guns N' Roses' – *Life Magazine*, December 1992

'Guns N' Roses Interview' – *Hit Parader*, July 1993

'Duff McKagan Talks' – *Kerrang!*, 1993

'Guns N' Roses' – *Okej*, November 1993

'Guns N' Roses Blazing Hot' – *Moving Pictures!*, 1994

'People' – 1994

'War Of The Roses!' – *Kerrang!*, 24 May, 1994

'Four Bust-ups And A Single!' – *RAW*, November 1994

'Welcome To Slash's Snakepit' – *Toronto Sun*, 24 January, 1995

'"I Spent A Week Jammin' With Guns N' Roses". Zakk Wylde to join GN'R?!' – *Kerrang!*, 28 January, 1995

'Coiled and Ready' – *Rolling Stone*, April 1995

'In Bed With . . . Slash' – *Kerrang!*, July 1995

'Excerpts from a Slash Interview' – *Folha De Sao Paulo Journal*, 21 July, 1995

'Guns N' Roses: Is It All Over? Does Anyone Care?' – *Metal Hammer*, November 1995

'Q&A with Slash' – *Kerrang!*, 1996

'It's All In The Wrist Action . . .' – *Metal Hammer*, February 1996

'Review of the Marshall 2555SL Slash Signature Amp' – *Guitar World*, April 1996

'At Home with Matt Sorum' – *Metal Hammer*, July 1996

'Outsiders responsible for Guns N' Roses reuniting?' – *Toronto Sun*, 4 September, 1996

'Neurotic Outsiders: Duff and Matt Talk Records' – *Kerrang!*, September 1996

'My Record Collection (Duff McKagan)' – *Kerrang!*, February 1997

'More than Blanks' – *Entertainment Weekly*, 31 July, 1998

'At Home with Slash' – *Metal Hammer*, August 1998

'Welcome To The Videos [press release]' – *Geffen*, October 1998

'At Home with Duff McKagan' – *Metal Hammer*, January 1999

'Duff McKagan: Laying Down His Guns' – *Hit Parader*, May 1999

'Snake, Rattle 'N' Roll' – *Guitar World*, May 1999

'Duff McKagan Interview' – *Hard Force Magazine*, June 1999

'Just A Little Patience' – *Spin*, July 1999

'Guns N' Roses 2-Part Article' – *Kerrang!*, August 1999

'"Oh My God" [press release]' – *Geffen*, September 1999

'Dirty Deeds Done Dirty' – *NME*, 25 December, 1999

'Axl Speaks' – *Rolling Stone*, January 2000

'Slash is still breathing' – *FHM*, March–April 2000

'What Happened To Axl Rose: The Inside Story of Rock's Most Famous Recluse' – *Rolling Stone*, 11 May, 2000

'Modern Life is Rubbish' – *Kerrang!*, 10 June, 2000

'Slash's Snakepit: For the Love of Art' – *Hard Rock Magazine*, October 2000

'Slash's Heroes & Villains' – *NME*, 7 October, 2000

'Axl Talks at the Pool Side' – *O Globo*, January 2001

'Interview with Beta Lebeis' – *O Globo*, January 2001

'GN'R Article' – *Clarin*, February 2001

'The History of Hard Rock: The Eighties (Appetite For Destruction)' – *Guitar World*, March 2001

'Didn't You Used To Be Axl Rose?' – *Q*, May 2001

'Slash Interview' – *Steppin' Out Magazine*, 16 May, 2001

'Democracy in Action' – *Q*, July 2001

'Matt Sorum Interview' – *Lawrence Journal-World*, 2001

'Inside The Lonely Mixed Up World Of Axl Rose' – *Classc Rock*, January 2002

'Gilby Clarke, Staying True to His Roots' – *Guitar Player*, April 2002

'Ready to Rock Again, or is Bloom off the Roses?' – *Florida Times Union*, 14 August, 2002

'Review of London Docklands Show' – *London Evening Standard*, 27 August, 2002

'Duff McKagan Interview' – *Classic Rock*, October 2002

'A new Bloom from GNR Veterans' – *LA Times*, 3 November, 2002

'We're Catching our Groove Again Now, (Richard Fortus interview)' – *Albany NY Times Union*, 21 November, 2002

'Meltdown' – *The Guardian*, 3 January, 2003

'Appetite For Self-Destruction' – *Classic Rock*, February 2003

'Welcome To The Jungle: A Timeline of Axl's Return to the Road' – *Classic Rock*, February 2003

'GN'R: The Inside Story' – *Total Guitar*, June 2003

'Appetite For Reconstruction (Velvet Revolver)' – *Kerrang!*, 2 July, 2003

'Velvet Revolver Set To Fire' – *Hit Parader*, October 2003

'Tommy Grows Up' – *Harper Magazine*, October–November 2003

'Geffen Guns N' Roses DVD Press Release' – *Geffen Records*, 15 October, 2003

'The Big Bang (Velvet Revolver)' – *Guitar World*, November 2003

'Guns N' Roses: The Scum Also Rises' – *Q*, November 2003, Issue 208

'Spotlight on . . . Camp Freddy' – *Metal Hammer*, January 2004

'Velvet Revolver Beating The Odds' – *Hit Parader*, February/ March 2004

'Appetite For Self-Destruction' – *Record Collector*, February 2004

'Guns N' Roses. GREATEST HITS. For the First Time (press release)' – *Geffen*, 19 February, 2004

'Gilby Clarke Moonlightin' With Sinatra' – *Guitar One*, March 2004

'Where Are They Now? The 411 on 46 Missing Guitar Heroes: Izzy Stradlin' – *Guitar One*, March 2004

'The Scum Also Rises' – *Revolver*, March 2004

'Welcome Back To The Jungle: Duff McKagan Reloads With Velvet Revolver' – *Bass Player*, March 2004

'Shooting from the Hip (Velvet Revolver)' – *Classsic Rock*, March 2004

'Welcome To The Jungle' – *Kerrang!*, 17 March, 2004

'Ten Reasons Why Guns N' Roses Still Rock' – *NME*, 20 March, 2004

'Guns N' Roses Not Able to Perform at Rock in Rio [press release]', *Sanctuary Records Group*, 30 March, 2004

'Matt Sorum Rocks with Velvet Revolver' – *Drum!*, April/May 2004

'Duff McKagan: Guns N' Roses/Velvet Revolver' – *Total Guitar Bass Special Issue 2*, April 2004

'Velvet Revolver: It's All Gonna Go so Wrong' – *Metal Hammer*, April 2004

'Velvet Revolver' – *Total Guitar*, April 2004

'Meet "The Most Dangerous Band in the World" . . .' – *Kerrang!*, 10 April, 2004

'Hanging With . . . Slash – Velvet Revolver' – *Kerrang!*, 10 April, 2004

'Paradise Lost' – *Classic Rock*, May 2004

'Bulletproof: Duff interview (Velvet Revolver)' – *Guitar World's Bass Guitar*, June/July 2004

'Slash Answers Your Questions' – *Guitar World*, June 2004

'Velvet Revolver The Ego Has Landed' – *Revolver*, June 2004

'Mexican Food With . . . Velvet Revolver' – *FHM*, June 2004

'I'm With Stupid (Velvet Revolver)' – *Q*, June 2004

'Gunning It (Velvet Revolver)' – *The Times*, 5 June, 2004

'Top Gun (Slash Interview)' – *Guitarist*, July 2004

'Slash and Burn' – *The Sunday Mail*, Brisbane, Australia, 29 August, 2004

'Velvet Revolver Cocked & Loaded' – *Circus*, October 2004

'Magnum Force (Duff interview / Velvet Revolver)' – *Guitar & Bass*, October 2004

'GN'R Set the Record Straight [press release]' – *Sanctuary/Business Wire*, 12 October, 2004

'Velvet Revolver – Drugs! Booze! Kung Fu! GN'R!' – *Classic Rock*, November 2004

'Guns at the Ready Indie legend Tommy Stinson Shoots Solo First' – *Guitar World's Bass Guitar*, December 2004

'An Appetite For Reconstruction: The Inside Story Of Velvet Revolver' – *Metal Edge*, December 2004

'Breaking The Big Machine (Velvet Revolver)' – *Metal Edge*, January 2005

'Tommy Gun' – *Classic Rock*, January 2005

'Radio Axl' – *Classic Rock*, January 2005

'Matt Sorum' – *Mojo*, January 2005

'Brain-Cheesy Fun And Cubist Funk' – *DRUM!*, March 2005

'Nowhere else to go but forward (Tommy Stinson)' – *Los Angeles Times*, 3 March, 2005

'Tom Zutaut Interview' – *New York Times*, March 2005

'Steven Adler Interview' – *Classic Rock*, April 2005

'The Complete Classic Axl Rose Interview' – *Hit Parader*, April 2005

'The Story Behind The Song: "Sweet Child O' Mine"' – *Q*, December 2005

'Axl Rose Responds To Lawsuit (press release)' – 6 March, 2006

'Hammerstein Preview' – *New York Times*, 13 May, 2006

'GN'R Get In The Ring! [press release]' – 19 May, 2006

'Guns N' Roses Storm New York [press release]' – 22 May, 2006

'Review of Hammerstein Ballroom Show' – *Hollywood Reporter*, 25 May, 2006

'Review of Hammerstein Ballroom Show' – *News Day*, May, 2006

'Review of Hammerstein Ballroom Show' – *Illinois Entertainer*, May, 2006

'Review of Hammerstein Ballroom Show' – *Reuters*, May, 2006

'Review of Hammerstein Ballroom Show' – *Chicago Tribune*, May, 2006

'Review of Hammerstein Ballroom Show' – *Variety*, May, 2006

'Review of Hammerstein Ballroom Show' – *New York Times*, May, 2006

'Review of Hammerstein Ballroom Show' – *New York Post*, May, 2006

'Tommy Hilfiger Fight' – *Associated Press*, May 2006

'Axl Vs. The World' – *Classic Rock*, May 2006

'Review of Hammerstein Ballroom Show' – *Blender*, June, 2006

'Review of Lisbon Show' – *El Diario Vasco*, Spain, May 2006

'Review of Madrid Show' – *MTV* Spain, 26 June, 2006

'Review of Hammersmith Apollo Show' – *London Evening Standard*, 9 June, 2002

'Review of Hammersmith Apollo Show' – *Daily Telegraph*, 9 June, 2002

'Review of Hammersmith Apollo Show' – *Channel Four Teletext*, June 2006

'Review of Hammersmith Apollo Show' – *NME*, June 2006

'Guns N' Babies! [press release]' – 21 June, 2006

'Axl Rose Held for 'Biting Guard'' – *Associated Press*, 27 June, 2006

'Guns N' Roses Knock Out Stockholm [press release]' – 28 June, 2006

'Axl in Fight with Security Guard' – *Expressen*, Sweden, June 2006

'Axl in Fight with Security Guard' – *Aftonbladet*, Sweden, June 2006

'Guns N' Roses Continue Through Europe! [press release]' – 30 June, 2006

'Guns N' Roses Heat Wave [press release]' – 22 July, 2006

'Guns N' Roses Win Big In Europe [press release]' – 11 August, 2006

'Axl Rose Could Be Kept In Jail Until Friday' – *Classic Rock*, August 2006

'The Final Comeback Of Axl Rose' – *American GQ*, September 2006

'Axl Rose article' – *New York Magazine*, September 2006

'Guns N' Roses Announce "Chinese Democracy" North American tour and Strategic Relationship with Major League Baseball Advanced Media [press release]' – 29 September, 2006

'Uncut' – October 2006 (grunge cover)

'A Polished Guns N' Roses Now More Brand than Band' – *Tribune*, 28 November, 2006

'Show in Portland, Maine Cancelled (press release)' – 6 November, 2006

'Christina Aguilera Feature' – *Blender*, November 2006

'GN'R line-up a thorn in Axl's Side' – *Boston Herald*, 10 November, 2006

'New Story' – *Los Angeles Business Wire*, December 2006

'Freedom du Lac, J. "Velvet Revolver, A Legal Substance"' – *The Washington Post*, August 2007

'And Now Let's Go Over to the Leather Report: Velvet Revolver' – Dan Gennoe, *Mail On Sunday*, March 2008

'Use Your Illusion' – *Classic Rock*, July 2011

'Axl Rose' – *USA Today*, October 2012

'Axl Rose' – *Revolver*, April 2014

'Axl Rose China Exchange Interview' – June 2016

'Axl Rose' – *NME*, May 2016

Online & Etc.

Special mention should also go here to the many well-intentioned people who emailed stories and information to my website, www.mickwall.com, many of which were exceptionally helpful in compiling my investigations for this book. Also, to www.contactmusic.com who filtered hundreds of related news items to my desk. Also to the brilliant www.metalsludge.com for providing laughs as well as good information and inspiration. And to the equally wonderful www.youtube.com for allowing me to view many related TV and video clips, both professional and amateur, from the past 20 years.

Specifically, though, I obtained useful information and quotes from the following sources:

Transcript of Slash online chat – Pepsi Live @ Ticketmaster Online, 16 October, 1996

Music West in 3-D: Duff, Dallas and Drugs, taken from the e-zine File, 1997

'For Slash, Life After Guns Is Grand' – <rollingstone.com>, October 2000

'Slash Exclusive: Appetite For Reconstruction' – <KNAC.com>, October 2000

Brain interview – <dwdrums.com>, 2001

Izzy Stradlin interview – <bol.com>, March 2001

GN'R press release with Axl interview – <gnronline.com>, 14 August, 2002

'Guns N' Roses Blooms Again' – Life & Mind Desk, 19 September, 2002

GN'R North American tour press release – <gnronline.com>, 25 September, 2002

'Beneath The Bucket, Behind The Mask: Kurt Loder Meets GN'R's Buckethead' – <MTV.com>, 21 November, 2002

'Use Your Delusion' – <RollingStone.com>, 3 June, 2003

'Scott & Slash Speak' – <RollingStone.com>, 17 June, 2003

Lonn Friend article – <lasvegasweekly.com>, 15 April, 2004

'This tastes like pretzels: the Tommy Stinson interview' – Here Today . . . Gone To Hell!, 10 October, 2004

'Sanctuary Music Publishing has signed Axl Rose to a publishing deal' – Sanctuary website announcement, 26 January, 2005

Steven Adler Interview, Metal Sludge, January 2006

Online review, Hammerstein ballroom show – <Rollinstone.com>, 15 May, 2006

Review of Hammerstein Ballroom show – MTV News, 18 May, 2006

'Tommy Hilfiger fight' – <PageSix.com>, 20 May, 2006

Sophie Anderston romance story – Digital Spy Showbiz, 29 May, 2006

Slash interview – <MTV.com>, June 2006 Axl ranting onstage on the 2002 US tour – <Youtube.com>, 27 June, 2006

Axl's appetite for destruction – Pop Bitch, 29 June, 2006

On the road by Del James – <GunsN'Roses.com>, 3 November, 2006

Concert review – <cinemablend.com/music>, November 2006

Concert review – <ifilm.com/video>, December 2006

Various clips:

<nme.com>

<photo.wenn.com>

<spıat.com>

<blabbermouth.net>

<holymoly.co.uk>

<allexperts.com>

<adlersappetite.com>

<mattsorum.com>

<knac.com>

<belowempty.com>

<rollingstone.com>

<classicrock.com>

<mtv.com>

<metalunderground.com>

<slashparadise.com>

<ultimate-guitar.com>

<seattletimes.com>

<nypost.com>

<reuters.com>

<mygnrforum.com>

<velvetrevolverforum.com>

<stereogum.com>

<alternativenation.com>

<theguardian.com>

<thetimesonline.com>

<gnrtruth.proboards.com>

Plus mostly unofficial, some claiming to be semi-official GN'R fan sites, most still active, some no longer so, such as: Aco's Guns N' Roses Unofficial Site; Belgian Democracy; Appetite Guns N' Roses; Chinese Democracy; Encyclopedia GN'R site; Evitaph's Guns N' Roses site; Garden Of Illusions: Guns N' Roses; Get. to/GnR; GnrDaily.com; GN'R en Español; GN'R Exclusive; GN'RLIVE.COM; Guns N' Roses: The Lost Rose Guns N' Roses Bootleg Page; Guns N' Roses Fans; Guns N' Roses In The Jungle; Guns N' Roses Videos; Gunz N' Roses; Here Today, Gone To Hell; Hugo's Guns N' Roses Bootleg Site; Intentional Illusions; John's GN'R bootleg page; Marcy's Guns N' Roses Page [Hungarian]; Mark's big GNR Collection; Nightrain; Portal Guns N' Roses; Rat's Guns N' Roses site; Right Next Door To Hell; Ryan's Guns N' Roses Page; Surfers Delight; The Tableture Incident; The Unofficial Uzi Suicide Homepage; Use Your Illusion; We Ain't Dead Yet; Welcome To The Jungle; and of coruse, the official sites such as www.newgnr.com, and Guns N' Roses - GN'R Online.

DVDs, TV AND RADIO
Axl on MTV in 1988 talking about One In A Million
Axl Rose – 'A conversation with Kurt Loder' – MTV US, 8 November, 1999
Axl interview – Radio Rock And Pop Chile, January 2001
Axl interview – Rock & Pop FM Argentina, January 2001
Post VMA interview – by Kurt Loder, MTV, 29 August, 2002
Axl interview – KISW Seattle, 8 November, 2002
Songs leaked on internet – MTV News, 23 February, 2006
Axl interview, KROQ, Los Angeles, May 2006
Plus:
Welcome To The Videos – DVD
Use Your Illusion World Tour 1992 In Tokyo – DVD
Axl Rose: The Prettiest Star – DVD
Guns N' Roses: Sex, Drugs N' Rock'n'Roll – DVD

INDEX